The Global Politics of Unequal Development

Also by Anthony Payne

Regionalism and World Order (*co-edited with Andrew Gamble*)
The New Regional Politics of Development (*edited*)

The Global Politics of Unequal Development

Anthony Payne

palgrave
macmillan

First published in 2005 by
PALGRAVE MACMILLAN
Houndmills, Basingstoke, Hampshire RG21 6XS and
175 Fifth Avenue, New York, N.Y. 10010
Companies and representatives throughout the world.

PALGRAVE MACMILLAN is the global academic imprint of the Palgrave Macmillan division of St. Martin's Press, LLC and of Palgrave Macmillan Ltd. Macmillan® is a registered trademark in the United States, United Kingdom and other countries. Palgrave is a registered trademark in the European Union and other countries.

ISBN-13: 978–0–333–74071–2 hardback
ISBN-10: 0–333–74071–8 hardback
ISBN-13: 978–0–333–74072–9 paperback
ISBN-10: 0–333–74072–6 paperback

This book is printed on paper suitable for recycling and made from fully managed and sustained forest sources.

A catalogue record for this book is available from the British Library.

A catalog record for this book is available from the Library of Congress.

10 9 8 7 6 5 4 3 2 1
14 13 12 11 10 09 08 07 06 05

Printed and bound in China

Contents

List of Tables

Preface

This book continues, and in some ways concludes, my personal project over the past few years to reinsert the issue of development more fully into the intellectual agenda of international relations and international political economy. I have pursued this agenda via the publication of an initial 'think-piece' which set out an embryonic case for a 'reframing' of the global politics of development; the subsequent clarification in another published paper of some of the theoretical ground on which this might be based; and the editing of a companion book to this, also published by Palgrave Macmillan and entitled *The New Regional Politics of Development*, which sought to explore the diversity of contemporary country development strategies by means of a comparison of the development experience of key regions of the world. The main innovation of this collection was perhaps the way that it deliberately cut across the familiar, and in my view highly problematic, analytical division between so-called 'developed' and 'developing' countries.

I concluded that book by identifying three projects that might sensibly be undertaken as the next steps in this general rethinking of development within international studies. The first would seek to put together a wide-ranging, comparative, cross-regional survey of development models, building on (but also going beyond) the old 'models of capitalism' and 'models of development' literatures. The second would endeavour to provide a comprehensive analysis of the impact of regionalism and regionalization on development, both retrospectively and prospectively. I am more than happy to leave these substantial tasks to other colleagues, should they catch their interest. But I have sought to bring to fruition my work in this field with an attempt to meet the challenge of my own third proposal, which called for an extended study of the inequalities which surely still sit at the heart of the global politics of development. We used to label this issue 'North–South politics' and I have occasionally and colloquially described my recent research to those who have asked me what I am 'working on' at the moment as an enquiry into 'whatever happened to "North–South" politics'. This book tries to give an answer to that question and will argue that the core questions which made up that agenda are not only still out there but continue to constitute some of the central issues confronting the contemporary world order, even though that well-known phrase may no longer be the most apt way to frame the basic dynamics of the politics to which they give rise.

As usual, in writing this book I have accumulated a host of debts that I would like to acknowledge here. Several colleagues and friends have read particular chapters of the book with a view to checking my interpretation of events against their expertise. Andrew Gamble gave me the benefit of his advice on Chapter 4, Randall Germain and Richard Woodward on Chapter 6, Dominic Kelly and Rorden Wilkinson on Chapter 7 and James Meadowcroft on Chapter 8. Each made a number of pertinent observations. Brendan Evans and Nicola Phillips exceeded even their efforts, for they read the whole of the manuscript with care, enthusiasm and a sharp eye for what was missing or not argued clearly. I wish to pay particular tribute to Nicola's support: I recognize her as a kindred thinker on the questions addressed in this book and I am enormously grateful for the friendship and collaboration she has offered to me on this and other projects. I should also like to thank Matthew Bishop for chasing down lots of references on my behalf and Chris Payne for compiling the statistical appendix. Steven Kennedy also displayed exceptional patience as the delivery of the manuscript passed ever further beyond the promised date.

Finally, I want to mention here the role that has been played in my career by my former PhD supervisor, Dennis Austin, with whom I still regularly debate news and views in the comfort of The Lamb Inn on Chinley Head. Dennis taught me many years ago that what those of us privileged to work in universities should endeavour to do, above all else, was write good books in plain English on important areas of enquiry. He has asked me over many lunches about my progress with this book and it would please me more than anything if he thought that in the end I had lived up to his injunction.

Sheffield   ANTHONY PAYNE

List of Abbreviations

ACP	African, Caribbean and Pacific states
AIA	Advanced informed agreement
AOSIS	Alliance of Small Island States
APQLI	Augmented Physical Quality of Life Index
ATC	Agreement on Textiles and Clothing
BEM	Big emerging market
BIS	Bank for International Settlements
CBD	Convention on Biological Diversity
CDM	Clean development mechanism
CDP	Committee for Development Planning
CEIT	Country with an economy in transition
CIS	Commonwealth of Independent States
CO_2	Carbon dioxide
COP	Conference of the Parties
DAC	Development Assistance Committee
DSB	Dispute Settlement Body
EU	European Union
EVI	Economic Vulnerability Index
FATF	Financial Action Task Force on Money Laundering
FSF	Financial Stability Forum
G7/8	Group of 7/8
G10	Group of 10
G20	Group of 20 (as formed by the G7 finance ministers)
G20	Group of 20 (as formed within the WTO)
G22	Group of 22
G24	Group of 24
G33	Group of 33
G77	Group of 77
G90	Group of 90
GATS	General Agreement on Trade in Services
GATT	General Agreement on Tariffs and Trade
GDP	Gross domestic product
GEF	Global Environmental Facility
GM	Genetically modified
GNI	Gross national income
GNP	Gross national product
HDI	Human Development Index

HIPCs	Heavily Indebted Poor Countries
IBRD	International Bank for Reconstruction and Development
ICSID	International Centre for the Settlement of Investment Disputes
IDA	International Development Association
IFC	International Finance Corporation
IFI	International financial institution
ILO	International Labour Organisation
IMF	International Monetary Fund
IMFC	International Monetary and Financial Committee
INC/FCCC	Intergovernmental Negotiating Committee for a Framework Convention on Climate Change
IPCC	Intergovernmental Panel on Climate Change
ISIC	International Standard Industrial Classification
ITO	International Trade Organization
JUS[S]CA[N]NZ	Japan, the United States, [Switzerland], Canada, Australia, [Norway] and New Zealand
LDC	Least Developed Country
LIC	Low Income Country
LMC	Lower Middle Income Country
LMG	Like-Minded Group
LMO	Living modified organism
LULUCF	Land-use, land-use change and forestry
MDG	Millennium Development Goal
MFA	Multi-Fibre Arrangement
MIGA	Multilateral Investment Guarantee Agency
NCCT	Non-cooperative country and/or territory
NEPAD	New Partnership for Africa's Development
NGO	Non-governmental organisation
NIC	Newly industrializing country
NIEO	New International Economic Order
NIFA	New international financial architecture
OAU	Organization of African Unity
ODA	Official development assistance
OECD	Organisation for Economic Cooperation and Development
OEEC	Organization for European Economic Cooperation
OFC	Offshore Financial Centre
OPEC	Organization of Petroleum Exporting Countries
PPP	Purchasing power parity
PRSP	Poverty Reduction Strategy Paper
PWC	Post-Washington Consensus

ROSC	Report on the Observance of Standards and Codes
S&D	Special and differentiated treatment
SDR	Special Drawing Right
SDRM	Sovereign Debt Repayment Mechanism
SP	Strategic Product
SSM	Special Safeguard Mechanism
TINA	'There is no alternative'
TNC	Trade Negotiations Committee
TRIMS	Trade-related Investment Measures
TRIPS	Trade-related Intellectual Property Rights
UK	United Kingdom
UMC	Upper Middle Income Country
UN	United Nations
UNCED	United Nations Conference on Environment and Development
UNCTAD	United Nations Conference on Trade and Development
UNDP	United Nations Development Programme
UNEP	United Nations Environmental Programme
UNESCO	United Nations Educational, Social and Cultural Organization
UNFCCC	United Nations Framework Convention on Climate Change
UNHCR	United Nations High Commissioner for Refugees
UNIDO	United Nations Industrial Development Organization
US	United States
USSR	Union of Soviet Socialist Republics
USTR	United States Trade Representative
WDR	World Development Report
WMO	World Meteorological Organization
WSF	World Social Forum
WSSD	World Summit on Sustainable Development
WTO	World Trade Organization

Part I

Introduction

Chapter 1

Framework of Analysis

Over the last few years it has come to be apparent to many of the more astute observers of contemporary international affairs that the most important line of division within the world order at the beginning of the twenty-first century is that which, broadly speaking, pitches the interests of the 'richer' countries against those of the 'poorer' countries. Indeed, there are those who would say that this has long been the case and that for the best part of the last half-century it was only the Cold War between the capitalist and communist countries which obscured this reality. The potentially enormous destructiveness of the Cold War conflict for all of humanity certainly meant that it overlaid even the many real dramas of the international politics of development during these years. The Cold War can of course be said to have fed off 'rich–poor' tensions in many parts of the world, but it is obvious that its core dynamic was something different. Nevertheless, it is now the case that, apart from a small number of outposts still mired in anachronistic disputes, the Cold War has passed into the history of the twentieth century. Since then the 'clash of civilizations' between the Christian and Muslim worlds has been widely touted as its natural successor as the key division in contemporary international politics, a claim to which the awful events of 11 September 2001 gave immediate and dramatic support. Yet it was not long before deeper reflection upon the provenance and significance of the terrorist attacks upon the United States (US) – above all, the realization that in several countries shock and outrage were accompanied by a widespread sense, almost of satisfaction, that the US had at last experienced something of the human horror that has become commonplace in many, less fortunate societies – brought to light the suggestion that underpinning September 11 was in fact this other, even more fundamental, divide: namely, that between the 'richer' and the 'poorer' parts of the world (again, as very broadly understood). This was seen as having the effect of exacerbating Christian–Muslim conflicts in much the same way as it had previously inflamed capitalist–communist tensions during the Cold War. It was commonly asserted, moreover, that *all* countries were now wrapped up together more closely than ever before within something called 'globalization', a phenomenon which, it should be said, many have found easier to applaud or condemn than analyse and understand. In short, it has not been difficult of late to find commentators who assert that the continuing question of relations between 'richer' and 'poorer' countries is *the* issue, above all others, which goes to the heart of contemporary international politics.

As suggested, this is in many ways an old and familiar fissure within the history of modern international politics. After all, it manifestly ran through every facet of the politics of colonialism; it fuelled much of the resentment which underpinned movements of decolonization; it underpinned the seminal Asian–African conference held in Bandung in Indonesia in 1955 from which grew the Non-Aligned Movement; and it gave rise generally to what has come in the era of independent statehood for most former colonies to be thought of as the development issue in international politics. Even more dramatically, it drove forward in the 1970s a powerful protest movement, led by many disaffected ex-colonial states, calling for the enactment of a so-called 'New International Economic Order' (NIEO) designed to bring about fairer economic relations between the countries of the world. This demand was first voiced in the United Nations (UN) General Assembly in 1974 and was subsequently prosecuted within a series of major international gatherings, most notably the Conference on International Economic Cooperation, which took place intermittently in Paris between 1975 and 1977, and the fourth UN Conference on Trade and Development (UNCTAD), which was held in Nairobi in 1976. For a period during these years the NIEO campaign occupied the centre of the stage in international politics. It acquired salience from, and of course itself contributed to, the general mood of uncertainty pervading the international political economy in the mid-1970s, and there is no doubt that it briefly commanded the attention of the richest and most powerful states in the world. However, in the final analysis the NIEO demand failed to shift the inherited hierarchies of the world order and the summit of selected heads of state held in Cancún in Mexico in 1981 explicitly to discuss international development could not even agree upon a final communiqué and can be said to mark the end of this particular phase of history. For quite a substantial period thereafter such questions were marginalized politically and attracted relatively little attention in most analyses of international affairs.

Needless to say, the core moral issues that have always lain at the root of 'rich–poor' tensions in international politics – matters such as poverty, inequality and injustice – did not disappear so easily. Indeed, as already argued, they have come back into focus much more starkly since the ending of the Cold War and the occurrence of events such as September 11. It can now again be said that, since at least the mid-1990s, there exists a range of arenas in contemporary international politics within which conflicts between 'richer' and 'poorer' countries are being pursued. The agenda is spread across several issues, including most prominently perhaps aid, debt, tax, trade and a number of environmental matters. These various points of pressure have yet to cohere into a collective demand for fundamental change in the world order along the lines of the old NIEO campaign and it is quite possible, indeed likely, that they will not. Yet they all derive from the same core dynamic and form part of the same big picture, and it is vital that they are not overlooked or treated as special and separate situations just because they reside in different institutional parts of the international system. In this book we have set ourselves the task of describing and analysing these various manifestations of the international politics that still divides 'richer' countries from 'poorer' countries. Above all, we seek to make sense of them as a whole, as aspects of a single theme, and to discern what sort of a portrait of international politics we can paint by so doing. We are only too aware that the range of both countries and issues which need to be covered is enormous and hope that all that can reasonably be expected by the reader is an initial remapping of this terrain. We also have no doubt that the map which will eventually emerge will be full of complexity and will be unlikely to sustain any simple notion of a single 'rich–poor' divide. It is important to stress that we deploy this notion cautiously and sensitively and have deliberately placed inverted commas around the two ostensibly defining terms in order to highlight the imprecision of these categories. We do not presume for a moment that such a sharp dichotomy can be said to exist in the real world. The language is designed simply to open up the problem that we want to address in this book.

Where, then, to begin? The initial problem that we face in embarking upon a study of the contemporary international politics of development is that we need to reassess the terms of the academic debate. This is necessary, even though many of the main features of this politics have *apparently* come to be well understood. Much of Asia, it has frequently been said, was developing, but has lately been hit by 'crisis'. Latin America has experienced a 'lost decade' of development. Africa has been 'marginalized'. The Middle East remains in 'turmoil'. Russia and Eastern Europe have been living through the travails of 'transition'. By contrast, the 'West' has continued to grow in wealth and has pushed even further ahead of other parts of the world. The terms used in the discussion may well be somewhat loose, but the overarching contours of the map nevertheless purport to be clear. All of this, moreover, is generally understood to have been taking place in the context of 'globalization'. In fact, everything is, unsurprisingly, rather murkier than these various clichés suggest. First, the debate about globalization, with which much of this is necessarily linked, is itself a vibrant one, with different schools of thought emerging and different phases in the process being detected even amongst those who believe in the significance of the concept – and there are still many who do not. Second, although it is the case that the many contributors to this debate do have views about the impact of globalization on the pattern of stratification of countries in the world, this part of their analysis – which is of the greatest interest here given the focus of this book – has not generally been probed as fully as it might and accordingly the literature on the development dimension of globalization is disappointingly sparse. Third, such discussion as there has been on the international politics of 'who wins' and 'who loses' from globalization has tended to be conducted in a vocabulary that originated in an earlier era and may be thought to be inappropriate, or at least not precisely designed, to comprehend the contemporary world order. As Bahgat Korany (1994: 7) noted several years ago, 'boundaries are not only territorial; they are also mental and conceptual ... Our global "conceptual geography" now needs reordering. Are basic categories such as the Third World or Nonalignment still relevant in the new global equation?'

This opening chapter seeks to initiate a response to that question and proceeds to explore ways of discussing the international politics of development in the context of Korany's new global equation. The first section briefly reconsiders the dominant conceptual frameworks deployed in the 1960s, 1970s and 1980s and finds them wanting as tools of analysis for the present era. The second section identifies two current and prominent paradigms in the field of political economy – liberal and sociological political economy respectively – and sets out the diverging interpretations of international development issues derived from them. As Jean-Philippe Thérien (1999: 723) has noted, these 'two tales of world poverty' were widely advanced in the real world of politics during the 1990s. Again, however, it is argued that these approaches are not adequate to the task at hand. Accordingly, the third section sets out a preferred method of analysis, grounded in what is known as critical political economy, which permits us to get to grips with the politics and the international relations of development in a more meaningful way than other available approaches.

The dominant concepts of the past

What is immediately striking in looking back at old ways of framing the international politics of development is the extent to which all approaches were grounded upon a very basic and rather crude categorization of the countries involved: if not a simple bifurcation, then generally not anything much more sophisticated. Several such formulations of this type can be easily identified in the compendious literature of four decades of analysis.

Central was, of course, the notion of the 'Third World'. Ironically, this was not itself, in origin, an indigenous 'Third World' conceptualization, but a European concept first deployed in 1952 by a French demographer, Alfred Sauvy, to refer to the 'third estate', the common people, before the French Revolution (Lewellen 1995). Because this usage implied poverty, powerlessness and marginalization, it was picked up by a number of scholars in the 1960s to refer to that whole category of emerging ex-colonial countries whose economic, social and political conditions, relatively speaking, replicated those of the French 'third estate' in pre-revolutionary times (Wolf-Phillips 1987). In other words, as Shu-Yin Ma (1998: 344) has observed, the original notion of the 'Third World' was 'not based upon the prior existence of the First and Second World'. However, given the numerical connotation of the term, it was hardly surprising that two other worlds were swiftly discerned: the 'First World' of the capitalist 'West' and the 'Second World' of the communist 'East', thereby implanting Cold War considerations at the very centre of the international development debate and keeping them there for the best part of three decades. In such an antagonistic geopolitical context the concept of the 'Third World' inevitably became political, expressing the attractions of keeping a neutral position, or finding a third way, between the capitalist and communist camps and, in so doing, adding the notion of non-alignment to the definition of 'Third World' (Willetts 1978).

As indicated, this whole literature could not but put politics in the foreground. The alternative starting-point was economics, which also again led in virtually all formulations, whether from the right or the left, to extraordinarily simple dichotomies. From a modernization perspective, the world was divided between 'developing countries' (viewed optimistically) or 'less developed countries' (viewed only a little less optimistically), on the one hand, and 'developed' countries, on the other. The latter were deemed to have offered a model of development to the former: all that the rest had to do within the modernization mind-set was follow in their path as closely and as quickly as possible (Hoselitz *et al.* 1960; Rostow 1960). From a dependency perspective, although the causal thrust of the argument as a whole was sharply divergent, the difference of categorization was only slight: it was 'underdeveloped' countries that were the antithesis of 'developed countries'. They were underdeveloped in this view because historically others had developed at a prior stage, and had done so by exploiting their resources and rendering them dependent (Baran 1967; Frank 1967). The world-systems approach used a different vocabulary – that of the 'core' and the 'periphery' – and sought to moderate the starkness of the bifurcation by introducing, albeit somewhat uneasily, the category of 'semi-periphery' to catch the possibility of countries playing an intermediate role in the system and even moving over time between 'core' and 'periphery' (Wallerstein 1974). Nevertheless, the fundamental thinking here was part and parcel of the dependency debate and the overall approach was still based on a bipolar analysis organized around the presumed existence of something that could be called a 'core' and something that equally could be called a 'periphery'.

A final, very popular way of setting out the issues characteristic of this period was the notion of a 'North–South' divide. This conceptualization drew a wavy line across the world broadly between the Northern and Southern hemispheres, thus separating North from South America, Europe from Africa, North Asia from South Asia and so on, deviating only to draw Australia and New Zealand into the economic and political 'North'. As classically formulated by the first report of the Brandt Commission (1980), which brought together in the late 1970s a group of eminent social democratic politicians to examine international development priorities, the idea expressed both the conflict which obviously was deemed to lie at the root of 'North–South' relations, but at the same time, and perhaps even more importantly, the essential linkage which bound the fates of 'North' and 'South' together in a world economy seen as increasingly interdependent in its functioning. Although this argument was fiercely criticized from a dependency position, which always saw 'North–South' conflict as fundamental rather than negotiable, this way of formulating the problem lent its name to the short-lived era of so-called 'North–South' dialogue (briefly mentioned earlier), during which governments from the two sides of the divide met in various conferences ostensibly to discuss ways of creating a 'new (and more equal) international economic order' (Jones 1983). However, as we noted, these political opportunities came to an end in the early 1980s, which meant that over the course of the next 10–15 years a 'North–South' dialogue was marked more by its absence than its vitality.

The point is that all of these various terms *remain* in widespread use within contemporary social science analyses of these issues. Some writers continue to make a positive case for particular formulations; others somewhat lazily inherit and do not question traditional ways of posing these problems. Only relatively rarely are the concepts still debated in an intensive and meaningful way (Berger 2004). The position taken up here, however, is that all of these conceptualizations are at best dated and at worst flawed, at least in part. As a consequence they should be largely abandoned. Take, first, the notion of the 'Third World'. At the beginning of the 1990s Hans-Henrik Holm (1990) was still prepared to suggest that the 'Third World' continued to be a powerful international actor in a number of arenas, whilst Marc Williams (1993) specifically identified the emerging global environmental agenda as something that could re-articulate the 'Third World' coalition. Others have argued that 'Third World' countries continue to constitute a distinct group identifiable by their 'tenuous, impermanent, fragmented' political culture (Kamrava 1995: 700). Against these points, it can be countered that the relevance of the 'Third World' as a collective actor needs to be demonstrated by reference to specific states and specific issues, and that the possession of an impermanent culture is not the firmest base on which to build a category of analysis. Indeed, as long ago as 1992 in reviewing two books, both of which claimed to be 'rethinking' aspects of the 'Third World', Vicky Randall (1992: 727, 730) noted somewhat sceptically that each held back from 'any explicit or sustained questioning of the validity of talking about a "Third World" as such'. She ended by asking directly: 'can we justify still holding on to the term?' As suggested earlier, a lack of clarity has always attached to the term. Given the manifest disappearance of a 'Second World' following the ending of the Cold War and the dramatic variations of development trajectory which different key parts of the 'Third World' experienced during the 1980s and 1990s, the answer to Randall's question offered by this book is firmly in the negative (see also Berger 1994 and several of the contributions to Berger 2004).

Turning to the various formulations deployed in the modernization and dependency discourses, the problem is not so much the concept of development itself (of which more in the next chapter), but the dichotomous way in which all countries have been assigned (usually) to one of only two groups. There are also political subtexts from which it cannot but be helpful to escape. The category of 'developing countries' now embraces countries in respect of which it is no longer apparent that they are developing at all. Perhaps we ought at least to ask if some countries, for various reasons, cannot ever develop satisfactorily. Others (predominantly in Asia) which many thought were developing are perhaps no longer doing so or at least doing so as effectively. If so, what does this mean? Equally, the phrase 'underdeveloped countries', if used precisely, can, and always could, refer only to countries whose 'underdevelopment' is thought to have been predominantly caused by their exploitation by the 'developed countries', and this is a position now held only by a few dependency zealots. As for the 'developed countries' themselves, one has to ask if it makes sense, in the light of all the social and economic problems which continue to beset the parts of the world embraced by this term, to categorize them still by reference to an apparently completed (for that is what the word developed implies) process of development. For its part, the world-systems approach also has its difficulties, which again have been well recognized over the years. Grugel and Hout have lately used the spectrum of 'core', 'semi-peripheral' and 'peripheral' countries in an ingenious way to probe the regionalist strategies now followed by many states, especially in the intermediate 'semi-peripheral' category. But even they rebel against the economic determinism for which all world-systems approaches have frequently and rightly been criticized and concede that they need to make these terms 'less theoretically rigid' (Grugel and Hout 1999: 8) to get analytical value out of them. Notions of 'core', 'semi-periphery' and 'periphery' still perhaps constitute useful metaphors to highlight the stratification at the heart of the global political economy, but they manifestly do not capture the full extent of the unevenness of the development actually experienced within the world. In other words, many of the categories of classification used in these various traditional literatures are surely too deeply loaded or too crude, or both, to be carried forward into continued unthinking usage.

The same can unfortunately be said for the terminology of 'North–South'. It is unfortunate because a commitment to recognition of a 'North–South' dimension to international affairs has generally been taken to indicate a genuine concern about unequal levels of development in the world. Nevertheless, for all the term's merit as a symbol of faith, it does not travel well into the post-Cold War, globalizing world. In the first place, there is more than one 'North'. It is too glib just to locate Japan automatically in the same camp as the US and the leading countries of Western Europe. Japan may have been trained to become a part of the 'West' in the Cold-War sense of that term; but it represents a different view of development and therefore stands for a different 'North' from that of the US. Given, too, the differences that are widely said to exist between Anglo-American and continental European forms of capitalism, with the former generally seen as a purer, free-market system and the latter as more trust-based and welfare-oriented, that fissure within the 'North' also differentiates the political economies of the two sides of the Atlantic alliance. In the second place, for reasons already noted, there are now many different 'Souths', whereas one of the principles which underpinned traditional 'North–South' politics was that the 'South' did constitute a relatively well identified and homogeneous group of countries (Ravenhill 1990). If there are several 'Norths' and multiple 'Souths', the case for working with a fundamentalist 'North–South' view of the world is much weakened. No purpose is served by aggregating too aggressively if one has instantly to disaggregate.

So where does that leave us? As we have said, the most fundamental questions raised by these debates have not gone away. Everyone knows that intuitively and the reality can be easily demonstrated by reference to a whole range of statistical material about different standards of living in different parts of the world. To put it at its simplest, there remain huge and unacceptable gaps in welfare between the 'richer' and the 'poorer' countries of the world. The task being embarked upon here is to make analytical sense of these gaps and, above all, the politics that is generated by them. The argument therefore moves on to consider the two accounts, or interpretations, of this divide most commonly advanced within official development circles over the last few years. As will be seen, they draw eclectically, and not always consistently, on the terminology discussed above, but nevertheless constitute new and important readings of the situation, not least because of the institutional locations from which they have originated.

Conventional contemporary interpretations and their problems

In a useful article published at the end of the 1990s Thérien pointed to the emergence during that decade of two competing official interpretations of international poverty which he dubbed the 'Bretton Woods paradigm' and the 'United Nations paradigm'. The former was associated with the discourse and practices of the international organizations initially conceived at Bretton Woods in 1944 – the International Monetary Fund (IMF) and the World Bank – and those subsequently established to work alongside them, namely, the secretariat of the General Agreement on Tariffs and Trade (GATT) and its successor, the World Trade Organization (WTO). The latter corresponded to the discourse and practices of the United Nations and, in particular, those of its specialized agencies, such as the United Nations Development Programme (UNDP), the UN Economic and Social Council and the International Labour Organisation (ILO), whose mandates have always been related to economic and social issues. Thérien noted that both paradigms explicitly sought to incorporate globalization into their thinking, thereby offering the prospect of greater contemporary resonance, although, as he also pointed out, they differed significantly in their analysis of the impact that it has had upon international inequality and development.

Perhaps unsurprisingly, given their function as the main international agencies of liberal capitalism, the Bretton Woods institutions have tended to take a broadly optimistic view of the historical achievements of post-1945 development. In a statement published in the middle of the 1990s the World Bank (1995b: 10) observed that:

> Over the last five decades, average per capita incomes in developing countries have more than doubled. The GDPs [Gross Domestic

Products] of some economies have more than quintupled ... There has been a 'green revolution' in South Asia, an 'economic miracle' in East Asia, Latin America has largely overcome its debt crisis, and substantial gains in health and literacy have taken place in Africa.

Prospects were also deemed to be good, provided that the countries either adopted or maintained the 'market-friendly' package of policies recommended by the institutions since the beginning of the 1980s. As is well known, these constitute principally the pursuit of 'sound' macroeconomic conditions, openness to world trade, the development of private enterprise and the attraction of foreign capital inflows. In effect, 'structural adjustment', initially presented as a drastic reorientation required to rebalance struggling 'Third World' economies, has come to be seen, and presented, as a necessary, permanent discipline.

Yet, as Thérien and indeed others have observed, the institutions did also concede in the 1990s that 'zones of extreme poverty' still existed in the world economy and they moved accordingly to make 'poverty alleviation' one of their new watchwords. Much of the World Bank's investment lending and the majority of its latest adjustment programmes were given an explicit poverty focus. In similar vein, the IMF made the financing of social safety nets a standard part of its macroeconomic programmes. However, it is important to stress that the attention paid to such matters by the Bretton Woods institutions during the 1990s emanated from a distinctively different worldview from that which drove the development debate and the 'North–South' dialogue in the 1970s and 1980s. For these institutions poverty did not derive from asymmetrical inequalities in the structure of the global political economy, but was 'more the result of a temporary misadaptation of markets' (Thérien 1999: 732). The causation was perceived to be domestic, not external. Thus poverty came to be treated by the Bank as a consequence of 'country-specific imbalances, policy errors, or political difficulties' (World Bank 1995a: 5). It had therefore to be countered with selective measures addressed to particular states and situations, not with global reforms that might challenge the core principles of a liberal international economic order. In sum, the vision, although superficially progressive, has also been deliberately restrictive and clearly political in its attempt to limit the range of possible, acceptable actions.

By comparison, the UN paradigm remained closer in spirit to the radicalism that drove much old thinking on international development questions, although it too moved on during the 1990s from the framework of these discourses to embrace and promote as its central idea the notion of 'global poverty'. While recognizing the extent of the social and economic progress generated by post-1945 development policies, the

UN position emphasized the unequal distribution of the fruits of development. As stated in the declaration adopted by the UN Summit for Social Development held in Copenhagen in 1995, 'we are witnessing in countries throughout the world the expansion of prosperity for some, unfortunately accompanied by an expansion of unspeakable poverty for others' (United Nations 1995: 6). In other words, globalization was openly recognized to be generating losers as well as winners. The extended liberalization of trade and finance was understood to have reduced the capacities of national governments to shape the social order within the countries over which they presided, producing 'states of disarray', the telling phrase by which the UN Research Institute for Social Development (1995) described the social effects of globalization.

As Thérien once again pointed out, this analysis had elements of both continuity and change in relation to the conventional 'North–South' approach. The UN paradigm still suggested that Asian, Latin American and African countries faced particular difficulties reacting to globalization because their economies tended to be more vulnerable to shocks emanating from global commodity and financial markets. For all that, it was the case that UN agencies no longer routinely treated these countries as a homogeneous group, instead fully acknowledging the differentiation that had taken place amongst them over the past 20 or more years. More importantly, however, the UN view also asserted that the broadening of the gap between 'rich' and 'poor' was genuinely global in impact and that poverty, although more severe in the 'South', also plagued the 'North'. The UNDP (1997: 3) thus reported in 1997 that there were 100 million people living below the poverty line in the countries that belong to the Organization for Economic Cooperation and Development (OECD). Indeed, from this conceptual perspective, poverty was more appropriately seen as a problem that affected individual human beings, rather than national states and societies. This was a shift of thinking of significance because it established a parallel between the poor of Asia or Africa, on the one hand, and the poor of North America or Western Europe, on the other. The lines of causation might be differently drawn between the two types of case and possible remedies might also diverge, but from the humanist position broadly adopted within the UN there was no intrinsic distinction to be made between the similar fate of a human being in one geographic location and that of another in a different location.

As can be seen, then, both the so-called Bretton Woods and UN paradigms offered strong, divergent accounts of the problem of international poverty and development. They emerged from different institutional complexes and have been sustained by different power blocs of markedly uneven weight within the current world order. The former remains very much the orthodoxy of our time; the latter still constitutes something of the critical opposition. As interpretations of events they are undoubtedly of great interest, but in the final analysis largely because of who it was that first articulated them. From our perspective the problem is that they do not lead us forward theoretically. It is not that they are *not* grounded theoretically, because they do connect to intellectual positions within the field of political economy that purport to be able to offer the very approach to the researching of the question of the international politics of development which this chapter explicitly seeks to elucidate. The difficulty is that the positions opened up, although very much focused upon the new global equation at the turn of the century and therefore not outdated, do not adequately serve our specific needs in this book.

Why is that so? The Bretton Woods paradigm can be quickly and easily dealt with in this respect. It is based directly upon the classic economic liberal position within political economy, the origins of which, as is well known, go back to the writings of John Locke, Adam Smith, David Ricardo and John Stuart Mill. This position derives from the founding premise that free individuals are best equipped to make social choices, and builds from this basic assumption a worldview which favours market solutions to development needs, tempered only by the establishment of a minimal state to secure the operation of the market. From the beginning of the 1980s onwards these classic ideas underpinned what John Toye (1987) described as a 'counter-revolution' (at least as seen from a broadly dependency perspective) in thinking about international development matters. This not only swept through the Bretton Woods institutions, as we have seen, but also had a forceful impact upon the academy, especially amongst economists. Although it could be said that these new neoliberal thinkers did not have much more to offer than a revitalization of some elements of modernization theory, they did seek to bury the notion of the situational peculiarity of the 'Third World' within a universalist liberal discourse which asserted that development was a process attainable all over the world, provided that the market was allowed to assert itself over the state. As such, they not only place at the centre of their analysis, but also welcome largely unreservedly, the increased liberalization of trade and financial flows that has been one of the key features of the reshaping of the world economy over the last 30 years.

The UN paradigm also has its associated political economy in a less prominent but still distinctive sociological strand within that field well represented by the recent work of such writers as Ankie Hoogvelt and William I. Robinson. Hoogvelt (1997: xii), for example, has argued that the fact that the new political economy was 'global from the very beginning' has had 'consequences for our understanding of the locational distribution of wealth and poverty, of development and underdevelopment'. Specifically, for her 'the familiar pyramid of the core–periphery hierarchy is no longer a geographic but a social division of the world economy'. In similar fashion, Robinson (1998, 2004) has called for a break with all analyses that put nation-states at their centre, a consequent reconsideration of the relationship between space and development and a rebuilding based not on the study of territory but of social groups, particularly classes. To use old concepts, in this vision the 'Third World' has come home to the 'First World', while the 'South' has got inside the 'North'. All nestle together, for sure, inside the world's major cities. The exemplar here is Los Angeles where, as Mike Davis (1990) vividly demonstrated, life in urban southern California for many African-Americans and other more recent immigrants from Latin America has turned out to be little different from that experienced by, say, Mexicans living south of the Rio Grande in the 'Third World' proper. Viewed more broadly, the concept of a global social structure is the necessary point of departure for this perspective. It can either be envisaged, in Hoogvelt's preferred terms, as composed of essentially three concentric circles, representing respectively the elites, the contented and the marginalized, each cutting across *all* national boundaries, or represented alternatively in the more classical Marxist categories of analysis deployed by Robinson in his work. Either way, it is the sociological dimension of a newly transnationalized world which is given primary emphasis.

The basic problem with both of these political economies is that they underplay international politics, most of which still goes on in and between states, globalization notwithstanding. Each makes the mistake of assuming that somehow the global restructuring of the last decade or so has led to traditional interstate political conflicts about development being superseded. Liberal political economy has long been criticized for presuming that political differences can be managed away amidst the interdependence and mutual advantage generated by economic contact and concomitant growth; it certainly makes that mistake in its approach to the analysis of globalization and development. But radical sociological political economy also takes us too far and too fast towards global class analysis, given that states, and all the vested interests (not to mention popular loyalties) which they generate, have scarcely yet disappeared. Although transnational class interests and alliances may well have formed and be in the process of strengthening, they are still required to assert their political influence mainly via pressure upon state actors. The focus of the discussion in this book on international politics certainly does not allow us to be as dismissive of the analysis of state action as sociological political economy generally allows. In sum, then, although both the intellectual perspectives within which Thérien's Bretton Woods and

UN paradigms are grounded have genuinely served to widen the debate about international development and take it beyond some of the simplistic dichotomies of the modernization versus dependency era, it remains the case that neither can provide the necessary theoretical foundation for the study of the politics underlying relations between the 'richer' and the 'poorer' states of the world which is being sought here.

The politics of critical political economy

So how, then, do we set about analysing what we have called the new international politics of development? It may seem as if the thrust of the argument being presented here is that all approaches are flawed and unsatisfactory, yet that is not ultimately the conclusion that we want to draw. It is the case that mainstream liberal political economy dominates this field of study and that a powerful, radical critique of this way of seeing the world has lately been made by an emergent sociological political economy. But the fact is that these approaches do not exhaust the field. This is not the place to set out a comprehensive review of the academic discipline of political economy. Other studies over the years have done that very well (Staniland 1985; Gill and Law 1988; Frieden and Lake 1991; Caporaso and Levine 1992; Balaam and Veseth 1996). The point to highlight and build upon is that there has lately advanced to prominence within political economy much 'critical' (or new, or heterodox, or counter-hegemonic) thinking. Drawing inspiration in the broadest sense from the critical theory of the Frankfurt School and within the field of political economy from the founding work of Robert Cox, as set out initially in a remarkable and pioneering article in the journal *Millennium* in 1981, this approach self-consciously set out to be 'critical in the sense that it stands apart from the prevailing order of the world and asks how that order came about' (Cox 1981: 129). In Cox's particular formulation, it was a theory of history concerned not just with the past but with a continuing process of change; it was directed to the social and political complex as a whole rather than to its separate parts; and it contained within its ambit the possibility of identifying the outlines of alternative distributions of power from those prevailing at any given time. In short, critical political economy was hitched from the outset to a different epistemology from most of the previously dominant frameworks of social science, both mainstream and radical. It favoured a reflectivist position that stressed the unavoidable relationship of subject and object in all forms of social analysis, rather than the conventional positivist insistence upon their separation.

On this basis Cox (1981: 137) proceeded to unfold his version of a critical theory appropriate to the study of the global political economy. He proposed a 'method of historical structures', with the latter conceived as configurations of forces (material capabilities, ideas and institutions) that do not determine actions but nevertheless create opportunities and impose constraints. Material capabilities were defined as natural resources transformed by technology and organization. Ideas were divided into two kinds: one connoted intersubjective meanings, or 'shared notions of the nature of social relations' (Cox 1981: 136), held broadly in common throughout a particular historical structure; the other consisted of contested ideologies about alternative social orders. Institutions reflected the particular amalgamations of ideas and material power in existence at the time of their formation, but nevertheless subsequently took on their own life. In an important ontological move, there is, for Cox (1981: 136) and those who think like him, presumed to be 'no one-way determinism' between these three forces. The question of which way the lines of influence run is always conceived as a research question likely to be answered in different ways in different historical circumstances. It is also important to stress that in this view of the world care is taken to make sure that structures are not reified: people are not just bearers of structures, they create them. For Coxian political economy, historical structures mean no more – *but no less* – than persistent social practices, made by collective human activity and transformed through collective human activity.

Within the global political economy, interaction between material capabilities, ideas and institutions was seen by Cox to take place across three interrelated levels: the social forces engendered by different and changing production processes; the varying forms of state derived from different state/society complexes, which, rather than states alone, were considered to be the basic entities of international politics; and types of world order. Again, the three levels were perceived to be interrelated, each bearing on the other, with the appropriate point of entry for analysts being a matter of preference *provided* that all levels are studied in connected fashion. That said, the last concept highlighted, that of world order, is an especially important feature of Cox's lexicon. He acknowledged the world-systems approach as a valuable radical alternative to conventional international relations theory, but argued that the notion of world order was preferable to that of world-systems because it indicated a structure which may only have a limited duration and which does not have the inevitable equilibrium connotation of system. The notion of order, Cox (1981: 152) suggested, should be 'used in the sense of the way things usually happen', not to imply 'orderliness' or lack of turbulence in international affairs.

What has been particularly appealing about Cox's formulation of a critical theory for political economy is the way he has consciously drawn upon the best insights of other preceding social science perspectives (see Cox 2002). For example, he argued in broadly conventional international politics terms that the varying forms of state which derive from different state/society complexes remained a crucial level of analysis, although it should quickly be added that the very fact that highly varied state/society complexes, rather than simple, self-interested states (as defined within so much conventional international relations theory), were seen as the actors in question makes his approach notably more subtle. In addition, however, he incorporated into his thinking the wide reach of world-systems theory, the traditional historical materialist concern with social forces and the particular Gramscian concern with ideas and ideologies as sources of power. This last aspect of the package, which was developed more fully by Cox in a later article which served to introduce Gramsci's ideas to the international studies community, was especially important because political economy has historically had a tendency to be preoccupied with materialist definitions of power. Yet, as Cox (1983: 168) himself put it, 'ideas and material conditions are always bound together, mutually influencing one another, and not reducible one to the other'. This insertion of an ideational dimension into the standard framework of analysis thus anticipated and took on board significant elements of the recent, fashionable application of social constructivism to issues of international politics (Wendt 1999).

Cox's work has been variously understood and received. In his assessment Sinclair (1996: 13) drew attention to an important difference of opinion. He noted that, for some, Cox offers no more than a 'watery Marxism', built upon concepts such as surplus, class forces and ideology which 'we have all seen before' (Adams 1989: 224). Yet others discern in Cox just the opposite: they criticize the absence of a notion of 'overall structure', lament the lack of genuinely 'determining' variables and end up condemning his approach as constituting an inadequate 'pluralist empiricism' (Burnham 1991: 78). We actually accept the validity of both charges, but are not in the least worried by their supposed force. In effect, we prefer our Marxism to be 'watery', rather than excessively dry; and we have no problem with 'pluralist empiricism'. Cox's wide-ranging and eclectic methods of analysis offer in our view a richness of resource unmatched by other perspectives in political economy. This is not to say that Cox's work is not without problems – as with all academic work it should be engaged, criticized and moved forward, not just admired – but it is to suggest that his innovativeness has been crucial in opening up the whole field of critical political economy. He has served to legitimize both a wider and a deeper range of thinking than was previously possible and, in so doing, to inspire a loose college of scholars working with a diverse range of critical political economy approaches. In short, the essence of the appeal of Cox's work is its very breadth, for what he offers is not so much a body of driven theory but rather an overarching framework of analysis.

For these reasons we suggest that this framework provides the most appropriate *starting point* for the generation of the particular method of analysis required to deliver the ambitions of this book. But we stress that it offers only our point of entry. We put it this way because we recognize that great care must be taken with all conceptualizations of political economy to ensure that an explicitly agency-oriented body of theory is inserted into the overall framework and excessive determinism thereby avoided. The latter is the great danger of any mode of analysis which foregrounds structures and there have been those who have argued that some of Cox's own substantive, empirical work has fallen prey to exactly this deficiency (Laffey 1992). However, critical political economy can, and should, be deployed in a way which avoids the tendency to overdetermine outcomes. Specifically, it must carry through into practice its commitment to give due weight to both structure *and* agency in its explanations, rather than privileging one to the exclusion of the other. This is very important and has been openly recognized by Cox himself. In one of his reflections on the development of his own thinking he draws an explicit distinction between the methodology of political science (including by implication international relations) and economics, on the one hand, and political economy, on the other. The former, he suggests, are actor-oriented studies which take off from fixed assumptions about the parameters within which actions take place; the latter, as we have seen, concerns itself primarily with the very historical structures within which political and economic activity occurs. For him, and for us, the two methodologies must be held in balance: 'the structural approach is not so much an alternative to the actor–interactions approach as a logical priority to it' (Cox 1989: 38).

In other words, the key notion with which we should be working is what might best be called 'structural context'. This is emphatically not to be understood as a cage, as with, say, much structuralist thinking within the dependency or world-systems schools. It is properly conceived as the source of both opportunities *and* constraints, as being both enabling *and* binding, as permitting agency *within* bounds. In a nutshell, what we are stressing is that agency-oriented concepts (which in our case will primarily be political or international relations concepts) must of necessity be embedded within structural (or political economy) concepts. In another statement made several years ago, a group of us suggested that the defining features of a critical (or, as we preferred to call it, 'new') political economy approach should be that it would reject 'the old dichotomy between agency and structure' and recognize the need to 'develop an integrated analysis, by combining parsimonious theories which analyse agency in terms of a conception of rationality with contextual theories which analyse structures institutionally and historically' (Gamble *et al.* 1996: 5–6). We stand by that prospectus and hope to live up to it in this study. Put directly and colloquially, therefore, what we seek to do is *the politics of critical political economy*, with the two methodologies wrapped up together, each mutually dependent on the other for their overall analytical purchase.

This chapter has thus worked its way towards an elaboration of the framework of analysis within which we propose to ground the ensuing elaboration of the new international politics of development at the end of the twentieth and the beginning of the twenty-first centuries. As will be seen shortly, the ensuing parts of the book are organized in a way that is designed to reflect this broad approach. Part II considers the 'structural context' within which this politics unfolds; Part III examines the activities of the various agents that then prosecute this politics in some of the major 'diplomatic arenas' within which development is presently pursued. However, there is one more stage in the argument that needs to be made before we can turn to the study proper. We need in a fuller way to orient the framework of analysis proposed here to the particular subject-matter of this book. This involves reviewing, and then taking up positions on, some of the most important debates about politics and international relations that have been generated within critical political economy over the past few years. In particular, we need to establish more precisely what we think about key concepts such as hegemony, globalization, states themselves and of course development. It is to this task that we turn in the next chapter.

Chapter 2

Founding Theses

As already indicated, critical political economy has not yet focused directly or intensively on the need to think through the new international politics of development in the context of globalization. But it is already the inspiration of a prolific academic literature on a range of closely related matters, and there is plenty of analysis and argument about contemporary politics that we can and should draw upon in order to orient ourselves to this particular line of enquiry. In this connection four particular debates stand out. Although they have often been pursued as if they are separate matters, they are in fact intrinsically linked. They need to be reviewed, and then brought together. The first focuses upon the notion of hegemony and examines the rise and fall of hegemonies as the means by which to comprehend changes in the nature of the modern world order. The second addresses the extent to which we can sensibly now talk about globalization and considers the meaning that we might attach to this popular but difficult term. The third explores changes and continuities in the role of states, and their relationship to the social forces that underpin them, within a putatively globalizing world order. The fourth returns to the core issue (for us) of development and asks again how that term might best be deployed in the new context of global restructuring. We shall chart a course through these debates, identifying and taking up positions in respect of each of them. These positions in effect constitute founding theses. *In combination*, they form the intellectual base upon which the rest of our endeavour to reframe the contemporary international politics of development will subsequently be built. They collectively generate an argument which has the following key characteristics: first, it views the contemporary world order as lacking a genuinely hegemonic state power; second, it takes globalization seriously, but at the same time is not overwhelmed by its supposed force; third, it recognizes the continuing realities of states and conventional international (interstate) politics, but acknowledges not only the historical variety of state forms but also the fact that states are being significantly restructured in the current era and that, as a result, different forms of state necessarily rub up against each other in the international arena; and, fourth, it does not reject the concept of development, but instead reinterprets it as a universal problem faced by all states and societies in

21

the world. These positions are explored further below in a fashion that is unavoidably more assertive than argumentative. This is necessitated by the voluminous character of the literatures from which these theses emerge and justified by the fact that the claims being made, although foundational for this work, are clearly not original to it.

The hegemony debate

Critical political economy's initial preoccupation was with the notion of hegemony. The initial contribution was made by Robert Cox at a time in the early 1980s when the dominant neorealist and neoliberal institutionalist strands within mainstream international relations theory were beginning to converge around three focal points: rational action theories of the state, the theory of hegemonic stability, and regime theory (Crane and Amawi 1991). The extent of the literature that had been generated in this vein was enormous. Charles Kindleberger (1973) and Robert Gilpin (1975) dominated the initial discussion about the need for a stabilizer to manage the world economy but did not actually use the term hegemony. As a result, the most-cited mainstream formulation of the problematic was provided by Robert Keohane (1984: 32), who described hegemony as a 'preponderance of material resources'. For him, the essential elements of hegemonic power, as they related to the world economy, were comprised of control over raw materials, markets and capital as well as 'competitive advantages in the production of highly valued goods ... involving the use of complex or new technology' (Keohane 1984: 33). These material resources then provided the means by which the hegemon could both make and enforce the rules of the world political economy. Power was thus conceived in traditional resource terms and hegemony was deployed as force.

This conception of hegemony set up a number of specific debates in mainstream international relations. One disputed the normative manner in which hegemonic power was exercised, positions ranging from the benign to the 'self-regarding' (Snidal 1985). Another concerned the impact of the loss of United States hegemony on the viability of the various post-1945 'regimes' designed to improve international economic cooperation (Krasner 1983). A third, and logically prior, debate addressed the very matter of whether the United States had indeed lost its hegemonic position (Huntington 1988/9; Kennedy 1988; Nye 1988). A final debate disputed how best to explain international cooperation, with neorealists contending that the importance of relative gains in conditions of international anarchy inhibited cooperation, and neoliberal institutionalists assuming that states were more concerned with absolute welfare maximization and were thus capable of learning to cooperate (Baldwin 1993). However, the problem with all of this literature was that its theoretical underpinnings were marked by a number of biases that rendered many of the attendant arguments deficient (Leaver 1989). For example, the definition of the core concept of hegemony was based upon a limited range of variables, largely drawn from a selective reading of the US post-war experience and minimally qualified by reference to aspects of the history of the United Kingdom (UK) in the nineteenth century. Other questions were also excluded from consideration, notably the matter of why some states came to accept and others to resist the rule of the hegemon. Additionally, the issue – vital for an approach which believed in the measurement of power – of exactly how much power was needed to engender hegemony was never satisfactorily resolved. One could go on. In the end, John Ikenberry (1989: 379) was right to suggest that 'the texture of hegemonic power' was not satisfactorily 'captured' in the major American international relations texts of this time.

The intellectual running was thereafter taken up by critical political economy. Cox himself advanced the classic neo-Gramscian definition of hegemony. For him it meant 'more than the dominance of a single world power' and was instead to be understood as:

> dominance of a particular kind where the dominant state creates an order based ideologically on a broad measure of consent, functioning according to general principles that in fact ensure the continuing supremacy of the leading state or states and leading social classes but at the same time offer some measure or prospect of satisfaction to the less powerful (Cox 1987: 7).

Thus 'there can be dominance without hegemony; hegemony is one possible form dominance may take' (Cox 1981: 153). Crucially, in this perspective (and in contrast to mainstream accounts) hegemony was seen as bringing together both coercive *and* consensual elements of power. It is worth emphasizing this. Although the novelty of this approach compared to most of the mainstream lay in the attention it gave to the role of ideology in establishing and maintaining a hegemonic world order, it did also theorize the objective elements of power that lead to the capacity for the exercise, ultimately, of coercion. Power was conceived, famously, as a centaur, part man, part beast, with different elements employed in different political situations. Broadly, the stronger the position of the ruling group or state, the less the need for the use of force. There are admittedly some difficulties with Cox's account of hegemony, notably a failure fully to separate out all the various elements that constitute hegemony across different structures of power (Payne 1994).

But, notwithstanding this, it is not difficult to see that Coxian theory is substantially more nuanced than mainstream approaches and enables analysts to catch much more of the essence of hegemony.

This understanding of hegemonic power was used by Cox and others to analyse the nature of the post-1945 world order. It was characterized as a *Pax Americana*, a period marked by the remarkably successful combination of two processes: the reassertion of liberal economic ideas and values across Western Europe and their espousal within the vast majority of the new states emerging out of colonialism, on the one hand, and the containment of the major alternative world order which had emerged after 1917 under the leadership of the Soviet Union and was legitimized by reference to the appeal of a Marxist–Leninist form of socialism, on the other. The steady, if uneven, reconstruction of a liberal international economic order, characterized by the freeing of trade between national economies and the eventual convertibility of other major currencies with the US dollar, thus went hand in hand with the development of national security states in the 'West', characterized by the acquisition of nuclear arsenals, a readiness to fight localized wars in the 'Third World' and the deployment of intelligence operatives for subversive purposes. In this sense, the Truman Doctrine was the other side of the coin from the Marshall Plan, the destabilization of radical regimes in Africa, Asia, the Middle East and Latin America the counterpoint to the many programmes of development aid. The rhetoric of the Cold War, extolling 'freedom' over 'repression', was the ideological cement which bound the whole system together, although it should be noted that the actual form of capitalism which mostly prevailed in this early post-war period was an 'embedded liberal' variant committed to a measure of state economic intervention and welfare provision (Ruggie 1982).

This order was managed by the United States with growing confidence until the late 1960s and early 1970s. The key event that marked the onset of crisis was the Vietnam War, the most ambitious expression of US post-war containment strategy. The 'long boom' of the so-called Bretton Woods era, which ran through the 1950s and into the 1960s restoring Western Europe and Japan to prosperity and buoying up the early developmental aspirations of many newly independent countries, had been largely funded by the willingness of the US to export liquidity to the rest of the capitalist world via official loans, corporate investment and military expenditure. This 'dollar overhang', as the jargon dubbed the gap between US foreign-exchange reserves and the extent of its financial liabilities overseas, was already considerable as involvement in Vietnam began to deepen (Triffin 1961). The dollar's status as the core currency of the system could not in the end survive the combination of enormous US expenditure on the war in Southeast Asia and the unwillingness of US politicians to tax their people sufficiently to cover the costs of the global operations of the US state. President Richard Nixon's devaluation of the dollar in August 1971 and the suspension of its convertibility into gold was the decisive moment that signalled the end of this era.

Precisely because the post-war world order was a *Pax Americana*, these problems affected the whole of the system. The inability of the US to manage the world economy in a financially responsible way served to transmit inflation internationally. This stimulated further cost pressures and falls in profit levels in all of the leading 'Western' countries, which in turn generated fiscal crises imperilling the welfare commitments of the post-1945 period. It also created pressures to push up raw material prices in 'peripheral' economies, as effected most dramatically of all by the Organization of Petroleum Exporting Countries (OPEC) in 1973 and as subsequently articulated in the widespread demand emanating from poorer countries for the negotiation of an NIEO. In the US, unlike Japan and the other leading Western European states, Presidents Nixon, Ford and Carter were still able to counter recessionary conditions by stimulating the economy towards full employment, but they did so only by continuing to run a deficit and thus in effect forcing US allies to take devalued dollars in exchange for the maintenance of its defence guarantee of the 'West'. In so doing, the dollar slipped from 'top-currency' to 'negotiated-currency' status (Strange 1971). The overall impact was to make the 1970s a period of great fluidity (and indeed turbulence) within the global political economy.

The reaction came in the form of an attempt by the US to reassert control of the system during the course of the 1980s by means of the political economy of 'Reaganism'. Feeding upon a popular emotional rejection of the new realities of US power, or 'weaknesses', which Jimmy Carter had asked the US people to confront, President Ronald Reagan offered the twin prospectus of 'militarism' and 'monetarism'. The former involved a major re-arming of the US military machine designed to allow the US once again to 'walk tall' on the world stage. More specifically, its purposes were to defeat so-called 'Third World nationalism', which was wrongly but deliberately interpreted as the advance of communism, and also to force the Soviet Union into a final decisive arms race which would divert resources away from its attempts to shore up its increasingly stagnant economy. The latter was premised upon increasing profit margins, weakening trade unions, eliminating inflation through the adoption of monetarist macroeconomic management and boosting growth by means of supply-side economics. It also sought to impose the same neoliberal economic doctrine within the multilateral financial institutions in which the US voice was critical. In other words, the thinking behind this strategy sought to re-create behind the rhetoric of the 'Second Cold War' a new mixture of consent and coercion comparable in effect to that which had characterized the establishment of the *Pax Americana* after 1945.

It only partly worked. It succeeded to the extent that the economic ideas of the neoliberals spread widely, whether adopted enthusiastically by allies of the US or forced upon reluctant reformist regimes in Africa, Asia and Latin America in the name of 'structural adjustment' by the combined pressures of the IMF, the World Bank and the US Agency for International Development. Under Reagan, the US also demonstrated again its willingness to intervene, by force if necessary, in intimidating regimes, such as those in Nicaragua and Libya, which stood out against its interests and its worldview. In 1985, in an even more dramatic shift, the Soviet Union embarked upon the process of *perestroika*, a restructuring of its own internal economic and political arrangements deliberately intended by the new leadership under Mikhail Gorbachev to open up Soviet society to outside influence from the West. Yet, in the final analysis, the US under Reagan was not able to reconstitute its control of the world order. In part, the failure was a consequence of the administration's unwillingness, like that of its predecessors in the 1960s and 1970s, to tackle the problem of the endemic trading and expenditure deficits of the US economy. It also obviously reflected the continuing growth in strength of the economies of Japan and Western Europe, the latter increasingly enmeshed and protected by the structures of the European Community, as well as the emergence of other successful export-oriented economies in the so-called newly industrializing countries (NICs) of East Asia.

This account of the post-1945 world order implies that during the course of the 1970s and 1980s US 'hegemony' gave way to US 'domination' (Cox 1987: 299). The key difference was the evaporation of that broad measure of consent more or less automatically and generally willingly given to the leadership of the most powerful state. Such a claim does not necessarily contradict the standard (neorealist) assertion that the US is the 'sole superpower' in the post-Cold War world of the 1990s, because it is made in a different conceptual vocabulary. But it does deliberately alter the emphasis of the argument. It fully acknowledges that, within a non-hegemonic world order, the power of the US unquestionably remains preponderant – certainly, as implied, in the military sphere given the demise of the Soviet Union, substantially too in the ideological domain given its continuing leadership of old and new organs of international management such as the IMF and the Group of 7/Group of 8 (G7/G8) summits, and also, not least, to a very considerable degree in economic matters. The size and technological vigour of the US economy, the origins of much capitalist enterprise in the US and the continuing centrality of the US dollar as an international currency are all factors which still very much matter and render the US still the most formidable national player in the world economy. They came together very effectively to generate the so-called 'Clinton boom' during which the US economy grew substantially and persistently through the 1990s (Aysha 2001; Gowan 2001).

What is different, though, and crucial, is that the US is no longer powerful enough to shape largely on its own the rules of a consensual hegemonic order. Even under Presidents George H. Bush and Bill Clinton, both of whom were internationalist in orientation, it was, for example, neither willing nor able to initiate a new 'Bretton Woods' whereby leadership was re-imposed upon the functioning of the world economy; it did not even consistently seek to use the G7/G8 process to shape the economic policies of the leading capitalist states. Although the US did succeed in putting together a powerful coalition to fight the Gulf War in 1991 it had to rely on German, Japanese and Arab funds to pay for its military effort and thereafter only became involved most reluctantly in managing the violent consequences in Europe of the disintegration of the former Yugoslav republic. In short, it can be suggested that the US no longer possesses that self-reinforcing and largely unchallenged primacy across *all* the necessary constituents of hegemonic power. It is still the world's preponderant state in terms of raw material power; it also remains wedded to a strong, if distorting, vision of 'American exceptionalism' (Pieterse 2003); but the reality is that it cannot call upon that old ideological command, that easy capacity to set and win support for its external agenda which marked the classic years of post-1945 *Pax Americana*. The US has in effect been reduced to mortal status.

We advance this argument even in the light of the ambitious and self-confident policies of the George W. Bush administration that assumed office in the US in 2001. Its apparent willingness to act unilaterally and to assert its perception of US interests increasingly aggressively over a wide range of policy areas, most notably of course Iraq, has swiftly given rise to a new analytical engagement with the notion of 'empire' as the most vivid way of portraying US power in the world at the beginning of the twenty-first century (Johnson 2000; Harvey 2003; Ignatieff 2003; Mann 2003; Ikenberry 2004). Although some of this work is undoubtedly insightful, it smacks on the whole of a rush to come to judgement about the impact of an administration which only moved in this direction after 11 September 2001 and might yet be viewed ultimately as an aberrant intervention within the wider tradition of US global policy over the last 50 years. Neither, for that matter, is it immediately obvious that some of the difficulties into which several of the policy initiatives of the Bush regime have run, again most notably in Iraq, are not evidence precisely of that loss of US *hegemony* and its replacement by a cruder US *domination* of which Cox spoke as early as 1987. There is a pressing need for critical political economy to return to the politics of hegemony and to endeavour to tease out more fully the potential of this concept as a tool for illuminating the power dynamics of the present era. For the moment, though, we propose as the first of our founding theses the marked absence within the world order of the past couple of decades of a truly hegemonic state.

The globalization debate

It is important to remember that the ending of US hegemony was the historical context within which the way was opened to the debate about globalization. The latter is often (wrongly) presented as if, to all intents and purposes, it came out of nowhere, either historically or conceptually. In fact, an important early thesis suggested that, during the crisis of US global hegemony in the 1970s and its attempted reconstitution in the 1980s, control of the world order had slipped not only beyond the capacity of the United States but also beyond that of any single state and perhaps even any group of states. This argument was built up as follows. Moving into the vacuum left by the vagaries of US financial policy after 1971 and then both inspiring and drawing sustenance from the ascendancy of neoliberal ideas during the Reagan years, a new 'transnational managerial class' (Cox 1993: 261) or 'an international business civilisation' (Strange 1990: 260) had come to the fore, based in the major private banks and global corporations. In combination with the political leaders of the US and other leading capitalist countries, as well as international bureaucrats working for the IMF and the World Bank, these social forces were seen by many critical political economists to constitute a 'transnational historic bloc' (Gramsci 1971; van der Pijl 1984; Gill 1990; Rupert 1995) committed to the overall management of the world economy. It was certainly widely argued that under these auspices a genuine global economy, grounded in production and finance, had been created, replacing the former post-1945 international economy premised upon exchange relations between national economies. Mostly, these early accounts of the 'sea-changes' deemed to have taken place in the nature of the world order since the era of US hegemony did not initially deploy the notion of globalization *per se*. But, of course, it was not long before the word was on everybody's lips and the point has now been reached where globalization has been used to launch a myriad of popular and academic analyses of the current global order, with the upshot that the term has been simultaneously overused and underdefined (Higgott and Reich 1998).

In these circumstances there is an undoubted attraction to turning away from the concept of globalization altogether. But the truth is that it connotes too important a phenomenon to be set aside, which means that there is no alternative but actually to grapple with the conceptual debate to which it has given rise. It is best understood, at least at first cut, as a social process unfolding at the global level and driven forward by a mixture of forces (public and private, political and non-political) within which states, although still likely to be highly significant, are not always necessarily the only or the most important influence. This sense of globalization as a very wide-ranging *process* has been well captured in the working definition adopted by David Held, Anthony McGrew, David Goldblatt and Jonathan Perraton in their commanding overview of the globalization debate. They say, specifically, that 'globalization may be thought of initially as the widening, deepening and speeding up of worldwide interconnectedness in all aspects of contemporary social life, from the cultural to the criminal, the financial to the spiritual' (Held *et al.* 1999: 2). From this conceptual starting point they then went on to identify and distinguish three broad schools of thought within the debate that they refer to as the 'hyperglobalizers', the 'sceptics' and the 'transformationalists'.

From our perspective these first two schools of thought offer too rigid a view of the process. The problem with the 'hyperglobalist' account is that it exaggerates, both in the form offered by neoliberals who effusively welcome the triumph of the market over states (Ohmae 1995), and by radicals or Marxists who bemoan what they see from their perspective as the ultimate victory of an oppressive capitalist system (Greider 1997). For all the difference of mood, they are agreed that globalization signals the arrival of a new era in human affairs which they see as largely created by a technological revolution in communications that has massively accelerated the exchange of people, ideas and money. A 'borderless world' has thus been brought into being, characterized by the establishment of proliferating transnational networks of production, trade and finance which operate according to a genuinely global dynamic. More generally, the 'hyperglobalizers' share 'a conviction that economic globalization is constructing new forms of social organization that are supplanting, or that will eventually supplant, traditional nation-states as the primary economic and political units of world society' (Held *et al.* 1999: 3). Accordingly, they foresee the inexorable rise and rise of global governance, global civil society and global cultural motifs. There is no doubt that there are trends in these directions that need to be taken seriously, but they are not problematized sufficiently by the 'hyperglobalizers' and that is par for their course. The 'hyperglobalist' account of globalization is too determinist, too sweeping, too apolitical.

Indeed, serious analysts of globalization do not give it much credence at all any more.

The 'sceptical' thesis has different faults. It is associated particularly with the critique of Paul Hirst and Grahame Thompson (1996, 1999) and was designed explicitly, in the words of the title of their book, to bring globalization into 'question'. Their analytical way into this debate (their 'trick', if you like) was to propose a highly demanding definition of the end-state of globalization – namely, a perfectly integrated global economy – against which evidence relating to the contemporary period, unsurprisingly perhaps, falls short. What it suggests, according to the 'sceptics', is no more than 'heightened internationalisation': in other words, intensified interactions between predominantly national economies, the conventional units of economic analysis. Even these, it is argued, do not significantly exceed the levels of economic interdependence witnessed historically at the end of the nineteenth century. In other words, globalization is more myth than new reality; the true 'global corporation' is still a rarity; national governments are far from immobilized, although they may have experienced a loss of nerve in the face of the powerful ideology of globalization; global governance, if it is anything, is a façade behind which the most powerful 'Western' countries continue to dominate the traditional international economic and political system. The line of argument here was fairly trenchant and sufficed initially as a counter to some of the hyperbolic (and populist) early claims about globalization. However, the globalization debate has itself unfolded in a series of waves and the 'sceptical' account has, to a considerable extent, been overtaken by events and is now in real danger of appearing as if it has an irredeemably closed mind on the matter, regardless of how much or how fast economic and political events still seem to move in a globalizing direction.

By comparison with these two readings, the so-called 'transformationalist' account of globalization, which Held and his co-authors derived particularly from the work of such as Anthony Giddens (1990), Manuel Castells (1996, 1997 and 1998) and James Rosenau (1997), is much more sensitive and persuasive and can be set out briefly as follows. It begins from the assumption that globalization as a concept draws attention to the recent emergence of what Held *et al.* (1999: 7) described as 'a powerful transformative force which is responsible for a "massive shake-out" of societies, economies, institutions of governance and world order'. Importantly, the direction of the shake-out remains uncertain, since globalization is understood as a long-term historical process characterized by contradictions, shaped by conjunctures and contested by increasingly aware and hostile political forces. There is thus no defined end-game, no single ideal-type of what a 'fully globalized' world would look like.

Of course, certain trends can be picked out, at least up to the present point of analysis. 'Transformationalists' do generally argue that there now exist historically unprecedented levels of global interconnectedness in trade, finance, production, culture and much else. They believe that virtually all parts of the world are functionally part of a global system in one or more respects, although they do not suggest that this is bringing about global convergence or a single world society. In fact, they are struck by the force of new, emerging patterns of stratification in which some states and societies, or rather *parts* of some states and societies, are becoming enmeshed in the globalizing order whilst others are being marginalized (see also Hoogvelt 1997). In the same uneven way the spread of global cultural forms is also having the paradoxical effect of revitalizing various highly local values and ways of living. Any sense of a clear distinction between international and domestic or external and internal affairs also collapses in this vision of the process of change. As Rosenau (1997) put it, politics takes place more and more 'along the domestic–foreign frontier'. In short, we are provided by these various writers with 'a dynamic and open-ended conception of where globalization might be leading and the kind of world order which it might prefigure' (Held *et al.* 1999: 7).

It is best in our view to proceed on 'transformationalist' terrain. Indeed, it could be said that we are all, or nearly all, 'transformationalists' nowadays. What this interpretation offers is a strong sense of globalization as an unfolding historical process. It succeeds in identifying the main contours of the changed structural context within which all economic, social and political actors have now unavoidably to operate, and that is realistically perhaps as much as the analysis of globalization can hope to do for the moment. It is certainly more than enough to capture the essence of the current phase of the emergence of a global economy. As we have seen, the 'transformationalist' approach also insists methodologically on the capacity of actors to alter structures by their actions, which means that they can and do influence the process of globalization. To paraphrase Alexander Wendt (1992), as many have done, globalization is indeed 'what we make of it'; it cannot be said of itself to cause anything. Indeed, this view of globalization fully allows for the way that the ideology of globalization, understood as an all-powerful, unidirectional force, can sometimes be used by economic and political leaders to promote acquiescence in what are in reality policies they happen to favour rather than inexorable processes that cannot be gainsaid (Hay and Marsh 2000; Hay and Rosamond 2002). What has been created at present is a particular sort of globalization, which some have labelled neoliberal globalization (Scholte 2000). In principle, it is possible that this current brand may be turned over time into another variant, or even that the process of globalization will itself be wound back. Nevertheless, an appreciation of the new reality of a 'globalizing' (but not yet fully globalized) liberal political economy is the second founding thesis that we want to draw out of the existing contemporary literature of critical political economy.

The state debate

In a related but equally relevant debate critical political economy has also devoted great attention to the matter of the vitality and capacity of states in just such a globalizing order. Many of the arguments mounted here have, to say the least, been rather crudely made: presented as either the 'retreat or the return' of the state, as Amoore *et al.* (1997: 184) put it in a useful early review of this literature. They too set out three different schools of thought analogous to the three positions identified by Held *et al.* in relation to globalization. As they noted, the initially dominant conceptualization viewed globalization as 'seriously undermining the basis of the nation-state as a territorially bounded economic, political and social unit' (Amoore *et al.* 1997: 185). State authority was seen to have been variously diffused: 'upwards' to international institutions and transnational corporations, 'sideways' to global financial markets and global social movements, and 'downwards' to subnational bodies of all shapes and sizes. In particular, states were deemed to have lost their old economic policy-making sovereignty and to have been reduced to competing with each other in the provision of the human and physical infrastructure that was now needed to attract footloose global capital. In the strongest, 'hyperglobalist' form in which this was put, the nation-state was rendered irrelevant; it was no longer, post-globalization, an appropriate unit of political analysis (Ohmae 1995). Against this interpretation, others insisted, sceptically but every bit as firmly, that the decline of the state was exaggerated. They based their reading on the notion of 'heightened internationalisation', rather than globalization, and asserted accordingly that such global restructuring as has taken place has been driven by the interaction of national capitalisms. Moreover, these capitalisms, rather than necessarily converging in type, remain characterized, as they always have been, by different institutions, processes and cultures (Berger and Dore 1996; Zysman 1996). As a consequence, states are held to continue to exercise considerable authority over their respective national economies and to contribute substantially still to the overall management of the global economy.

Neither of these sets of arguments was completely convincing when expressed in full-blown fashion. What was required was a more perceptive grasp of what has lately happened to the state in relation to the process of globalization. Fortunately, a third, much more subtle, position has now been widely advanced and is much the most interesting and useful. In the words of Amoore *et al.* (1997: 186) again, this suggests that 'the usual understanding of a dichotomy between the state and globalization is an illusion, as the processes of global restructuring are largely embedded within state structures and institutions, politically contingent on state policies and actions, and primarily about the reorganisation of the state'. This last phrase is the most significant, for the point being made here is precisely that the changing nature of the state is at the very heart of the process of globalization. *The* state is neither transcended nor unaltered in some overarching, all-encompassing fashion: instead *each* state (whether located in the old 'First', 'Second' or 'Third Worlds') is finding that its relationship to key social forces both inside and outside its national space is being restructured as part and parcel of all the other shifts to which globalization as a concept draws attention.

As indicated, the claim that the state has been reorganized has now been taken forward in a variety of forms and by a variety of analysts (Hobson and Ramesh 2002; Phillips 2005b). Cox (1981: 146) initially described the process as the 'internationalisation of the state', understood as a process that 'gives precedence to certain state agencies – notably ministries of finance and prime ministers' offices – which are key points in the adjustment of domestic to international economic policy'. Jan Aart Scholte (1997: 452) suggested that globalization has yielded 'a different kind of state [which has] ... on the whole lost sovereignty, acquired supraterritorial constituents, retreated from interstate warfare (for the moment), frozen or reduced social security provisions ... and lost considerable democratic potential'. From the left, Peter Burnham (1999: 43–4) highlighted the widespread shift in the politics of economic management in advanced capitalist societies from 'politicised management (discretion-based)' to 'depoliticised management (rules-based)', the latter being characterized by attempts to reduce the former political nature of economic decision-making and re-position it as far as possible at one remove from government. Peter Evans (1997: 85), reflecting on 'stateness' in an era of globalization, stressed the centrality of the hegemony of Anglo-American liberal ideology in limiting belief in the efficacy of state action and charted the 'project of constructing a leaner, meaner kind of stateness' which has come to be associated with the 'Third Way' thinking of the Clinton, Blair and Schröder administrations in the US, the UK and Germany respectively. Linda Weiss (1997: 17) similarly insisted on the variety of 'state capacities' and argued that 'adaptation is the very essence of the modern state by virtue of the fact that it is embedded in a dynamic economic and inter-state system'. Although in some states certain policy instruments, particularly those associated with macroeconomic adjustment strategies, may be enfeebled by globalization, others, such as those related to industrial policy, may and do change in all manner of creative ways. She thus cautioned that one should therefore always look to a country's governing institutions and expect differences according to national orientation and capability (see also Weiss 1998).

This last cautionary point is especially well taken. In his survey of what he called 'the rise and rise of the nation-state', Michael Mann rightly insisted that states have *always* varied greatly in their degree of democracy, level of development, infrastructural power, national indebtedness and regional location. He asked: 'can contemporary capitalism, even if reinforced by environmental limits, "cultural postmodernity" and demilitarization, render all this variation irrelevant, and have the *same* effects on all countries?' (Mann 1997: 474, his emphasis). His answer – emphatically in the negative – constitutes a warning against overgeneralization, even about the thesis of the reorganization of the state. The patterns of change and continuity are simply 'too varied and contradictory, and the future too murky, to permit us to argue simply that the nation-state and the nation-state system are *either* strengthening *or* weakening' (Mann 1997: 494, his emphasis). Nevertheless, what one can discern through the fog depicted by Mann is, first, that the state remains crucial to contemporary economic and political practice, but, second, that great sensitivity must always be displayed to the enormous variety of *forms of state* and, above all, to the full complexity of the processes by which they are presently being reorganized in different ways in different parts of the globe in response to the differing impacts of globalization on their modes of operation. Indeed, the sheer diversity of these mechanisms of adjustment is still not sufficiently appreciated, for, as Nicola Phillips (2005b) has recently shown, the literature of the 'state debate' remains overwhelmingly biased towards analysis of the situation of countries within the OECD world.

Such a continuing focus on the role of states is sometimes still misinterpreted as connoting a simplistic statism or, indeed, an overpreoccupation with states, a failing with which political economists of all genres have long taxed traditional international relations analysis. On the contrary, it is only to note the obvious, which is that what admittedly should more accurately be described as the state–society relationship still remains central to any explanation in politics and political economy. In fact, in his path-breaking article in *Millennium*, Robert Cox (1981: 127) took great pains to make clear that the appropriate units of analysis for critical political economy were not states *per se*, but what he called 'state/society complexes'. It is also the case, conveniently, that state theory in political analysis (if not, sadly, in all that much international relations analysis) has always sought to embrace a view of the varied relationships between non-state actors and states, rendering it an attractively broad-based literature. Indeed, there has lately occurred something of a convergence in thinking amongst the main extant traditions in state-society theory: namely, pluralism, elitism and Marxism (Marsh 1995). All now agree that the state needs both to be located socially and disaggregated institutionally. They all also accept – although they do not always work this through – that the interests and/or social forces which limit the autonomy of the state, and the policy networks and communities through which state and other actors exercise their relative autonomy, are as likely to be transnational as national. Finally, all strands of state– society theory further acknowledge that the structural constraints imposed on state behaviour reflect both ideational and material sources of power. In short, we can note that there has been forged new common ground in contemporary trends in state–society theory and that, in consequence, there exists a wealth of compatible intellectual tools with which to set about the dissection of particular state strategies and the general relationship of states to social and other forces at work within national political economies as well as within the global political economy as a whole.

There is, then, every reason to believe too that the notion of the state, specifically understood as being reorganized, restructured, re-engineered in conjunction with the current global shift, should remain at the centre of our enquiries, viewed still as a key *political* actor on the global stage. What has to be grasped, though, is that states are not all hewn from the same stone. There exist different forms, types and shapes of state, states that have led different histories and come to be motivated by varying rationales. It is too simple to say, as do so many neorealist analysts of international relations, that at the end of the day a state is a state is a state, each to be understood as a rational, self-maximizing, calculating actor. Yet, at the same time, we should be careful not to throw the baby out with the bathwater. There is undoubtedly still something of great value to be derived from this kind of traditional approach to the analysis of international relations, some 'timeless wisdom' which can be said to reside within this way of thinking (Buzan 1996). The core point here is that, no matter how differently they are set up both institutionally and socially, states cannot but come into interaction with each other as they proceed to pursue their perceived interests beyond their boundaries within the international, or inter-state, environment. To a considerable degree, this remains an arena in which self-help, selfishness and sheer survival are necessarily ever-present watchwords and, to that extent, we need not shy away from adding to the mix of analytical tools at our disposal many of the classic tenets of mainstream international relations analysis, including most notably the notion that a state's interests, whether 'real' or 'constructed', are the driving force behind its actions. Since this kind of argument has been much debated over the centuries and is generally very widely understood, we probably do not need to say anything more about it here. Perhaps the only point that needs reiterating by way of summary is our insistence on the continuing need to focus on the actions of states and, in so doing, to utilize the full range of analytical mechanisms identified in this discussion. This is the third founding thesis on which we intend to build.

The development debate

The debate about development long preceded the birth of what we have called critical political economy. As Björn Hettne (1995: 30) has shown more elegantly than anyone else, classical development theory unfolded historically in dialectical fashion, oscillating between 'mainstream' and 'counterpoint' paradigms. In the post-1945 phase of that history, modernization theory and dependency theory proposed contrasting accounts of the problem of development. For the former, the task lay in eliminating the various internal obstacles, mostly deriving from 'tradition', which lay in the way of emulating the path to development seemingly blazed successfully by modernized, 'Western', liberal democratic states. For the latter, the challenge was to overcome the external obstacles to development, with the strongest arguments suggesting that a dependent location within the international economy inevitably created underdevelopment. It is not clear, though, that there was ever that much actual engagement between the two competing perspectives. Dependency theorists typically mounted polemical attacks upon modernization orthodoxies; modernization thinkers typically ignored the attacks in the most studied of fashions. Over time what became apparent was that each body of theory had the reverse defect of the other: an excessive endogenism in the case of the modernization school and an excessive exogenism in the case of the *dependentistas*. There was created, in consequence, an 'awkward theoretical vacuum' in the field (Hettne 1995: 104). This sense that development theory had lost its way became the academic orthodoxy of the 1980s and was persuasively captured in the declaration of David Booth (1985: 761) that an 'impasse' had been reached.

Yet the reality was that classic development theory had been undone not so much by theoretical failures, as by fundamental changes in the world order: namely, the ending of the era of US hegemony and the attendant unwinding of the original Bretton Woods system of regulated capital movements and international trade. As Colin Leys (1996: 41) put it, 'if the end of the Bretton Woods system spelled the end of national

Keynesianism, it also spelled the end of national development as it had hitherto been conceived'. Although this new phase in the world order inevitably had a significant impact on all states, it proved particularly destabilizing for states in Africa, Latin America and the Caribbean seeking to establish some limited room for manoeuvre in the international economy. The 1980s saw a swathe of such states run into intractable debt and balance of payments problems, which pushed them inexorably into the hands of the IMF and the World Bank. As noted earlier, these institutions in turn used the conditionalities attached to their loans to impose 'structural adjustment programmes' (routinely involving deregulation, privatization, devaluation, the removal of price controls and trade tariffs, increased indirect taxation, and public sector demanning), the declared purpose of which was to make the recipient economies ready to withstand the rigours of the international market place. Again, to quote Leys (1996: 42), 'it is hardly too much to say that by the end of the 1980s the only development policy that was officially approved was not having one – leaving it to the market to allocate resources, not the state'. These trends angered many of those working in development studies and attention came to focus strongly on exposing the many damaging consequences for the well-being of the states and societies being 'structurally adjusted', a task which was generally carried out with great energy and understanding.

For all the merits of this body of empirical work, the wider theoretical problem was that, in this new set of circumstances, any body of theory premised upon the possession by national state governments of a variety of policy tools which they could deploy in the pursuit of development could not but hit an impasse. Hettne (1995: 111) suggested that, as a consequence, the classical debate between modernization and dependency perspectives became transmuted from the national stage, where it had hitherto been exclusively conducted, into a global contest between what he dubbed 'world development ideologies'. In this arena there was no doubt that neoliberalism moved into the ascendant during the 1980s. As we have already seen, as a body of ideas it came to dominate the thinking and policies of many governments and all the major international financial institutions (IFIs), such as the IMF and the World Bank. It also drove forward the planned extension of global free trade that the Uruguay Round of trade talks sought to effect from the middle of the decade onwards. Neoliberalism was, of course, the quintessential 'world development ideology' since its core claim was that development was a process attainable all over the world, provided that the 'market' was allowed to assert itself over the 'state'. The critical positions in this global battle of ideologies were taken by 'neo-Keynesianism', exemplified by the efforts of the Brandt Commission (1980) and the Socialist International to promote belief in the notion of a fundamental interdependence binding the 'developed' and 'developing' worlds; 'neomercantilism', illustrated by the continuing interest shown by some development theorists in forms of national or regional economic protection (Hettne 1993); and the 'neopopulism' of the green movement, which called in different ways for a rejection of all forms of industrial development, irrespective of whether they were led by the market or the state (Goodin 1992). These various alternative arguments were energetically pursued both in the academic and political literatures, but they had great difficulty in shaking the ideological hold of the neoliberal counter-revolution on both development theory *and* practice. Moreover, while the arguments raged, structural adjustment proceeded apace.

In short, neoliberalism has laid effective claim to be the new mainstream development paradigm. This is not to say that it has been an unchanging paradigm. Over time some of the most fundamentalist features of 'early' structural adjustment programmes have been softened. More time for implementation has been allowed and more emphasis has been placed on social measures, in pursuit of 'adjustment with a human face'. During the 1990s, in particular, important debates were also opened up by the World Bank about the appropriate role to be played by the state in a market economy, about corruption and about so-called 'good governance', a phrase used to catch the essence of all that was considered to be best about 'Western' liberal state forms (Williams 1996; Doornbos 2001). Yet it is still argued by many that these changes constitute no more than piecemeal additions to the core of the original neoliberal consensus in a series of attempts to rescue it from some of its inadequacies. Indeed, they make the paradigm even more embracing, and have thus given rise to even more potential conditionalities, precisely by inserting into it a stronger social and political dimension. It is certainly striking that neoliberalism has been challenged as the 'counterpoint' not by a new, radical, post-dependency thinking or even a revival of statist social democracy, but rather by a postmodernism which has advanced what is, to all intents and purposes, an anti-development position. This body of thought deliberately turned away from political economy to emphasize culture and aggressively dismissed all existing notions of development as 'Eurocentric' by virtue of their approval of technology, innovation and growth (Esteva 1992; Said 1992; Escobar 1995). It preferred instead to laud local, non-governmental initiatives, more or less for their own sake, and certainly regardless of their likely economic or political efficacy. Although this approach has been much criticized within development studies (Ziai 2004), it still remains fashionable in some circles. However, it has also always been characterized by a preoccupation with its own internal debates and language and, as a consequence, has signally failed to impact to any degree upon either mainstream ideas or policy practice. The result has been that neoliberals and postmodernists have never found a way to talk creatively to each other. In that sense, perhaps even more markedly than in the era dominated by competing modernization and dependency perspectives, there manifestly now exists no central, agreed terrain of debate within development studies.

However, the good news is that, within the broad field of critical political economy, useful insights – which can be built up into a new approach to development – have begun to be thrown up in the literature. It is true that no scholar or group of scholars has yet had the self-confidence, or self-consciousness, to declare the birth of such a 'new' development studies in the title of a book, although Frans Schuurman (1993) did edit a collection as long ago as 1993 deliberately called *Beyond the Impasse*. Indeed, in the most important chapter in the book, Booth (1993) indicated that he saw signs of a 'new agenda' emerging from the enormous expansion of actual field research undertaken in different development contexts. The cumulation of this work served, in his view, to reveal the thin empirical foundations on which much early dependency theory (in particular) rested. It was all too general, too dogmatic, too pessimistic, too class-reductionist. Put the other way round, it neglected gender, ethnicity, religion and culture; de-emphasized the local; and in a whole range of ways was insufficiently sensitive to the great diversity of situations in Africa, Asia, Latin America and the Caribbean. Leys (1996: 44) subsequently criticized Booth and his colleagues for viewing the transcendence of the 'impasse' in essentially idealist terms: for substituting 'development studies' for 'development theory', as he put it. However, given that good studies are a necessary prelude to good theory, it was an important first step to have returned to the critical political economy of development a stronger sense of variety and situation.

It was on this basis that Hettne thereafter moved the agenda on a stage further. He argued in the mid-1990s that the problem for the field of development studies was that it had become 'trapped somewhere between an obsolete "nation state" approach and a premature "world" approach' (Hettne 1995: 262). A stance needed to be taken, he suggested, at a mid-point between these two extreme positions, thereby constituting a synthesis that would transcend the dichotomy of the successive endogenism and exogenism of previous modernization and dependency analyses. In his words, there were 'no countries that are completely autonomous and self-reliant, and no countries that develop (or underdevelop) merely as a reflection of what goes on beyond their national borders' (Hettne 1995: 262). This was a crucial insight because it laid the basis for a universalization of the study of development within which no country enjoyed more than a relative autonomy in charting its relations with the rest of the world (although manifestly the degree of that relativity varied). The key task for the future was 'to analyse development predicaments stemming from the fact that most decision makers operate in a national space but react on problems emerging in a global space over which they have only partial and often marginal control' (Hettne 1995: 263). In undertaking this analysis it was also necessary to appreciate that the decision-makers in question had to react to forms of power that were ideational as well as materialist. Development studies has in fact always been better at grasping this than some other mainstream areas of political economy – for example, dependency theory long ago incorporated discussion of cultural dependency or 'colonialism of the mind' – but it was important to give full acknowledgement to this other form of power, especially given the many emerging new means of communication and knowledge dissemination by which the battle of different development ideologies was being conducted by the end of the 1980s.

From these beginnings, it is now just about possible to identify the main features of a new critical political economy of development. Such an approach requires 'a marriage between certain strands of development theory and certain strands of international political economy' (Hettne, Payne and Söderbaum 1999: 354). It can be assembled, as it were, in four stages. First, it rejects the 'exceptionalism' of a special category of countries deemed to be in particular need of development and endeavours to recast the whole question of development as a universal question, as 'a transnational problematic' grounded in the notion that '*all* societies are developing as part of a global process' (Pieterse 1996: 543, our emphasis). Second, it focuses attention on development strategy, principally as still pursued by a national economy, society and/or polity, albeit within a global/regional environment. Hettne (1995: 263) himself can thus describe development as no more (but also no less) than 'societal problem solving', implying that 'a society develops as it succeeds in dealing with predicaments of a structural nature, many of them emerging from the global context'. Third, it recognizes that such strategy necessarily involves the interaction, and appropriate meshing, of internal *and* external elements, even if in many cases the latter do seem to be increasingly overbearing. In this vein Philip McMichael (2000: 150) has lately noted that 'states still pursue development goals, but these goals have more to do with global positioning than with management of the national "household" '. Fourth, it insists upon due recognition of variations of time, place and history in development predicaments, something which Stuart Corbridge (1990) called for a decade or more ago and which, as pointed out earlier, was not characteristic of a lot of classical development theory in both its modernization and dependency guises.

To sum up these claims, then, development can be redefined for the contemporary era as the collective building by the constituent social and political actors of a country (or at least in the first instance a country) of a viable, functioning political economy, grounded in at least a measure of congruence between its core domestic characteristics and attributes and its location within a globalizing world order, and capable on that basis of advancing the material well-being of those living within its confines. It is not necessary in this conceptualization to incorporate issues such as freedom and identity; it is not necessary even to define the moral or ethical content of development, conceived as some ultimate condition, in the way that has historically always been done by modernization, dependency and other 'alternative' bodies of theory. The records of achievement of country development strategies will always be contested ideologically, precisely for the reasons that competing notions of the 'good society' have always been debated over the centuries. Different people value different things. The purpose of this approach is to allow analytically for many types or forms of *actual* development. For, as Hettne (1995: 266) has repeatedly reminded us, 'the "three worlds" are disintegrating and development is becoming a global and universal problem ... too important to be left to a special discipline [development studies] with low academic status'. Redefined in this way, development is thus just as much a problem for the ex-hegemon as the smallest ex-colonial territory, for the new industrializer as much as the former communist country in 'transition'. The problems faced by some countries may in practice be much more serious and intractable than in others, but on this account they are *not* conceptually different. As the editorial in the first issue of *Progress in Development Studies*, the newest academic journal to be devoted to these questions, put it in a simple and attractive formulation, 'development is everywhere' (Potter 2001: 3).

The next stage in the rethinking being undertaken here is to specify how we are in practice to set about researching development when conceived in this way as the building by a country of a distinctive and viable political economy. As it happens, there is already a substantial amount of good work on which we can draw. Interestingly, and perhaps revealingly, it comes from both sides of the old divide between study of the 'developing' and the 'developed' worlds. We refer to the now relatively old 'models of development' literature and the much newer 'models of capitalism' literature. In its day the former strand was central to the political economy of development. It reaches right back to studies of the various state-led strategies of import-substitution industrialization pursued in Latin America in the 1960s and 1970s. Some studies emphasized institutional variation from an explicitly historicist perspective (Roxborough 1979); others, notably the highly influential work of Cardoso and Falletto (1979: 15, 172), operated within the dependency tradition, but sensitively so, seeking to deploy the concept of dependence 'to make empirical situations understandable in terms of the way internal and external structural components are linked' and yet still trying 'to demonstrate that the historical situation in which the economic transformations occur must be taken into account'. Similar analytical themes, notably the character of state institutions and their degree of autonomy *vis-à-vis* the relative strengths of domestic and external class forces, were also subsequently addressed in the African context, particularly in discussion of Tanzanian socialism and Kenyan capitalism (Randall and Theobald 1998), and then reinterpreted yet again in relation to the economic successes enjoyed by the 'newly industrializing countries' of East Asia during the 1980s. These striking achievements were aggressively claimed by the neoliberals as evidence of the virtues of a market-led strategy until the research of Clive Hamilton (1986), Gordon White (1987), Alice Amsden (1989), Robert Wade (1990) and many others served cumulatively to undermine such an assertion. Even if the neoliberals had a point in arguing that states were sometimes more corrupt than rational, these various studies demonstrated in broad terms exactly the opposite of their core argument: namely, that forceful and focused economic intervention by a strong state over a sustained period of time and in the context of a supportive social structure and a growing international economy was a necessary developmental ingredient. All in all, this rich, but now largely quiescent, literature showed the considerable merits of analyses of particular development strategies, in whatever preferred mode, whether institutionalist or Marxist, which sought to integrate an understanding of the domestic state–society context with a grasp of the constraints and opportunities posed by the external environment.

The latter strand of writing, that which has addressed 'models of capitalism' in the industrial and post-industrial world and which has been fashionable of late within what might be called comparative rather than international political economy, can in fact be dissected along much the same lines. It too is marked by a tension between its (dominant) institutionalist and (critical) Marxist wings. For most contributors to this literature institutions are seen as both socially embedded and nationally constrained. They are not produced randomly but rather reflect a 'logic in each society [which] leads institutions to coalesce into a complex social configuration' (Hollingsworth and Boyer 1997: 2). By its nature such a configuration is not easy to specify precisely, although most interpretations have lately stressed the importance of variables such as labour and management skills, systems of industrial relations, financial markets, industrial structures and political systems. An interesting variation on the general theme is provided by the concept of 'embedded autonomy' identified by Peter Evans (1995) as the defining variable in patterns of industrial transformation in a study which focused on the computer industries of three countries conventionally deemed to be 'developing': India, Brazil and South Korea. He characterized the 'developmental states' of these countries as constituted by the co-existence of a certain kind of autonomy *and* yet at the same time an embeddedness in a set of social ties which allowed for continual renegotiation of policy. These institutionalist perspectives have, however, been subjected to powerful criticism from a Marxist direction by David Coates who has argued that, for the most part, they lack a conception of the class underpinnings of all institutional arrangements under the capitalist system. Accordingly, in his view:

> The pattern of different performance between national capitalist economies ... is best re-specified as a set of shifting national trajectories on a map of combined but uneven development, where the spaces for catch-up and convergence were predetermined by the prior character of class relations distributed across that map by almost five centuries of class struggle, capital accumulation, production and trade (Coates 2000: 227).

Even so, his actual account of contemporary models of capitalism, which focused on the US, the UK, West Germany, Japan and Sweden, gave only passing consideration to the way that the national basis for capitalist organization may have been seriously affected by recent globalizing trends. In this respect at least his approach is not much of an advance upon institutionalist writing.

Nevertheless, from the perspective of this study the argument to emphasize is what Phillips (2004: 22) has identified as the 'very striking similarity between the research agendas of influential strands of development theory and the contemporary models of capitalism debate'. What can be drawn from them is a strong sense of the key foundational components of a development *strategy* upon which analysis must necessarily focus. These are various. We need to understand the character of the national political economy of the country pursuing the strategy, incorporating a consideration of its core economic attributes as well as an assessment of the institutional basis of the state and the domestic forces which either sustain it or challenge it; we need to consider the impact of any regional arrangements within which the key economic, social and political actors of the country in question are enmeshed (indeed, we might have to contemplate a regionalist body becoming the dominant agent charting development strategy); and we need to explore and evaluate the positioning, actual and intended, of the national (and, as indicated, regional) political economy within the wider global order and the mechanisms available to leading actors to adjust and, conceivably, reshape that position. An additional consideration may, or may not, be the ideological claims made (or not made) on behalf of the particular strategy in question. This is a contingent political question dependent mainly on circumstances. All these matters in combination might be said to constitute the overall development strategy within which specific policies (e.g. macroeconomic, industrial, educational, foreign) are then pursued as component parts. As indicated in the earlier discussion, these are also universal questions that can be asked of *all* types of strategy and country. They offer 'an authentic universalism' in contrast to the putative universalism of modernization theory or neoliberalism: in other words, a universalism derived from the commonality of the problem, rather than the proposed solution (Hettne 1995: 15). This rethinking of the notion of development thus constitutes the fourth and final, and most important, founding thesis on which the remainder of the analysis rests.

The agenda of the book

We have reached the point at the end of these introductory chapters when we can both try to sum up what has been said so far and set out in summary the ensuing agenda of the book. Chapter 1 began by reviewing many of the familiar concepts by which relations between the 'richer' countries and the 'poorer' countries of the world have conventionally been discussed, and largely found them wanting in respect of their relevance to the present era. In particular, it turned away from the bipolar thinking which characterized much of the classic terminology of the field. It went on to consider popular interpretations of the contemporary international politics of development deriving from liberal and sociological schools of political economy and drew attention to the underplaying of politics to be found in these two approaches. Finally, it introduced, and made a case for, the deployment of a critical political economy method broadly as proposed by Robert Cox over 20 years ago, in good part because such an approach facilitates the interaction of agential and structural variables and thus, as it were, allows the politics to come back into political economy. Chapter 2 then trespassed across much of the best recent work on politics and international relations within critical political economy, with a view to presenting a number of founding theses on which the subsequent analysis could rest. In turn, these theses interpreted the end of US hegemony in the 1970s as the beginning of a new phase in the world order; conceptualized globalization as a process of ongoing structural change in the world economy; insisted upon the continuing centrality of states (or, more precisely, varying state/society complexes) as key political actors in contemporary international politics; and re-defined development as the strategy by which all countries seek to orient themselves (that is, their economies, polities and societies) to the new globalizing order.

We suggest, moreover, that these various readings of key debates in critical political economy complement each other very nicely. They lay the basis for a research agenda that focuses directly on development (conceived essentially as strategy) as part of an integrated account of structure (conceived essentially as globalizing) and agency (conceived essentially as states, or states-societies), with the whole analytical enterprise located historically within a specific world order (conceived essentially as non-hegemonic). The rest of this book seeks to explore this agenda. We have in effect reformulated our initial point of entry – a desire to probe that strand of international politics which appears to pose a tension between 'richer' countries and 'poorer' countries – into a broader concern with what we will henceforth call 'the global politics of development'. This phrase is adopted for two reasons. First, we refer to *global politics* (rather than, say, international politics) primarily in order to signal that international (inter-state) politics now takes place – and has to be understood as taking place – in the changed, and still changing, structural context which the concept of globalization, however imprecisely, seeks to capture. Much more could be said here on this theme, but it should be enough just to note that the phrase 'global politics' serves above all to highlight the greater intensity and complexity of the connections that bind states, societies and other institutions in the present era. For all the reasons previously adduced earlier in this chapter, this broad ontological change is of sufficient significance to merit this terminological adjustment. Second, we address specifically the 'global politics of *development*' as our way of highlighting the full complexity of the pattern of inter-state conflicts that emerge from the intrinsically competing development strategies of the whole range of states now in existence in the world. In other words, country development strategies are seen as inevitably having an external dimension. They cannot avoid reaching outwards in pursuit of advantage, interests and position and, in so doing, they come into conflict with the strategies of other countries working to exactly the same dynamic. Indeed, in an old-fashioned turn of phrase, this might even be described as the international relations of development. It is certainly not presumed *a priori* that these relations fall into a neat 'rich–poor' dichotomy. Indeed, from what has already been said about the fracturing of old concepts such as 'North' and 'South' one would expect to find a great variety of positions taken up by states on all of the development issues around which they have to negotiate. But that, strictly speaking, remains to be seen.

The text now proceeds into two more parts. Part II paints in a number of relevant structural considerations in an attempt to establish the deeper context in which this inter-state bargaining is pursued. It is composed of three chapters that examine in turn the different material capabilities (Chapter 3), different ideas (Chapter 4) and different institutions (Chapter 5) that establish the structural context (in Cox's phrase, the 'historical structures') within which the global politics of development unfolds. Part III turns directly to the actions and behaviour of states and other actors. It also constitutes three chapters that address in their turn the current key diplomatic arenas within which countries (predominantly) work out the conflicts generated by their diverse development strategies. The arenas highlighted are finance (Chapter 6), trade (Chapter 7) and the environment (Chapter 8). Part IV consists of a concluding chapter (Chapter 9) that endeavours to tie the various strands of the argument together and identify the main distinguishing features of the global politics of development at the beginning of the twenty-first century. In seeking to do this, it highlights as a central theme of the analysis the notion of unequal development.

Part II
Structural Context

Chapter 3

Material Capabilities

As indicated, the three chapters in Part II of the book seek to depict the structures within which the contemporary global politics of development takes place. They reflect Robert Cox's identification of such a context as being made up of a particular combination of material capabilities, ideas and institutions that has a discernible coherence amongst its constituent elements. This first chapter in this part of the book addresses the matter of material capabilities which, it should be remembered, Cox defined straightforwardly as natural resources transformed by technology and organization. In principle the notion of material capabilities can be tracked down to the potential to exert material force exercised by each individual; in practice it makes sense to think in terms of organized collectivities of people wielding material power. From the perspective of this enquiry it is countries (or in Cox's terms state/society complexes) which stand as the most significant collectivities in question and thus it is the differing material capabilities of the large number of independent countries active within global politics which form the focus of investigation of this particular chapter.

This is a trickier task than it may seem. The problem is not access to data, because the UN, the World Bank, the IMF and many other global institutions provide a mass of relevant information about countries and their economies. There are gaps in relation to the smallest countries and some of those that have only lately moved out of the communist world, but for the most part the necessary data are available. They are set out as clearly as is possible, given the range of information that we want to include, in a Statistical Appendix at the end of the book. The reader should refer as necessary to the data on particular countries as he or she works through the ensuing analysis. The problem that we face in making sense of all of these statistics is actually much more to do with the deployment by the various organizations that gather them of systems of classification which endeavour, for understandable 'managerial' reasons, to group countries into different 'types' in accordance with specific, chosen criteria. What is more, many of these terms of classification continue to refer to the different levels of development of countries, which is something that we suggested earlier is a dubious and increasingly inappropriate vocabulary of analysis. Such terms, as and when they are used, clearly need to be noted, understood and, above all, set in their political and institutional context. But, for reasons already advanced, we are of the view that it is important to avoid the temptation to prejudge the needs and likely actions of different states and societies in the contemporary world order by categorizing them in advance of analysis. One of the tasks of this chapter is therefore to draw attention to which countries are, or are not, included in the various categorizations deployed by different international bodies for their varying purposes and, where necessary, to deconstruct the political significance of the patterns of inclusion and exclusion which emerge.

Size

For the moment, let us proceed with the exercise of investigating as objectively as we can the material capabilities of the 191 countries of the world that presently constitute the membership of the United Nations. Such a working definition of a country elides a number of disputes concerning representation, but for present purposes it suffices. The best starting point is the size of countries, as measured both by their land area and population. Tables 3.1 and 3.2 present the basic information for the ten largest, the ten median-sized and the ten smallest countries of the world.

The two lists are very interesting, especially for the slight but significant variations between surface area and population as indicators of size. In general, it is clear that a good deal of care has to be taken in drawing broad conclusions, not least because large land areas and big populations obviously generate not only substantial potential material capabilities but also more borders to defend, more mouths to feed and so on. By the same token, small size may mean access to fewer resources, but it may also involve facing fewer problems. That said, it is not possible to be anything other than struck by the extraordinary range of the sizes of countries, almost to the point where one thinks that they cannot sensibly be compared like for like. In terms of land area, the spread is from the Russian Federation as the largest (at 17,075 thousand sq. km.) to Nauru as the smallest (at a minuscule 21 sq. km.). In terms of population it runs from China (with some 1,281 million people in 2002) to Nauru (again) and Tuvalu (each with a mere 10,000 people in 2001, the latest year for which figures are available). Some countries, of course, appear either high or low on both lists, which suggests that concepts of 'bigness' and 'smallness' can perhaps be made to work as useful analytical categories. They are certainly terms that are quite widely used in economic and political analysis and yet, as soon as specific definitions for such categories are examined, we find that we run into politics.

Table 3.1 *Surface area of countries of the world (in rank order)*

Country	Thousands of sq. km.
1. Russian Federation	17,075
2. Canada	9,971
3. China	9,598
4. United States of America	9,329
5. Brazil	8,547
6. Australia	7,741
7. India	3,287
8. Argentina	2,780
9. Kazakhstan	2,725
10. Sudan	2,506
... ...	... ...
92. Bangladesh	144
93. Tajikistan	143
94. Greece	132
95. Nicaragua	130
96. Korea, Democratic Republic	120
97. Eritrea	118
98. Malawi	118
99. Benin	113
100. Honduras	112
101. Liberia	111
... ...	... ...
182. St Kitts and Nevis	0.4
183. Malta	0.3
184. Grenada	0.3
185. Maldives	0.3
186. Monaco	0.2
187. Marshall Islands	0.2
188. Liechtenstein	0.2
189. San Marino	0.1
190. Tuvalu	0.03
191. Nauru	0.02

Source: Data from The World Bank, *World Development Report 2004* (Oxford University Press for the World Bank, Oxford, 2004), Tables 1 and 7.

Table 3.2 *Population of countries of the world (in rank order)*

Country	Millions, 2002
1. China	1,281
2. India	1,048
3. United States of America	288
4. Indonesia	212
5. Brazil	174
6. Pakistan	145
7. Russian Federation	144
8. Bangladesh	136
9. Nigeria	133
10. Japan	127
... ...	... ...
92. Benin	7
93. Burundi	7
94. El Salvador	7
95. Honduras	7
96. Switzerland	7
97. Israel	6
98. Lao PDR	6
99. Paraguay	6
100. Tajikistan	6
101. Turkmenistan	6
... ...	... ...
182. Andorra	0.07
183. Antigua and Barbuda	0.07
184. Marshall Islands	0.05
185. St Kitts and Nevis	0.04
186. Monaco	0.03
187. Liechtenstein	0.03
188. San Marino	0.03
189. Palau	0.02
190. Tuvalu	0.01
191. Nauru	0.01

Source: Data from The World Bank, *World Development Report 2004* (Oxford University Press for the World Bank, Oxford, 2004), Tables 1 and 7.

Attempts to define big countries almost always seem to imply a concern for markets. For example, during the mid-1990s the US administration of President Bill Clinton began to refer to what it dubbed the 'big emerging markets' (BEMs). The phrase was first used in a speech given in January 1994 by Jeffrey E. Garten, Clinton's Undersecretary of Commerce for International Trade. Based on estimates that the bulk of the growth in world trade over the next two decades was going to occur outside the mature markets in Europe and Japan in which the US had traditionally traded, he drew the attention of US business to a number of other markets which were thought to show the greatest future growth potential (Garten 1994). These so-called BEMs were all deemed by Garten and the staff of his department to share a number of common characteristics. They were all physically large; they had significant populations and represented considerable markets for a wide range of products; virtually all of them had strong rates of growth or held out the promise of future economic expansion; almost all were in the process of undertaking substantial economic reforms; and all were 'regional economic drivers', meaning that their growth engendered further expansion in neighbouring markets. On the basis of these key criteria, the ten countries identified in Table 3.3 were thus selected as BEMs.

However, Garten himself subsequently admitted in a book written after demitting office that the selection criteria deployed by the Department of

Table 3.3   *The 'big emerging markets'*

Country	Population (millions, 1997)
Argentina	35
Brazil	165
China	1,200
India	914
Indonesia	194
Mexico	88
Poland	39
South Africa	41
South Korea	45
Turkey	61

Source: Data from Jeffrey E. Garten, *The Big Ten: The Big Emerging Markets and How They Will Change Our Lives* (Basic Books, New York, 1997), pp. 4–12.

Commerce had been as much political as economic. It seems that several other countries were considered for inclusion, but were ultimately left off the list. They included Russia (characterized at the time as 'not far enough along with its economic reforms, its political leadership too precarious, and consequently the prospects for progress ... simply too uncertain'), Pakistan ('nowhere near the global influence' of India), Thailand (less 'weight on the global scene' than Indonesia), Venezuela (its economic policies were 'in a total shambles, with little prospect ... that they would improve') and Greece (lower 'geopolitical significance' than Turkey) (Garten 1997: 15). The incorporation of such considerations amply reveals the political nature of the exercise that was being undertaken by the US and renders any notion that the BEMs constitute a firm category of analysis of countries in the world order distinctly implausible.

In a similar fashion smallness has also usually been proclaimed for a purpose. Amongst international organizations the lead here has lately been taken by the Commonwealth Secretariat representing the former colonial states of the British Empire, the majority of which are very small in size. As early as 1983 the Commonwealth Heads of Government commissioned what turned out to be a pioneering report on small states, entitled *Vulnerability: Small States in the Global Society* (1985). This study built on economic evidence that it made sense to define smallness by reference solely to population criteria (since a high correlation existed between population and other measures of economic size) and adopted the working definition of a small state as one with a population of around one million people or less. A decade later, in 1995, the Commonwealth Secretariat was asked to produce an updated report (Commonwealth Secretariat 1997) and, in deference to the steady worldwide rise in population in the intervening period, revised its cut-off point to around 1.5 million people. It also argued that an additional consideration was the importance of region, by which it meant that the common circumstances and collective identities of the Caribbean, the South Pacific and Southern Africa warranted the inclusion in the category of small states of, in turn, Jamaica, Papua New Guinea, Botswana, Lesotho and Namibia, even though their populations exceeded 1.5 million. Using this Commonwealth definition, but not limiting the category to Commonwealth member states, this means that there are presently no fewer than 54 small states in the world, as shown in Table 3.4.

During 1998 the Commonwealth lobbied intensively amongst international organizations in order to have the category of small and, as it saw it, vulnerable states recognized as a case for special treatment, and it did succeed in persuading the World Bank to set up a joint task force to examine the question in greater detail. The report of this group did not, however, take the issue any further: it agreed that small states did

Table 3.4　*Small states*

Country	Population (thousands, 2002)	Country	Population (thousands, 2002)
Andorra	70	Malta	397
Antigua and Barbuda	69	Marshall Islands	53
Bahamas	314	Mauritius	1,212
Bahrain	672	Micronesia,	122
Barbados	269	Fed. States	
Belize	253	Monaco	30
Bhutan	851	Namibia	2,000
Botswana	2,000	Nauru	10
Brunei	351	Palau	20
Cape Verde	458	Papua New	5,000
Comoros	586	Guinea	
Cyprus	765	Qatar	610
Djibouti	657	Samoa	176
Dominica	72	San Marino	30
Equatorial Guinea	481	São Tomé and	154
Estonia	1,000	Príncipe	
Fiji	823	Seychelles	84
Gabon	1,291	Solomon	443
Gambia	1,376	Islands	
Grenada	102	St Kitts and Nevis	46
Guinea-Bissau	1,253	St Lucia	159
Guyana	772	St Vincent	117
Iceland	284	Suriname	423
Jamaica	3,000	Swaziland	1,088
Kiribati	95	Timor-Leste	78
Lesotho	2,000	Tonga	101
Liechtenstein	30	Trinidad and Tobago	1,318
Luxembourg	444	Tuvalu	10
Maldives	287	Vanuatu	206

Source: Data from The World Bank, *World Development Report 2004*, Tables 1 and 7.

have special characteristics which should be noted by global institutions, but was not persuaded that a new country category should be created (Commonwealth Secretariat/World Bank Joint Task Force on Small States 2000). Once again, then, the only conclusion that can be drawn is that smallness as a means of classifying countries within the world order remains a contested notion: a cause for continuing campaigning rather than, as yet, a firm and accepted category.

Gross national income

Size is only a starting-point and, as we have seen, is not necessarily as clear an organizing concept as one might imagine. The core indicator of the material capabilities of countries, to which we must therefore devote the greatest attention, is their Gross National Income (GNI), generally as calculated by the World Bank by means of converting national currencies into current US dollar figures. GNI is the broadest measure of national income, measuring the total value added from domestic and foreign sources claimed by a country's residents. It provides the best evidence of the size of a country's economy within the world economy, but it does not necessarily indicate the wealth of the people of that country or tell us much about the nature of the economy in question. In particular, it is flawed by its inability to measure the many, extensive inequalities of income that exist in all societies or to give any insight into the vital structural differences between economies of the same or similar overall economic size. Nevertheless, we have to make do with the data that we have. Notwithstanding these problems, the best available indicator of wealth remains GNI per capita, calculated by dividing GNI by mid-year population. Tables 3.5 and 3.6 draw upon the most recent available figures for GNI and GNI per capita for all World Bank member economies and all economies with populations of more than 30,000 people (thus including some economies of non-independent political units) and again set out on both counts the ten countries with the highest incomes, the ten that gather around the median and the ten with the lowest.

Yet again the effect of presenting the figures in this way is to highlight the massive disparities that exist between countries within the world economy. At the top end of the scale the US has a GNI of US$10,110 billion, a long way ahead of even its closest rivals: Japan at US$4,266 billion, Germany at US$1,870 billion, the UK at US$1,486 billion, France at US$1,343 billion, China at US$1,209 billion and Italy at US$1,098 billion. At the other end of the scale the World Bank often does not show figures for the smallest economies, but does record the GNI of São Tomé and Príncipe at a mere US$45 million and of Kiribati at a scarcely bigger US$77 million. Differences in per capita income are just as striking. They run from a top figure of US$38,830 (Luxembourg) to a low of US$90 (Democratic Republic of Congo). It is also immediately apparent that nine of the ten economies with the lowest per capita income figures in the world are to be found in Sub-Saharan Africa.

The World Bank in fact uses per capita income figures to classify economies. It presently identifies four groups defined as follows: low income (LIC) as US$735 or less; lower middle income (LMC) as between US$736 and US$2,935; upper middle income (UMC) as between US$2,936 and US$9,075; and high income as US$9,076 or more. For 2002 it thus came up with the following classification:

Table 3.5	Gross national income of countries of the world (in rank order)

Country	Billions of dollars, 2002
1. United States of America	10,110.1
2. Japan	4,265.6
3. Germany	1,870.4
4. United Kingdom	1,486.2
5. France	1,342.7[1]
6. China	1,209.5
7. Italy	1,097.9
8. Canada	700.5
9. Mexico	596.7
10. Spain	594.1
... ...	... ...
83. Jordan	9.1
84. Cameroon	8.7
85. Trinidad and Tobago	8.5
86. Latvia	8.1
87. Iceland	7.9
88. Bolivia	7.9
89. Jamaica	7.4
90. Bahrain	7.2
91. Turkmenistan	6.7
92. Paraguay	6.4
... ...	... ...
166. Guinea-Bissau	0.2
167. Micronesia, Fed. States	0.2
168. Samoa	0.2
169. Vanuatu	0.2
170. Comoros	0.2
171. Marshall Islands	0.1
172. Tonga	0.1
173. Palau	0.1
174. Kiribati	0.08
175. São Tomé and Principe	0.04

Table 3.6	Per capita national income of countries of the world (in rank order)

Country	Dollars, 2002
1. Luxembourg	38,830
2. Switzerland	37,930
3. Norway	37,850
4. United States of America	35,060
5. Japan	33,550
6. Denmark	30,290
7. Iceland	27,970
8. United Kingdom	25,250
9. Sweden	24,820
10. Netherlands	23,960
... ...	... ...
83. Romania	1,850
84. Colombia	1,830
85. Bulgaria	1,790
86. Namibia	1,780
87. Jordan	1,760
88. Guatemala	1,750
89. Algeria	1,720
90. Iran	1,710
91. Macedonia, FYR	1,700
92. Kazakhstan	1,510
... ...	... ...
166. Tajikistan	180
167. Niger	170
168. Malawi	160
169. Eritrea	160
170. Guinea-Bissau	150
171. Liberia	150
172. Sierra Leone	140
173. Burundi	100
174. Ethiopia	100
175. Congo, Democratic Republic	90

[1] Includes French Overseas Departments of French Guiana, Guadeloupe, Martinique and Réunion.

Sources for Tables 3.5 and 3.6: Data from The World Bank, *World Development Report 2004*, Tables 1 and 7.

Low income (65 in number): Afghanistan, Angola, Azerbaijan, Bangladesh, Benin, Bhutan, Burkina Faso, Burundi, Cambodia, Cameroon, Central African Republic, Chad, Comoros, Côte d'Ivoire, Democratic Republic of Congo, Democratic Republic of Korea, Equatorial Guinea, Eritrea, Ethiopia, Gambia, Georgia, Ghana, Guinea, Guinea-Bissau, Haiti, India, Indonesia, Kenya, Kyrgyzstan, Lao PDR, Lesotho, Liberia, Madagascar, Malawi, Mali, Mauritania, Moldova, Mongolia, Mozambique, Myanmar, Nepal, Nicaragua, Niger, Nigeria, Pakistan, Papua New Guinea, Republic of the Congo, Rwanda, São Tomé and Principe, Senegal, Sierra Leone, Solomon Islands, Somalia, Sudan, Tajikistan, Tanzania, Timor-Leste, Togo, Uganda, Ukraine, Uzbekistan, Vietnam, Yemen, Zambia, Zimbabwe.

Lower middle income (53): Albania, Algeria, Armenia, Belarus, Bolivia, Bosnia and Herzegovina, Brazil, Bulgaria, Cape Verde, China, Colombia, Cuba, Djibouti, Dominican Republic, Ecuador, Egypt, El Salvador, Fiji, Guatemala, Guyana, Honduras, Iran, Iraq, Jamaica, Jordan, Kazakhstan, Kiribati, Macedonia FYR, Maldives, Marshall Islands, Federation States of Micronesia, Morocco, Namibia, Paraguay, Peru, Philippines, Romania, Russian Federation, Samoa, Serbia and Montenegro, South Africa, Sri Lanka, St Vincent, Suriname, Swaziland, Syria, Thailand, Tonga, Tunisia, Turkey, Turkmenistan, Vanuatu, West Bank and Gaza.

Upper middle income (34): American Samoa, Argentina, Belize, Botswana, Chile, Costa Rica, Croatia, Czech Republic, Dominica, Estonia, Gabon, Grenada, Hungary, Latvia, Lebanon, Libya, Lithuania, Malaysia, Mauritius, Mayotte, Mexico, Northern Mariana Islands, Oman, Palau, Panama, Poland, Saudi Arabia, Seychelles, Slovak Republic, St Kitts and Nevis, St Lucia, Trinidad and Tobago, Uruguay, Venezuela.

High income (members of the OECD) (24): Australia, Austria, Belgium, Canada, Denmark, Finland, France, Germany, Greece, Iceland, Ireland, Italy, Japan, Luxembourg, Netherlands, New Zealand, Norway, Portugal, Republic of Korea, Spain, Sweden, Switzerland, United Kingdom, United States of America.

Other high income (32): Andorra, Antigua and Barbuda, Aruba, Bahamas, Bahrain, Barbados, Bermuda, Brunei, Cayman Islands, Channel Islands, Cyprus, Faeroe Islands, French Polynesia, Greenland, Guam, Hong Kong, Isle of Man, Israel, Kuwait, Liechtenstein, Macao, Malta, Monaco, Netherlands Antilles, New Caledonia, Puerto Rico, Qatar, San Marino, Singapore, Slovenia, United Arab Emirates, US Virgin Islands.

This method of classification is again very interesting, but it is also not without its politics. The system adopted is apparently straightforward, involving the 'banding' of countries by level of per capita income; but in such a system it matters considerably where the thresholds are placed by the Bank. The effect of adjusting them even slightly either upwards or downwards can make the difference between classifications for certain countries, with all the attendant differences of perception and provision that then follow from apparent movement from either LIC to LMC or LMC to UMC status, or vice versa. It is notable too that the Bank divides the high income category into two not on the grounds of any distinction in levels of per capita income, its core classificatory principle, but rather in relation to membership of a particular body, the Organization of Economic Cooperation and Development. This is extraordinarily revealing: it is OECD membership – in other words, a political phenomenon – which is used by the Bank to establish the 24 economies which are somehow the 'real' economic centres of the world order. The economies embraced within the 'other high income' category are, by contrast, a very mixed bag, being composed largely of small non-independent units and independent states which have found a successful niche within the world economy, generally via the provision of financial services, oil or tourism. Their peoples enjoy high incomes but, unlike the OECD countries, they are not for the most part significant players in international affairs.

Nevertheless, despite these limitations, the Bank's own income classificatory system, potentially adjustable every year according to per capita income movements, may be as far as one can go in drawing out 'types' of economy from these particular data. It has certainly been the case that some other attempts to derive categories from the comparative analysis of GNI and other associated evidence of economic growth have not always stood the test of time in the best of shape. Illustrative of this is the experience of the so-called 'newly industrializing countries'. The term has been widely used not only in academic discussion of the impact of different models of political economy upon economic growth (where it is actually the case that imprecision surrounding the matter of which countries are, or are not, NICs does not of itself undermine the merits of the substantive debate that has been generated about the efficacy of the means towards growth that have generally been adopted), but also by international organizations for official purposes. As long ago as 1979 the OECD defined the common characteristics of NICs as: (i) rapid penetration of the world market in manufactured goods; (ii) a rising share of industrial employment; and (iii) an increase in real GDP per capita relative to the more advanced industrial countries. On this basis it identified ten such countries: Singapore, the Republic of Korea, Hong Kong (strictly speaking, of course, an overseas territory of the UK at the time), Taiwan, Brazil, Mexico, Spain, Portugal, Yugoslavia and Greece (OECD 1979: 19). The World Bank, on the other hand, adopted a characterization of countries where manufacturing accounted for 20 per cent of total GDP, thereby adding to the OECD list Malaysia, Argentina, Turkey, the Philippines, Colombia and South Africa (World Bank 1979: 87). Two decades later neither list appears especially robust. The economic fortunes of these putative NICs have varied considerably over the period, to say the least, and, as we have seen, the World Bank no longer classifies by reference to the term 'industrializing countries', whether new or old. Indeed, in its 2002 survey the 16 NICs identified in 1979 were to be found spread across three income groups, from LMC through UMC to 'high income', including those with OECD membership.

There is, however, one area where it is possible and instructive to push these World Bank figures further, and that concerns the relativities between them. The Bank itself does some of this. For example, it averages per capita incomes by category and then unpicks the figures by region for all except the 'high income' category. Its results are set out in Table 3.7.

Table 3.7 *Average per capita incomes of World Bank groupings of countries*

Groupings of countries	Per capita dollars, 2002
Low income	430
Middle income	1,840
Lower middle income	1,390
Upper middle income	5,040
Low and middle income	1,170
East Asia and Pacific	950
Europe and Central Asia	2,160
Latin America and Caribbean	3,280
Middle East and North Africa	2,230
South Asia	460
Sub-Saharan Africa	450
High income	26,310
World	5,080[1]

[1] Weighted average

Source: Data from The World Bank, *World Development Report 2004*, Table 1.

Even these figures are striking. The desperate income position of South Asia and Sub-Saharan Africa by comparison with all other parts of the world is fully exposed. What is more, it is notable that the average per capita income figure for the upper middle income category (at US$5,040) is actually just below the world average (at US$5,080). The extent of the gap between the high income countries and all of the rest is indeed marked.

Another way of assessing the 'relative economic command' of the core economies of the world has been provided by Giovanni Arrighi. In an important, but not very widely cited, article published in *New Left Review* in 1991, he presented a series of calculations which showed the Gross National Product (GNP) per capita of a number of regions and countries as a percentage of the GNP per capita of the countries which he defined as constituting the 'organic core' of the capitalist world economy. He argued that:

> What the ratio of GNPs per capita is an indicator of – and a better indicator than anything else that is readily available – is the command of the inhabitants of the region or jurisdiction to which it refers over the human and natural resources of the organic core, relative to the command of the inhabitants of the organic core over the human and natural resources of that region or jurisdiction (Arrighi 1991: 46).

What is more, he suggested, the relative economic command measured by this indicator was in effect 'an expression ... of the totality of power relations (political, economic and cultural) that has been privileging the inhabitants of the organic core in their direct and indirect deals with the inhabitants of the regions and jurisdictions that lay outside the organic core' (Arrighi 1991: 46).

Arrighi's method was innovative and can be updated for the contemporary era. His concern was with the historical perpetuation of 'world income inequalities' and he thus defined his 'organic core' as 'the states that over the last half-century or so have occupied the top positions of the global hierarchy of wealth': namely, those in Western Europe (the Benelux and Scandinavian countries, West Germany, Austria, Switzerland, France, the UK) and North America (the US and Canada), along with Australia and New Zealand (Arrighi 1991: 42). Accordingly, Japan and the 'economic miracles' (Arrighi's term) of Italy and Spain were excluded. For the most recent period it seems more sensible to re-define the 'organic core' as the 'high income OECD' countries identified by the World Bank in 2000 (although noting, in passing, that they do not comprise the total current membership of the OECD). Table 3.8 thereby sets out the economic performance of these countries against the weighted average of that of the 'core' as a whole as of the year 2000.

Table 3.8   *The economic performance of the 'organic core' (2000)*

Country/region	Ratio	Country/region	Ratio
Australia	72.9	New Zealand	46.5
Austria	89.6	Norway	119.6
Belgium	87.5	Portugal	39.3
Canada	74.8	Spain	53.2
Denmark	113.8	Sweden	95.2
Finland	88.5	Switzerland	135.5
France	84.1	United Kingdom	87.1
Germany	89.0	United States of	121.7
Greece	42.5	America	
Iceland	110.5	*Western Europe*	81.2
Ireland	81.6	*North America*	116.8
Italy	71.1	*Australia/*	68.6
Luxembourg	157.6	*New Zealand*	
Netherlands	89.3	Weighted average	100.0

Note: The figures represent the GNP per capita of each country/region divided by the GNP per capita of the 23 countries taken together times 100.

Source: Author's calculations from data in The World Bank, *World Development Report 2002*, Table 1.

The table shows clearly the diverse levels of wealth that exist within the economic 'core' of the current world economy, even though the ratios have to be considered against demographic mass to get an accurate sense of real economic power. Luxembourg and Switzerland are thus not more substantial economies in respect of their capacity to treat with other economies than the US. But the positions of the US and Japan at around 20 *above* the average for the 'core' and of Germany, France, Italy and the UK, Western Europe's leading economies, all at least 10 *below*, does tell its own not unimportant comparative story. Where, however, the Arrighi method comes into its own is in the making of comparisons between the economic performance of the 'rest', as it were, against that of the 'organic core'. Table 3.9 goes on to show these ratios for the key regions identified by the World Bank.

These are the principal figures that testify to the continuing world economic inequalities in which Arrighi was fundamentally interested (see also Arrighi, Silver and Brewer 2003). The economic ascent of the Republic of Korea is obvious, although its relatively limited extent is given away by the fact that its ratio to the 'core' (at 31.6) is still substantially below that of Greece, the 'weakest' country in the 'core' (at 42.5). Other than that, the message that is revealed is stark in the extreme and provides the most compelling evidence of the continuing command of the contemporary global economy exercised by its 'core' members. To put the

Table 3.9 *The economic performance of the 'rest' (2000)*

Region/country	Ratio
1. Eastern and Central Europe	12.70
2. Russian Federation	5.89
3. Former USSR (including Russia)	4.47
4. Middle East and North Africa	7.42
5. Latin America and the Caribbean	13.46
6. South East Asia	4.07
7. China	2.98
8. Republic of Korea	31.66
9. South Asia	1.63
10. Sub-Saharan Africa	1.69

Notes:
(i) The figures represent the GNP per capita of each region/country divided by the GNP per capita of the 23 countries taken together times 100.
(ii) Aggregate 1 consists of Bosnia and Herzegovina, Bulgaria, Croatia, Czech Republic, Hungary, Macedonia FYR, Poland, Romania, Slovak Republic and Slovenia.
(iii) Aggregate 3 consists of Armenia, Azerbaijan, Belarus, Georgia, Kazakhstan, Kzrgyzstan, Moldova, Russian Federation, Tajikistan, Turkmenistan, Ukraine and Uzbekistan.
(iv) Aggregate 4 consists of Algeria, Bahrain, Djibouti, Egypt, Iran, Jordan, Lebanon, Morocco, Oman, Saudi Arabia, Syria, Tunisia, United Arab Emirates and the Yemen.
(v) Aggregate 5 consists of Antigua and Barbuda, Argentina, Bahamas, Barbados, Belize, Bolivia, Brazil, Chile, Colombia, Costa Rica, Dominica, Dominican Republic, El Salvador, Grenada, Guatemala, Guyana, Haiti, Honduras, Jamaica, Mexico, Nicaragua, Paraguay, Peru, St Kitts and Nevis, St Lucia, St Vincent, Suriname, Trinidad and Tobago, Uruguay and Venezuela.
(vi) Aggregate 6 consists of Brunei, Cambodia, Indonesia, Lao PDR, Malaysia, Papua New Guinea, Philippines, Singapore, Thailand and Vietnam.
(vii) The Republic of Korea has subsequently been reclassified by the World Bank as a 'high income OECD' economy.
(viii) Aggregate 9 consists of Bangladesh, Bhutan, India, Maldives, Nepal, Pakistan and Sri Lanka.
(ix) Aggregate 10 consists of Angola, Benin, Botswana, Burkina Faso, Burundi, Cameroon, Cape Verde, Central African Republic, Chad, Comoros, Democratic Republic of Congo, Republic of the Congo, Côte d'Ivoire, Equatorial Guinea, Eritrea, Ethiopia, Gabon, Gambia, Ghana, Guinea, Guinea-Bissau, Kenya, Lesotho, Madagascar, Malawi, Mali, Mauritania, Mauritius, Mozambique, Namibia, Niger, Nigeria, Rwanda, São Tomé and Principe, Senegal, Seychelles, Sierra Leone, South Africa, Sudan, Swaziland, Tanzania, Togo, Uganda, Zambia and Zimbabwe.

Source: Author's calculations from data in The World Bank, *World Development Report 2002*, Tables 1 and 1a.

point numerically again, the Arrighi indicator tells us that the average command of the inhabitants of Eastern and Central Europe over the human and natural resources of the 'core' is about eight times less than the average command of the inhabitants of the 'core' over the human and natural resources of Eastern and Central Europe. For the former Union of Soviet Socialist Republics (USSR), even including Russia, it is around 22 times less, for the Middle East and North Africa around 13 times less, for Latin America and the Caribbean around seven times less, for Southeast Asia around 24 times less and for South Asia and Sub-Saharan Africa approximately 60 times less – a staggering disparity by any standards.

The preceding analysis in this section has treated the economies of countries holistically and has sought to assess and compare on this basis. However, as a final contribution to analysis of the available data on the Gross National Income of countries, it makes sense to try to explore the composition of this income for each country by *sector*. The World Bank provides figures for 'value added', defined as the net output of an industry (that is, after adding up all outputs and subtracting intermediate inputs), for the three most frequently defined economic sectors: agriculture, industry and services. In this data set agriculture 'value added' corresponds to International Standard Industrial Classification (ISIC) divisions 1–5 and thus includes forestry and fishing; industry 'value added' comprises mining, manufacturing, construction, electricity, water and gas (ISIC divisions 10–45); and services 'value added' corresponds to ISIC divisions 50–99. Table 3.10 sets out the percentage contributions of each sector to the Gross Domestic Product of most World Bank member economies for the year 2002.

These figures must not be allowed to mislead: they only capture the relativities between a country's main economic sectors, giving no indication themselves of the absolute size of a particular sector. For example, several countries with very low figures for the contribution of agriculture to GDP (e.g. Australia, France, Poland, the UK) nevertheless possess agricultural sectors of substantial size and, more to the point, political weight. The same can be said of the US economy, even though sectoral figures are not provided for the US in the World Bank indicators. Equally, relatively low percentage figures for the contribution of industry (e.g. Germany at 30 per cent, Italy at 29 per cent, and the UK at 26 per cent) should not lead to any underestimation of the continuing absolute level of industrialization attained by these countries.

Yet, for all this, the figures do tell a story of some significance about the priority which particular countries might attach to the defence of their position in certain sectors. For example, only five countries (the Central African Republic, the Democratic Republic of Congo, Lao PDR, Myanmar and Sierra Leone) now derive more than half of their

Table 3.10 Value added as a percentage of the GDP of World Bank member economies (2002)

Country	Agriculture	Industry	Services
Albania	25	19	56
Algeria	10	53	37
Angola	8	68	24
Argentina	11	32	57
Armenia	26	37	37
Australia	3	25	72
Austria	2	32	66
Azerbaijan	16	52	32
Bangladesh	23	26	51
Belarus	11	37	52
Belgium	1	27	72
Benin	36	14	50
Bolivia	15	33	52
Botswana	2	48	50
Brazil	6	21	73
Brunei	n.a.	n.a.	n.a.
Bulgaria	13	28	59
Burkina Faso	32	18	50
Burundi	49	19	31
Cambodia	36	28	36
Cameroon	43	20	38
Canada	n.a.	n.a.	n.a.
Central African Republic	57	22	21
Chad	38	17	45
Chile	9	34	57
China	15	51	34
Hong Kong, China	0	13	87
Colombia	14	30	56
Congo, Dem. Rep.	56	19	25
Congo, Rep.	6	63	30
Costa Rica	8	29	62
Côte d'Ivoire	26	20	53
Croatia	8	30	62
Czech Republic	4	40	57
Denmark	3	27	71
Latvia	5	25	71
Lebanon	12	21	67
Lesotho	16	43	41
Lithuania	7	31	62
Macedonia, FYR	12	30	57
Madagascar	32	13	55
Malawi	37	15	49
Malaysia	9	47	44
Mali	34	30	36
Mauritania	21	29	50
Mexico	4	27	69
Moldova	24	25	51
Mongolia	30	16	54
Morocco	16	30	54
Mozambique	23	34	43
Myanmar	60	9	31
Namibia	11	31	58
Nepal	41	22	38
Netherlands	3	26	71
New Zealand	n.a.	n.a.	n.a.
Nicaragua	18	25	57
Niger	40	17	43
Nigeria	37	29	34
Norway	2	38	60
Pakistan	23	23	53
Panama	6	14	80
Papua New Guinea	27	42	32
Paraguay	22	29	49
Peru	8	28	64
Philippines	15	33	53
Poland	3	30	66
Portugal	4	27	69
Romania	13	38	49
Russian Federation	6	34	60

Dominican Republic	12	33	55
Ecuador	9	28	63
Egypt	17	33	50
El Salvador	9	30	61
Eritrea	12	25	63
Estonia	5	30	65
Ethiopia	40	12	48
Finland	3	33	64
France	3	25	72
Georgia	21	23	56
Germany	1	30	69
Ghana	34	24	42
Greece	7	22	70
Guatemala	22	19	58
Guinea	24	37	39
Haiti	30	20	50
Honduras	13	31	56
Hungary	4	31	65
India	23	27	51
Indonesia	17	44	38
Iran	12	39	49
Ireland	n.a.	n.a.	n.a.
Israel	n.a.	n.a.	n.a.
Italy	3	29	69
Jamaica	6	31	63
Japan	2	36	62
Jordan	2	26	72
Kazakhstan	9	39	53
Kenya	16	19	65
Korea, Rep.	4	41	55
Kuwait	n.a.	n.a.	n.a.
Kyrgyzstan	39	26	35
Lao PDR	53	22	25
Rwanda	41	21	37
Saudi Arabia	5	51	44
Senegal	15	22	63
Serbia and Montenegro	n.a.	n.a.	n.a.
Sierra Leone	53	32	16
Singapore	0	36	64
Slovak Republic	4	29	67
Slovenia	3	36	61
South Africa	4	32	64
Spain	3	30	66
Sri Lanka	20	26	54
Sweden	2	28	70
Switzerland	n.a.	n.a.	n.a.
Syria	23	28	49
Tajikistan	24	24	52
Tanzania	44	16	39
Thailand	9	43	48
Timor-Leste	n.a.	n.a.	n.a.
Togo	40	22	38
Tunisia	10	29	60
Turkey	13	27	60
Turkmenistan	27	45	28
Uganda	32	22	46
Ukraine	15	38	47
United Kingdom	1	26	73
United States	n.a.	n.a.	n.a.
Uruguay	9	27	64
Uzbekistan	35	22	44
Venezuela	3	43	54
Vietnam	23	39	38
Yemen	15	40	44
Zambia	22	26	52
Zimbabwe	17	24	59

n.a. = not available

Source: Data derived from http://devdata.worldbank.org.

GDP output from agriculture; only a further eight countries accrue 40 per cent or more from this sector, all but one of them Sub-Saharan African states. These are, in a proper sense, the 'agricultural countries', even if their combined total agricultural output counts for less than that of one or two larger, but less agriculturally dependent, country economies. By the same token, only six countries accrue more than 50 per cent of their GDP from industry (which of course in this measurement includes mining, gas and oil): they are Algeria (53 per cent), Angola (68 per cent), Azerbaijan (52 per cent), China (51 per cent), the Republic of the Congo (63 per cent) and Saudi Arabia (51 per cent). A further 11 countries derive above 40 per cent of their GDP from this sector, only one of which (the Czech Republic) is to be found in Europe. In the sense deployed above, these are now the 'industrial countries'. The term does not apply so neatly any more to what might more accurately be referred to as the early industrializing countries, for their economies have moved on to become oriented around services. The figures again reveal the relative contribution of services to GDP for some key 'early industrial' states: Belgium 72 per cent, France 72 per cent, Germany 69 per cent, Italy 69 per cent, the Netherlands 71 per cent and the UK 73 per cent. They suggest in a very clear fashion what sorts of issues these countries are likely to be most agitated about in present and future international trade talks. They are perhaps now better described in shorthand as the 'post-industrial countries'.

As suggested at the beginning of this part of the discussion, we must not seek to make too much of these relativities: they should always be interpreted in the context of absolute economic size. But they do have the one major merit of again showing how difficult it has become to classify any set of countries by reference to a single, easy characteristic of, or even set of characteristics about, their economic activity.

Human development

It may plausibly be objected that assessment of the material capabilities of countries solely or even predominantly by reference to Gross National Income is too crude or basic a means of measurement. After all, Cox understood material capabilities to connote natural resources *transformed* by technology and organization. The latter concepts unavoidably introduce a human dimension to the calculation and suggest the need to add to per capita income analysis and surveys of sectoral contributions to economic activity some mechanisms by which to evaluate and compare the capacity of countries to *utilize* their residual economic assets either to good or bad effect. To this end, the United Nations Development Programme has produced each year since 1990 a so-called Human Development Index (HDI) for as many countries of the world as it can gather the necessary statistics. The HDI, as presently composed, seeks to measure the average achievements of a country on three main dimensions of human development, as follows: (i) a long and healthy life, as measured by life expectancy at birth; (ii) knowledge, as measured by the adult literacy rate (with two-thirds weight) and the combined primary, secondary and tertiary gross enrolment ratio (with one-third weight); and (iii) a decent standard of living, as measured by GDP per capita (calculated in relation to the purchasing power parity (PPP) of the US dollar) (UNDP 2001: 240). In other words, the UNDP conceptualizes development as cumulative achievement and seeks to press beyond measures of economic success or failure to incorporate a wider social dimension. In so doing, it inevitably has to work with more judgemental data, as well as to grapple with real inadequacies of data collection in some parts of the world. However, over time the number of countries included in the index has risen and a figure of 177 was reached in the most recent 2004 report. Table 3.11 sets out a sample of the entries in this latest index, focusing once more on those at the top, in the middle and at the bottom.

Table 3.11   *Human Development Index*

HDI rank	Life expectancy at birth (years), 2002	Adult literacy rate (% ages 15 and above), 2002	Combined gross enrolment ratio for primary, secondary and tertiary schools (%), 2001–2	GDP per capita (PPP US$), 2002	HDI value, 2002
High human development					
1. Norway	78.9	99.0	98	36,600	0.956
2. Sweden	80.0	99.0	114	26.050	0.946
3. Australia	79.1	99.0	113	28,260	0.946
4. Canada	79.3	99.0	95	29.480	0.943
5. Netherlands	78.3	99.0	99	29,100	0.942
6. Belgium	78.7	99.0	111	27,570	0.942
7. Iceland	79.7	99.0	90	29,750	0.941
8. USA	77.0	99.0	92	35,750	0.939
9. Japan	81.5	99.0	84	26,940	0.938
10. Ireland	76.9	99.0	90	36,360	0.936
… … … …					
51. Bahamas	67.1	95.5	74	17,280	0.815
52. Cuba	76.7	96.9	78	5,259	0.809
53. Mexico	73.3	90.5	74	8,970	0.802
54. Trinidad and Tobago	71.4	98.5	64	9,430	0.801
55. Antigua and Barbuda	73.9	85.8	69	10,920	0.800

Table 3.11 *Continued*

HDI rank	Life expectancy at birth (years), 2002	Adult literacy rate (% ages 15 and above), 2002	Combined gross enrolment ratio for primary, secondary and tertiary schools (%), 2001–2	GDP per capita (PPP US$), 2002	HDI value, 2002
Medium human development					
56. Bulgaria	70.9	98.6	76	7,130	0.796
57. Russian Federation	66.7	99.6	88	8,230	0.795
58. Libya	72.6	81.7	97	7,570	0.794
59. Malaysia	73.0	88.7	70	9,120	0.793
60. Macedonia, FYR	73.5	96.0	70	6,470	0.793
... ...					
137. Swaziland	35.7	80.9	61	4,550	0.519
138. Bangladesh	61.1	41.1	54	1,700	0.509
139. Sudan	55.5	59.9	36	1,820	0.505
140. Nepal	59.6	44.0	61	1,370	0.504
141. Cameroon	46.8	67.9	56	2,000	0.501
Low human development					
142. Pakistan	60.8	41.5	37	1,940	0.497
143. Togo	49.9	59.6	67	1,480	0.495
144. Congo	48.3	82.8	48	980	0.494
145. Lesotho	36.3	81.4	65	2,420	0.493
146. Uganda	45.7	68.9	71	1,390	0.493
... ...					
168. Congo, Dem. Republic	41.4	62.7	27	650	0.365
169. Central African Republic	39.8	48.6	31	1,170	0.361
170. Ethiopia	45.5	41.5	34	780	0.359
171. Mozambique	38.5	46.5	41	1,050	0.354
172. Guinea-Bissau	45.2	39.6	37	710	0.350
173. Burundi	40.8	50.4	33	630	0.339
174. Mali	48.5	19.0	26	930	0.326
175. Burkina Faso	45.8	12.8	22	1,100	0.302
176. Niger	46.0	17.1	19	800	0.292
177. Sierra Leone	34.3	36.0	45	520	0.273

Source: Data from http://hdr.undp.org/statistics/data, which also specifies the sources from which the various figures were obtained.

As set out in the table, the UNDP divides countries into three categories of human development: low (with an HDI of less than 0.500), medium (0.500–0.799) and high (0.800 or above). These divisions are no more than arbitrary divisions on a scale and do not carry any analytical weight. The UNDP does, however, also provide some regional HDI calculations that broadly bear out the familiar set of variations across the major world regions noted earlier in the chapter. Its latest figures for these are: Eastern Europe and the Commonwealth of Independent States (CIS) 0.796; Latin America and the Caribbean 0.777; East Asia and the Pacific 0.740; Arab states 0.651; South Asia 0.584; and Sub-Saharan Africa 0.465. They compare with an HDI of 0.935 for the World Bank's 'high income OECD' group of countries.

Conclusion

We have ranged over a lot of statistical material in this chapter in an attempt to paint a picture in words and numbers of the material capabilities of all of the countries that play some part in the contemporary global politics of development. We have looked in particular at indicators of size, GNI and human development. They have each transmitted certain messages about the distribution of resources (of varying kinds) between countries, messages which do accumulate to provide a strong, general sense of which countries matter the most and which the least when it comes to power relations.

One question that legitimately arises is whether or not some composite index could be created which would have enough authority to propose and then affirm an agreed categorization of countries according to their capabilities. It might be said that some advance has been made in this direction in relation to the notion of the Least Developed Countries (LDCs) first created by a resolution of the UN General Assembly in 1970. The origins of this initiative can be traced to the work of a group of experts initially convened in 1968 by the UN Conference on Trade and Development and subsequently reporting to the UN Committee for Development Planning (CDP). Three criteria were eventually adopted as the means of identifying LDCs: (i) per capita income of less than $100 (in 1968 US dollars); (ii) a share of manufacturing in GDP of 10 per cent or less; and (iii) literacy rates of 20 per cent or less. At first the list of criteria had extended to eight items, but it was later simplified to three on the grounds that, 'arbitrary though it was, the distinction and its simplified method was necessary if a concrete expression was to be given to the political will to implement special measures' (Committee for Development Planning 1971). The reference to political will was significant, for the context in which the initiative was launched was precisely that of the beginning of the Second UN Development Decade and the early stages of the movement which flowered in the campaign to bring about an NIEO. At any rate, on this basis a total of 25 countries were initially designated as LDCs. Over time the CDP has refined its method of classification on a number of occasions. In 1991 it added a criterion of size (a population of under 75 million, except for Bangladesh which had already been included) and now focuses on the following three considerations:

(a) low income, based on a three-year average estimate of per capita GDP;
(b) human resource weakness, as measured by a composite Augmented Physical Quality of Life Index (APQLI) embracing indicators of nutrition, health, education and adult literacy; and
(c) economic vulnerability, as assessed by a composite Economic Vulnerability Index (EVI) based on indicators of: (i) the instability of agricultural production; (ii) the instability of exports of goods and services; (iii) the economic importance of non-traditional activities (share of manufacturing and modern services in GDP); (iv) merchandise export concentration; and (v) the handicap of economic smallness (as measured by population and the proportion of people displaced by natural disasters).

A lot of evidence is embraced here, drawing on many of the strands of data set out earlier (including some of the arguments about vulnerability pushed forward by small states in their bid for attention). A country qualifies to be added to the list of LDCs if it meets inclusion thresholds on all three criteria and comes under consideration to be graduated if it meets the upward limits of the thresholds on two of the criteria. On this basis the CDP proposed in 2000 the admission of Senegal and in 2003 added Timor-Leste at the time of its independence, thereby bringing the total number of LDCs presently recognized by the UN to 50, as follows: Afghanistan, Angola, Bangladesh, Benin, Bhutan, Burkina Faso, Burundi, Cambodia, Cape Verde, Central African Republic, Chad, Comoros, the Democratic Republic of Congo, Djibouti, Equatorial Guinea, Eritrea, Ethiopia, Gambia, Guinea, Guinea-Bissau, Haiti, Kiribati, Lao PDR, Lesotho, Liberia, Madagascar, Malawi, Maldives, Mali, Mauritania, Mozambique, Myanmar, Nepal, Niger, Rwanda, Samoa, São Tomé and Principe, Senegal, Sierra Leone, Solomon Islands, Somalia, Sudan, Tanzania, Timor-Leste, Togo, Tuvalu, Uganda, Vanuatu, Yemen and Zambia. Of these 50 countries, 34 come from Africa, ten from Asia, five from the Pacific and one from Latin America and the Caribbean.

As indicated, it might be thought that this method effects as good a job as can technically be done in assembling appropriate criteria for identifying the 'least developed countries'. Indeed, one might derive from it the thought that categories of, say, 'most' or 'middling' developed countries might, with ingenuity and hard work, also be established by the UN. However, the idea that the LDC classification represents some kind of authoritative composite indicator, and thus shows the way forward, cannot in the end be sustained. In reality, political considerations have scarcely ever been set aside in either its construction or its operation. We noted earlier the political circumstances which gave birth to the very notion of LDCs and it has frequently been the cause for political commentary that the number of countries so designated has almost doubled in 30 years. It is also the case that the governments of countries have to acquiesce in the designation, which they do not always do. The governments of Ghana and the Republic of the Congo, for example, have refused what they interpreted as 'demotion' to LDC status from the broader category of 'developing countries' (which, by comparison, is largely undefined by the UN). More predictably, countries resist being 'graduated' from the list, so much so that only one country, Botswana, has moved up from being an LDC in all of the years since the classification was introduced. In 1994 and 1997 the CDP recommended Vanuatu for graduation, but the country's representatives persuaded the General Assembly not to implement the proposal. In 2000 the CDP considered Cape Verde, Samoa and the Maldives as candidates for graduation, and in the end recommended that the latter did indeed meet the graduation criteria. However, the Maldives' government also vigorously challenged the assessment, arguing in particular that its economy was threatened by a possible rise in the level of the sea. In 2003 the CDP again concluded that Cape Verde and the Maldives qualified for graduation and that Samoa would do so in 2006. The government of Cape Verde has indicated that it will accept this redefinition of its status within the UN, although viewing it in good part as a mixed blessing, which means that the number of LDCs may soon drop again to 49. Finally, as part of the evidence that politics always rears its head in these matters, it is worth noting that, even within the UN itself, the category of LDC is 'adjusted' around the edges for political reasons. Thus the CDP itself has identified at least another 16 countries (including such as China, India, the Democratic Republic of Korea and Zimbabwe) as meeting some, but not all, of its three LDC criteria, whilst the UNDP has developed a similar category of 'As-If' LDCs to signify countries that are close to this status (including, notably, Nicaragua and Vietnam).

At the end of all of this, the key point to emphasize is that the whole business of categorizing countries is irredeemably political. Although this should not, of course, be a surprising conclusion, it is a salutary one. It means that we need to proceed in this book on the basis of analysing the political strategies and international relations of countries by reference to what they do and say, not which grouping they are supposed to belong to according to the judgements of institutions which, as we shall see later, are themselves actors within the global politics of development. Our earlier theoretical argument that it is time to move on and away from classifications of countries according to notional levels of development has thus been reinforced by the examination in this chapter of the practical difficulties of rendering such categories operational on an authoritative basis. We shall certainly note when, where and why such categorizations are deployed in political action. But, in the main, in subsequent discussions of the role and behaviour of particular countries in later chapters it will be important that the reader refers back mentally, as necessary, to the specific data presented here (and in fuller detail in the Statistical Appendix) about their material and other capabilities. That is the only proper way to treat the complexity that we have already uncovered.

Chapter 4

Contending Ideas

This second chapter in this part of the book turns to consider the role played by contending ideas in the constitution of the framework of action within which the global politics of development is presently pursued. Ideas here are understood in the Gramscian sense as setting out the patterns of thinking that are largely taken for granted in any society. They contend because the dominant 'common-sense' of any era is always under challenge, however ineffectually it may seem on some occasions, by alternative ways of framing issues, of defining what is important or unimportant and of laying down the apparent limits of what can, or again cannot, be done. Ideas are thus always political in their impact. To cite Robert Cox again, 'any general organization of power ... sustains ideas which legitimate it. Such a dominant ideology justifies the existing order of power relations by indicating the benefits accruing (or accruable) to all the principal parties, including in particular the subordinate or less favored.' Yet, he went on, 'where there is a general challenge to the prevailing structure of power, then the articulation of counter-ideologies becomes a part of the action, and the possibility of reaching reasonably durable agreement on the practical issues of policies and institutions becomes bound up with the possibility of reaching a new consensus on theories and modes of analysis' (Cox 1979: 259). It is important to establish this general argument clearly. Ideas can have real power in the political world. They can effect significant changes in the definition of interests and the conduct of both individual and collective behaviour. But, as Peter Hall (1989: 390) has also insisted, 'they do not acquire political force independently of the constellation of institutions and interests already present' in political and economic life. In short, the contention of ideas is an important dimension of the general framework of action we are trying to set out, but it is only *part* of a wider context that we must see as a whole. Ideational determinism is very much to be avoided.

The ideas that we need to address, given the concerns of this study, are inevitably quite wide-ranging. They concern fundamental matters of political economy, embracing debates about the merits of different types of capitalism, different strategies of development and different modes of governance. They stretch too, as we will see, into the terrain of foreign

73

policy and international relations. These various 'global political-economic visions', as Craig Murphy (1999: 289) has described the systems of ideas in question, can also be seen to flow, backwards and forwards, between national arenas and the global stage, creating complex patterns of influence that require some unpicking. As with the previous chapter, we want to assess the contemporary position, exploring the contending ideas that bear upon the issue of international development at the turn of the century. This requires us, in the main, to focus upon two contrasting global visions. The first is the emergence within the Anglo-American world of what became known as 'Third Way' thinking and its shaping of a so-called post-Washington Consensus; the second is the recent, swift rise to prominence within the US of a powerful neoconservative strand of thinking and the consequential damage that this has done to the maintenance of ideational consensus within the 'Western' world. Both visions can only be understood by reference to the firm hold that neoliberalism, broadly defined, gained upon the parameters of political economy debate during the 1980s and we must start therefore by going back to consider the origins of its ascendancy.

Neoliberalism and the Washington Consensus

It should hardly need saying that neoliberalism did not spring upon the world fully formed and fully armed. During most of the post-1945 era it lurked in the minds of a small number of heretical economists working away largely on their own in the academy or in think-tanks, rather than advising governments. The intellectual orthodoxy of this period permitted, even encouraged, forms of state management and intervention in economic and social matters. In the old industrialized world this was legitimized by reference to the key tenets of Keynesian economic theory which made the case for governments managing economic demand in order to iron out excessive fluctuations in the natural economic cycle; in the so-called 'developing world' it was justified by the argument of the 'special case' which asserted that market imperfections in these countries significantly vitiated the conventional laws of neoclassical economics, thereby necessitating the formation of a distinctive 'development economics'. In other words, neoliberal economic ideas extolling the classical virtues of the market had initially to fight their way into the mainstream from the periphery of debate (Gamble 2001). It is worth emphasizing this, given the way in which their subsequent rise to prominence, their 'triumph' in Thomas Biersteker's (1995: 174) phrase, has so often been presented by their advocates as both inexorable and inevitable. In fact, as Biersteker (1995: 180) himself noted, the process by which neoliberalism actually spread across the world was 'lumpy, jerky, and uneven in important respects'.

The neoliberal counter-attack against Keynesian orthodoxy was also first launched in specific national contexts – in the United Kingdom and the United States – rather than on the global stage or within global institutions. It both contributed to, but then drew great strength from, the emergence into office in these two key countries of the Thatcher and Reagan administrations in 1979 and 1981 respectively. As became widely known all over the world, both these leaders brought several neoliberal ideas directly to bear on national economic policy making, seeking to reduce the role of state bodies in economic management, giving greater freedom of action to business corporations, curbing trade unions and generally allowing the market to shape major social and political decisions. But, even under Thatcher and Reagan, rhetoric always ran ahead of reality and in practice the proclaimed neoliberal 'revolution' was often implemented incrementally, partially and sometimes almost by accident. For example, the Thatcher administration did not fully embrace privatization as a policy option until it had been in office for several years, and the Reagan administration always gave a higher priority to spending than sound finance. Nevertheless, it cannot be denied that these two governments, led by strong personalities who also saw each other as kindred spirits joined in struggle, emerged symbolically as the leading national flagships of neoliberal thinking and, as such, constituted important models for other leaders in other countries.

Yet, for all its appeal and apparent success, the Thatcher–Reagan approach did not succeed in eliminating the residual appeal of other existing forms of capitalist organization within the leading post-industrial countries. In fact, it gave rise to a vigorous intellectual debate about the competing merits of contrasting national 'models' of capitalism, of which that represented by the UK and the US during the 1980s was but one type. For example, writers such as Michel Albert (1993) drew striking, albeit simplified, distinctions between the Anglo-American variant, which he theorized as grounded upon notions of individual success, short-term financial profit and the glorification of the market, and what he termed a 'Rhenish' model, founded on ideas of group success, long-term planning and the pursuit of consensus. The latter, in his view, stretched from the northern fringe of Europe through Germany to Switzerland, as well as including a Japanese variant. It was assuredly still capitalism, but 'capitalism with built-in regulators and corrective mechanisms' (Albert 1992: 20). Many others followed up on this argument and in particular picked out more sharply an East Asian (principally Japanese) neocorporatist model, characterized by the leadership of a 'developmental state' seeking to 'govern' the market (Wade 1990). Some still insisted upon the continuing vitality of a European social democratic alternative, named by Lipietz (1992) the 'Kalmarian model' because of the location in Kalmar of the main Volvo plant in Sweden. The plant was organized around a labour process wherein workers were directly involved in the regulation of production and the pursuit of quality improvements, and thus arguably less alienated from capitalist exploitation. The objective here is not to review these various models comprehensively, but simply to note that throughout the 1980s the rise of Anglo-American neoliberalism faced stubborn and persistent ideological opposition within several other major 'Western' countries, as well as domestically from opposition elements within the UK and the US themselves. Indeed, so apparently strong was this opposition that, following the sudden and complete destruction of Soviet-bloc Communism in the aftermath of the fall of the Berlin Wall in 1989, most predictions of the future foresaw not the triumph of liberalism and the 'end of history' famously heralded by Fukuyama (1989), but rather a 'rebalancing' of the ideological landscape, with social democracy and democratic socialism gaining renewed impetus from their release from the legacy of the Soviet experience, and Japanese/Rhenish capitalisms displaying greater social equity and superior economic efficiency than their Anglo-American rival versions.

In the event, these expectations proved to be fanciful, for what neoliberalism did eventually achieve, with stunning success, was arguably even more important than victory in this 'battle of national capitalisms' within the post-industrial countries. It was nothing less than the capture of the intellectual high ground within the major global institutions, notably the IMF and the World Bank. This can only be fully understood in the context of the internal power structure of these institutions (to which we will turn in the next chapter). For the moment it is enough to note that the adherence to neoliberal ideas in US and UK government circles during the 1980s was sufficiently extensive to bring in its train their rise to the position of dominant ideology also within the Fund and the Bank (although it should be noted *en passant* that many neoliberals remained unreconciled to the IFIs, believing them to be essentially Keynesian bodies which properly functioning markets should not require). Nevertheless, the conversion of the Fund and the Bank was of huge significance because these two bodies, more than any others, have been able throughout the post-1945 era to set the terms of the official debate about development: to lay down in precisely the Gramscian manner previously articulated what can be thought legitimately and what can be done practically. It was for this reason – the location in Washington, not just of the Reagan White House, but of these two organizations – that John Williamson (1990, 1993) so aptly coined the phrase the 'Washington Consensus' to describe the essential components of the neoliberal take upon development which dominated 'Western' thinking from the end of the 1980s through into the 1990s. As Paul Krugman (1995: 28–9) observed:

> By 'Washington' Williamson meant not only the US government, but all those institutions and networks of opinion leaders centered in the world's *de facto* capital – the IMF, World Bank, think tanks, politically sophisticated investment bankers, and worldly finance ministers, all those who meet each other in Washington and collectively define the conventional wisdom of the moment.

As with the spread of all systems of ideas, the new ascendancy of neoliberalism within the IMF and the World Bank, especially the latter, was not effected without having to overcome dissent. Staff had to come and go and, amongst those that stayed, minds had to be changed. A significant political challenge also had to be resisted. As Robert Wade (1996) has shown, the Japanese government pressed hard in the early 1990s to have some of the distinctive statist features of its successful development strategy recognized more fully in World Bank thinking. It succeeded in overseeing the publication in September 1993 of a major Bank report, entitled *The East Asian Miracle*, which considered the role played by government intervention in modern East Asian development. But, by the time of publication, as a result of internal battles within the Bank, the role attributed to interventionism had been rendered ambiguous at best and irrelevant at worst. The key argument advanced in the report was that the miracle was non-replicable in other countries. At this point the Japanese government decided 'to calm relations with the World Bank in order to avoid causing even more turbulence in Japan's relations with the US' (Wade 1996: 125); this allowed the Bank, with some relief, to leave the East Asian agenda behind and move on to focus more on Africa. The upshot, nevertheless, was that over the course of this period all models of capitalism, other than the Anglo-American version, were effectively sidelined in the assertion of a new ideological orthodoxy within the global economic institutions. Reflecting this shift in orientation, the Bank moved steadily away from the large-scale infrastructural loans and projects that were typical of its work during the Keynesian era and embraced instead the promotion of market institutions and the dismantling of public enterprises as part of a series of 'structural adjustment' programmes introduced into countries all around the world. For its part, the IMF similarly widened its remit beyond its original role as a short-term stabilization instrument and entered the same 'structural adjustment' territory. It hardly needs adding that these were shifts of practice of great moment in the context of the broader contest of ideas about the political economy of development.

It is important, too, to stress that the Washington Consensus only ever existed as a loose set of ideas: it was never formally set out in any document or officially endorsed by any body. In fact, in his initial analysis Williamson (1990) was seeking to do no more than address the policy reforms deemed to be appropriate to bring Latin America, his particular area of concern, back into economic growth following the recession in which it had been cast by the emergence of the 'debt crisis' at the beginning of the 1980s. Accordingly, he set out ten generalizations that he suggested were the 'common core of wisdom' on this issue, in that they were 'embraced by all serious economists' within 'the economically influential bits of Washington' (Williamson 1993: 1,334 and 1,329). These market-oriented prescriptions straddled both macroeconomic and microeconomic changes and focused specifically upon the linked objectives of fiscal discipline, altered public expenditure priorities, tax reform, financial liberalization, exchange rate adjustment, trade liberalization, privatization, deregulation and support for property rights. Although Latin America was the prompt which drew Williamson into this analysis, he drew attention to the fact that, in Washington by 1990, proof of 'the superior economic performance of countries that establish and maintain outward-oriented market economies subject to macroeconomic discipline' was not perhaps 'quite as conclusive as the proof that the Earth is not flat', but was nevertheless 'sufficiently well established as to give sensible people better things to do with their time than to challenge its veracity' (Williamson 1993: 1,330). In a brutal turn of phrase, he observed that only 'cranks' contested the new orthodoxy: the Washington Consensus reflected nothing less than the emergence of a 'universal convergence' (Williamson 1993: 1,334).

In a valuable commentary on all of this, Charles Gore from UNCTAD has argued that the establishment of this new consensus in Washington represented more than just a swing in real-world development strategy from state-led to market-oriented policies, as significant as this was in its own right. Deploying Kuhn's notion of paradigm change to highlight the creation of new standards of what was 'normal' within a field of scientific enquiry, he suggested that there also took place 'a deeper shift in the way development problems were framed and in the types of explanation through which development policies were justified' (Gore 2000: 790). This had two aspects. The first was what he described as the partial globalization of development policy analysis. That is to say, it was the norms and disciplines of a liberal international economic order that were increasingly used to show why countries which did not follow Washington Consensus policies would be cut off from the intensifying, and beneficial, global field of flows and, concomitantly, why those that did pursue the 'right' policies would be rewarded. Country trends could thus still be attributed to domestic policy choices, since the key issue was deemed to be whether to embrace or reject the liberalization that was somehow happening outside the countries in question. The second aspect was the shift to ahistorical performance assessment. In Gore's view, this connoted a departure from the presumption that development analysis was based on some understanding, however much disputed in its essence, of large-scale historical sequences of economic and social change in favour of the adoption by the global institutions of a mode of ahistorical performance assessment by which countries could be crudely divided into 'success stories' or 'failures' according to how well they implemented the supposedly necessary policy reforms. Understood in these terms, the Washington Consensus can be seen to have represented an even more meaningful reconfiguration of some of the core tenets of political economy than is usually assumed.

Third Way thinking and the post-Washington Consensus

In these formative manifestations the ideology of neoliberalism was generally cast in fundamentalist terms. It was strong meat, and deliberately so. Although its implementation as a programme of government was necessarily characterized by all manner of pragmatic adaptations, its proponents understood that the core proclamations of neoliberalism and the Washington Consensus had to be enunciated with vigour and confidence in order to muster the ideological resources needed to overcome the hold of the old statist ways on the popular mind of a whole range of countries. As the slogan most frequently associated with Mrs Thatcher put it quite brilliantly, 'there is no alternative' (TINA). The more complex cause of neocorporatist capitalism could not find a way of matching these overweening simplicities and consequently did not for the most part succeed in presenting itself to the newly emerging democracies of Eastern and Central Europe, Latin America and elsewhere as a workable alternative to the all-conquering Anglo-American model of development.

By the mid-1990s, then, it seemed as if an era of fundamentalist neoliberal hegemony had been initiated. But political ideas always develop dialectically and it was only a matter of time before new, or seemingly new, ideological constructions began to be articulated. Again, it was initially within the context of the national political debates taking place in the US and the UK that this occurred. Bill Clinton and Tony Blair emerged in turn as the leaders of political parties widely portrayed as ideologically exhausted and fated to experience continuing electoral defeat. From 1968 to Clinton's election in 1992 the Democrats had held

the US Presidency only for the period of Jimmy Carter's four-year term
(1977–81); when Blair assumed the leadership of the Labour Party in the
UK in 1995 Labour had been out of office since 1979. As Norman
Birnbaum (1999: 439) noted, 'the conventional opinion to which the
two leaders deferred was fabricated by the ideologues of market capitalism, but that did not make it any less effective'. If they were to arrest
these trajectories of decline, both Clinton and Blair realized that their
historic task was to bring about some measure of reconciliation between
neoliberalism and the very different ideological histories of their respective parties. For reasons of pragmatic politics they needed a phrase with
which to seek to promote a new 'common-sense', something preferably
that could be deployed in a reinforcing way on both sides of the Atlantic.
The name that they gave to their joint project to do precisely this was the
Third Way.

The Third Way did reject the fundamentalist neoliberalism of the
Washington Consensus. Enough was said and done by Clinton and Blair
to show that they were genuine in wanting to move a step or two away
from full-blooded market principles; but to place the emphasis here
misses the main point about the politics of the Third Way. The mission,
above all, was to lay to rest the legacy of American social reform of the
style of Franklin Roosevelt and of British social democracy of the type
pioneered after 1945 by the Labour government of Clement Attlee. As
John Westergaard (1999: 429–30) observed of the prospectus as set out
by Blair in a Fabian pamphlet published in 1998 a year after winning
power in the UK:

> It involves turning backs as much or more against 'fundamentalism'
> of left-wing ilk as against market fundamentalism: against both for
> dogmatism; against the latter for social divisiveness and failures of
> economic performance; against the former ... for 'statist' hang-ups,
> public spending zeal, urges to 'second guess' decisions more properly
> and effectively made by business, and leanings to stifle 'opportunity in
> the name of abstract equality'.

Although the official rhetoric may have sought to pitch the Third Way's
tent on centre ground ('beyond left and right', in the phrase used by
Anthony Giddens (1994), one of Blair's intellectual mentors), the bulk of
the emotional energy associated with the project in both the US and the
UK was devoted to seeing off key ideological nostrums of the 'old' politics.
Clinton thus pronounced again and again that 'the era of big government'
was over, Blair intoned repeatedly that the politics of 'tax and spend' was
dead. Neither followed their own exhortations all that closely in office,
but that is not the point. What was significant was that neither felt

that they needed to put the same effort into establishing the case for the basic tenets of the market economy. By the mid-1990s these had come to be taken for granted by most people in these two critically important 'Western' societies. Interestingly too, both Clinton and Blair insisted with the same rhetorical repetitiveness that 'globalization' had to be accommodated – for, again, there was simply 'no alternative' (see Coates and Hay 2001; Weir 2001). They in effect used globalization as an ideology in precisely the way that was highlighted earlier in the general discussion of the trend in Chapter 2: namely, to promote the widespread acceptance of policies chosen for specific political reasons by means of proclaiming the enormous power and potential threat of the economic and social forces bearing in upon them and constraining their room for manoeuvre. The Third Way was thus associated with an embrace, rather than a rejection, of the shift towards neoliberal globalization.

In this spirit, when seeking at the turn of the century to capture 'the trend of the time', Perry Anderson (2000: 10) suggested that it could most accurately be defined as 'the virtually uncontested consolidation ... of neo-liberalism'. He went on:

> Ideologically, the neo-liberal consensus has found a new point of stabilization in the 'Third Way' of the Clinton–Blair regimes. The winning formula to seal the victory of the market is not to attack, but to preserve, the placebo of a compassionate public authority, extolling the compatibility of competition with solidarity. The hard core of government policies remains further pursuit of the Reagan–Thatcher legacy ... [b]ut it is carefully surrounded with subsidiary concessions and softer rhetoric. The effect of this combination ... is to suppress the conflictual potential of the pioneering regimes of the radical right, and kill off opposition to neo-liberal hegemony more completely. One might say that, by definition, TINA only acquires full force once an alternative regime demonstrates that there are truly no alternative policies. For the quietus to European social-democracy or the memory of the New Deal to be consummated, governments of the Centre-Left were indispensable. In this sense ... we could say that the Third Way is the best ideological shell of neoliberalism today (Anderson 2000: 11).

Anderson is a Marxist of long standing and this analysis was contained in the 'renewal' document of the journal, the *New Left Review*. It unquestionably offers a harsh reading of the ideas advanced by the Third Way, for they did present real alternatives and were not necessarily insincerely generated. But it does nevertheless capture well the way in which Third Way thinking in the two leading national centres of ideological production in the world (as well as in Germany and parts of Eastern Europe, and indeed Latin America to which it spread, albeit in simplified and less intensive form) did succeed in loosening some of the features of fundamentalist neoliberal political economy, the better perhaps to consolidate the hold of core elements of the programme in the long run. To this extent, at least, it can be understood as 'the "second phase" neo-liberal approach' (Cammack 2004: 165).

The same impulse to ameliorate the worst excesses of fundamentalist neoliberalism that gave birth to the Third Way in the US and the UK was also felt in relation to the global political economy as a whole. By the mid-1990s it was increasingly recognized that there was a need for a period of consolidation. In particular, it was becoming clear, even to neoliberals, that the rapid spread of globalization was generating its own instabilities, manifested most markedly by the onset of financial crises in Latin America, Asia and Russia during the course of the decade. A number of public intellectuals who were not hitherto known for possessing a critical outlook began to speak out and articulate a number of ideas that chimed with the Third Way thinking being developed around Clinton and Blair. Initially, it was the alleged excesses of financial liberalization that were most frequently picked up and highlighted in the editorial pages of leading US newspapers and other elite journals. For example, Paul Krugman (1995) argued after the Mexican crisis of 1994 that Washington Consensus policies had worked to create a speculative bubble in 'emerging markets' such as Mexico and that the bubble had inevitably burst. He even made the case for exchange controls as a response to the crisis. Jagdish Bhagwati (1998), a leading liberal economist, similarly came to decry free capital mobility across borders as the fetish of a 'Wall Street–Treasury complex' created by the ease with which financiers directly entered, as well as indirectly influenced, the US government. Jeffrey Sachs of Harvard University, who had once been an advocate of 'shock therapy', the sudden introduction of neoliberal policies, in Russia after the end of the Communist era, turned his attack upon the IMF. He accused the Fund of pursuing policies that turned liquidity crises into financial panics and eventually into collapsed economies in an expanding list of countries. 'Instead of dousing the fire', he wrote, 'the IMF in effect screamed fire in the theater' (Sachs 1998: 17). None of these eminent economists retracted their underlying support for free trade, but they had come to doubt the wisdom of instituting free markets via short-term capital flows and argued that the global institutions needed to rethink some of their instinctive commitments and policies. In particular, these sorts of criticisms opened the way to serious consideration of an improved 'international financial architecture' capable of heading off financial frailties before they became crises.

The growing dissent from orthodoxy of these various US-based economists was, however, overshadowed by the even louder voice of

Joseph Stiglitz, chief economist of the World Bank from 1996 until he was, to all intents and purposes, dismissed from that office in late 1999. Although, in retrospect, Stiglitz can be seen to have begun his critique of the neoliberal consensus when he was Chairman of the US Council of Economic Advisers within the Clinton administration, he first went public with his doubts in a significant way in his World Institute for Development Economics Research lecture delivered in Helsinki in January 1998 whilst in post at the Bank, and continued in the same vein in calling for a 'new paradigm for development' (no less) in another lecture given to UNCTAD in Geneva in October of the same year. The first lecture concentrated on the failings of the Washington Consensus, which *inter alia* were deemed to include the following:

> That consensus all too often confused means with ends: it took privatization and trade liberalization as ends in themselves, rather than as means to more sustainable, equitable, and democratic growth ... It focused too much on price stability, rather than growth and the stability of output. It failed to recognize that strengthening financial institutions is every bit as important to economic stability as controlling budget deficits and increasing the money supply. It focused on privatization, but paid too little attention to the institutional infrastructure that is required to make markets work, and especially to the importance of competition (Stiglitz 1998b: 1).

At the end Stiglitz called vaguely, but tellingly, for continued movement towards a 'post-Washington consensus' (hereafter PWC), an intellectual and political construction that he thought was already beginning to emerge. It should be defined, he said, by two principles: first, it should not be based in Washington, for, 'if policies are to be sustainable, developing countries must claim ownership of them'; and, second, it should be characterized by 'a greater degree of humility' and an acknowledgement that the Bank and the Fund 'do not have all the answers' (Stiglitz 1998a: 15).

Measured against such ambitions, Stiglitz's substantive prescription for the future, set out in the second lecture, could not but disappoint. Essentially, he offered a reformulation of neoclassical economics (sometimes referred to as the information-theoretic approach) that acknowledged the existence of a range of different market imperfections and provided accordingly a rationale for various microeconomic and macroeconomic interventions. He insisted that a 'development strategy outlines an approach to the transformation of society' (Stiglitz 1998b: 10) and must therefore address all components of society, including the private sector, the state, the community, the family and the individual; he called for new institutions and regulations and for more emphasis on capacity-building; he urged the end of conditionality in the making of loans; and he set out a vision of the World Bank as a 'knowledge bank' which could 'provide the cross-country experience that, when melded with local knowledge, makes possible effective choices of development policies, programs, and projects' (Stiglitz 1998b: 12). As Guy Standing (2000: 739) amongst others noted, it was 'regrettable' that he did 'not acknowledge that there has been ... a critique all along'. As a consequence, he did not address 'the nuances of the debates that those criticisms have generated' and left himself open to the charge that all he was trying to do was 'create a new Washington consensus, in which institutional structures would be given more prominence and in which the policy package would be more flexible, according to the structure of the economy and society of the country concerned' (Standing 2000: 739, 748).

That said, Stiglitz was absolutely critical to the intense contestation of ideas that characterized the end of the 1990s not because of the merits or otherwise of his specific take upon development or political economy, which were not in themselves all that original, but because of his pivotal position in the World Bank and the fact that he was challenging entrenched orthodoxies from that standpoint (see Mittelman 2004). What he symbolized in his person was a period of renewed intellectual debate within the Bank and the global institutions as a whole. He had obviously been given some space to open up discussion by the then President of the Bank, James Wolfensohn, who himself expressed growing awareness of some of the social and environmental costs of Washington Consensus policies. Indeed, Wolfensohn (1999) reiterated elements of Stiglitz's thinking when, in January 1999, he introduced a proposal for a 'Comprehensive Development Framework' designed, in his words, to achieve a better balance in the Bank's policies between the macroeconomic and the human aspects of development. But, in taking up these issues in the way he did, Stiglitz arguably went too far and in particular attracted the ire of the US Secretary of the Treasury in the Clinton administration, Lawrence Summers. In a dramatic *dénouement* he was eventually forced to resign his post by Wolfensohn (ostensibly as part of a deal which kept Wolfensohn as President of the Bank for a second term (Wade 2001: 1,438). Far from retreating at this point, Stiglitz chose to add even greater stridency to his message in an article published in a US magazine, and later posted on the internet, in April 2000. In this piece, which again provoked impassioned discussion amongst those concerned with the trend of global ideas, he turned his fire directly upon the IMF and its handling of the Asian financial crisis of 1997–8. The problem, he said, was not 'imprudent government ... but an imprudent private sector'; the IMF could not see that imposing higher interest rates and demanding reductions in government spending in classic neoliberal fashion would only increase bankruptcies; its staff were generally 'third-rank students from first-rate universities'; for its part the US Treasury Department was 'so arrogant about its economic analyses and prescriptions that it often keeps tight – much too tight – control over what even the president sees'; and so it went on (Stiglitz 2000).

Needless to say, the epistle represented Stiglitz's final, decisive break with the Washington Consensus elite, but it did not immediately bring to an end disputation within the Bank on major matters of strategy and presentation. Whilst still in post, Stiglitz had appointed a British-educated Indian economist, Ravi Kanbur, to head the team charged with preparing the Bank's 2000 *World Development Report* (WDR). The WDRs are the Bank's ideological flagships: each takes a theme, is lavishly produced and has an extensive print-run (at least 50,000 copies in English, as well as another 50,000 copies of the Report's summary in seven different languages). As again Wade (2001: 1,435) has noted, 'the WDR is a political document in the sense that ... its message must reflect the ideological preferences of key constituencies and not offend them too much; but the message must also be backed by empirical evidence and made to look "technical" '. By means of close contacts with Bank staff, Wade has also been able to piece together the story by which early drafts of Kanbur's WDR, which was subtitled 'Attacking Poverty', were thought to overemphasize problems of inequality of income and the case for empowering the poor at the expense of liberalization and the pursuit of economic growth by conventional means. Apparently, the comments of the US Treasury on the first draft were especially tart and influential. In the end, in May 2000, Kanbur also resigned, thereby allowing the production of a final version of the Report that tilted back considerably in the direction of the 'free markets' argument made by his critics inside the Bank and the US Treasury.

The dramas occasioned by Stiglitz's and Kanbur's departures from the Bank were highly illuminating and served to draw direct attention to the proposition that a PWC had slowly, and perhaps painfully, been coming into being over the last few years of the 1990s. It is time now to focus directly on this claim. The phrase certainly took hold and has been widely deployed in academic analyses (Broad and Cavanagh 1999; Higgott 2000; Fine, Lapavitsas and Pincus 2001). However, the problem that we face is that there was even less formally set out or codified than there was in relation to the Washington Consensus itself. The PWC was always a much murkier construct and is perhaps best understood as the piecemeal addition of a number of new ideas to the core of the original consensus in a series of attempts to rescue it from its own inadequacies. This is not at all to say that the breadth and depth of external economic intervention lessened, or even that the theoretical basis upon which these interventions were defended moved very much, if at all, beyond mainstream neoclassical economics. In the words of Ben Fine (2001: 4), the 'intellectual narrowness and reductionism [of the PWC] remain striking', for it replaced 'an understanding of the economy as relying harmoniously on the market by an understanding of society as a whole based on (informational) market imperfections'. Nevertheless, on this basis the remit of the Bank and the Fund began to reach out more extensively than ever before into social and political arenas well beyond the parameters of conventional economic policy making (thereby perhaps giving force to earlier neoliberal suspicions that the IFIs were irredeemably interventionist bodies). The PWC was also invested with a more pronounced international, indeed global, dimension, which was itself revealing and important.

Unpicking these various accretions in turn, the embrace of the social was marked most characteristically by 'the forward march of social capital' (Fine 1999: 4). Fine has shown how Stiglitz himself drew somewhat tentatively upon the concept of social capital and, more importantly, how, from the mid-1990s onwards, it came to be adopted by the World Bank and other global institutions as the vital 'missing link' (World Bank 1997a) in development theory. Even Fukuyama (1996: 13), in his sequel to his 'end of history' thesis, was prepared to concede that neoclassical economics was only, say, 'eighty per cent correct', the 'missing twenty per cent of human behaviour', of which it gave only 'a poor account', being made up of 'the customs, morals, and habits of the society' within which economic life takes place. Yet, as again Fine and indeed many others (Harriss and de Renzio 1997; Putzel 1997; Woolcock 1998) have demonstrated, it is hard to define with any precision what social capital means, beyond saying that it refers to other types of capital from those (physical, financial and human) usually distinguished within neoclassical orthodoxy. In Fine's (1999: 5) acidic summary, 'it seems to be able to be *anything* ranging over public goods, networks, culture etc. The only proviso is that social capital should be attached to the economy in a functionally positive way for economic performance, especially growth' (his emphasis). Of course, its very scope and ambiguity was exactly what made it attractive to reformers of the Washington Consensus. It also did not stray far from the mainstream. In effect, what it proposed was the addition of the idea of social imperfections to the existing, relatively orthodox, economic notion of market imperfections, thereby legitimizing a range of social policies premised on their capacity to build up social capital in societies where the latter was deemed to be deficient.

The political side of the PWC debate was provided by the promotion of the concept of governance and the partial rehabilitation of the state that ran alongside it. The origins of this process again lay in the Bank's realization that the kind of transformation initiated by structural adjustment had to be even more fundamental than had been realized. Specifically, 'getting the prices right' had to be accompanied by 'getting the politics right'. Accordingly, the Bank turned enthusiastically to the concept of governance, breaking it down into five elements: public sector management, accountability, the legal framework, transparency and information, and civil society (World Bank 1992). Crucially, however, these aspects of governance had to be assembled together in a prescribed fashion. As David Williams (1996: 163) summarized the desired mix:

> The state being held accountable by civil society is necessary for effective public sector management, the activities of the state must be transparent for this to occur, information is necessary both for the accountability of the state, and for the state to carry out its development functions successfully ... The new model of the state requires both a smaller state and one which functions more effectively, providing an enabling environment for private sector growth and poverty reduction.

From these beginnings the imperative of 'good' governance spread quickly throughout the whole international donor community. In particular, it opened up space for a new chapter of conditionalities that broke through past inhibitions about interfering in 'politics' and thus substantially extended the terrain upon which it was thought plausible to seek to intervene in the internal affairs of other countries.

Again, from an analytical perspective what was striking about this usage of the concept of governance was its malleability. Martin Doornbos (2001: 98) has pointed out that it was 'somehow broad enough to comprise public management as well as political dimensions, while at the same time vague enough to allow some discretion and flexibility in interpretation as to what "good" governance would or would not condone'. For all that, the character of the overall vision offered by the Bank and all the other institutions which picked up the concept and ran with it was recognizably still a liberal one (Williams and Young 1994). The fact that World Bank functionaries, amongst others, paid lip service to the need to build on the 'indigenous' and to reflect 'cultural values' (Dia 1991) did not obscure this central truth. As Williams (1996: 170) put it in a telling turn of phrase, it was possible to say that governance, in this usage, was 'part Hobbes (disciplining state), part Locke, Smith and de Tocqueville (civil society, property rights, legal system), with a healthy dose of contemporary management theory thrown in (efficiency, quality control, auditing)'. An extension of the point would be to say that it was definitely not part Friedrich List, because one of the unspoken agendas of the revival of interest in the state on the part of the Bank was a concomitant rejection of the particular notion of the 'developmental state' associated with Japan and other fast-growing East Asian economies. This harked back to the controversy surrounding the publication of *The East Asian Miracle* in 1993. In this light nobody should have been fooled (although some were) by the devotion of the 1997 WDR to an analysis of *The State in a Changing World* (World Bank 1997b). Although it was a significant advance, at least at the level of discourse, that the state had been reintroduced, the concept of the state espoused was very much the 'lean and mean' state of neoliberal provenance. The prominence given to this vision in the 1997 WDR showed only that the Bank and its associated thinkers were by then confident enough of the spread of the governance agenda to feel that it was 'safe to re-introduce the subject of the state into polite conversation' (Moore 1999: 69).

The final addition to the package of ideas that made up the PWC also drew upon the notion of governance, but promoted the case for 'global governance'. This meant in the first instance reform and consequential strengthening of the various global organizations, principally the UN, the World Bank and the IMF. The first body to articulate this argument was the self-named Commission on Global Governance, a group of senior politicians and public figures brought together in the early 1990s by the former Swedish prime minister, Ingvar Carlsson, and the former Commonwealth Secretary-General, Shridath Ramphal, with the explicit purpose of suggesting ways of consolidating the presumed revival of the UN in the aftermath of the Gulf War of 1991. Its preference for the notion of governance and its particular usage of the term was interesting and indicative. According to the Commission, governance was 'a continuing process through which conflicting or diverse interests can be accommodated and cooperative action may be taken' (Commission on Global Governance 1995: 2–3). The Commission thus sought to shift attention away from the specificities of the particular powers of international organizations *per se* and reframe global governance as a process founded on accommodation and continual interaction between public and private actors. However, the moment was not yet fully ripe, or perhaps globalization was not yet thought to be in sufficient trouble, and the many (broadly social democratic) reform proposals of the Commission generally fell by the wayside. However, after the Asian financial crisis of 1997–8 the mood in and around Washington was rather different, as we have already seen. Not only did a specific debate begin about reform of the structures of the international financial system, but renewed interest was also shown in theorizing the concept of global governance. The prospectus that caught the mood was offered up, with a considerable fanfare, by a group of economists linked to the UNDP. Their organizing insight was that 'today's turmoil reveals a serious underprovision of global public goods' (Kaul, Grunberg and Stern 1999: xxi), understood in conventional terms as goods that were unlikely to be provided by unregulated markets. As this way of posing the problem revealed, the UNDP study was firmly cast within the framework of liberal economics. That does not mean that some of its suggested global public policy initiatives were not thoroughly worthy; after all, they sought to address problems as genuine and wide-ranging as distributive justice, equity, health, the environment and peace. It is rather that the thrust of the thinking was always biased towards the provision of a technocratic fix to political problems. There was in this view nothing that could not be 'governed away'. Regardless of the detail of particular proposals – and plenty of others were advanced in the late 1990s, such as the Global Compact between global institutions and corporations proposed by UN Secretary-General Kofi Annan in 1999 (United Nations 1999) – the promotion of programmes of global governance in this period seemed always to fall solidly within the broader embrace of liberal ideology (Payne 2005). Although that was part of what made it such an appealing component within the construction of the PWC, it was also what generated its lack of a sharp grasp of politics and, in particular, of the obstacles which routinely impeded implementation of its vision.

What, then, did all of these additional dimensions to the original Washington Consensus add up to? The PWC was manifestly a broader, more wide-ranging 'global-economic vision' than its predecessor. Although, intellectually speaking, that body of ideas was far from tight, the PWC was looser still. Indeed, part of its strength was that it did not have to be propagated as a total package, but could be decomposed, if appropriate, into a more flexible menu of options. This was deliberate. It is also the key insight into what was in effect a considered, political response to some of the failings of the former consensus, an attempt to legitimize globalization by mitigating some of its worst excesses. Neither the Bank nor the Fund was required to abandon the substance of the practices developed during the 1980s. Indeed, the two bodies could even disagree and squabble on occasion about the merits of some of the new arenas of intervention as long as the core activities of stabilization and structural adjustment went on in more or less conventional fashion. The principal achievement of the PWC was to head off opposition to the most fundamental principles of a liberal international economic order by coopting potentially challenging ideas, bringing them into the service of the neoliberal mainstream and thereby rendering their radicalism redundant. Its colour was accordingly paler than that of its predecessor, its tone more muted, its generalities perhaps worthier; but it was still recognizably neoliberal at root and there was much of the old consensus still present. It is also worth noting that the PWC represented another single vision of the good political economy with the same universalist pretensions and that, *contra* Stiglitz's initial exhortation, it remained firmly based in Washington. It was, then, a huge irony that, when the PWC came in turn to be challenged, it was not from a leftist or radical direction at all, but rather the result of an ambitious reassertion of right-wing politics and political economy mounted, once again, in Washington in the very heart of the new US administration formed by George W. Bush in early 2001.

Neoconservatism and the disintegration of 'Western' consensus

The political character of the Bush administration was initially widely misunderstood, and even after its re-election in November 2004 remains uncertain and much debated. Bush initially campaigned for the US presidency as a 'compassionate conservative'. As a candidate he certainly talked in a fundamentalist way about the merits of tax cuts and, in general, deployed a completely different rhetorical armoury from Clinton. But, beyond a greater willingness to enthuse about markets, he did not articulate a distinctive approach to matters of international development. Indeed, in his first months in office it did not appear that the Bush administration would seek to lead the global polity and the global political economy in any particular direction. It was instead a new US isolationism, marked by a withdrawal of interest in a number of international treaties, which seemed to emerge as the most striking initial characteristic of US foreign policy. Everything changed, of course, with the events of 11 September 2001. Since that day the US government has viewed every problem and every policy option through the prism of its security concerns. What is more, it was possible to see that an extraordinarily important argument was taking place within the administration about the extent and nature of US foreign policy, and indeed about the US role in the world order as a whole, in the aftermath of 9/11. The nature of this argument and the policies that flowed from it had, and still have, vital implications for the kinds of debates about political economy and development that we have hitherto been examining. But, at the same time, it was obviously the case that these latter matters were far from being the central focus of the administration after 9/11. They were generally approached only when security questions permitted or demanded and were addressed consistently from a security perspective. This means that, in seeking to set out the context of ideas within which the global politics of development has been pursued since late 2001, we cannot avoid grappling with the different positions taken up in Washington about how the US should respond to terrorist attack.

The Bush strategy after 9/11 is best thought of as an uneasy marriage of three linked, but ultimately separable, approaches to the articulation of US power (Fidler and Baker 2003; Leonard 2004; Nye 2004). The first is an orthodox foreign policy realism, grounded in a traditional conception of the national interest, necessarily pragmatic in practice, anxious above all about the stability of the international system and instinctively ready to use all of the longstanding resources of the diplomatic system, including international agencies and institutions. It looks back favourably to the era of the George H. Bush administration and was articulated most determinedly within the first George W. Bush administration by Colin Powell as Secretary of State. The second has sometimes been described as an 'assertive nationalism': it is indicative of a conventional Republican conservative or 'hawkish' position, pessimistic about the world and ready accordingly to deploy US power, aggressively but yet sparingly, in order to keep the US mainland safe and defend core US interests. It too is pragmatic in orientation, preferring to work via coalitions of willing states but at the same time ready to use international institutions in what has sometimes been dubbed 'multilateralism *à la carte*'. It has been represented thus far in the Bush administration by Dick Cheney as Vice-President and Donald Rumsfeld as Secretary of Defense; the view of Condoleezza Rice as Bush's national security adviser in the first term was more oblique, most likely straddling the realist and nationalist stances. The third approach is the most novel and interesting, and has possibly been decisive. It is the neoconservative position and needs to be examined here in somewhat greater depth.

The first neoconservatives in the US were intellectuals, often Jewish, who converted from the political left during the 1950s and 1960s. They included Norman Podhoretz, editor of *Commentary* magazine, and Irving Kristol, editor of *The Public Interest*. They came of age during the Vietnam years in the US, rejecting both the critique of US intervention in Vietnam mounted by the Democrat left and the cynical, as they saw it, realism of the Nixon/Ford era which dominated US foreign policy in the early 1970s. Instead, the neoconservatives celebrated US power as a force for moral good in the world. The Soviet Union was indeed an evil empire, a phrase later used by Ronald Reagan, who became one of their heroes. Containment was insufficient, *détente* no better than appeasement. The Reagan administration subsequently gave office to a number of younger neoconservatives who did not have a left-wing past and came to the creed with even more zeal. They included such men as Richard Perle, Elliot Abrams and Frank Gaffney, all of whom had also admired and worked for Senator Henry Jackson, a Democrat who was, however, known for his readiness to confront 'democracy's enemies' early and, if necessary, far from home shores. Thereafter this emergent neoconservative cabal tended to inhabit a number of distinctive, new think-tanks, often funded by the US defence industry; bodies such as the American Enterprise Institute, the Project for a New American Century, the Center for Security Policy and the Hudson Institute. Its members used these platforms to articulate a powerful neoconservative critique of Clintonian Third Way politics and were then able in 2001 to acquire a number of middle-ranking positions in and around the first Bush administration. Their most senior representatives in office were Paul Wolfowitz as Deputy Secretary of Defense and Douglas Feith as Under-secretary for Policy at the Pentagon. The neoconservatives were thus involved in the making of policy under Bush, but initially (that is, before 9/11) they were overshadowed by the conventional 'hawkish' nationalists.

Neoconservatives have been described by Daalder and Lindsay (2003) as 'democratic imperialists'. They have also been called 'Wilsonians of the Right' in a reference to US President Woodrow Wilson, who asserted that he wanted to 'make the world safe for democracy' after the end of the First World War. Their approach to US foreign policy is characterized by a willingness to use US power to advance ideological goals. They believe in the active promotion of democracy and, in particular, have wanted lately to effect the complete transformation of the economic and political order of the Middle East so as to bring this region fully into line with classical liberal democratic norms. They are not really conservatives at all, but rather crusading liberals with a belief in the power of activist government to bring about liberal ends, a consequentially huge and ambitious agenda and a willingness to create instability in the short term in order to achieve longer-term gain (Stelzer 2004). They do not, however, share all of Woodrow Wilson's beliefs, for, as Francis Fukuyama has noted, they stand for 'Wilsonianism minus international institutions' such as the UN (cited in Leonard 2004: 19). It is important to note too that neoconservatives are in turn bitterly criticized and seen themselves as a threat to American liberty by genuine libertarians, as most effectively represented in the US think-tank world by the Cato Institute, precisely because of their readiness to use US state power and money to advance their cause (Crane and Niskanen 2003). Nevertheless, the neoconservative message has never been less than completely clear and consciously strident. What it has lacked in subtlety it has more than made up in fervour.

In practice, Bush's foreign policy statements and actions since September 2001 have been an uneasy amalgam of all of these approaches. There were, for example, strands of each mode of thinking apparent in the new, and seminal, 'National Security Strategy of the United States of America' presented to Congress in September 2002. Traditional patterns of alliance-building with other great powers, increased military spending, the doctrine of 'pre-emptive attack', the desire to extend 'the benefits of freedom across the globe' – all made their appearance (US Government 2002). Each approach also had its moments of bureaucratic triumph during the course of the first Bush administration. But, that said, and viewed over time, 9/11 can be seen to have projected the neoconservative take on the world to a greater degree of prominence within the administration than appeared likely or even possible before that cataclysmic event. As the focus of the war on terror moved from the invasion of Afghanistan to the invasion of Iraq, there developed a growing convergence of view between the 'assertive nationalists' and the neoconservatives, with the realists led by Powell in the Department of State placed more and more on the defensive. This certainly does not mean that Bush's has been a neoconservative administration, as some simplistic journalistic analyses have suggested. The neoconservatives were always in a minority in the administration during the President's first term and did not hold any of the most senior offices of state. Their voice was, however, a self-confident one and it was persistently heard, working to push the administration to focus on Iraq (Wolfowitz is alleged to have proposed regime change in Baghdad within five days of 9/11) and then to embark on a process of national rebuilding in that country. Notwithstanding the direction of US policy so far in Iraq and the extent of its current involvement, the argument within the administration between the three foreign policy approaches described here has not been concluded and, to a substantial degree, depends on the unfolding of events within the Middle East. It is not a straightforward matter to predict which way the balance of the argument will move, and we do not need to try to do so for present purposes.

From our perspective the point to stress is that the US approach to questions of international development under George W. Bush has been mediated via this wider foreign policy and security debate. The 2002 'National Security Strategy' did not discuss issues of political economy at great length, but they surfaced in revealing ways. For example, one of 'the lessons of history' was declared to be that 'market economies, not command and control economies with the heavy hand of government, are the best way to promote prosperity and reduce poverty'. The IMF was told that it needed to improve its efforts to prevent financial crises and ensure stability in emerging markets. By contrast, the World Bank was not mentioned at all. 'Free trade' was applauded 'as a moral principle' as well as 'a pillar of economics'. In addition, although 'decades of massive development assistance' were deemed not to have spurred economic growth in the poorest countries, 'significant new levels of assistance' were promised from within the US federal budget, but only 'where governments have implemented real policy changes'. Conditionality was in effect being demanded in advance. Finally, it was asserted that the events of 9/11 'taught us that weak states, like Afghanistan, can pose as great a danger to our national interests as strong states' (US Government 2002). As Susan Rice (2003: 2) commented, 'weak states' were understood as countries 'in which the central government does not exert effective control over, nor is it able to deliver vital services to, significant parts of its own territory due to conflict, ineffective governance, or state collapse'. Although they were not explicitly defined in the document as poor countries, that implication was left hanging in the air (Soederberg 2004). This last theme added a notably harder and more threatening edge to a philosophy of development which in any case had already moved a long way from the tenets of the post-Washington Consensus in the direction of mainstream liberal Republican economic values, suspicion of aid and relative hostility to the management of the global political economy by the multilateral institutions.

As is well-known, the Bush administration has not been too concerned to build support amongst its traditional 'Western' allies for its 'revolution' (Daalder and Lindsay 2003) in US foreign policy. It preferred to act pre-emptively and unilaterally and has seen global institutions, particularly of course the UN Security Council in respect of Iraq, as sources of constraint rather than legitimacy or sustenance. With the marked exception of the United Kingdom in the form of the Blair government, 'old Europe' was found wanting in Washington, condemned as cowardly, conservative and cynically preoccupied with preserving the status quo rather than crusading to make the world a better place. One important consequence of the rise of neoconservatism in the US and the degree of influence that it has had on the first Bush administration has therefore been to bring an end, at least temporarily, to much of the traditional ideological consensus that bound the 'West' together throughout the Cold War. Fukuyama (2002) posed the problem in the most plaintive of fashions in a syndicated newspaper article published in September 2002:

> What is going on here? The end of history was supposed to be about the victory of western, not simply American, values and institutions, making liberal democracy and market-oriented economies the only viable choices ... Yet an enormous gulf has opened up in American and European perceptions about the world, and the sense of shared values is increasingly frayed. Does the concept of 'the west' still make sense in the first decade of the 21st century? Is the fracture line over globalisation actually a division not between the west and the rest but between the US and the rest?

The latter are good questions. The best available answers at present suggest that the spontaneous outpouring of support for the US and its people immediately after 9/11 has been replaced by new expressions of anti-Americanism felt almost as strongly in Europe as in other parts of the world. The ending of the Cold War of itself removed the major strategic linkage that held Europe and the US in close alliance for so many years. Its passing enabled France and Germany, in particular, to oppose the war in Iraq, as a consequence of which they now enjoy awkward relations with the US under Bush. Western European governments, including even the Blair government in its domestic policy orientation, also remain committed to an approach to welfare at home and development abroad which is much closer to the old PWC than either the old neoliberal or new neoconservative worldviews. In short, for perhaps the first time since 1945 there no longer exists a 'Western' consensus on the core ideas that should underpin the political economy of development.

Radical challenges

In order to provide a complete picture of the contest of ideas at work in the contemporary world order we still need to examine and assess the appeal and coherence of other radical ideologies that seek to challenge mainstream 'Western' thinking. As Caroline Thomas (2000: 47) has observed, there can be detected 'a variety of resistance responses in different localities', taking many forms 'from micro-scale to large-scale movements'. Indicative examples at different levels of resistance which she cites include: peasant protests in the southern Indian state of Karnataka; the Zapatista movement in Chiapas in Mexico; workers' strikes in South Korea; the Malaysian government's attempt to create an East Asian Economic Group exclusive of the US, Australia and Canada; street demonstrations in Seattle during the WTO meeting held there in 1999; and the forums now organized by non-governmental organizations (NGOs) in parallel with most major gatherings of the global institutions. The diversity of these forms of politics is obvious, as Thomas herself concedes, and it is clearly difficult to discern much more to bind them together than a motif of 'resistance'. She sets out the core ideas and assumptions of this 'alternative view' of development as embracing the following concepts:

- sufficiency;
- the inherent value of nature, cultural diversity and the community-controlled commons (water, land, air, forest);
- human activity in balance with nature;
- self-reliance rather than reliance on the market or external agents;

- democratic inclusion [and] participation, e.g. voice for marginalised groups such as women, indigenous groups; and
- local control (Thomas 2000: 38).

One can recognize here clearly enough the ethical basis of the prospectus, with its mix of ecological, humanistic and local dimensions. But at the same time it cannot be seen plausibly as a 'global economic-political vision', to use Murphy's phrase again, capable of matching the rigour and sheer ideological force of either of the Washington consensuses or indeed contemporary neoconservatism. It is simply too woolly and unspecific to stand up to scrutiny as a coherent, alternative *package* of ideas. Nevertheless, there are or have been strands of non-mainstream thinking about development which have had a measure of appeal and arguably some real-world impact over the last few years and which, as a consequence, we need to examine.

The first such strand has been called 'a latent "Southern consensus" ' – latent in the sense that, even according to its proponent, it does not presently 'exist as a political reality' and has not, as yet, been 'articulated analytically'. It is suggested that its existence is apparent in 'the convergence between the policy conclusions of Latin American neostructuralism', set out initially by the UN Economic Commission for Latin America, and 'the deeper understanding of East Asian development models', advanced again mainly by UN bodies, notably the UN Economic and Social Commission for Asia and the Pacific and UNCTAD (Gore 2000: 795). In common with neoliberalism, these approaches remain focused on the achievement of economic growth as the central objective, but reject the notion that a general blueprint can be prescribed, especially for 'late' industrializing countries seeking to 'catch up'. By contrast, a more subtle historical analysis is deployed by means of which policy measures are adapted to initial conditions and the external environment, as well as changing over time as an economy matures. Although Gore acknowledges that there are differences between Latin American and East Asian thinking, and admits that for the moment he cannot really discern an African ideological contribution to his putative 'Southern consensus', he nevertheless identifies, as follows, five general policy orientations that ostensibly characterize the model:

(i)   the process of growth is best achieved through the 'strategic integration' of the national economy into the international economy via selective tariffs and gradual capital account liberalisation, rather than either de-linking from the rest of the world or rapid across-the-board opening up of the economy;

(ii) national economic strategy should *combine* a growth-oriented macroeconomic policy designed to reduce both inflation and fiscal deficits and a supply-side-oriented 'productive development policy' embracing *inter alia* technology policy, human resource development, physical infrastructure development and industrial organisation;

(iii) this requires government–business cooperation within the framework of a 'pragmatic developmental state' whereby a capable economic bureaucracy advances a common set of societal objectives and succeeds in harnessing the 'animal spirits' of the private sector;

(iv) the distributional dimension of the growth process is managed in order to ensure legitimacy, but is pursued mainly by means such as wide asset ownership and widespread employment rather than direct redistributive transfers; and

(v) regional integration and cooperation supports all of the above, especially the pursuit of increased international competitiveness and the creation of larger regional markets to reduce the demand-side constraints on growth (Gore 2000: 796–8, his emphasis).

In many respects, obviously, these ideas make a firm bow to the neoliberal view of development: they accept multilateral rules and arrangements and they acknowledge the imperative of competitiveness. To this extent, they are perhaps not radical at all. Nevertheless, they do surely represent something at least a little distinctive even from the PWC. They are rooted in a continuing economic nationalism and take a notably realistic, rather than idealistic, view of how market economies actually work, with all their vulnerabilities, imperfections and instabilities, especially when viewed from outside the core countries. The approach also rescues a modestly developmental conception of the state and, in so doing, joins ideological battle from the other side, as it were, with those deliberate efforts by the World Bank and others to re-describe the East Asian 'miracle' as compatible with the virtues of liberal market economics. Of late, the economic difficulties into which many Latin American and East Asian countries have run have worked to weaken the short-term political appeal of this 'Southern consensus', to the point, certainly in respect of Latin America, where one can question whether states really have either the fiscal or institutional capacity to implement successfully the various strategies proposed. Nevertheless, this does not mean that the ideas underpinning the so-called 'Southern consensus' have themselves been undermined, and indeed they remain a part of the policy debate about development.

The second and the more serious 'Southern' challenge to mainstream Western thinking is anything but latent, for it derives its ideological appeal from the extraordinary economic growth achieved over the last decade by

China. What can this be said to represent in terms of development strategy? It is still perhaps rather early to expect to be able to answer that question. But it is striking and potentially of great significance that Joshua Cooper Ramo has recently sought to set out the essential elements of the 'new physics of power and development' in China, which he deliberately names the 'Beijing Consensus'. Indeed, he explicitly argues that it is replacing 'the widely-discredited Washington Consensus, an economic theory made famous ... for its prescriptive, Washington-knows-best approach to telling other nations how to run themselves' (Ramo 2004: 4). According to this argument, the Beijing Consensus is made up of three theorems. The first 'repositions the value of innovation', reversing the old argument that 'developing countries must start development with trailing-edge technology (copper wires)' and insisting instead on 'the necessity of bleeding-edge innovation (fiber optics) to create change that moves faster than the problems change creates' (Ramo 2004: 11–12). The second part of the package 'looks beyond measures like per-capita GDP', focuses instead on 'quality-of-life' and advocates a model of 'balanced development' where 'sustainability and equality become first considerations, not luxuries'. The third element is constituted by 'a theory of self-determination ... that stresses using leverage to move big, hegemonic powers that may be tempted to tread on your toes' (Ramo 2004: 12). Ramo's language is colloquial in tone and his conceptualization of some of the features of the Chinese model rather loose; others, however, have expressed not dissimilar arguments in more academic fashion, Breslin (2003), for example, talking of China's commitment to an 'embedded socialist compromise'. What matters, though, from the perspective of the argument here is the evidence that is now emerging of the growing 'intellectual charisma of the Beijing Consensus' (Ramo 2004: 27). For instance, in just the last year or so leading development policy makers and thinkers from countries as diverse as Brazil, India, Thailand and Vietnam have all expressed admiration for different aspects of China's attempt to practise 'Globalisation with Chinese Characteristics' (Ramo 2004: 33). Much of course remains dependent upon events (and continued success), whilst it is also important to note those aspects of China's record which damage its standing as a development model: namely, its internal empire and unsatisfactory human rights regime. But, even with that said, it is already clear that China has the potential to change the contest of ideas about development in very significant ways.

The third and final body of radical ideas worth exploring briefly is that associated with what is commonly called the 'anti-globalization movement', although, as has often been observed, this is neither wholly against globalization nor a single movement. The many diverse strands of action that are encompassed by this label are, in fact, as much 'for' certain causes and values as they are 'against' others (Cohen and Rai 2000; Klein 2001; Ashman 2004). Yet, because activists run the full gamut of attitudes from reactionary to progressive, they have been difficult to characterize in more positive fashion: hence the 'anti' prefix has stuck. Even the conscious attempt to escape from this trap made by the organizers of the World Social Forum (WSF) in Porto Alegre in Brazil in January 2002 in choosing for their slogan for that meeting the phrase 'Another World is Possible' failed to establish precisely what vision of the future the movement held. Subsequent WSFs have not done much more to clarify the matter. Attempts to classify the anti-globalization movement ideologically have thus been many and various. In a useful review Duncan Green and Matthew Griffith (2002: 55) tentatively propose a tripartite division between 'statists', 'alternatives' and 'reformists'. On this conceptualization the 'statists' seek straightforwardly to defend and rebuild the role of the state in economic management after the neoliberal onslaught of the last 20 years. They are to be found mainly on the traditional left, in some sections of labour movements and amongst activists in Asia and Latin America. The 'alternatives' are best understood in cultural terms: they believe in smallness and decentralization and are strongly anti-corporate. The 'reformists', the biggest group, are brought together only by a general desire to offset the worst injustices perpetrated by globalization. However, even the authors of this categorization are quick to point out its weaknesses. It does not, they say, allow for the fact that many individuals and groups span more than one current, or do justice to the role played by a number of prominent writers and campaigners from outside the post-industrial world, such as Vandana Shiva (India), Martin Khor (Malaysia) and Walden Bello (Philippines). Lastly, none of the postulated ideological strands of the movement adequately describes the 'nihilists' who 'rage against the machine', rather than engage in political debate.

It is also the case that the movement does not have any major intellectual statements of position around which they can agree to cohere or which they can even collectively admire. Naomi Klein (2000) has unquestionably become one of the anti-globalization movement's heroines since the publication in 2000 of her book *No Logo*; but she speaks mainly to the anti-corporate dimension of the movement and offers only a cultural, rather than a political economy, critique of globalization. Noreena Hertz (2001) and George Monbiot (2000, 2003) have also achieved considerable media visibility without coming close to setting out the compelling vision of 'anti-globalization' that is missing (see Thompson 2003, 2004). Sometimes the work of Amartya Sen (1999) is cited approvingly, although his approach is philosophically entirely consistent with liberal principles and more obviously underpins the UNDP's reformist endeavour to build interest in its Human Development Index than any genuinely radical challenge to neoliberal orthodoxy. Perhaps it is the case in the age of internet communication, which has been a central, practical sustaining force of the anti-globalization movement, that activists within the various movements do not read that widely or feel the need to locate their grievances against the system within any acknowledged theoretical framework. Their gut beliefs tend towards libertarianism, in that any and all can join and believe in whatever they choose. At the broadest level, too, a strain of anti-capitalism, or what the *Financial Times* (11 September 2001) delicately described as a 'queasiness' about capitalism, can be said to pervade the movement. For all that, the intellectual basis of the opposition to capitalism is, as we have noted, rarely (if ever) articulated in serious and grounded terms and in the end it is questionable whether or not the anti-globalization movement has yet generated a systematic set of ideas with which it can expect to challenge globalization orthodoxy in real ideological combat.

In concluding this section of the chapter we should perhaps note the bodies of thought that we did not need to revisit: the longstanding systems of ideas that once posed the toughest of radical challenges to the mainstream, namely, dependency theory and Marxism. During the 1960s, and certainly the 1970s, these separate, but linked, bodies of thought were fully engaged in the business of offering alternative visions of political economy to governments, intellectuals, activists and peoples around the world. No similar survey of the contest of ideas at that time could have ignored them. Yet, to all intents and purposes, they live on now only within the academy, and generally in remote and marginal parts even of these circuits. In fact, one could plausibly argue that in the real world of contending ideas elements of dependency theory have transmuted into the latent 'Southern consensus' and the embryonic Beijing Consensus, and elements of Marxism into the anti-capitalist protestations of the anti-globalization movement. There is ample space still for radical ideas to come to the fore; in fact, there are many peoples and groups in many countries looking somewhat desperately for them. But the truth is that they have yet to be authoritatively articulated, let alone embedded as the new 'common-sense' of the times.

Conclusion

We have sought in this chapter to range over a wide span of contemporary ideological debate in order to describe and analyse a further part of the framework of action within which we suggest that the global politics of development is currently being forged. In particular, we have wanted to establish exactly what are the dominant ideas in the realm of political economy at the turn of the century and, just as importantly, to assess *how* dominant they are. It is immediately apparent that the main sources of the ideas that we have been discussing have been the US and the UK – the Anglo-American world (even other parts of Western Europe have, by comparison, been only token contributors). In successive phases the Washington Consensus and the post-Washington Consensus unquestionably commanded the stage. The former constituted the self-conscious assertion of a new neoliberal development paradigm and manifestly succeeded in changing the terms of the debate. For all that, the PWC was more formidable as a panoply of ideas: it was more flexible than the first Washington Consensus, more sensitive to the pressures that had begun to be experienced by neoliberal globalization, more able to roll with the punches. Yet, as Richard Higgott has written, it was actually 'no less universalizing', and attempted to be 'no less homogenizing', than its forerunner. 'Global policy debates', he noted, were still 'reliant on a set of "generalizable", but essentially Western liberal, principles and policy prescriptions'. Even while they offered 'a more subtle understanding of market dynamics than in the early years of global neoliberalism', they still demonstrated 'a penchant for universalizing notions of a "one-size-fits-all convergence" on issues of policy reform under conditions of globalization' (Higgott 2000: 16). To that extent, it was a *post*-Washington Consensus only in the temporal, rather than the substantive, sense of that phrase. From this perspective, the more significant change has come about since 2001 with the sudden disintegration of 'Western' (even Anglo-American) consensus on key development, political economy and international relations questions. The growing influence of neoconservative ideas within George W. Bush's America has pushed US policy and rhetoric in the direction of a cruder, security-oriented approach to the global politics of development which, as we have seen, has begun to open up a gulf between current official US and mainstream European thinking. In this important respect we are beginning to move into uncharted territory.

It is not that other more radical impulses do not exist within many states and societies, including the US itself: they do, probably more widely than at any time in the last quarter of a century. But they have failed thus far to express their resistance to the various different faces of Washington's ideological dominance of the last 20–30 years in a form which constitutes a plausible counter-hegemonic project. Generally speaking, 'movements of rage', in Kenneth Jowitt's (1991) felicitous phrase, considerably outnumber 'movements of position', which was Gramsci's preferred term for emergent political forces capable of challenging and ultimately overthrowing hegemony. Perhaps only the constellation of ideas gathering around the Beijing Consensus can be said to have that potential. For the moment, we can best sum up the present global balance of ideological power as an uneasy dissensus between a 'harder', crusading neoconservatism in the US and a 'softer', more accommodating Third Way neoliberalism in Europe, tempered only by the rising pitch of a distinctively Chinese soundtrack and the continuing voice in the background of 'an increasingly angry international cadre committed to the kind of accountable humanitarianism that justifies an endless struggle to support those excluded and victimised by an unequal world order' (Murphy 1999: 302).

Chapter 5

Global Institutions

This chapter completes our background survey of the framework of action within which we have suggested that the global politics of development is being conducted. It moves on to consider the third category of forces identified by Cox as fundamental to the make-up of any historical structure: namely, institutions. Cox does not, in fact, specify precisely how he defines institutions. It is likely that he was thinking of institutions conventionally as firm organizational structures rather than as the general 'rules of the game' that shape the behaviour of actors, which is how the concept has come to be used in much contemporary so-called 'institutionalist' political science (Hall and Taylor 1996). He has noted that 'institutionalization is a means of stabilizing and perpetuating a particular order'; that 'institutions reflect the power relations prevailing at their point of origin and tend, at least initially, to encourage collective images consistent with these power relations'; that institutions can become 'a battleground of opposing tendencies, or rival institutions may reflect different tendencies'; and, in an important point of connection to his other two organizing concepts, that 'institutions are particular amalgams of ideas and material power' (Cox 1981: 136–7). This suggests an insightful way of analysing institutions, but does not, of course, tell us which institutions should be the focus of our attention.

From the perspective of this study we can best deploy Cox's method by focusing upon the many international or intergovernmental organizations (to use a somewhat old-fashioned but nevertheless unambiguous formulation) that now patrol the global politics of development. The reality is that these bodies play a hugely significant role in the political conflicts that are the subject of this enquiry. We have already had cause to talk at length about the IMF and the World Bank in preceding chapters and have seen some of the many ways in which they shape the formation of ideas, not only about categories and definitions of types of countries but also more widely about the parameters of acceptability within which countries are permitted to pursue their chosen economic and political strategies. Reference has also been made in passing to the role of some of the agencies of the UN system and to the WTO, the newest global institution on the block. However, what we have not yet done is analyse systematically the leading global institutions of the current world order, with a view to filling in what they do and, above all, how they operate internally. We will thus focus in this chapter on their organizational shape and style, membership and rules and procedures.

We will seek to review all of the major institutions, dividing them into two broad camps roughly equivalent to a distinction between an 'old' economic multilateralism, generally perceived as supportive of the post-1945 liberal international economic order founded at Bretton Woods, and a 'new' or 'newer' political multilateralism, symbolically located in the UN General Assembly and characterized by a greater readiness to challenge some of the traditional features of that order (Cox 1992). It should be stressed that this is primarily a presentational device, for the distinctions drawn here between old and new and economic and political cannot be expected to be particularly sharp. We need, however, to begin by considering the emergence of an important institutional nexus within global politics that does not quite fall into either of these categories, namely, the Group of 7/Group of 8 system.

The Group of 7/Group of 8

At its most basic the G7/8 is a summit of leaders. Since 1975 the heads of state or government of the leading post-industrial democracies have been meeting annually to discuss the major economic and political issues facing their societies and the international community as a whole. The six countries that attended the first summit, which took place at Rambouillet in France, were France, the US, the UK, West Germany, Japan and Italy. They were joined by Canada at the 1976 meeting in San Juan, Puerto Rico. Since then the summit has met every year for two or three days, usually some time between May and July, with each country acting as host and taking the chair in an agreed order. In the period since 1976 membership of the G7 has been modified only twice, once quite early and once relatively recently. The European Community was invited to attend (in the person of the President of the European Commission) in 1977, but this did not represent the addition of a new state. Russia is the one other country that has eventually been formally admitted, albeit after a long apprenticeship (http://www.g7.utoronto.ca). Courtesy of the momentous political changes taking place in the Soviet Union in the late 1980s and early 1990s, its leader was asked to take part in a post-summit dialogue with the G7 from 1991 onwards. Starting with the 1994 Naples summit this was extended into a formal meeting with Russia at each G7 gathering (referred to as the P8 or Political 8 summit). Russia then attended the summit as a participant for the first time at Denver in 1997, but at Japan's insistence this was called the 'Summit of the Eight' and

Russia was only allowed to take part in the political, not the economic and financial, discussions. Its continuing, severe economic difficulties were deemed to make 'full' membership absurd. Nevertheless, in the following year at Birmingham in the UK, it was agreed that the nomenclature of the G8 would henceforth be used. Unsurprisingly, Russia's leaders chafed at their exclusion from key meetings and at the Kananaskis meeting in Canada in 2002 it was decided that Russia would have full rights of membership from the following year, including responsibility for taking its turn to host the annual summit. This at last resolved the formal question of Russia's membership and removed some of the confusion caused by the fact that, from 1998 until 2003, the G7 and G8 in effect co-existed, meeting more or less alongside each other. What it did not do was solve the substantive issue. Russia is neither a proven democracy, nor one of the world's most powerful post-industrial economies. It has had, to put it mildly, a highly distinctive modern history and was only admitted into the G7 family of states as a diplomatic tactic by which to finesse the ending of the Cold War. As such, it does not sit at all comfortably alongside the other states in the grouping. In fact, Russia's membership is, potentially, a serious flaw in the constitution of the G8.

In the meantime, there is no doubt that the agenda of the summits has expanded considerably since the early days, which of itself made the distinction drawn in relation to Russia between 'political' and 'economic' matters increasingly hard to sustain. The leaders have consistently discussed the macroeconomic management of the world economy, international trade, financial matters and aid. But they have over time broadened their remit to include microeconomic issues (such as employment and information technology), transnational issues (such as the environment, crime and drugs), and a host of security issues (such as arms control, terrorism and human rights). The style of the summits has similarly altered. From being conceptualized initially as private, informal gatherings of 'those who really matter in the world', which was the reported comment of the then West German Chancellor, Helmut Schmidt (Putnam and Bayne 1987: 29), they have come to be prepared more meticulously, with representatives of the leaders, known colloquially as 'sherpas', in constant contact throughout the year and working with many other officials towards the satisfactory evolution of the annual communiqué. All in all, no fewer than 30 summits have now been held in the series. Achievements have of course varied. Even Nicholas Bayne (2000: 195), who has studied the history of the G7 and the G8 more closely and supportively than anyone else, has judged that on several occasions 'nothing significant' was gained from the meetings. Nevertheless, on other notable occasions the leaders have given a decisive steer to the making of policy in key areas of global concern, including many matters that are the focus of this book. To put it another way, they have wielded the agenda-setting power available to them as heads of the most powerful (seven) countries in the world. Even so, the G7/G8 process can still be said to have crept up somewhat surreptitiously on observers of world affairs and it has often not been given the attention that its centrality to global political decision-making has lately come to merit (Baker 2000; Dobson 2004). It is the case that this body is the closest institutional representation of an organizing political intelligence at the summit of the world order presently in existence. Indeed, John Kirton (1999: 46) has gone further and described it as 'prospectively the effective center ... of global governance'.

This claim is reinforced by the fact that the G8 network also now embraces meetings of foreign, finance, trade, justice, environment, home, employment, energy and education ministers, as well as *ad hoc* meetings, task forces and working groups to address pressing issues. These ministerial gatherings are inevitably backed up by associated meetings of officials, thereby adding to the sense that a system of rule may be emerging in and around the annual summit of leaders. We should note two specific features of this system, which are that the finance ministers meet as the G7 (that is, without a Russian representative), and the trade ministers meet as the 'Quad' (that is, as Canada, the European Union (EU), Japan and the US). These groupings have slightly different histories. The G7 finance ministers meeting has its roots in the 'Library Group' (so called because it initially met in the White House library) formed in 1973 between the then finance ministers of France, West Germany, the US and the UK (Armstrong 1996: 42). When Japan joined it became the Group of 5 and met irregularly and largely in secret until 1986 when Canada and Italy also joined, converting the Group of 5 into the G7. These ministers now meet every three months or so, often alongside their central bank governors and routinely also with the managing directors and other senior officials of the IMF and the World Bank. Over time, as Bayne (2000: 34) puts it, the G7 finance ministers 'steadily increased their institutional independence and took over the initiative from the leaders in economic policy-making'. As indicated, they can and do meet more frequently than the heads of state or government; they usually attract less media attention, which can facilitate effectiveness; and they can bring to bear on issues formidable amounts of technocratic support. By comparison, the 'Quad' trade ministers meeting dates back only to 1981, but it too convenes three or four times a year and plays a key role in giving political direction to the various rounds of trade negotiations conducted under the auspices of initially the GATT and latterly the WTO. The finance ministers and the trade ministers are without doubt the two most influential of the ministerial groupings within the G7/G8 system.

Global economic institutions

The International Monetary Fund

The IMF, along with the World Bank, was actually conceived at the Bretton Woods conference in July 1944, formally coming into being (with headquarters in Washington) just over a year later in December 1945 when the first 29 countries signed its Articles of Agreement. According to these articles, the purposes of the Fund were: (i) to promote international monetary cooperation; (ii) to facilitate the expansion and balanced growth of international trade; (iii) to promote exchange stability; (iv) to assist in the establishment of a multilateral payments system between members; (v) to correct maladjustments in the balance of payments of members by making the general resources of the Fund available to them on a temporary basis; and (vi) to reduce the duration and severity of disequilibria of members' balance of payments (http://www.imf.org). Although these statutory purposes have not altered over the succeeding half-century, the institutional arrangements and wider policy thrust of the Fund have changed substantially (de Vries 1986; James 1996; Bird 2001). Initially it was mainly concerned to establish and manage an international regime of fixed, but adjustable, exchange rates; it was required to intervene with member governments only relatively infrequently.

However, following the move to widespread 'floating' of exchange rates after 1971, the IMF in effect reinvented itself, opening up an expanded 'second generation' agenda of new policy areas. These have been identified as: comprehensive and detailed surveillance of the economic performance of member states; the imposition of structural adjustment packages for medium- and long-term economic reconstruction; extensive training and technical assistance activities; and various initiatives to restore stability to global financial markets (O'Brien *et al.* 2000: 161–3). Unsurprisingly, in order to handle such an enlarged remit, the Fund has had both to draw upon more resources and to increase the size of its staff. The IMF's resources come mainly from the quota, or capital, subscriptions which countries pay when they join: these have gone up from the equivalent of 21 billion Special Drawing Rights (SDRs), which are the IMF's own money form, in 1965 to 213 billion SDRs in the latest adjustment which took effect from January 1999. This represented about US$290 billion at that time. Staff numbers had reached approximately 2,700 persons by late 2004, with the Fund now having 'resident representatives' in around 80 countries, as well as other offices in Geneva, Paris, New York and Tokyo. Finally, membership of the IMF has risen over the period of its existence to no fewer than 184 states at present.

The IMF is formally accountable to these member countries via its Board of Governors, on which all countries are represented and which usually meets once a year at the Annual Meetings of the Fund and the World Bank, and, more routinely, via its Executive Board, which consists of just 24 executive directors and generally meets three times a week in full-day sessions. From the outset the internal structure of the Fund was designed to balance the perceived requirements of 'universality' and 'effectiveness'. On the one hand, its universal character was acknowledged by the allocation of so-called 'basic votes' – 250 – to each country (Horsefield 1969). As Joseph Gold (1972: 18) noted, these votes 'were to serve the function of recognizing the doctrine of the equality of states', whilst also avoiding 'too close an adherence to the concept of a private business corporation'. On the other hand, the effective dimension was met by ensuring that the interests of the most powerful member states were protected by the introduction of a weighted element whereby additional votes were granted in relation to a country's quota in the Fund, which in turn was calculated in some accordance with relative economic strength. The initial quotas were drawn up by the US government as early as 1943. They were nominally based on measurements of national income, foreign exchange reserves and international trade, but also involved, according to Raymond Mikesell (the man who actually devised them), overt political considerations. Asked to undertake this task over a weekend by Harry Dexter White, the main US negotiator at Bretton Woods, he was told that 'our military allies (President Roosevelt's Big Four) [the US, the UK, the USSR and China] should have the largest quotas, with a ranking that the President and Secretary of State had agreed' (Mikesell 1994: 21). In the intervening period technical adjustments in the formulae by which quotas, and hence votes, are calculated have been made several times, always with political undertones, but the practice of 'basic votes plus quota' has always been maintained (Buira 1996). As of late 2004 the allocation of IMF quotas and voting power for the most influential member states was as shown in Table 5.1.

As can readily be seen from the table, the disparities in the allocations, even of economically significant countries, are stark: from a high of 371,743 votes (17.14 per cent) for the US via a big gap to the next largest, Japan, with 133,378 votes (6.15 per cent) to a low of 24,205 votes (1.12) for Sweden. No fewer than 164 countries possess under 1 per cent of the votes each and only amass 29.68 per cent between them. The lowest allocation is given to Paleu, which has just 281 votes (0.013 per cent of the total). What is more, these latter countries are generally the ones in which the IMF has lately been most likely to intervene. It has also been observed that countries such as Brazil (1.41 per cent of the votes), Spain (1.42 per cent) and Mexico (1.20 per cent), whose GDP and population are higher than countries such as Belgium (2.13 per cent), the Netherlands (2.39 per cent)

Table 5.1 *Member quotas and voting power in the IMF, December 2004*

Member	Quota Millions of SDRs	Quota Percentage of total	Votes Number	Votes Percentage of total
United States	37,149.3	17.46	371,743	17.14
Japan	13,312.8	6.26	133,378	6.15
Germany	13,008.2	6.11	130,332	6.01
France	10,738.5	5.06	107,635	4.97
United Kingdom	10,738.5	5.05	107,635	4.96
Italy	7,055.5	3.32	70,805	3.26
Saudi Arabia	6,985.5	3.28	70,105	3.23
China	6,369.2	2.99	63,942	2.95
Canada	6,369.2	2.99	63,942	2.95
Russia	5,945.4	2.79	59,704	2.75
Netherlands	5,162.4	2.43	51,874	2.39
Belgium	4,605.2	2.16	46,302	2.13
India	4,158.2	1.95	41,832	1.93
Switzerland	3,458.5	1.63	34,835	1.61
Australia	3,236.4	1.52	32,614	1.50
Spain	3,048.9	1.43	30,739	1.42
Brazil	3,036.1	1.43	30,611	1.41
Venezuela	2,659.1	1.25	26,841	1.24
Mexico	2,585.8	1.22	26,108	1.20
Sweden	2,395.5	1.13	24,205	1.12
Rest (i.e. 164 countries)	51,460.2	28.54	650,855	29.68

Source: Data from http://www.imf.org

and Switzerland (1.61 per cent), have fewer voting rights within the IMF system (Buira 1996: 48). One could go on, too, to highlight a number of other apparent disparities. As a way of mitigating some of them an alternative way of calculating quotas (based on the use of purchasing power parities rather than official exchange rates in measuring GDP) has been proposed and investigated. However, the political problem with this, as Ngaire Woods (2000: 830) has noted, is that it would alter the distribution significantly in favour of the poorer, less industrialized countries and it has consequently never been adopted. Table 5.1 does not show it, but it is also the case that the original balance between 'equality' votes and 'weighted' votes has changed considerably over time: from basic votes counting for 11.3 per cent of total votes in 1946, rising to a high of 14 per cent in 1955, the proportion has slipped to around 3 per cent at present, thereby increasing significantly the overall impact of the weighting element and the inequalities inherent within it (Woods 2000: 828).

The make-up of the membership of the Executive Board, the key decision-making forum within the IMF, is also rather revealing. The Fund's five largest shareholders – the US, Japan, Germany, France and the UK – have permanent seats, along with China, Saudi Arabia and Russia. The other 16 executive directors are elected for two-year terms by groups of countries, known as 'constituencies', gathered together on the basis of a rough mix of cultural, historical and geographical connections (thereby producing some odd alliances, such as Ireland being linked with Canada and the English-speaking Caribbean countries). These constituencies run from the influential (Austria, Belarus, Belgium, Czech Republic, Hungary, Kazakhstan, Luxembourg, Slovak Republic, Slovenia and Turkey, with their director wielding 5.15 per cent of the votes) to the weak (24 African countries, with their representative being empowered to cast a mere 1.42 per cent of the votes). It is often objected within the Fund that formal voting power is not really an issue, that the Executive Board operates by consensus and that this eliminates, or at least eases, such irritations as flow from anomalies and discrepancies in the distribution of votes (Gianaris 1991; Bichsel 1994; Thomas 2000). Yet, as has been said, such arguments are misleading. As Woods (2000: 829) has commented:

> Even where formal voting is not used to make decisions, formal powers have an underlying force of which all participants in meetings are aware: typically during Board discussions ... the Secretary will keep a running tally of votes on a particular decision which assists the Chairman in formulating the 'sense of the meeting'.

Knowledge of the pattern of votes can also be expected to have an even deeper effect, influencing the informal politics and negotiations that take place before proposals ever come before the Board itself. Country representatives are especially likely to be reluctant to speak out against powerful member states on broader issues if their own programmes are under consideration at around the same time.

The particular consequence of the Fund's organizational shape is that there has been established a structural bias in its decision making in favour of a small group of countries, principally, of course, the US and the other leading post-industrial countries. The percentage share of voting power held by the US has, in fact, fallen over the years (it held approximately 33 per cent at the time of the first Executive Board meeting in 1946). But this has been more than offset by the force of the wider arguments about influence elaborated above, as well as the steady advance within the Fund of a system, promoted by the US, whereby 'special majorities' of 85 per cent majority are required for many of the most important decisions, giving the US alone amongst member countries a veto power in its own right (Lister 1984; Gianaris 1991; Thacker 1999; Woods 2000). Several analysts have therefore argued that the US can, to all intents and purposes, manipulate the IMF in accordance with its economic and political interests, whether these necessitate the creation of 'minilateral' cooperative initiatives with other major economic players (Ruggie 1993) or the reward of friends and clients (Kahler 1990). By comparison, and notwithstanding the fact that the 25 EU countries now control well over 30 per cent of the votes, nearly double the share of the US, 'the EU's influence on IMF matters is rather limited' (Smaghi 2004: 230). This has led one or two academics and other observers to propose the idea of a single seat for the EU within the IMF, although everybody agrees that this is 'not on the agenda for the immediate future' (Smaghi 2004: 247).

It is perhaps odd, given these contentions, that by a 50-year old tradition the Managing Director of the IMF has always been a (Western) European. This does not mean, however, that the weight of US opinion is not fully brought to bear upon the process of selection. In November 1999 Michel Camdessus, the Frenchman who had been Managing Director for the previous 12 years, announced his retirement. As a protest against the traditionally closed nature of the appointment process, the Japanese government nominated Eisuke Sakakibara, its former Vice-Minister of Finance; a number of African countries nominated Stanley Fischer, the existing First Deputy Managing Director, who, although a naturalized US citizen, was born in Zambia; whilst the EU countries proposed Caio Koch-Weser, formerly Managing Director of the World Bank. Although Koch-Weser secured the strongest support in an initial informal round of voting within the Executive Board, the Clinton administration expressed US disfavour and over a third of the votes cast were abstentions (Lee 2002). Koch-Weser had in effect been vetoed and the succession eventually went to the EU's second-choice candidate, Horst Köhler, then the President of the European Bank for Reconstruction and Development. The defeated Fischer subsequently himself resigned and was replaced, again as tradition demanded, by an American chosen by the US administration, Anne Krueger, an academic economist. In his (by then) familiar acidic tone Joseph Stiglitz (2001: 1–2) deduced the message: 'despite the demise of colonialism candidates from developing countries – the focus of the IMF's activities – need not apply'. A similar pattern provoking just the same unease emerged in March–April 2004 when Köhler in turn announced his forthcoming resignation in order to become the federal president of Germany. A number of executive directors, representing Africa, Asia, Latin America and the Middle East, backed by the directors from Australia, Russia and Switzerland, immediately issued statements calling for the selection of his successor to be both transparent and open to talent from all countries. However, in reality the contest for the post was once again fought out primarily within the EU, with Spain's Minister of Finance, Rodrigo Rato, eventually emerging as the favoured choice over rival French and Italian candidates. Rato had the support of the US and managed also to win the backing of the Latin American countries. The Egyptian executive director did formally nominate a fellow countryman and former senior IMF member of staff, Mohamed El-Erian, but did so in the end just to set the precedent that a country such as Egypt could break into the process. Rato took over the headship of the IMF in June 2004, with Europe once more having succeeded in controlling the appointment.

The World Bank

The World Bank is often described as the IMF's twin, the other Bretton Woods institution. This is correct in that the International Bank for Reconstruction and Development (IBRD) was also conceived at the Bretton Woods talks and came into being in 1946 with its office in Washington. It was formally linked too in that, under its Articles of Agreement, a country has to belong to the IMF before it can become a member of the IBRD. The IBRD's mission was to provide development loans to assist in the reconstruction and restoration of the economies of its members, which were then mainly war-torn European countries. However, the IBRD has since been joined within what is now described as the World Bank Group by four other institutions: the International Development Association (IDA), formed in 1960 to provide concessional loans to poorer countries; the International Finance Corporation (IFC), established in 1956 to lend to private-sector enterprises willing to invest in poorer countries; the Multilateral Investment Guarantee Agency (MIGA), founded in 1988 to insure foreign direct investors against non-commercial risks; and the International Centre for the Settlement of Investment Disputes (ICSID), set up in 1966 to deal with investment disputes between states and foreign investors. Each of the five bodies is an autonomous organization, with varying numbers of member countries (IBRD 184, IDA 165, IFC 176, MIGA 164 and ICSID 140). However, the IBRD and the IDA work together especially closely and the term World Bank is often deployed to refer just to these two organizations.

As can be seen, the collective remit of the World Bank Group is wide-ranging in the extreme. It has often been suggested that there has always existed a fundamental tension between its identity, on the one hand, as a bank, with continuing pressure to raise money in the capital markets, and, on the other, as a 'development organization', with an equivalent pressure to adjust to changing theorizations of development. Like the Fund, it has extended the range of its operations over time and has lately been pulled by its commitment to the prevailing neoliberal notion of development to intervene more extensively than ever before in the social and political affairs of the countries to which it advances loans. We saw in the previous chapter the extent to which it has itself also become a source, perhaps even the key source, of official thinking about development within the leading 'Western' countries. The Bank has thus always been more involved than the Fund with debates about economic and political ideas. This has made it even less the monolithic or monological body that it has often been charged with being by overhasty critics on the left and the right.

It is the case, however, that the World Bank shares many of the organizational features of the IMF. The IBRD and the IDA (the narrow definition of the Bank, if you like) are accountable in the same way to an annual meeting of their Board of Governors and regular meetings of their Executive Board. The latter also has 24 members, with eight permanent seats held by the same countries as in the IMF and the remaining 16 chosen from constituencies that are almost (but not exactly) identical in country composition. World Bank subscriptions also vary slightly from Fund quotas because of the use of different technical measures to do the calculations, but the same principle of equal basic votes and weighted extra votes is used to determine voting power (Gianaris 1991). The precise allocation within the IBRD, as of late 2004, is given in Table 5.2. Only slight variations are apparent by comparison with the allocation of voting power within the IMF Executive Board. The US still has the biggest bloc (but with a marginally lower percentage at 16.35 per cent); Japan is relatively more influential (at 7.86 per cent), having fought a determined campaign in the mid-1980s to move itself from fifth-placed to second-placed shareholder in the Bank; and Iran and Argentina enjoy more than 1 per cent of votes each, which they do not in the Fund. Again no fewer than 163 countries account for slightly less than 30 per cent of the votes. The IDA in effect shares the same Executive Board as the IBRD, but the directors wield different weights of vote. The power structure of the IDA favours the poorer countries rather more, chiefly because they are allowed to pay the bulk of their subscriptions in their own currency. Members are divided into (28) Part I countries ('mostly developed countries which contribute to the resources of the IDA'), which hold between them 62 per cent of the votes, and (137) Part II countries ('mostly developing countries, some of

Table 5.2   *Subscriptions and votes in the IBRD, December 2004*

	Subscriptions		Votes	
Member	*Amount (1944, US$ millions)*	*Percentage of total*	*Number*	*Percentage of total*
United States	26,496.9	16.85	265,219	16.35
Japan	12,700.0	8.08	127,250	7.86
Germany	7,239.9	4.60	72,649	4.49
France	6,939.7	4.41	69,647	4.30
United Kingdom	6,939.7	4.41	69,647	4.30
China	4,479.9	2.85	45,049	2.78
Canada	4,479.5	2.85	45,045	2.78
India	4,479.5	2.85	45,045	2.78
Italy	4,479.5	2.85	45,045	2.78
Russia	4,479.5	2.85	45,045	2.78
Saudi Arabia	4,479.5	2.85	45,045	2.78
Netherlands	3,550.3	2.26	35,753	2.21
Brazil	3,328.7	2.12	33,537	2.07
Belgium	2,898.3	1.84	29,233	1.81
Spain	2,799.7	1.78	28,247	1.75
Switzerland	2,660.6	1.69	26,856	1.66
Australia	2,446.4	1.56	24,714	1.53
Iran	2,368.6	1.51	23,936	1.48
Venezuela	2,036.1	1.29	20,611	1.27
Mexico	1,880.4	1.20	19,054	1.18
Argentina	1,791.1	1.14	18,161	1.12
Rest (i.e. 163 countries)	157,266.1	28.16	1,618,661	29.94

Source: Data from http://www.worldbank.org

which also contribute to the resources of IDA'), which account for the remaining 38 per cent. All in all, though, the power politics of the World Bank work in an analogous fashion to those of the Fund. The US government operates as the dominant force within the councils of the Bank and, by virtue of the original Bretton Woods compromise with the countries of Europe over appointments to the two top jobs in these institutions, in effect chooses the President of the Bank. It is noteworthy too that the US has always been concerned to protect its position of ascendancy. For example, when Japan succeeded in increasing its voting share within the IBRD, thereby reducing somewhat the relative power of the

US, it responded by pushing forward an increase in the majority required for a change in the Bank's articles to 85 per cent, so as to be sure to maintain its veto over this important aspect of Bank politics (Ogata 1989). As before, then, a predominantly consensual style of decision making on the surface should not be allowed to mask the underlying reality of where and how the votes stack up.

Two other factors further reinforce the role of the US. They apply also to the Fund but make themselves felt with most effect in relation to the World Bank. One highlights the extent of the role played by the very sizeable staffs of the Fund and the Bank. As we have seen, the Fund has something close to 3,000 employees, whilst the Bank has substantially more – approximately 9,300 persons in total – with the vast majority based in Washington and the remainder in the field. As a consequence they have sometimes been described as 'staff-driven [as opposed to member-driven] organisations' (Woods and Narlikar 2001: 573). The point is that, on a routine basis, especially perhaps within the Bank (which has historically always been more project-oriented), staff work directly with government representatives to design agreements and programmes which they are then responsible for monitoring and enforcing. Although it is true that they operate only under the authority of the Executive Boards, the reality is that they enjoy a good deal of autonomy and can themselves set agendas (Williams 1994). However, it has been suggested that the make-up of the staff of both organizations does not at all accurately reflect the diversity and range of the country membership. From the earliest days the US successfully resisted pressures for national quotas in hiring and imposed a commitment to English as the only working language. The consequences were several. Employment was skewed significantly in favour of graduates of US and, to a lesser extent, UK universities, with studies revealing as many as 80–90 per cent of high-level staff in this category (Stern and Ferreira 1993; Clark 1996), the majority of them Americans. Courtesy of their British imperial legacy, South Asian applicants also gained *vis-à-vis* those from East Asia. Other commentators noticed too that, in respect of staff from non-English-speaking countries, 'fluency in English tended to be correlated with preferred economic and social status' (Kapur, Lewis and Webb 1997: 1,167). Add to this the neoliberal bias already discussed in connection with most mainstream UK and US economics over the past 20 years and one can see a further channel of Anglo-American influence over these major global institutions. As Wade (1996: 36; his emphasis) has explained, 'this channel of influence is obscured by talking of "professionalism" as a source of ... autonomy, without also talking about the *content* of that professionalism and from which member state's intellectual culture it comes'.

The other factor which needs to be mentioned concerns the way that the Fund and the Bank, especially again the Bank, have opened up considerably during the 1990s to the ideas and values of non-governmental organizations (O'Brien *et al.* 2000). This is conventionally interpreted, and not necessarily wrongly, as a progressive move, an indicator of the desire of the institutions to ground their activities on a wider political base. The main problem with this reading is the matter of to whom the NGOs themselves are accountable, if indeed they are accountable at all. Although some NGOs do genuinely emanate from poor countries, and many profess to work on behalf of the interests of the people of those countries, the reality is that the majority of the most active and influential, those with the most prolific resources at their disposal, are based in the richest countries. The danger is therefore that this new type of citizen activism, contrary to intention, serves further to entrench the several other inequalities of power at work within the institutions to which we have already drawn attention. For example, one recent study by Charles Abugre and Nancy Alexander (1998: 116) specifically concluded that 'activism by US NGOs has probably expanded the already disproportionate role of the United States in the international financial institutions, especially the World Bank'.

The World Trade Organization

Although the WTO only came into being on 1 January 1995, it can to some extent be thought of as a young sister institution to the Bretton Woods twins, conceived at around the same time, one might say, but long in gestation and very late in delivery. For it is the case that the WTO's origins can be traced back to December 1945 when the US government invited a modest number of other countries to begin negotiations on the post-war liberalization of trade. These led to the signing in late 1947 of the GATT, presumed only to be a provisional tariff-reducing agreement pending the establishment of an International Trade Organization (ITO) as the third pillar, along with the Fund and the Bank, of the post-1945 international economic order. A wide-ranging draft charter for an ITO was signed in Havana in 1948, but crucially the US Congress refused to ratify the agreement, largely because liberal critics in Congress thought that the US negotiators had made too many concessions in the direction of economic nationalism to the other would-be signatories (Kock 1969). The ITO's demise left the GATT as the only trade organization in town – specifically Geneva, not Washington – and it subsequently operated as the world's *de facto* trade coordination body for the best part of the next 50 years.

GATT was a weak organization, albeit not ineffective. As O'Brien *et al.* (2000: 69) observed accurately, it 'did not demand the politically impossible – that all nations liberalise immediately and unconditionally'. What happened was that members of GATT (which were always increasing in number as colonies acquired their independence and signed up as a token of their new maturity and respectability) met eight times in a series of multilateral trade negotiations, or 'rounds', in which they painstakingly drafted further agreements to reduce tariffs and regulate non-tariff trade measures and policies. Major concessions were regularly made to liberal principles, with member countries constantly balancing the protection of key domestic interests with their obligations to an open trading regime (Finlayson and Zacher 1981). Nevertheless, by the beginning of what became the last GATT round, the Uruguay Round (1986–94), trade liberalization, at least in goods, had come a long way and the mood existed in the US in particular to push the process further into the areas of services, intellectual property and investment measures. The opportunity was also taken to make up for the stillbirth of the ITO and to create the WTO as GATT's successor organization. In legal terms the WTO is a single undertaking, with member countries having to agree, with only some exceptions, to accede to the entire set of agreements, including the inherited body of GATT trade law. In addition, of course, the WTO continues to sponsor further multilateral trade talks, to manage trade disputes and to promote predictable and transparent trade policies. At the end of 2004, it had 148 member countries, accounting between them for over 97 per cent of world trade. A further 25 or so countries were also in various stages of negotiating membership. In short, just as the IMF and the World Bank also expanded their memberships and range of activities during the 1980s and 1990s, so the WTO is a much more intrusive actor on the world stage than GATT had ever been.

It is significant too that the WTO is set up organizationally on a very different basis from the IMF and the World Bank. Although that was true also of the GATT, the WTO is 'GATT-plus' in two respects. One innovation has been the establishment of a biennial Ministerial Conference as its foremost decision-making organ; the other has been the considerable strengthening that has taken place, compared to the GATT, in its internal dispute settlement system. The first confirms the important point that the WTO is a member-driven institution: it is in essence 'a forum' in which member states undertake multilateral trade negotiations (Woods and Narlikar 2001: 573). Certainly, the staff and management of the WTO play a lesser role than their counterparts in the Fund and the Bank. The Secretariat is headed by a Director-General who has a high political profile and some symbolic importance, but no power other than his capacity, or otherwise, to persuade. That has not eliminated conflict over the appointment, member countries in 1999 being able only to resolve the rivalry of two candidates to succeed the WTO's first

Director-General, Renato Ruggiero from Italy, by agreeing that one, Mike Moore from New Zealand, should serve in post for three years from September 1999 and the other, Supachai Panitchpakdi from Thailand, should take over for his three years from September 2002. For all the intensity generated by the contest, the Secretariat is small, employing only some 600 staff, and it provides no more than administrative and technical support for the member-state representatives who attend the Ministerial Conferences and sit on the General Council (mainly ambassadors and heads of delegations to the WTO). This latter body, which also meets as the Trade Policy Review Body and the Dispute Settlement Body (DSB), convenes officially about 12 times a year and, like the Ministerial Conference, includes representatives of all WTO members on an equal basis. There are no weighted voting schemes in the WTO. Below the General Council are Councils for Trade in Goods, Services and Intellectual Property, plus a range of committees and working parties that report directly to the General Council and to the other three councils. Again, all these levels are constituted by official representatives of member countries wielding one vote each.

In theory, the WTO is thus a more egalitarian organization by far than either the Fund or the Bank. It is also important that it is not located in Washington. That said, the formal equality of the WTO's procedures does not, by common consent, describe the way that decisions are actually taken. It is true that the WTO works by consensus, not voting (Woods 1999), but any consensus needs to be hammered out, often in informal meetings before proposals are brought formally before the councils. The WTO uses the so-called 'Green Room' process whereby a senior figure, usually but not always the Director-General, gathers together the representatives of about 20 or so countries, perhaps those deemed to have a vital interest at stake in the matter under discussion, in an informal consultation to try to agree a position. The reality is that these meetings nearly always include representatives of the 'Quad', namely, the US, EU, Japanese and Canadian participants within the G7/8 trade ministers grouping. They often also include ministers or delegates from, say, Brazil and India, countries which have always played a big role in GATT politics. Inevitably, though, in an organization with over 140 member countries (and rising), most weaker, poorer countries are excluded from the 'Green Rooms'. They may well not even know that such meetings are happening and, even if they did, given the sheer number of WTO meetings now taking place – estimated even two or three years ago to be about 1,200 a year (Hoekman and Kostecki 2001) – they do not have the knowledge, resources or personnel to service more than a tiny fraction of them. The result is the assertion within the WTO of something akin to an old-fashioned form of realist power politics.

As Ngaire Woods and Amrita Narlikar (2001: 573) have put it, 'the reality of trade negotiations is that states with large market-shares enjoy significant input and influence over decisions; indeed one might describe them as decision makers, while states with smaller market-share are effectively decision takers'.

In this respect the WTO operates in a different political context from the GATT. Multilateral trade talks have always been shaped in the main by the biggest traders; that is not new. But what is different, and highly problematic, for the WTO is the combination of the large number of countries that are already, or desire to be, members and the awareness, possessed now by all of them, of the impact of trade decisions on their national well-being, even if many struggle to know what to do to affect these decisions. By way of emphasizing the contrast, only ten countries signed the original GATT accord, of which only Cuba and Haiti were from the poorer parts of the world. Early trade rounds often had no more than 20–30 country participants. The point is that GATT grew up as a club of largely satisfied members who did not need to worry too much about those outside the framework. It was not really until the Uruguay Round that the impact of emergent globalization began to push rich countries to demand significant concessions from poorer ones, and not until after the formation of the WTO itself that this need became pressing. At this point the procedures inherited from the GATT era, particularly the exclusive nature of the 'Green Room' process, started to show their limitations and, in so doing, to undermine the legitimacy of WTO decision making. In the last couple of years or so some attempts have been made to open up the process of consensus building within the organization by means such as notifying meetings more widely on bulletin boards, permitting self-selecting attendance and publishing minutes. However, it is obvious that these steps are only palliatives and do not come close to addressing the core problem of how to resource sufficiently the smaller, weaker, poorer countries so that they too can work the WTO's relatively representative procedures to their advantage. The difficulty for the WTO is that, to the extent that they do increasingly succeed in doing so, it becomes 'a club no more' (Kerr 2002). It may then find that its current mode of decision making no longer delivers decisions (Narlikar 2004).

The second organizational innovation introduced by the WTO is a more robust dispute settlement mechanism. However political is the process by which rules are made, a rules-based system of trade relations requires methods of resolving disputes which do not have recourse directly to power. Under the GATT a dissatisfied contracting party to a dispute could veto the process at numerous stages – by blocking the creation of a panel, opposing the adoption of its report and refusing to abide by the outcome – leaving the aggrieved party with the option only of undertaking retaliation in some form. The new WTO system reversed the need for unanimity, so that panel reports are now automatically adopted by the Dispute Settlement Body after 60 days unless there is a consensus that they be rejected. In normal circumstances such a consensus is unlikely to be agreed by the benefiting party, thereby promoting a norm wherein panel reports are generally adopted. If thereafter the state in question does not comply with the proposed remedy, the DSB may authorize limited trade sanctions against the violating state. It can be objected that, at the final stage, the dispute settlement process is therefore political, not legal. Against this, the DSB is the General Council in another guise and contains representatives of all member countries. It can thus be said that members police themselves and that there is no involvement of the Secretariat or the staff of the WTO. Confidence in the system is borne out by the number of cases that have already been brought forward: almost 250 in the WTO's first seven years of existence, compared to approximately 300 during the entire life of the GATT. As argued earlier, resources do facilitate access to all complex procedures and it is not surprising that one analyst has already suggested that 'complaints brought by developed states are more likely to result in the establishment of a panel (that is, proceed further through the dispute settlement process), whereas those brought by their developing counterparts are more likely to be settled after bilateral negotiations' (Wilkinson 2002: 136). Even so, it must be conceded that the WTO has taken a major step towards the implementation of a rules-based global trading system.

For a variety of reasons, then, the WTO challenges – and some would say violates – what Destler (1986: 34) described as 'the policy tolerance which had been a central, if largely implicit, element of the international consensus that had created and maintained the GATT'. It rides like 'a sheriff' (WTO official, cited in O'Brien *et al.* 2000: 72) into places that the GATT never dared to tread, and does so generally in the cause of the biggest and most efficient trading states. For this reason the WTO has quickly come to attract political attention (and NGO criticism and popular protest) on a par with the two Bretton Woods institutions (with which it has, incidentally, lately signed formal cooperation agreements). Some of the invective to which it has been subjected has probably been unjustified, but the attention is merited, for the WTO matters these days just as much as the IMF and the World Bank.

The Organisation for Economic Cooperation and Development

The OECD is an odd organization, difficult to pin down. It has been variously described as a think-tank, a monitoring agency, a rich man's club and a non-academic university (Woodward 2004). It has elements of all of these features, but yet none quite captures the essence of the OECD. It grew out of the Organization for European Economic Cooperation (OEEC), which was formed in 1948 to administer US and Canadian aid for the reconstruction of Europe under the terms of the Marshall Plan. The OEEC effectively collapsed late in 1958 following the signing by just six of its members of the treaty establishing the European Economic Community. Some continuing means of institutionalized transatlantic cooperation was still favoured and in December 1960 some 20 countries signed the original convention setting up the OECD: Austria, Belgium, Canada, Denmark, France, West Germany, Greece, Iceland, Ireland, Italy, Luxembourg, the Netherlands, Norway, Portugal, Spain, Sweden, Switzerland, Turkey, the UK and the US. The Organization has since expanded to 30 member countries, moving sometimes controversially beyond its Atlantic origins to include Japan in 1964, Finland in 1969, Australia in 1971, New Zealand in 1973, Mexico in 1994, the Czech Republic in 1995, Hungary, Poland and South Korea in 1996 and the Slovak Republic in 2000. The OECD currently defines itself as a group of 'like-minded countries' that share a commitment to the principles of the market economy, pluralist democracy and respect for human rights (http://www.oecd.org). That claim cannot be scrutinized too closely, given the nature of the social and political systems of some member countries, including one of the original members, Turkey, but it does reveal the OECD's overt ideological tone and global pretensions. For example, its web-site proclaims in exactly that vein that it now actively seeks to reach out beyond its member countries to 'offer its analytical expertise and accumulated experience to [approximately 70] developing and emerging market economies' (http://www.oecd.org).

As indicated, it is not easy to define the precise character of the OECD as a global institution. It is like the IMF and the World Bank in that it depends heavily on the professional policy analysis of a substantial secretariat (of approximately 2,300 staff members), but different from them in that its base is Paris, not Washington (although the US government still contributes the largest part, a quarter, of the budget). It is like the WTO in that it operates as an intergovernmental body managed by means of a Council that includes a representative of every member country (plus the European Commission) and meets routinely at the level of resident ambassadors and annually at the level of ministers. The Council prefers consensus decision making and disgruntled members can effectively veto proposals they oppose, in turn irritating some other member countries which believe that the OECD's effectiveness is hampered by this *modus operandi*. Yet, unlike all these other bodies, the OECD does not actually run anything. It has 'no regulatory responsibility, no independent source of funds, no money to lend and no instruments within its control' (Wolfe 2001: 1,180). What it principally does, in the wording of Article 1 of its convention, is 'promote policies': that is to say, it works in the background of governments and other institutions to detect and frame emerging issues, bring forward ideas and proposals, set out behavioural guidelines for multinational enterprises and, in general, suggest 'rules of the game' in any multilateral policy arenas where they might be deemed to be required. All of this is grounded in detailed research and gathering of data (the OECD publishes around 250 titles a year) and disseminated by means of intense and deliberate networking (some 40,000 senior officials from national administrations attend OECD committee meetings each year). In a nutshell, then, the OECD is an important source of thinking about a range of policy matters, running from economic management to the environment, trade, science and technology, agriculture and energy. Of particular significance from our perspective is its Development Assistance Committee (DAC) founded at the beginning in 1961 and charged with helping member countries reach a collective understanding of their responsibilities for assisting in the 'development' of other countries. DAC principles have come to be used to define the grant element which qualifies as official development assistance (ODA) in OECD countries and it is no more than apt that the DAC should have been described recently as 'the donor's [sic] club' at which matters of aid policy are discussed, aid data collected and reported, and periodic reviews of donor performance carried out (White 2001a: 340). The DAC, it should of course be noted, lacks meaningful representation from aid recipients.

The Bank for International Settlements (BIS)

The BIS was founded in Basel in Switzerland in 1930 as part of the mechanism for managing the reparation payments imposed on Germany at the end of the First World War. From these origins it has subsequently developed into the leading forum for international monetary and financial cooperation between central banks and also acts as a bank for central banks. Some 120 central banks and international financial institutions presently place deposits with the BIS, generating a foreign exchange holding equivalent to approximately 7 per cent of the world's reserves. Although it operates as a global economic institution, the Bank itself is actually owned and controlled by the central banks or monetary authorities of only 55 countries, each of which has rights of representation at an annual general meeting. These countries do, however, extend beyond the OECD world to include, *inter alia*, Argentina, Brazil, China, Hong Kong, India, Malaysia, Russia, Saudi Arabia and Thailand.

That said, the management of the BIS is routinely overseen by its Board of Directors which has only 17 members, comprising the governors of the central banks of Belgium, France, Germany, Italy and the UK and the Chairman of the Board of Governors of the US Federal Reserve System, each of whom is entitled to appoint another member of the same nationality. The Bank's statutes further provide for the election of a small number of other central bank governors, currently those of Canada, Japan, the Netherlands, Sweden and Switzerland. The locus of control is obvious and exposes the reality that one of the main political functions of the BIS is to impose as effectively as possible around the world standards of bank supervision agreed upon in core BIS countries. It seeks to do this, in the main, via the Basel Committee on Bank Supervision, established in 1974 and presently chaired by the President of the Federal Reserve Bank of New York. The Committee does not possess formal supranational supervisory authority; rather, it formulates broad guidelines and statements of best practice 'in the expectation that individual authorities will take steps to implement them through detailed arrangements ... best suited to their own national systems' (http://www.bis.org). The BIS provides a secretariat for the Committee which means that it always meets in Basel, usually three or four times a year. The BIS does not attract much political attention, but its contribution to the wider dissemination of ('Western') 'good practice' in banking methods should not be underestimated.

The Paris Club

The Paris Club is an informal group of official creditors, with no legal basis or status, whose role is to seek solutions to the payment difficulties experienced by debtor countries. Nineteen countries are permanent members (Australia, Austria, Belgium, Canada, Denmark, Finland, France, Germany, Ireland, Italy, Japan, Netherlands, Norway, Russia, Spain, Sweden, Switzerland, the UK and the US), with other creditor countries invited to participate as necessary and provided that they agree to follow the rules of the Club. They meet 10 to 11 times a year, either to discuss debt issues amongst themselves or to negotiate with the governments of specific debtor countries. The meetings are always chaired by a senior official of the French Treasury, which provides the Club with a small part-time secretariat. These arrangements began in 1956 when the Argentinian government agreed to meet its public creditors in Paris. Since then, the Paris Club has reached approximately 384 agreements concerning in total some 79 debtor countries, which have fallen, in the main, in the World Bank's lower middle income, rather than low income, classification. The Club works closely with the IMF because the creditor countries have come to insist that a country approaching them to negotiate debt rescheduling will already have in place an active Fund-supported adjustment programme, thereby bringing in to the negotiations the disciplinary force of the IMF. It should be noted again that the outcome of any negotiation is not itself a legal agreement; indeed, it is no more than an 'agreed minute'. But this is in effect a recommendation to the relevant creditor countries to sign bilateral agreements with the debtor country concerned. As Howard White (2001b: 1197) has observed, the Paris Club can be accurately labelled 'a creditors' cartel ... since it deals with each country on a case-by-case basis, undoubtedly increasing the relative bargaining position of the creditor against the debtor'. In substance and impact, as he suggests, it is far from being the 'non-institution' which it proclaims itself (http://www.clubdeparis.org).

United Nations institutions

The United Nations

A distinction needs to be drawn at the outset of this part of the chapter between the UN and the so-called UN system. The UN is made up of the six major organs set up under the auspices of the UN Charter in 1945: the General Assembly, the Security Council, the Economic and Social Council, the Trusteeship Council, the International Court of Justice and the Secretariat. The UN system embraces the many separate and subsidiary organs subsequently established by the major UN bodies as well as the various other agencies created by separate international agreements to deal with particular issues which have come to be affiliated to the UN and are known as its 'specialized agencies'. Some members of the UN system have already been discussed (e.g. the IMF and the World Bank, both of which – formally at least – are UN 'specialized agencies') and others will be highlighted shortly. In this section we focus on the roles of the General Assembly, the Security Council and the Secretariat.

The General Assembly is the emotional heart of the UN. All 191 member states are represented in it and each has one vote. They can raise any item within the purview of the Charter. Unsurprisingly perhaps, voting patterns have always been fluid and complex, although regional blocs have emerged and often shape outcomes. Decisions on ordinary matters are taken by simple majority, although on more important issues, such as proposals for amendments to the Charter, a two-thirds majority is required. The Assembly has accordingly been described as 'the favorite principal organ of the weak states, which have always constituted a majority of the UN's membership, because it gives them an influence over decisions that they lack anywhere else in the international system' (Peterson 1986: 2). Inevitably, however, it is somewhat cumbersome in its operation and only generally has the power to make recommendations to members. As a result, its main political role has come to be that of agenda setting via the passage of resolutions, the number of which has increased markedly with time. Meetings of the General Assembly are routinely held for three months in the last quarter of each year, although special sessions have not infrequently been called to deal with specific problems.

The Security Council is the body charged with maintaining international peace and security. It was deliberately designed to be small and effective, being composed of just 15 members, five of which are permanent (P-5) – the US, the UK, France, Russia (as successor state to the USSR in 1992) and the People's Republic of China (taking over from Taiwan in 1971) – and enjoy a veto power over resolutions, the other ten being elected by the General Assembly for a two-year term on the basis, since 1965, of the so-called 'equitable geographic distribution formula' which allocates five seats to Africa and Asia, two each to Latin America and Western Europe, and one to Eastern Europe. Resolutions – which, in theory at least, have to be implemented by all member states – require nine votes to pass, including the concurring vote of all five permanent members. Yet, in practice, most of the Security Council's business is conducted in informal negotiations behind the scenes, which inevitably magnifies the effect of the unequal political resources available to different members (Caron 1993). The initial designation of permanent members reflected the realities of the distribution of military power at the time of the inception of the UN, but there have always been doubts raised about its legitimacy and reform of the Security Council's membership, in particular its potential enlargement, has been a longstanding issue of contention within the UN. Following the end of the Cold War, an 'Open-ended Working Group on the Question of Equitable Representation' was set up in December 1993 and a specific reform plan, the Razali Plan (named after the Malaysian then President of the General Assembly), was tabled before the Assembly in March 1997. It called for five new permanent and four new non-permanent members of the Security Council, to be chosen again on a geographical basis but giving extended representation to Africa, Asia, Latin America and the Caribbean, and Eastern Europe. Although the plan was widely hailed as representing a realistic compromise, it sparked off acrimonious debate in subsequent Assembly sessions. Italy objected to the popular presumption that two of the new permanent seats would be allocated to Germany and Japan, whilst even fiercer conflicts were generated over the destination of the other three proposed new permanent seats. As two analysts of the ensuing diplomatic battle asked, 'who would represent Asia – India or Indonesia? Would Brazil or Mexico fill the Latin American seat? Who would speak for Africa – Nigeria, South Africa or Egypt? Who would represent the Islamic states, which claim that, by representing more than 1 billion people, they are entitled to a permanent seat?' (Bourantonis and Magliveras 2002: 27). As many predicted, no changes were agreed.

However, the intense debates that took place within the Security Council during late 2002 and early 2003 over policy towards Iraq further exposed the structure and *modus operandi* of this body to global scrutiny. Yet another 'High Level Panel' on 'Threats, Challenges and Change' was established, chaired by the former Thai prime minister, Anand Panyarachun, and charged with again reviewing the composition of the Council. It reported in December 2004 and proposed that membership be substantially extended to 24 countries via one of two methods: either by adding six new permanent but non-veto-wielding members (two from Africa, two from Asia, one from the Americas and one from Europe) and three new rotating seats, or by creating a new second-tier of eight semi-permanent members (two each from Asia, Africa, the Americas and Europe) chosen for four-year terms, plus one more rotating seat. One member of the panel, Amre Moussa, Secretary-General of the Arab League, reportedly pressed for one of the proposed new African seats to be reserved for a Muslim country, but this did not form part of the eventual recommendations. Several countries have been lobbying hard over the last few years to gain admission to the Security Council. They include Brazil, Germany, India, Japan, South Africa, Nigeria and Egypt. Just to list them indicates the formidable difficulties that will have to be faced, and overcome, if a reformed Security Council is to be brought into being in the foreseeable future.

The Secretariat, based in New York, is another complex organization, comprising some 9,000 staff, which has been frequently charged with inefficiency and weak management. At its head is the Secretary-General, elected for a five-year renewable term by two-thirds of the General Assembly on a recommendation from the Security Council in respect of which the permanent members play a decisive part. Despite the high political profile that always attaches to the Secretary-General, his role is ill-defined, being in essence only that of chief administrative officer of the UN organs. From that base the person holding the office has to carve out a niche from the available political opportunities. There have so far been only seven UN Secretary-Generals and, because of the unwillingness of the P-5 states to allow one of their number to take hold of the post, incumbents have tended to come from either relatively weak or, in the context of the Cold War, neutral states, namely (in turn) Norway, Sweden, Burma, Austria, Peru, Egypt and Ghana (which is the home of the present incumbent, Kofi Annan).

Finally, something needs to be said briefly about the funding of the UN. The General Assembly has a Committee on Contributions which re-evaluates member states' contributions every three years on the basis of total national income, per capita income, the impact of economic dislocations and ability to obtain foreign currencies. Initially the highest rate (for the US) was set at 40 per cent of the assessed budget, with the minimum rate at 0.04 per cent. However, over time these rates have been adjusted, with the US share reduced to 25 per cent and the minimum for a country dropping eventually to 0.0001 per cent in 1997. Other changes of significance include a rise in the contributions paid by Japan (from 11.82 per cent in 1985 to 17.9 per cent in 2000) and Germany (from 8.26 per cent to 9.6 per cent over the same period) and a dramatic fall in the payment expected from Russia (from 11.98 per cent in 1985 during the existence of the USSR to a mere 2.87 per cent in 2000). As might be expected, the UN has regularly experienced difficulties in getting states to pay their assessments (for a whole variety of reasons including, in the case of the US in the 1980s, political hostility to the perceived anti-US stance of the General Assembly), with the consequence that many UN organs have had to live with endemic financial crisis throughout their existence.

United Nations Educational, Social and Cultural Organization (UNESCO)

UNESCO came into being in November 1946, based in Paris and charged with promoting collaboration between countries by means of education, science and culture. It might thus be thought to be a rather apolitical organization. However, the US withdrew its membership in December 1984, followed a year later by the UK and Singapore. The US claimed that 'UNESCO had politicized virtually every subject it dealt with, had exhibited hostility towards the basic institutions of a free society (especially a free market and a free press) and had demonstrated unrestrained budgetary expansion' (El Kahal 2001: 1,639). Shorn of the 30 per cent of its income that the US contribution alone constituted, UNESCO has since been under pressure to restructure itself internally and to reorient its programmes to make them more acceptable to its critics. The UK resumed its membership in July 1997, following the election of the New Labour government of Tony Blair, and the US rejoined in October 2003, proclaiming that the organization had been successfully reformed.

United Nations High Commissioner for Refugees (UNHCR)

The Office of the UNHCR is the primary international agency concerned with the welfare and rights of refugees. Established by the UN General

Assembly in 1950, it began operations in January 1951 with a temporary three-year mandate to resettle 1.2 million European refugees left homeless by the Second World War. It did not initially even have a budget to conduct operations in the field. But, as various refugee crises continued to arise, it was seen that there was a need to extend the UNHCR's mandate and set it up on a more substantive basis. It is fair to say that it was hampered in its work during the Cold War by the political dynamics of superpower rivalry and that it has grown considerably in visibility and significance in the post-Cold-War era. The UNHCR now works with a US$1 billion budget, has offices in 116 countries and claims presently to be helping an estimated 17 million people (http://www.unhcr.org). The organization is led by a High Commissioner for Refugees – most recently Ruud Lubbers, the former Prime Minister of the Netherlands – appointed by the General Assembly for a five-year term from nominations made by the Secretary-General. He has been able to make sure that the UNHCR's voice is widely heard, and sometimes listened to, in the growing number of contentious discussions of refugee problems that now take place in and between so many countries.

United Nations Conference on Trade and Development

UNCTAD is both a series of conferences, normally held every four years, and a permanent organization based in Geneva and currently headed by Rubens Ricupero from Brazil. It was established in 1964 by the General Assembly with the purpose of maximizing the trade and investment opportunities of 'developing countries' and assisting them in their efforts to integrate into the world economy on an equitable basis. Its creation owed much to the earlier work of the UN Economic Commission for Latin America where dependency and neo-Marxist ideas about development flourished under the leadership of the Argentinian economist, Raúl Prebisch. Prebisch was appointed the first Secretary-General of UNCTAD and immediately positioned the organization in the forefront of debates about the structure of the international economy. The first UNCTAD conference in 1964 thus focused on the problems faced by exporters of primary commodities, whilst the second in 1968 called for preferential treatment of the exports of 'developing countries' and paved the way for the introduction of the Generalized System of Preferences by the major industrial countries during the early 1970s. The so-called Group of 77 (G77) countries (named after the number of countries which signed an early declaration calling for change in the working of the world economy) emerged as the dominant force within UNCTAD and, as we have seen, skilfully used the organization, along with other bodies, during the course of the 1970s to push for the introduction of a New International

Economic Order which would improve the prospects of development for the majority, rather than a minority, of the world's countries (Williams 1994).

The problem is that UNCTAD has become trapped by this early history. It is still seen from one perspective as dangerously radical, from another as disappointingly conformist (Taylor 2003). In fact, its influence began to lessen as soon as neoliberal economic policies were introduced in the US and the UK in the early 1980s, and its decline only accelerated further as these ideas steadily spread to most of the countries which UNCTAD had traditionally seen as its 'clients'. Ricupero has on occasion spoken boldly of UNCTAD becoming a 'global parliament on globalization' (http://www.unctad.org), and it is the case that the organization has produced several authoritative studies that show some of the inequalities involved in contemporary patterns of trade and investment. In particular, its annual *Trade and Development Report* generally represents a distinctive and alternative reading of global economic and political trends to that offered in, say, World Bank publications. But it is produced on a shoestring budget and only has a print-run of about 12,000 copies in English, plus another 7–8,000 split between the five official languages of the UN (Chinese, Russian, French, Spanish, Arabic). One has only to compare this with the huge dissemination effort put into the World Bank's annual *World Development Report* (discussed in the last chapter) to appreciate the point. The fact is that, despite genuine efforts, UNCTAD has not been able to stand in the way of the emergence of the WTO as the main forum in which trade and investment issues are debated and resolved. The organization has in effect recognized the nature of the position in which it now finds itself and, for example, works in close partnership with the WTO Secretariat within the so-called International Trade Centre to foster 'trade-related capacity building' within countries that do not have the resources to cope with the complexities of the contemporary multilateral trading system. In short, despite the hopes of some radical activists such as Walden Bello (2001), who has proclaimed that it is 'time to lead, time to challenge', UNCTAD has lost much of its former political character and is now primarily an organization devoted to the worthy matters of technical support and research within its spheres of interest.

United Nations Development Programme

The UNDP was established by the General Assembly in 1965 as the UN's principal provider of 'development advice' to member states. It has its headquarters in New York, but also appoints resident representatives to over 130 recipient countries. These representatives are expected to assess local needs, coordinate technical assistance programmes, act on behalf of other UN 'specialized agencies' as (probably) the highest ranking UN official in the country, and generally link the UN with the country's government in whatever ways are necessary. The UNDP has built up high levels of trust with recipient governments and associated NGOs and is conventionally regarded by them as a partner rather than an adversary. However, the resources at its disposal have been, and remain, limited by comparison with those of the World Bank and the major bilateral aid donors, and this has inevitably constrained the UNDP's capacity as the effective coordinator of all country-based activities. As noted previously, the UNDP also produces annually the *Human Development Report* containing its novel Human Development Index. This has become increasingly influential over the decade or so in which it has been produced and, strikingly, has a print-run even larger than the WDR of the World Bank (approximately 100,000 in 12 languages).

United Nations Industrial Development Organization (UNIDO)

UNIDO was set up in 1966 following pressure within the UN General Assembly from would-be industrializing countries to create an international body to help to promote their industrialization. Opening for business in Vienna in January 1967, it initially saw the public sector as the most likely leading edge of industrialization strategies. However, with the general shift to neoliberal thinking from the late 1970s onwards, it came under pressure, again principally from the US and the UK, to limit its role to the support of private enterprise. Even though it did respond by placing more emphasis on technical work, the US government in particular grew impatient with what it saw as UNIDO's slow pace of reform and announced its withdrawal from the organization at the end of 1996. As a consequence UNIDO had to scale back its budget very considerably and has also lately switched its focus, sectorally to agro-based industries and regionally to the group of Least Developed Countries first identified by a resolution of the General Assembly in 1970.

United Nations Environmental Programme (UNEP)

UNEP was created following the 1972 UN Conference on the Human Environment held in Stockholm. It reflected growing international concern about environmental issues and was charged with coordinating, encouraging and catalysing environmental action within the UN system. It consists of a governing council of 58 member states elected on a rotating basis for four years by the General Assembly, backed by a small secretariat located in Nairobi, the first time a UN agency has been based outside either the US or Europe. UNEP publishes an annual 'state of the environment' report, runs a modest environmental fund principally to assist the collection and dissemination of data through such programmes as Earth Watch, and helps to organize the many meetings and conferences through which international environmental diplomacy is now conducted, being centrally involved, for example, in the establishment of the Intergovernmental Panel on Climate Change (IPCC) and the convening of the UN Conference on the Environment and Development (the 'Rio Earth Summit') in the early 1990s. Along with the World Bank and the UNDP, UNEP is also responsible for the Global Environmental Facility (GEF) set up in 1991. This fund gives concessional support for major global environmental programmes and was set up because the post-industrial countries wanted something done about environmental degradation. However, it was realized from the outset that the cooperation of other countries was essential and a number of Asian and Latin American countries made it clear that they would not participate if the GEF was structured in the same way as the World Bank and the IMF (Sjoeberg 1994). As a consequence the GEF formally requires a 60 per cent majority of participants in the Facility and a majority representing 60 per cent of total contributions before an approval can be given. Yet again, though, consensus decision making tends to prevail (Woods 1999) and in practice the World Bank carries out most of the operations of the GEF, for UNEP lacks the Bank's project expertise. In general, UNEP is handicapped by a lack of leverage over other agencies and national governments, by its small budget and by its location away from the other main centres of the UN system.

The International Labour Organisation

The ILO is best considered as a UN institution even though it was established (in Geneva) in 1919 in the aftermath of the First, rather than the Second, World War. The motivation for its creation at that time was anxiety about the emergence of a revolutionary politics in other parts of Europe than Russia and a consequent desire to lay down acceptable international labour standards. However, the ILO only moved to adopt the key conventions which enshrine the principles of democratic labour rights in the period after 1945 when again the dominant political ideas in the US and Western Europe recognized the need to incorporate labour into a new post-war social settlement. Indeed, the initial planning of the post-war system of international economic management at Bretton Woods envisaged the ILO as a fourth institution, albeit of lesser importance, alongside the IMF, the World Bank and the ill-fated ITO (Gardner 1956). Yet, when GATT emerged to fill the vacuum left by the stillbirth of the ITO, its preamble paid little respect to the notion of a 'social contract' between government, capital and labour and made no mention at all of the ILO (Wilkinson 2000). Arguably, the best political moment to embed labour standards fully and comprehensively into the edifice of the global institutional order had already passed. Since then the ILO has unquestionably been on the back foot, even though it was incorporated into the UN system as its first 'specialized agency' in 1946. Like several other UN institutions, it found the shift to neoliberalism difficult to handle since this body of ideas manifestly had short shrift for notions of worker representation and organization. Of late, the ILO has also run into conflict with the WTO on the matter of the appropriate relationship that should exist between trade liberalization and the maintenance of labour standards.

Conclusion

We have now worked our way through a consideration of all of the major global institutions that bear upon the contemporary global politics of development. In particular, we have identified and flagged the growing significance of the G7/8 system. We also drew a distinction at the outset of the chapter between the Bretton Woods institutions and the various UN bodies. Although of itself this should not be pushed too far, it has served to highlight important differences of power and effectiveness between the various bodies represented within the two categories. To put it baldly, the Bretton Woods institutions have always carried much, much more clout in their spheres of operation than UN bodies generally have done in theirs. Moreover, it is probably the case that the UN has lost still more of its standing since 9/11, given the new emphasis which states now feel that they need to place on their immediate national security. There has also been shown to exist revealing variations of style, attitude and perception between the component elements of the two camps. Indeed, some analysts have gone so far as to comment upon the 'separation' of the World Bank, the IMF and the WTO from the UN system (Mingst and Karns 2000: 135); it should be remembered here that we too identified in Chapter 1 of this book the contrasting institutional homes of the two contemporary 'tales of world poverty' described by Jean-Philippe Thérien. This separation is marked in a number of ways: in the contrast between enthusiasm and acquiescence in response to neoliberal ideas, in the starkly different implications of weighted versus equal voting in internal decision-making systems (which either marginalize or privilege the large majority of the world's states in the day-to-day functioning of particular organizations) and, not least, in the varying role of the United States in these many institutions.

This last point is worthy of further emphasis. Within the IMF and the World Bank the US is, by a substantial margin, the most powerful state actor, its position additionally protected, as we have seen, by special rules and procedures. Within the more open councils of the WTO it is unquestionably a major player by virtue of its economic weight, but nevertheless it still has to battle with the other economic powers. Within the UN system, notwithstanding its considerable budgetary contribution and with the sole, highly significant, exception of the Security Council, it has often found its views swallowed up amidst the mass of other positions being articulated by the huge number of independent states that now exist in the world. Under the leadership of George W. Bush, in particular, the US finds these constraints inhibiting and irritating and has been increasingly prepared of late to act unilaterally against the wishes and policies of UN bodies, most notoriously of course in deciding to invade Iraq in March 2003. At the same time, though, the US is often able to use global institutions to its advantage. Robert Wade (1996: 36) exaggerates the relationship when he suggests that the World Bank 'forms part of the external infrastructural power of the US state', but he is quite right to put the point the other way round and note how much 'the US state ... relies upon its dominance of international organizations like the World Bank and the IMF to keep these organizations pursuing goals that augment its external reach' (see also Wade 2002).

With this we have reached the end of Part II of the book. What has been exposed in successive chapters is a cumulative pattern of structured inequality in the very context within which the global politics of development takes place. This manifested itself initially in the appraisal that was undertaken of the fundamental material and other capabilities possessed by contemporary states and the marked divergence of resources that were apparent. It was further demonstrated by the discussion of the main contending ideas that have constituted the development debate over the last two decades and the realization that these have been drawn overwhelmingly from what is really, in global terms, an extraordinarily narrow Anglo-American base. Finally, in this chapter, the same broad picture has emerged via our exploration of the membership and working procedures of the major global institutions of our era, and the exposition in detail of precisely how a few leading countries dominate these bodies to the detriment of the large majority of other countries. We must hold these interim conclusions firmly in mind as we proceed. At this point, however, with what we have called the framework of action for the global politics of development duly established, we turn in the next part of the book to the 'action' itself. Three chapters address the main policy arenas within contemporary development diplomacy, beginning, as one must, with finance.

Part III

Diplomatic Arenas

Chapter 6

Finance

As explained earlier, the three chapters that make up Part III of the book address the main policy arenas within contemporary development diplomacy. They cover, in turn, finance, trade and the environment. Each of these policy arenas in effect constitutes a particular space within the global politics of development. Within these different spaces all states necessarily pursue national strategies of development, thereby generating contact, competition and conflict with other states doing precisely the same. Although other non-state actors join the fray in the cause of their specific civil or corporate interests, they still endeavour, most of the time, to achieve their goals by influencing the stances of states. What we are highlighting, in other words, are the principal stages on which the inter-state politics of development is presently played out. These are the spaces in which states seek to create room to manoeuvre for themselves, in which they work to resist external pressures and in which they try to find niches that permit successful development. To put it at its most political, these are the diplomatic arenas where the main deals are done. All of this, it should be reiterated, takes place not in a vacuum but in a specific historical context, shaped by the distribution of material capabilities, the contention of ideas and the patterns of behaviour of the global institutions described and analysed in Part II.

We begin with finance because it constitutes the base upon which all strategies of development that are to be viable must rest. Nothing wrecks a country's prospect of development more quickly or severely than a financial crisis, whether it be the incidence of financial defaults by leading enterprises, or balance of payments and foreign exchange difficulties within the national economy, or fiscal crises of the state and the accumulation of debt. The financial sphere is also, by general consent amongst analysts of globalization, the sector of the world economy where global economic integration has proceeded furthest, with both capital and currency markets lately linked on a virtually continuous basis over the 24 hours of the day, thereby enabling huge sums of money to be moved around the world in various different forms, often on a very short-term basis (Held *et al.* 1999: 189–235). Such financial globalization has also been accompanied by, and perhaps has even been responsible for causing, extensive turbulence in financial markets, leading to the spread of so-called 'financial-crisis contagion' over the course of the 1990s. According to this account, the collapse of the Mexican peso in 1994–5 prompted further substantial outflows of capital from a number of other countries in Latin America; the devaluation of the Thai baht in 1997 led to other currencies in neighbouring countries coming under speculative attack and ultimately being forced into being a full-blown 'Asian financial crisis' with devastating consequences for the economic fortunes of the region; as an oil exporter likely to suffer from the contraction of the Asian economy Russia became the next target of currency sales, with the consequence that by mid-1998 the rouble had also been devalued and the Russian government had effectively defaulted on its short-term debts; finally, the process of contagion came full circle and returned to Latin America when Brazil was pushed into devaluing the real and introducing an austerity programme in early 1999.

These events are by now well known and have been much debated (Higgott 1998; Bulmer-Thomas 1999; Haggard 2000; Higgott and Phillips 2000; Robison *et al.* 2000) and there is no need or intention to explore them further here. But they do represent the essential backcloth to a number of inter-state conflicts over financial issues which came to the fore in the late 1990s and early 2000s and which it is the purpose of this chapter to describe and analyse. In the main, they revolve around three key areas of policy contention: debt, offshore finance and aid. Although these conflicts take different forms, are being carried out within several dispersed institutional settings and involve a diverse group of countries, it will be seen that they are being shaped by certain common imperatives and are unfolding in not dissimilar ways. They also consistently have at their epicentre the activities of the IMF and the various other 'international financial institutions' introduced in the preceding chapter. Nevertheless, no single institution or framework embraces all that we need to consider under the heading of finance and so we shall take the various issues in turn. We must start, however, with the fundamental question of the nature of the 'financial architecture' of the global economy, the adequacy of which was very much brought into doubt by the rolling financial crises of the 1990s.

The financial architecture

The body that has come more and more to take the major responsibility for the direction and stability of the global financial system is the G7. As we noted earlier, this body has evolved substantially over time, growing from its origins as an informal summit of leaders discussing general matters of economic policy to become the key location at which international financial initiatives are undertaken and then carried forward via regular meetings of G7 finance ministers and central bankers and ongoing contacts between finance officials. In specifically financial matters the G7 is supported by four other countries – Belgium, the Netherlands, Sweden and Switzerland – within the misnumbered Group of 10 (G10), these being the original participants in the IMF's so-called 'general arrangements to borrow' agreed in the 1960s (Kapstein 1994). Effective decision making within the 'old' financial architecture extended no further than these 11 countries; indeed, even in that forum, the G7 countries were always central. Meeting in Halifax in Canada in 1995 in the aftermath of the Mexican peso crisis, the leaders of the G7 spoke for the first time of the need to reform the existing mechanisms of global financial governance and thereafter continued to press the issue at succeeding summits. As Porter and Wood (2002: 244) describe the process, 'by announcing priority initiatives in their communiqués', the G7 leaders 'effectively issue directives to the IMF and other international financial institutions'. Initially it was generally thought that a number of technical adjustments in the management of the interface between national financial systems and the global financial system was all that was required, but this was quickly deemed to be insufficient. A political agenda, sometimes dubbed 'the new international financial architecture' (NIFA), has instead been advanced, centred on one overarching question: how to enable the formerly excluded countries to acquire a genuine stake in the decision-making structure of the global financial system (Germain 2002: 21). According to Germain (2002: 21), the 'mechanisms of inclusion' have consisted of three specific institutional developments, which are discussed below in what he considers to be their 'descending order of significance'.

The first was the creation of a new forum. This emerged from a series of *ad hoc* meetings that took place during 1998 and 1999 in direct and emergency response to the Asian financial crisis (Eichengreen 1999). Known by their participants variously as the Willard Group, the 'Group of 22' (G22) and the 'Group of 33', they were generally called into being by the US (although the initial suggestion can be traced to a suggestion made by Mahathir Mohamed, the Prime Minister of Malaysia, at the 1997 Asia–Pacific Economic Cooperation summit). At one level the US was interested in creating some kind of wider political forum in which it could bring in new allies to help counter the rather different voice of the European countries which were so well represented in the G10 (eight of the 11 members). At another it realized that there was a pressing need to legitimize the trajectory of post-Asian crisis reform. Crucially, therefore, all these various groupings included representatives of some of the 'emerging economies' directly involved in the crisis in an explicit attempt to chart a more collective response to the situation.

The merits of this idea were obvious and in September 1999 the G7 finance ministers formalized it by announcing the formation of the Group of Twenty (G20) as the fulfilment of the commitment made by the G7 leaders at their summit earlier that year in Cologne to 'establish an informal mechanism for dialogue among systemically important countries within the framework of the Bretton Woods institutional system' (Group of Seven 1999).

In addition to the G7 countries and representatives of the European Union, the World Bank and the IMF, the countries invited to join – 'under the watchful eye of the USA', as Soederberg (2002: 613) put it – were Argentina, Australia, Brazil, China, India, Mexico, Russia, Saudi Arabia, South Africa, South Korea and Turkey. In a further demonstration of the vetting operation at work here Indonesia was subsequently added once the situation regarding Timor-Leste's independence was considered to have been sufficiently resolved. By contrast, Malaysia was excluded, even though it had participated in the Willard Group and the G22; some felt that it was being punished for having flirted briefly with controls on the outflow of capital from its economy during the Asian financial crisis (Soederberg 2001: 462). The core concept underpinning G20 membership was this notion of 'systemic importance', which was a polite way of referring to countries whose financial problems, as and when they occurred, had the potential to become problems for the system as a whole. As Soederberg (2002: 614) again was quick to point out, 'the key objective of this inter-state initiative was integrate emerging market economies more fully and flexibly into the world economy' and its main management mechanisms; it was 'not an attempt to shift the balance of power between the developing and developed world but to strengthen the existing system through collective surveillance'.

Nevertheless, the significance of the establishment of the G20 should not be instantly or entirely dismissed. It does constitute an extension of international decision making beyond the G7 countries, with its member states representing some 87 per cent of the world's GDP and some 65 per cent of its population, according to its own publicity statements. It is true that it has no permanent secretariat and was seen by its first chairman, Canada's Finance Minister, Paul Martin (2000), only as a 'network', not 'a bricks-and-mortar edifice'. It has now met (at the level of finance ministers and central bank governors) on six occasions, most recently in Berlin in November 2004, Germany being the latest country to assume the chairmanship (after Canada, India and Mexico). It would have to be said too that its agenda has not, as yet, been anything other than orthodox. Its internal working arrangements are, however, designed to facilitate even-handed involvement since only two representatives of each country are permitted in the room at meetings. The G20 obviously has the potential to become a radical addition to the structure of international financial governance and it might be presumed that over time countries such as China and India, or even Russia, will seek to use the Group to argue for policies appropriate to their development strategies. But the reality is that, in its short existence to date, it has not sought to move in a radical direction. There are no plans, for example, to summon a G20 summit of state leaders, or to fold it into the G7. For the moment at least, the G20's role in the financial architecture remains very much secondary to the G7.

The second institutional development was the establishment of a new regulatory initiative, the so-called Financial Stability Forum (FSF), first convened in April 1999. Emanating from a report prepared by Hans Tietmeyer, the then President of the German Bundesbank, this too was part of the G7's response to the threat of financial contagion spreading outwards from the 'emerging market economies'. It brought together 21 representatives of the G7 countries (three each) and 14 representatives of the Basel-based and Bretton Woods institutions with a view to promoting international financial stability through improved information exchange and enhanced cooperation in financial supervision and surveillance. It was provided with a small secretariat at the BIS in Basel and its first chair was the English general manager of the BIS at the time, Andrew Crockatt. These last two features of its design were particularly revealing: although the FSF inevitably acquired a political mandate by virtue of its efforts to develop standards that constituted international benchmarks for prudential financial regulation all over the world, the reality was that it sought to address the perceived problem of systemic instability solely from a G7 perspective (Andresen 2000). Crockatt recognized this and pressed the G7 leaders at their 1999 Cologne summit to make a token gesture to remedy this deficiency by expanding the FSF's membership to include Australia, Hong Kong, the Netherlands and Singapore (but with these new countries having an entitlement to only one, not three, representatives), and by permitting non-G7 countries to participate in working groups. Other countries have since taken part in some of the FSF's work, but these changes have not altered the obvious fact that the Forum is not an inclusive institution. Optimists on this front have only been able to claim that the club is at least 'open to adaptation' (Germain 2002: 27).

The third institutional innovation within the NIFA agenda highlights a relatively minor change in the form of governance of the IMF itself. This occurred in September 1999 and involved the transformation of its 'Interim Committee' of the Board of Governors (originally formed in October 1974 at the time of the initial collapse of the Bretton Woods fixed exchange-rate system) into a new International Monetary and

Financial Committee (IMFC), to be chaired by Gordon Brown, the UK Chancellor of the Exchequer. This sensibly recognized that in the new era of globalization financial and monetary issues were best handled by the Fund under the same jurisdiction. The IMFC was also given a stronger mandate, being required to hold preparatory meetings before the spring and autumn joint sessions of the Fund and the Bank (which have long been the key political moments in the calendar of the IFIs) and encouraged to review the IMF's role in the financial system as a whole. Furthermore, IMFC membership was recast in line with the IMF's constituency system. On this basis some observers, and indeed some participants, hoped that the IMFC would become a broader-based committee, more open to divergent opinions. However, it is far from clear to what extent, if at all, these changes have enabled the 24 countries represented on the IMFC 'to raise issues without in principle being hampered by their allocation of votes on the IMF's Executive Board', which some initially suggested would be a possible outcome (Germain 2002: 21). Frankly, the experience of the first five years of the IMFC's operation offers little support for such a contention and it is probably fair to add that the Committee, which is still chaired by Brown, has by now settled into its *modus operandi*.

The question thus remains: even when understood as parts of a whole, how 'new' (see Kenen 2001) is this new international financial architecture? Certainly, it has been newly acknowledged that the present global financial order – built, as indicated, on extensive capital mobility – has come to be vulnerable to unanticipated movements and shifts taking place in the 'emerging economies' located at some distance still from the core of the system. Accordingly, some of these countries have been drawn a little more closely into the decision-making apparatus of the system and pressed into playing rather more in accordance with the orthodox rules of the game. But, notwithstanding the addition of the G20 and the FSF as new pillars, at the centre of the international financial architecture there still sit the G7 countries and of course the IMF, itself at the centre of a web of other IFIs including the World Bank, the BIS and bodies such as the International Organization of Securities Commissions. To put it mildly, the 'old' architecture still matters hugely. In fact, a very important strand of the international politics attaching to this whole issue during the first few years of this century has related directly to the role of the IMF and has concerned the controversial question of whether or not its mission needed to be re-thought in the context of financial contagion and globalization.

The opening shot in this debate was fired in December 1999 by Lawrence Summers, the Treasury Secretary in the Clinton administration in the US, when he observed to journalists that the increasing availability of private capital for 'emerging economies' implied 'some reduction of the IMF's role as a steady provider of medium and long-term finance' (*Financial Times*, 14 December 1999). By implication, the US view was that the IMF should focus on preventing financial crises, leaving the matter of lending to countries that could not access private capital markets to the World Bank. In early 2000 Summers followed up these remarks by persuading G7 finance ministers to set in train a comprehensive review of the roles of the Fund, the Bank and the other regional development banks. Even before this decision was taken, Republican Party forces within the US Congress, hostile for ideological reasons to the extensive IMF 'bail-outs' of Asian economies required by the dramatic collapse of currencies in that region in 1997 and 1998, had secured agreement on the establishment of a commission, chaired by the US monetarist economist Allan Meltzer, to review the role of the IFIs in similar root-and-branch fashion. The Meltzer Commission duly reported in March 2000, calling by a majority verdict for a radical contraction in the remits of the two Bretton Woods institutions, with the IMF reduced to a lender of last resort to countries that had already met certain financial preconditions and the World Bank to a provider of grants to the world's poorest countries (International Financial Institutions Advisory Commission 2000). The IMF, in particular, felt that it was under real political attack and it initially struggled to respond effectively, not least because it was at the same time going through the bitter battle described earlier in Chapter 5 over the succession to Michel Camdessus as Managing Director.

However, the eventual appointment of Horst Köhler to this position did stabilize the situation. In his first public statement he conceded the need for some reform, but hastened to add that there was 'no need to turn the IMF upside down' (*Financial Times*, 29 March 2000). He also spoke highly critically of the Meltzer proposals. Summers too sought to reduce the political pressure on the IMF by making it known that the Clinton administration considered that the idea of denying emergency lending to countries unless they pre-qualified for assistance was unlikely to be of much help in the key matter of dealing with systemic financial crises. In short, Köhler was enabled to undertake a reappraisal of the Fund's role in close conjunction with the World Bank in conventional technocratic fashion. In his early months in post he did undertake a grand tour of Africa, Asia and Latin America in order to listen to views expressed in these parts of the world, but he knew that, as always, the only national political arena that mattered in the context of his work was that of the US. The outcome of all these deliberations was a 'joint statement' by Köhler and the World Bank President, James Wolfensohn, issued at the time of the autumn 2000 joint meetings (held that year in

Prague), which announced 'an enhanced partnership' between the Fund and the Bank 'based on a clear sense of the complementarities of our two institutions'. Most importantly, the 'core mandate' of each body was reiterated in traditional terms, with the Fund expected 'to promote international financial stability and the macroeconomic stability and growth of member countries' and the Bank required 'to help countries reduce poverty, particularly by focusing on the institutional, structural and social dimensions of development'. As suggested, there was nothing new in these terms of reference. Nevertheless, the statement served to clarify the nature of the continuing, close working relationship of the two bodies and did not hesitate to make the boldest of cases for the adoption of 'a comprehensive approach' to address what it described as 'the multidimensional nature of sustainable growth and poverty reduction' (Köhler and Wolfensohn 2000). The Köhler–Wolfensohn declaration should therefore be seen as an expression of renewed self-confidence on the part of the two leading agencies of global financial governance and a validation of the existing post-1945 international financial architecture.

However, in another important statement to the Prague sessions Köhler (2000) set out proposals for earlier, and better, detection and management of financial vulnerability. These in effect constituted the IMF's input into the would-be NIFA. The watchwords here were surveillance and standards and the technique the elaboration of no fewer than 11 areas where 'standards are important for the institutional underpinning of macroeconomic and financial stability' (IMF 2001b: 105). These ranged widely, covering data dissemination, fiscal practices, monetary and financial policy transparency, banking supervision, insurance supervision, securities market regulation, payments systems, corporate governance, accounting, auditing, insolvency regimes and creditor rights. In each area Reports on the Observance of Standards and Codes (ROSCs) were to be prepared, laying out 'internationally agreed standards' which were then to be 'benchmarked' against existing country practices in order to improve transparency and reduce the opportunities for countries to 'cheat' or 'free ride'. Although standard setting by the IFIs was not in itself new, the ROSCs undoubtedly spread the tentacles of surveillance further than ever before, embracing even private sector practices. It should not therefore be surprising that these proposals were met with suspicion in some quarters. Criticism derived in the main from a part of the international financial architecture that had been largely ineffective since its heyday 30 years ago, namely, the Intergovernmental Group of Twenty-Four on International Monetary Affairs (G24). The G24 was set up in 1971 at the beginning of the wider push on the part of many newly independent countries to establish a New International Economic Order. It consists of countries from Africa,

Asia and Latin America and the Caribbean and was designed to concert their positions on monetary and financial issues in advance of IMF and World Bank meetings. It has doggedly continued to meet over the intervening years (Mayorbre 1999), although its representations have generally had little impact and, on the matter of the policing of standards, were firmly brushed aside by the G7 countries. Nevertheless, the point that the G24 (2000) made in its statement was entirely fair, for it described the proposed application of the ROSCs as 'highly asymmetrical', arguing that they were being 'pressed upon' its member states 'without a commensurate application of corresponding obligations for disclosure' in the G7 world, especially in respect of 'currently unregulated highly-leveraged' hedge funds.

The ongoing debate about the reformulation of the global financial architecture has now all but fizzled out. The new US administration of George W. Bush, which came into office at the beginning of 2001, was not that interested in these matters. It was the case that several of his senior appointees, including his first Treasury Secretary, Paul O'Neill, had been schooled in the same Republican tradition of opposition to substantial IMF 'bail-outs' of crisis-hit emerging economies which had fed into the Meltzer report. As we noted in Chapter 5, he had the opportunity to press upon the Fund the appointment as First Deputy Managing Director, by convention always a US citizen, the Republican development economist and robust advocate of free trade, Anne Krueger. The Bush team also picked up from Meltzer the idea of abolishing a substantial part (around 40 per cent) of the soft loans made to the poorest countries of the world by the IDA arm of the World Bank and replacing them with grants that did not have to be repaid. Although this also appealed for quite different reasons to some development campaigners in the NGO world, it was opposed by a number of European G7 countries, such as France and the UK, on the grounds that it would gradually erode the Bank's finances and thus over time undermine its very rationale and existence. Although the argument and the bargaining ran on for a time, it never became a touchstone issue for either side and a compromise was eventually reached at the G7 finance ministers' meeting in Halifax in June 2002 by which grants would be reserved for certain categories of assistance, including combating HIV-AIDS, and yet would not constitute more than 15–20 per cent of IDA support for the poorest countries. Generally, though, the Bush administration was not inclined to think that the global financial architecture needed any further refinement; in so far as it possessed a coherent view of the matter, it perceived it to be cumbersome enough already.

In sum, the current financial architecture is a complex mix of the old and the new. The architects themselves have remained essentially the same.

What has changed is that the G7 countries have been forced to admit the 'emerging market economies' into the system, precisely because they realized that it could not function securely without them. But the latter have been permitted entry only on a partial basis and very much on terms as set by the G7 and its main financial agent, the IMF. There has been no substantive negotiation of the type that characterized the making of Bretton Woods. Instead, as Jacqueline Best (2003: 364) has argued, in a conscious reference to John Ruggie's (1982) description of the 1944 arrangements as a form of 'embedded liberalism' marked by the grounding of liberal principles in the distinctive social and political norms of participant countries, advocates of the new international financial architecture have sought, largely successfully, to 'embed a singular global liberalism by imposing a set of Western "universal" financial norms and institutions', rather than to 'facilitate a plurality of liberalisms suited to particular domestic norms and practices'. For, as she again says, the task has not even been conceived as one of *'engaging'* the emerging countries in a dialogue about the merits of the typical financial practices of the G7 countries; it has instead been seen as a matter of *'convincing'* them by political means of the would-be universality of such practices (Best 2003: 376, her emphasis).

Debt

Debt has long been one of the most salient of global financial issues. It also has a particularly marked capacity to reveal the inequalities at the heart of the relationship between 'richer' and 'poorer' countries (see Payer 1974; Roddick 1988; George 1992). From the beginning of the 1980s onwards the debt problem had generally been perceived by official and Paris Club creditors as one of liquidity (Evans 1999). In consequence, the typical approach to debt relief was to refinance or reschedule payments, provided the debtor country was committed to an IMF-supported adjustment programme. Moreover, despite much talk of the existence of a 'Latin American' or an 'African' debt crisis, debtor countries were always treated separately in this period, largely in accordance with the extent of their potential threat to system instability. On this basis some of the early and larger 'problem countries', such as Mexico and Brazil, were enabled to regain, at least temporarily, the means to continue operating as viable financial entities. Yet over time it came to be seen that such an approach led only to a steady increase in both the overall stock of outstanding debt and the severity of the debt burden ratios of many of the poorest countries of the world (Sachs 1989). The realization slowly grew in the financial centres of the world that the core problem was one of solvency, rather than liquidity. Starting in 1988, following the G7 summit in Toronto, Paris Club members thus agreed to provide the poorest rescheduling countries with debt relief of up to one-third of its value by either forgiving part of the debt or by granting concessional interest rates. These 'Toronto terms' were then enhanced on two subsequent occasions, facilitating a debt reduction of up to one-half from December 1991 under the 'London terms' and of up to two-thirds from January 1995 under the 'Naples terms'. Nevertheless, even these arrangements could not maintain the service capacity of some of the most severely indebted poor countries; in September 1996 the politics of debt relief entered a distinctive new phase when the boards of the IMF and the World Bank approved the first Heavily Indebted Poor Countries (HIPC) initiative. This was explicitly presented as the putative means to a 'comprehensive solution' to what was referred to as 'unsustainable' debt (Boote and Thugge 1997).

The key to the HIPC initiative was this notion of sustainability. According to the World Bank (1998: 55), a debt would be considered sustainable if 'a country is able in all likelihood to meet its current and future external obligations in full without resorting to rescheduling in the future or the accumulation of arrears'. In other words, it would be a mistake to think that the policy was ever designed to eliminate debt; the objective was merely to reduce it to a sustainable level. This meant that the specific rules which were used to define what was, or was not, sustainable and which countries were, or were not, eligible were especially crucial. They proved to be complex to understand and laborious to implement. Countries could apply to be considered possible beneficiaries if they were (i) classified as poor, which was deemed to mean that their annual income per person on 1993 figures was US$695 or less; (ii) eligible to borrow from the IDA, the World Bank Group's concessional lending window; (iii) eligible for assistance from the Enhanced Structural Adjustment Facility, set up by the IMF in 1987 for low-income countries; and (iv) already taking full advantage of the traditional debt-relief terms already in existence. On this basis some 41 countries were initially identified as HIPCs: Angola, Benin, Bolivia, Burkina Faso, Burundi, Cameroon, the Central African Republic, Chad, the Republic of the Congo, the Democratic Republic of Congo, Ethiopia, the Gambia, Ghana, Guinea, Guinea-Bissau, Guyana, Honduras, the Ivory Coast, Kenya, Lao PDR, Liberia, Madagascar, Malawi, Mali, Mauritania, Mozambique, Myanmar, Nicaragua, Niger, Rwanda, São Tomé and Principe, Senegal, Sierra Leone, Somalia, Sudan, Tanzania, Togo, Uganda, Vietnam, the Republic of Yemen and Zambia. Four were Latin American and Caribbean countries; three were East Asian; one was Middle Eastern; and all of the rest, the vast majority, were African.

However, before applying for assistance, the rules further required that the eligible countries establish a three-year track record of 'economic and social reform' (which meant adherence to stabilization and structural adjustment programmes), at which 'decision point' a 'debt sustainability analysis' would be undertaken by IMF and World Bank staff to determine if the country was actually faced with an unsustainable debt burden. Generally, this was assessed by reference to export earnings, rather than GDP or the size of the government's budget, both of which were arguably as appropriate, if not more so. The specific figures used were a debt–exports ratio of between 200 and 250 per cent (in present value terms) and a debt service–exports ratio of between 20 and 25 per cent. Yet even this calculation did not bring the process to an end or immediately qualify the countries for debt relief. At the 'decision point', if a country was deemed to be eligible (and it should be noted that there were also conceived two other potential outcomes, 'exit' and 'borderline', which befell a few of the 41 countries), a case-by-case promise of extra assistance was indeed made by the multilateral institutions. But this could not actually be accessed by the debtor country until it had demonstrated a *further* three-year record of good performance, during which time the only gain to the HIPC thus far from the whole process was that Paris Club creditor countries would provide rescheduling on slightly enhanced 'Lyon terms' applicable to up to 80 per cent of the present value of the debt. Finally, if this second stage was eventually carried through successfully, the 'completion point' was deemed to have been reached and all creditors would take the previously agreed action to bring the country's debt to a supposedly sustainable level.

To say the least, the HIPC initiative, as originally conceived, was a highly elaborate and controlling policy framework. It is hardly surprising that it drew sustained criticism, especially from NGOs concerned with development matters, such as Oxfam (1998), Christian Aid (1998) and Jubilee 2000, an umbrella group set up specifically to demand the cancellation of all poor country debt by the beginning of the new millennium. These bodies complained that the key sustainability criteria were narrowly economic in character and thereby overrode a range of other more welfare-oriented or rights-based ways of assessing the capacities of countries to service debt (Castillo-Ospina 2002). They also drew attention to the absence of any link in the initiative between debt reduction and the positive benefits that might be derived from the saving within the recipient countries. As one commentator with close links to the NGO community put it, 'the HIPC debt cancellation process is based entirely on reducing debt to a level which can be repaid. It asks no questions about development, poverty or post-war reconstruction' (Hanlon 2000: 887). Above all, though, the critics exposed to public scrutiny the slow and cumbersome procedures that the HIPCs were being forced to undergo. For the reality was that, by mid-April 1998, only seven countries had got as far as the 'decision point': of these, six had been deemed eligible (in order of decision, Bolivia, Burkina Faso, Guyana, the Ivory Coast, Mozambique and Uganda) and one (Benin) had been judged able to reach sustainable debt levels through traditional mechanisms (Esquivel, Larraín and Sachs 1998: 20).

The political impact of this performance assessment was intensified because the G7 countries were scheduled to hold their annual summit in Birmingham in the UK in May 1998. In the run-up to the meeting various NGO statements, newspaper articles and a report from the UK House of Commons International Development Select Committee combined to attract extensive public interest in the debt question amongst the British people and Jubilee 2000 managed to organize a huge 'human chain' around the summit venue which attracted still more publicity. The effect was to transform the HIPC initiative from being a highly technical matter of concern in the main only to the IMF, the World Bank and their immediate clients and critics to a major political issue that demanded the attention of all of the leaders of the G7 states. At this level political divisions were also very apparent. The British and French governments pressed for an acceleration of the HIPC process and drew particular attention to the case for 'fast-tracking' seven African countries (Burundi, the two Congos, Liberia, Rwanda, Sierra Leone and Somalia), all of which were struggling to recover from recent civil wars. Both administrations professed to adhere, albeit in different ways, to broadly social democratic values, but also could be said to have more to gain from the whole initiative than other G7 countries in that many of the HIPCs were from Commonwealth or Francophone Africa. By contrast, Germany, Italy and Japan were resistant to any proposals to speed up disbursements of debt relief. The United States was equivocal, with President Clinton supportive at the rhetorical level but the US Treasury seemingly content with the existing pace and mechanisms. The other linked issue that split the summit was the idea of providing extra funds for the initiative by selling off some IMF stocks of gold. Again, the political divisions ran along similar lines.

In the end, no agreement on reform of the HIPC initiative could be reached at Birmingham. It took more pressure, a change of government in Germany in September 1998 which saw the replacement of the conservative administration of Helmut Kohl by a social democratic and green government led by Gerhard Schröder, extensive discussions at the spring 1999 joint meetings of the Fund and the Bank, another G8 (as the body had by now been renamed) summit in Cologne in June 1999 at which Germany took more of a lead (Kampffmeyer and Taake 1999) and further bargaining at the autumn 1999 IMF/World Bank joint sessions before 'HIPC II' could be enunciated. The main bases of the improved deal were:

(a) the revision downwards of the key definition of sustainable debt from a debt–exports ratio of 200–250 per cent to 150 per cent;
(b) the introduction of interim debt relief between the 'decision point' and the 'completion point';
(c) the creation of a 'floating completion point' to enable a country to be judged by the actual extent of its 'reforms', rather than the passage of an arbitrary period of time; and
(d) the inclusion of a new dimension in the qualification process whereby a beneficiary country was required to produce by the 'decision point' a Poverty Reduction Strategy Paper (PRSP), worked up in conjunction with staff from the multilateral institutions but also, significantly, drawing upon a measure of participation by elements of local civil society.

The various changes were positive in that in their different ways they clearly responded to some, but not all, of the criticisms mounted against HIPC I by the NGO development community (Killick 2000). More to the point, agreement was also eventually reached between the leading creditor countries to raise some more money to sustain the HIPC trust fund, to be derived partly from some revaluation of IMF gold stocks, use of some of the profits made by the World Bank on its loans to middle-income countries and additional bilateral contributions from the US, the EU states and Japan.

The package did at least enable more countries to be processed. By May 2001, IMF data showed that 23 HIPCs had debt relief arrangements in place, with relief already flowing and the total cost of the commitment to these countries valued at US$19.5 billion. Out of the 23, two countries – Uganda and Bolivia – had reached their 'completion points'. Of the remaining countries from the original list, four (Angola, Kenya, Vietnam and the Republic of Yemen) had been deemed likely to be able to achieve debt sustainability under the usual Paris Club mechanisms and 14 still awaited approval. On this basis, the IMF was prepared to claim partial success for its HIPC initiatives. It produced figures that suggested that the total external debt stock of the 23 beneficiaries would eventually be cut by as much as two-thirds, from US$54 billion to around US$20 billion. What is more, expressing external debt as a percentage of GDP, it projected that the ratio would fall from 57 per cent before the initiatives to 29 per cent in 2003: a level that, according to the IMF, would be lower than the average of 36 per cent for what it described as 'non-HIPC developing countries' (IMF 2001a: 5). There was also evidence at this stage that in a small number of the lucky countries debt relief had generated increased social spending, with consequent real impacts on education and healthcare. Madagascar and Malawi were the countries most frequently cited as exemplars in this regard. However, against these claims, what critics of the HIPC process continued to highlight was the way that new repayments as they became due often pushed up the total debt owed even by a country that had received HIPC relief. Falling commodity prices, as experienced from 2000 onwards by a number of African agricultural producers, also impacted damagingly on the debt sustainability calculation, given that it rested essentially on a debt–exports ratio. This affected even the best performers under HIPC, such as Uganda, which still remains heavily dependent economically on coffee exports.

It is also the case that much of the heat has now gone out of debt politics. The Okinawa G8 summit in July 2000 was attended by three African leaders – Abdelaziz Bouteflika of Algeria, Thabo Mbeki of South Africa and Olusegun Obasanjo of Nigeria, representing respectively the Organization of African Unity (OAU), the Non-Aligned Movement and the Group of 77 within the UN – who called collectively for a debt programme that went beyond even the enhanced HIPC initiative. But their pleas fell on deaf ears. The Blair government, in particular, continued to talk up possibilities and at one point went so far as to propose the extension of the HIPC concept to former Soviet states such as Armenia, Georgia, Kyrgyzstan, Moldova and Tajikistan. But the truth was popular pressure, which had been so important in the late 1990s in forcing the problem of debt on to the centre stage of global politics, had also fallen away somewhat. As the old millennium passed into the new, Jubilee 2000 transmuted into 'Drop the Debt', a similar organization but one with a much less realistic ambition given the relativities of power that have always existed between creditor and debtor countries. As a result, IMF and World Bank officials tended increasingly to take the line that they had already done all that could be done on debt for the foreseeable future.

For its part, the incoming US administration of George W. Bush was profoundly unconcerned by the impasse into which HIPC had run. As already indicated, its initial gut instinct was that too many governments irresponsibly ran up debts via reckless macroeconomic policies precisely because they thought that the IMF and the World Bank would lend them money cheaply as and when desired. Indeed, it pressed Anne Krueger's appointment upon the Fund in the belief that, *inter alia*, she would stand firmly in opposition to such policies. However, Krueger surprised many commentators by setting as her first priority the drawing-up of a plan for what was, to all intents and purposes, an international bankruptcy procedure whereby the IMF could impose temporary standstills on debt payments while countries worked out restructuring deals with their private sector creditors. She even went so far as to describe such a plan as 'the missing element we must provide' in the global financial system (*Financial Times*, 28 November 2001). This had not hitherto been regarded as 'thinkable' in official circles, but it seems that the IMF was responding in part to recent unsatisfactory debt restructurings in Ecuador, where a unilateral default had effectively cut the country off from international capital markets, and Peru, where the government had been more or less held to ransom by a 'vulture fund' which bought up its debt and forced it to pay the full face value on pain of seizing other assets. By late 2001 the growing financial crisis in Argentina was also threatening to bring a 'systemically significant' country into the frame and Krueger was clearly determined to try to use the Argentinian situation to push through her agenda.

The IMF can be seen here as seeking to act on behalf of the financial system as a whole, rather than any particular country interests within it. As Krueger (2002) saw it, a balanced mechanism was needed which would both 'create incentives for a debtor with unsustainable debts to approach its creditors promptly – and preferably before it interrupts its payments' and yet also 'avoid creating incentives for countries with sustainable debts to suspend payments rather than make necessary adjustments to their economic policies'. Initially, she had the support of the Bush administration in the person of O'Neill as Treasury Secretary, and she did succeed for a brief period in committing the IMF to work out the details of a new Sovereign Debt Repayment Mechanism (SDRM), as the proposed framework came to be called, in time for the spring 2003 joint meetings of the Fund and the Bank. However, the initiative also generated opposition from an odd but effective coalition: on the one hand, powerful Wall Street banking interests in the US itself, concerned at the potential reduction of profitable debt 'work-outs' in which to get involved, and, on the other hand, leading Latin American countries, such as Brazil and Argentina, alarmed that enforced restructuring which overrode the claims of private creditors would only raise the initial cost of financing in the money markets. O'Neill's resignation from office in December 2002 and his subsequent replacement by John Snow led to a reversal in the position of the US Treasury, at which point the prospect of an SDRM being agreed came to an end. Krueger's plan was accordingly shelved at the spring 2003 joint IMF/World Bank meetings. In its stead the US Treasury is now pushing the incorporation of 'collective action clauses' into sovereign debt contracts as an alternative means to encourage a majority of creditors to re-work a debt before the point of default is reached. Progress has not yet been very great and it may well not be, given that the 'threat' of a statutory framework being imposed has now been removed (Ghosal and Miller 2003).

In the meantime, the debt of middle-income countries has continued to be handled in the way it always has been: on a case-by-case basis, shaped by the politics of the situation. To highlight some of the most obvious recent cases, Turkey has been treated favourably by the IMF because of its geopolitical position in relation to the Middle East. It has benefited from a series of stand-by agreements running continuously since December 1999. Brazil was also granted a big new loan in August 2002 as a way of tying a prospective new radical government into the Fund's embrace. By comparison, successive Argentinian governments have endured a tense and troubled relationship with the Fund since its support was initially suspended at the height of that country's financial crisis in late 2001. In the end, its economy has been sustained by decisions to 'roll over' significant portions of its debt to the IFIs, the views of IMF staff (supported by some state representatives on the Executive Board) having ultimately been overruled by political pressures emanating from within the Bush administration (notwithstanding its initial ideological hostility to generous 'bail-outs'). However, this pales by comparison with the political arm-twisting in which the US has engaged since the end of the ground war in Iraq in 2003 to engineer under the auspices of the Paris Club a significant 'write-off' of Iraqi government debts. At the outset, France and Germany in particular – two countries which were major creditors of Iraq and which also, of course, had opposed the Iraqi invasion – were opposed to anything more than a partial forgiveness of the debt. But, in November 2004, aware of the extent of the transatlantic discord generated by the Iraqi war and, significantly, just after Bush's re-election to the US Presidency, they moved to concede an eventual 80 per cent 'write-off' of Iraq's US$39 billion debt owed to Paris Club members. It was less than the US was demanding, but nevertheless the deal still represented a telling benchmark against which bargaining around the rest of Iraq's enormous sovereign debt could take place.

As for HIPC, it had almost been forgotten, as we have seen. The spring 2003 joint IMF/World Bank meetings were the first for several years where it was not a major item on the agenda. Instead, SDRM and Iraq dominated talk about debt. Yet, paradoxically, the determination of the Bush administration to push through favourable treatment for Iraq did open up enough political space for HIPC's longest-standing supporters amongst the G8 states to propose a further injection of money into the scheme at the June 2004 heads of state summit held on Sea Island in Georgia in the US. The UK, under the joint leadership of Blair and Brown, took the lead in this discussion, calling for a more extensive cancellation of HIPC debt to be funded by a revaluation of IMF gold stocks. The US gave support, although it muddied the waters by suggesting again that, as part of the overall package, grants should replace loans in multilateral support programmes, thereby undermining by the back door, as it were, the future resource base of the IFIs. However, the other G7 countries could not be shifted and in the end all that was agreed was a modest US$1 billion increase in HIPC funding, an extension of the initiative for an additional two years until the end of 2006, and further study of options. The whole HIPC project thus stands as evidence of the limits of the possible in respect of debt relief in the current world order (Teunissen and Akkerman 2004). A long-running grassroots campaign, the support of some leading G7/8 governments and the active engagement of the Fund and the Bank has collectively produced no more than a relatively minor dent in the problem. According to one UNDP source, even though 27 countries were benefiting from HIPC by the autumn of 2004, the total debt reduction involved amounted to only US$34 billion, marginally more than the sum involved in Iraq's recent Paris Club deal (Watkins 2004). Even so, the HIPC initiatives have still to be seen as an advance because they did promise, and then deliver, some alleviation of the debt owed to multilateral bodies by a handful of relatively small, but poor, countries. HIPC II was also an improvement on HIPC I. Moreover, as indicated, HIPC is not yet concluded and there is thus still a possibility that it can be further deepened and extended. It is also the case that the vehicle of the PRSP, as initially trialled with the HIPCs, has since been deployed more widely by the World Bank in relation to 'low-income countries' in general. It has been criticized as 'a generalised means of intervention in economic and social policy and political governance' (Cammack 2002: 50) and thus it would be perverse, to put it mildly, if the wider implementation of such an extensive system of World Bank surveillance turned out to be one of the consequences of all the global pressure built up around the question of poor country debt over the past several years.

Offshore finance

Offshore finance is, by comparison with debt, a new issue in global financial politics. For the first time in the late 1990s, again prompted in the main by the Asian financial crises, the regulatory ambitions of the would-be financial architects of the G7 countries were deliberately widened to embrace so-called Offshore Financial Centres (OFCs). Offshore is a notoriously tricky concept to define precisely. Palan (1998: 626) uses the term to connote 'special territorial or juridical enclaves ... in which the state's regulation and taxation are fully or partially withheld'. Although popular conceptualizations tend to emphasize the territorial dimension, conjuring up images of islands detached physically from the prying eyes of state authorities, the real significance of offshore lies in its juridical properties. As Woodward (2002: 3, his emphasis) notes, 'offshore is a legal as well as a physical domain. *Where* an activity takes place is secondary to the *rules* under which it takes place.' Offshore financial activities undoubtedly developed extensively during the 1970s and 1980s when they were generally viewed benevolently. It is also widely agreed that the 'provision of offshore financial facilities has lifted a host of small jurisdictions from the poverty of the developing world to levels of affluence few would have believed within their grasp' (Hampton and Abbott 1999: 1). However, as financial crises within the global system began to occur with growing frequency in the 1990s and it was realized just how substantial were the financial flows passing through OFCs, the whole offshore sector came to be viewed more and more in the G7 world as a pariah zone that had the capacity to threaten global financial stability and consequently needed much tighter regulation. Three initiatives were set in motion, addressing in turn issues of taxation, money laundering and prudential regulation.

The first emanated from the OECD, which was itself interesting because it exposed the kind of political role sometimes played by this body. The initiative grew out of a call from the OECD Ministerial Council for the organization to develop measures 'to counter the distorting effects of harmful tax competition' (OECD 1998: 7) and the subsequent publication of a major report on this 'emerging global issue' in April 1998. The argument was that tax havens and preferential tax regimes – which, although different, were collectively described as harmful tax practices – were diminishing global welfare because they allowed wealth and income to be transferred to offshore locations, thereby weakening the ability of states to levy taxes on individuals and corporations for fear of stimulating further capital flight. The OECD stressed that it was not hostile to low taxation *per se*; the latter only became 'harmful' when combined with a lack of effective exchange of information between tax authorities and a general absence of transparency in legal, administrative and legislative matters. Accordingly, it was proposed that a Forum on Harmful Tax Practices be set up as a subsidiary of the OECD Committee on Fiscal Affairs and given two tasks: one, to ask OECD member states to appraise their own preferential tax regimes and then report any harmful aspects to their peers within Forum working groups; the other, to conduct external reviews of tax havens and then require them to commit publicly to the elimination of harmful practices by a specified date. The difference in methodology was stark and apparent to all.

In June 2000 the OECD reported on its work to date. It announced that potentially harmful tax regimes existed in 21 of the 30 OECD member countries and called for these to be adjusted appropriately. More dramatically, it listed some 35 OFCs which were deemed to deploy harmful practices; they were given a year to make a commitment to eliminate such practices, with failure to do so leading to them being formally dubbed 'uncooperative' tax havens and subjected thereafter to a range of sanctions (OECD 2000). The listed territories were: Andorra, Anguilla, Antigua and Barbuda, Aruba, the Bahamas, Bahrain, Barbados, Belize, the British Virgin Islands, the Cook Islands, Dominica, Gibraltar, Grenada, Guernsey, the Isle of Man, Jersey, Liberia, Liechtenstein, the Maldives, the Marshall Islands, Monaco, Montserrat, Nauru, the Netherlands Antilles, Niue, Panama, St Kitts and Nevis, St Lucia, St Vincent, the Seychelles, Tonga, the Turks and Caicos Islands, the US Virgin Islands, Vanuatu and Western Samoa. It seems that a further dozen tax havens had also been investigated, with six passing the OECD tests (Costa Rica, Jamaica, Dubai, Brunei, Macao and Tuvalu) and another six pledging to cooperate just before the list was announced (Bermuda, the Cayman Islands, Cyprus, Malta, Mauritius and San Marino).

As might be expected, the publication of the list generated a hostile political reaction from the governments of many of the tax havens on the grounds that the central feature of their economic strategies was being undermined, with likely disastrous consequences. Over two-thirds of the listed territories were members of the Commonwealth – which also includes the OECD members Australia, Canada, New Zealand and the UK – and their complaints about the initiative crystallized at an angry meeting of Commonwealth finance ministers in September 2000. This gathering highlighted in particular the 'double standards' inherent in the OECD's whole approach to harmful tax and expressed the fear that tax funds would be drained from small, island states to larger jurisdictions either within the OECD itself or at least not censured by it. It was unquestionably true that the OECD was ambiguous as to whether or not it was seeking to mount counter-measures to deal with its own non-compliant members. Switzerland and Luxembourg had in fact abstained from the initial report, citing their disagreement with the criteria set out and their desire to protect the client confidentiality of their financial enterprises. Portugal and Belgium also later abstained from the 2001 Progress Report prepared by the OECD. However, the biggest blow to the OECD's political solidarity emerged from an unexpected source: it was dealt by the new Bush administration in the US when in May 2001 Paul O'Neill issued a statement that, although supporting the case for greater transparency and improved information exchange, went out of its way to insist that the project was not only 'too broad' but also dependent on the dubious underlying premise that 'low tax rates are somehow suspect' (US Treasury Department 2001). The politics of the situation was that an unholy alliance of big business, right-wing think-tanks and development campaigners in the US had played effectively not only upon the conventional low tax convictions of most American Republicans but also the fact that the sort of tax competition being prosecuted by the OECD (albeit with the Clinton administration's initial backing) was itself a longstanding feature of the US tax regime. Needless to say, the antipathy of the US government did more to check the progress of the OECD initiative than any amount of hostility from Barbados and other listed countries.

Faced with faltering political support, the OECD postponed its various deadlines and did not announce its inaugural list of uncooperative tax havens until April 2002. Intensive negotiations resulted in all but eight of the original 35 territories making the necessary commitment (thereby becoming what the OECD glibly termed 'participating partners'). Barbados refused to do so but, in detailed discussions with OECD representatives, managed to convince them that its mechanisms for information exchange and transparency were adequate after all. As a result, seven countries were named on a second list (Andorra, Liberia, Liechtenstein, the Marshall Islands, Monaco, Nauru and Vanuatu) and told that they faced sanctions from mid-2003 onwards. Vanuatu and Nauru have since signed up, reducing the non-compliant list to just five. However, as Woodward (2002: 24) has put it, 'the OECD juggernaut' has in effect 'ground to a halt'. Although discussions continue and there remain fears in the tax havens that their eventual negotiation with the OECD has accorded this body a certain legitimacy in the governance of globalization which might open 'the floodgates to a raft of other demands by an organisation with no authority except the coercive power of its member states' (Sanders 2002: 53), the reality is that it will not be easy to get this particular juggernaut rolling again, not least because the pledges that were made by OFCs were only offered on the explicit condition that the OECD treated its members in like fashion. Given the positions of Luxembourg and Switzerland, such a 'level playing field' is simply unachievable. The OECD presents the situation as a substantial advance and it is the case that the 'participating partners' have made some attempts to fulfil commitments to greater transparency and effective information sharing. The five recalcitrant jurisdictions also, notionally at least, remain liable to sanction. That said, after more than six years of OECD pressure the political space available to tax havens to go about their business is still largely intact.

The second strand in the attempt to construct a more elaborate system of governance for OFCs emerged out of a different intergovernmental body, the Financial Action Task Force on Money Laundering (FATF). The FATF was first established as a new policy-making unit in the financial architecture in 1989 by a decision of the G7 summit of that year in explicit response to mounting concern about money laundering. It does not have a tightly defined constitution and technically it has only a limited life span, although it has lately been agreed that it should continue in existence until at least 2012. Over time its membership has grown to 31 countries (mostly OECD member states, but also including Argentina, Brazil, Hong Kong, Singapore and South Africa), plus two regional bodies, the European Commission and the Gulf Cooperation Council. It works closely with a number of equivalent FATF-style bodies in Asia, the Caribbean, Europe, Eastern and Southern Africa and South America, and has a small secretariat housed at the headquarters of the OECD in Paris. It is not, however, a part of the OECD.

The FATF enters this discussion because in 1999 it too launched a new initiative to identify those parts of the world which were weak links in the fight against money laundering and for this reason were again seen as imperilling the integrity of the whole financial system. What is more, it set about the task by 'naming and shaming' in analogous fashion to the OECD in its pursuit of harmful tax competition; indeed, in one respect it exceeded the OECD by having the nerve to coin a new acronym to describe its targets: the NCCTs, or non-cooperative countries and territories. It began by publishing universal criteria by which to determine detrimental rules and practices and then in June 2000 produced its first list of 15 jurisdictions that either had 'critical deficiencies' in their anti-money laundering systems or had demonstrated unwillingness to cooperate with the FATF. They were: the Bahamas, the Cayman Islands, the Cook Islands, Dominica, Israel, Lebanon, Liechtenstein, the Marshall Islands, Nauru, Niue, Panama, the Philippines, Russia, St Kitts and Nevis and St Vincent. The political reach of this list was clearly wider than just OFCs: it included, for instance, Russia, a member of the G8. Since this first declaration the FATF has both added and withdrawn countries as its investigations and ensuing discussions have unfolded. Despite complaints about the hypocrisy of the leading states represented in the FATF, given that most laundered money has always made its way into US and European banks, many targeted countries were driven to bring their laws into line with the guidelines. Russia has thus been removed (and has since been invited to join the FATF), but six countries or territories are still listed as NCCTs, namely, Indonesia, Myanmar and Nigeria as newer additions and the Cook Islands, Nauru and the Philippines from the original grouping. FATF member states have also gone so far as to impose counter-measures, including enhanced surveillance, against the Ukraine, Nauru and Myanmar, but these were only temporary moves and have since been withdrawn, even though the latter two countries remain on the NCCT list. It is not evident as yet that there exists the political will to impose meaningful sanctions via the FATF process, although there is no doubt as to the renewed support of the Bush administration following 9/11 and the connection it has officially drawn between money laundering and terrorism.

The final element in the intensified international pressure brought to bear upon OFCs in the last few years has concerned their so-called 'prudential regulation' and involved the Financial Stability Forum discussed in the first section of this chapter. Official diagnoses of financial contagion once more drew attention to the role of deficiencies in the oversight of OFCs in exacerbating the crises and the FSF was charged with setting up a working group to look at remedies. Reporting in April 2000, it too engaged in 'list politics' and the language of 'cooperation and non-cooperation' by discerning three 'groups'. Group I included 'jurisdictions generally viewed as co-operative ... with a high quality of supervision, which largely adhere to international standards'; Group II comprised 'jurisdictions generally seen as having procedures for supervision and co-operation in place, but where actual performance falls below international standards, and there is substantial room for improvement'; and Group III was made up of those 'jurisdictions generally seen as having a low quality of supervision, and/or being non-co-operative with onshore supervisors, and with little or no attempt being made to adhere to international standards' (Financial Stability Forum 2000: 46). Hong Kong, Luxembourg, Singapore and Switzerland, for example, were placed in Group I; Andorra, Bahrain, Barbados, Bermuda, Gibraltar, Macau, Malta and Monaco were in Group II; but no fewer than 25 OFCs were graded in Group III: Anguilla, Antigua and Barbuda, Aruba, the Bahamas, Belize, the British Virgin Islands, the Cayman Islands, the Cook Islands, Costa Rica, Cyprus, Lebanon, Liechtenstein, the Marshall Islands, Mauritius, Nauru, the Netherlands Antilles, Niue, Panama, St Kitts and Nevis, St Lucia, St Vincent, Samoa, the Seychelles, the Turks and Caicos Islands and Vanuatu. For these countries and territories the FSF did not rule out the possibility of sanctions, but astutely passed the buck to the IMF to take responsibility for enforcing adherence to international standards. As we saw earlier, this tied in closely with the IMF's renewed engagement from 2001 onwards with policies of surveillance and standard setting.

These various approaches to the global management of OFCs all manifestly reveal the same political style. The favoured recipe seems to have involved a similar three-stage process, whereby rules were laid down by an appropriate 'technical' body as to the bounds of acceptable behaviour, countries were then appraised and exposed for their failings in the expectation that this would generate immediate voluntary compliance, and finally counter-measures were threatened or deployed as further means of persuasion for those still uncowed. Although the OECD initiative in particular has lost some of its initial momentum, it cannot be denied that this methodology has served to impose different policies from those that would otherwise have been chosen on some of the smallest and weakest countries in the world. As was noted in relation to the 'emerging market countries', the political point that needs to be made is again that the standards being enforced are not genuinely universal, but instead reflect the particularities of the current, broadly neoliberal norms of the powerful G7 states.

Aid

Aid is the final piece in the finance jigsaw as far as the global politics of development is concerned. Formally described as 'overseas development assistance', aid has conventionally been taken to refer to loans and grants provided for poor countries which (i) come from the public sector, (ii) are granted with a view to fostering development and (iii) contain a concessional element (OECD 1985: 171–3). Despite the ideological offensive against aid mounted by many neoliberal economists during the 1980s (see Riddell 1987), it has continued to be an important issue, especially for the poorest countries least likely to be able to attract extensive flows of foreign direct investment. However, far from sparking an 'aid dividend', the end of the Cold War saw levels of aid fall and by the late 1990s some commentators took the view that ODA provision was facing an unprecedented crisis (Grant and Nijman 1998). Between 1992 and 1997 international aid from member countries of the OECD's Development Assistance Committee decreased by 21 per cent, the sharpest decline since the creation of the DAC in 1960. Total aid amounted to only US$49.6 billion by the end of that period, which meant that the ODA/GNI ratio for DAC members stood at 0.22 per cent, 'a far cry', as Thérien (2002: 458) accurately put it, from the international target of 0.7 per cent agreed at the UN more than 30 years earlier. Indeed, only Denmark, Norway, the Netherlands, Sweden and most recently Luxembourg have ever reached these standards, prompting their ministers for development cooperation to dub themselves, with heavy but appropriate irony, the 'G-0.7' (Bundegaard *et al.* 2001). What is more, within these falling sums ODA flows to the LDCs (never that big a proportion of the total in the first place) were not protected, but also dropped from approximately US$17 billion in 1990 to approximately US$12 billion in 1999, and a substantial amount of the aid provided was still 'tied aid', which meant that recipients were required to spend it on goods supplied by the donor country (a factor which at that time, according to various aid NGOs, limited the effectiveness of aid by about 25 per cent of its value).

However, a shift in the tenor of aid politics occurred in September 2000 when over 150 heads of state, meeting in New York at the end of the millennium and responding to the prompting of Kofi Annan as Secretary-General, adopted a bold 'Millennium Declaration'. As regards development and poverty eradication they resolved:

- to halve, by the year 2015, the proportion of the world's people whose income is less than one dollar a day and the proportion of people who suffer from hunger and, by the same date, to halve the proportion of people who are unable to reach or afford safe drinking water;
- to ensure that, by the same date, children everywhere, boys and girls alike, will be able to complete a full course of primary schooling and that girls and boys will have equal access to all levels of education;
- by the same date, to have reduced maternal mortality by three-quarters, and under-five child mortality by two-thirds, of their current rates;
- to have, by then, halted, and begun to reverse, the spread of HIV/AIDS, the scourge of malaria and other major diseases that affect humanity; and
- to provide special assistance to children orphaned by HIV/AIDS (UN General Assembly 2000).

These were not new commitments – they dated back in fact to the early 1990s – but they were given a rhetorical flourish by political leaders eager to appease millennium fever and have since come to be known as the 'Millennium Development Goals' (MDGs). More to the point, from early 2001 they were also adopted by the finance ministers and central bankers of the G7 countries with whom, of course, actually lay the power to do something about them.

It is true that new initiatives did ensue. The Italian government marked the holding of the annual G8 summit in Genoa in July 2001 by soliciting financial commitments to a proposed US$2 billion 'global health fund', and the UK Prime Minister, Tony Blair, used the same occasion to make the first of several calls for a new aid programme for Africa which he pronounced to be one of the priorities of his second term in office. At this point, 9/11 intervened, as it were. Whilst the US administration preoccupied itself with initiating the war on terrorism, the MDG baton was picked up in a significant and effective way by Gordon Brown. In a series of speeches in late 2001, the key ones deliberately delivered in

New York and Washington, the UK Chancellor of the Exchequer argued that September 11 proved that 'what happens to the poorest citizen in the poorest country can directly affect the richest citizen in the richest country' (Brown 2001). On the back of this claim he called for the enunciation of a 'new Marshall Plan' based on the raising of a '2015 fund' which would increase existing levels of aid provision each year by some US$50 billion, thereby doubling the overall sums available. The *quid pro quo* – in classic IMF/World Bank fashion – was that recipient countries should commit themselves to bring in, 'over time', international codes for setting monetary and fiscal policy and reducing corruption. Brown's figure of US$50 billion was the extra amount that a 'high-level panel' of financial leaders chaired by former Mexican President Ernesto Zedillo had judged to be necessary each year to implement the MDGs (Zedillo *et al.* 2001). This group had been set up by Annan following the Millennium Summit with a view to identifying the practical means needed to fulfil the declared UN goals, as well as building political momentum for the forthcoming UN conference on 'Financing for Development' scheduled to be held in Monterrey in Mexico in March 2002. This conference was the first international gathering specifically charged with addressing the issue of aid to have been held for more than two decades, and it was the place at which all the politics attaching to these various ideas for increasing the global aid budget was played out.

By general consent, the 'Monterrey Consensus', which was the name given to the statement agreed by the conference (International Conference on Financing for Development 2002), was a disappointing document. It was imprecise, highly orthodox and generally failed to address the main systemic issues relating to the financing of development. One NGO observer described it witheringly as no more than 'the Washington Consensus wearing a sombrero' (*Financial Times*, 25 March 2002). Even in the preliminary talks there emerged differences of approach between the EU countries and the US, some of which could be traced to their ongoing dispute at that time about the balance of grants and loans in World Bank funding. The UK government, which under Blair had slightly increased its aid budget (albeit to no more than 0.34 per cent of GNI), was also openly critical of the less generous stance taken by many of its EU partners. In the end the main achievement of the Monterrey meeting was that its very happening provoked some of the G7 countries to announce modest increases in ODA. The EU eventually committed itself to raising average ODA to 0.39 per cent of GNI by 2006, with all member countries aiming for a minimum of 0.33 per cent. Within the EU Ireland promised that it would reach the longstanding 0.7 per cent target by 2007. Other EU countries subsequently pledged to do the same by 2015. The Bush administration in the US also announced plans

to raise its existing ODA of approximately US$10 billion by almost
50 per cent by 2006, but indicated that it would place these new funds
in a new 'Millennium Challenge Account' to be distributed only to countries with strong records on good governance and macroeconomic stability (Soederberg 2004). Although hailed by some as a step in the right
direction, it should be noted that in 2001 US aid constituted a mere
0.11 per cent of its GNI, was skewed in the direction of a small number
of countries that supported its wider strategic goals (an extra US$600
million was allocated to Pakistan after 9/11), offered accordingly only
the most limited assistance to the LDCs, was delivered in a notoriously
complex and bureaucratic fashion and was still widely tied. Indeed, the
OECD itself admitted that, even if all the commitments made around
Monterrey were fully realized over time, the overall ODA/GNI ratio
for DAC countries would rise by only 0.02 per cent (to 0.24 per cent)
by 2006. It was a bitterly telling calculation that unquestionably put
Monterrey in perspective.

In the meantime Africa has been accorded at least a measure of priority
in the politics of aid. At their June 2002 meeting in Kananaskis in
Canada the leaders of the G8 gave their public endorsement to what has
been called the New Partnership for Africa's Development (NEPAD).
Assembled from a number of parallel initiatives launched in 2000–1 by
the presidents of Algeria, Nigeria, Senegal and South Africa and subsequently approved by the OAU, NEPAD is, in Alex de Waal's (2002: 464)
phrasing, 'both a "big idea" and an umbrella for best practices'. Its professed aim is to achieve the 7 per cent annual economic growth which
has been calculated to be necessary to halve poverty in Africa by 2015;
its methodology enshrines the conventional neoliberal wisdom on structural adjustment, debt management and the merits of agro-processing
and mineral exploitation; its political strategy has been to frame its
ambitions explicitly in terms of the Millennium Development Goals,
thereby directly challenging aid donors (described euphemistically as
'development partners') to put their money in the same place as their
mouths. The G8 countries only partially responded. At Kananaskis they
signed an agreement with NEPAD's four founding leaders in which
promises were made to direct at least half of the (approximately US$12
billion) extra resource flows committed at Monterrey to Africa, to erad-
icate polio by 2005 and combat aggressively other diseases, including
HIV/AIDS, to increase funding for basic education and, in respect of the
trade agenda, to improve access for Africa's exports. But, as John Loxley
(2003: 127) has said, this level of support was 'hopelessly inadequate to
meet NEPAD's own estimates of Africa's needs, and it could be argued
that it did not add up to a nickel more than had already been committed'. It seems that, although Blair and the Canadian Prime Minister, Jean

Chrétien, pressed for more support, the Japanese prime minister indicated that his country was cutting back sharply on ODA in the light of its own economic problems and George W. Bush expressed deep scepticism about the robustness of the 'peer review mechanism' contained within NEPAD by means of which African leaders were supposed to hold each other to account for lapses of good governance.

The same African leaders also attended a working dinner with the G8 leaders at the next summit held in Évian in France in 2003, but discussion focused on the possible establishment of a regional peace-keeping force and certainly no new money was put up to support NEPAD. Indeed, it is possible that Africa's best political opportunity to generate substantially increased aid has already passed. Tony Blair has at least stuck to his rhetoric and in early 2004 established a new Africa Commission (the historical reference point being the Brandt Commission) to chart another way forward for the continent. This group reported in early 2005 at the time when the UK was chairing the G8; this means that the planned annual summit to be held in Gleneagles in Scotland will provide one further moment when Africa will, albeit briefly, be the focus of global concern.

On other fronts, too, the picture is mixed at best. In October 2002, in his first progress report on the implementation of the MDGs, Annan (2002) was forced to concede that, 'if we carry on as we are, most of the pledges are not going to be fulfilled'. A full five-year review conference will be held at the UN in September 2005, but nothing has been identified in subsequent reports by Annan which suggests that these basic goals will come close to being met in the ways promised by 2015. The Global Fund to fight AIDS, Tuberculosis and Malaria has now been set up and has begun to disburse some modest grants. However, the reality is that it is desperately short of funds: many promised commitments have not been made in full and the US, in particular, seems to be determined to bypass it in favour of bilateral health programmes (Sachs 2003). Here is further evidence of the reluctance of the Bush administration to participate in multilateral initiatives that it does not control. On a more optimistic note it is commendable that Gordon Brown has not forgotten his notion of a modern Marshall Plan designed to double aid flows over the next decade or so. In early 2003 he came up with a novel way of raising the resources for such a scheme by proposing a new 'International Finance Facility' which could borrow against future aid flows on the international capital markets (Brown 2003). The idea is an ingenious one and Brown has doggedly pursued it within G7 financial circles, as well as more widely, securing the support, for example, of the Papacy. France and Italy have expressed public support, albeit with qualifications; the German government was initially sceptical, but has to some extent been brought round; whilst the US administration has indicated a lack of interest and, indeed, opposition. However, the plan is not yet dead and could go ahead still on a partial basis. It does at least have the merit of breaking the deafening silence within the G7 community about where the money is actually to come from to meet the Millennium Development Goals and shift the aid business into a higher gear.

At the end of 2004, however, the general position is that the aid agenda, briefly revived at the beginning of the millennium around the MDGs and Monterrey, has been overwhelmed by the politics of the war on terrorism. James Wolfensohn, President of the World Bank, declared at a major poverty-reduction conference held in Shanghai in May 2004 that, in his judgement, interest in global poverty was 'near a low point' (*Financial Times*, 26 May 2004). He had earlier told the spring joint sessions of the Bank and Fund that US$900 billion was spent globally on defence, compared to US$50–60 billion on development, adding with heavy irony that, 'if we spent $900bn on development, we probably would not need to spend more than $50bn on defence' (*Financial Times*, 26 April 2004). The impassioned popular response in so many countries to the Asian tsunami disaster in late December 2004 showed that there is still a dynamic of support for aid which can be mobilized, at least temporarily, in particular crises. Nevertheless, the deeper truth is that what has begun to be revived over the past two or three years is something akin to the pattern of the Cold War era where aid flows were predominantly dictated by perceived security concerns rather than humanitarian needs. There is thus a real danger that over the next few years global aid policies will be driven back towards unhelpful past practices, rather than forward to fulfilment of the MDGs.

Conclusion

Finance emerges as an arena where there exists sustained evidence of domination of the diplomatic and policy agenda by the most powerful countries of the world gathered together with increasing effectiveness and purpose within the G7/8. The G10 is almost wholly supportive of the G7/8, and the G20 has not as yet carved out a distinctively different niche for itself. It is true that, via this last new grouping, the 'emerging market economies' have 'breached the citadel' (Germain 2001: 419) of G7/8 power, but, as has been made clear, they have been permitted entry on guarded and limited terms with a view in the main to legitimating G7/8 initiatives to contain systemic financial crisis. For the rest, the OFCs have been exposed to the punitive processes of what we have called 'list politics' and many have adjusted their regimes in line with externally imposed standards. The HIPCs, for their part, have been led slowly and awkwardly down a road signposted by 'decision points' and 'completion points', with some eventually arriving, exhausted, at the threshold of debt relief only to find that declining commodity prices have pushed them back into the debt trap. Would-be aid recipients, the LDCs, the poorest of the poor countries of the world, appear, as ever, as supplicants, dependent on the fluctuating political support for aid in the major G7/8 states and particularly vulnerable at the moment to even greater marginalization amidst preoccupation with Iraq and the war on terrorism. Finally, it should be noted that the role in this story of the G24, the group set up specifically to articulate the view of African, Asian and Latin American and Caribbean countries in international monetary and financial issues, has been important only for its absence.

It is also strikingly the case that the sources of ideas about matters of finance and financial governance are overwhelmingly to be found within the institutions and agencies of the G7/8 countries. Amongst these, of course, the IMF and the World Bank, both now almost 60 years old, continue to predominate and might even be said to possess a greater institutional autonomy than for several years. The leaders and staff of the two institutions work together closely, although not of course without occasional clashes, and have built their 'enhanced partnership' in financial affairs with some effect since the autumn of 2000. There is no doubt that the Fund–Bank nexus constitutes the intellectual nerve centre of the contemporary global financial order. By contrast, as Norman Girvan (1999: 417) has noted, 'a clearly defined position on system reform' from what he called 'a Southern perspective' has 'not been articulated'. Of itself, this is a failure of significance that seriously undermines the prospect of a different and possibly more equitable global politics of development being achieved in the arena of finance for the foreseeable future.

Chapter 7

Trade

Trade is the next policy arena to which we turn in our analysis of contemporary development diplomacy. Even more fundamentally than finance, trade has always expressed the outward orientation of a country's development strategy, constituting its most obvious point of contact and, by extension, competition with other countries. Trade has also been the centrepiece of both mercantilist and liberal international economic theory. The former justified state intervention to regulate trade in order to cultivate a national trade surplus in a world in which international trade was considered to be in essence a zero-sum game. The latter posited the case for free trade between countries on the basis of a founding principle of comparative advantage. This claims that the pattern of international trade is determined by relative cost differences in the production of traded goods and thereby encourages countries to focus their productive resources upon the commodity in which they have a comparative advantage. In the contemporary era, of course, liberal arguments are heard much more widely than mercantilist ones. But it is certainly worth noting that, for all their difference of perspective and philosophical orientation, the common assumption of both these contending schools of thought is that trade policy, with all its external implications, is central to a country's chosen strategy of development.

Pragmatic questions immediately arise from the establishment of this linkage. Sheila Page (2002: 4) argues that, in thinking about the trade dimension of its strategy:

> A country must assess whether its economic structure is expected to change: does it need to negotiate for new trading patterns? Is it overly dependent on some commodities or some markets? ... Are there types of domestic policy which it wants to follow which might conflict with particular trading patterns or rules? Are there particular commodities which are so important to it that they determine its trade policy?

Other questions could easily be added to her list and the list then multiplied by the number of countries participating in the negotiations. It is apparent that the precise terms and conditions by which international trade is conducted cannot but be a major bone of contention in relations

167

between states. The dominant trading states of all eras tend to have an obvious general interest in extending the reach of free trade (although not necessarily in every particular commodity). The UK in the nineteenth century and the US after 1945 both took this view and succeeded for the most part in imbuing the ideological climate within which modern international trade politics has taken place with a free trade orthodoxy. Yet, as Paul Krugman (1997: 114) has observed, 'anyone who has tried to make sense of international trade negotiations eventually realizes that they can only be understood ... [as] a game scored according to mercantilist rules, in which an increase in exports ... is a victory, and an increase in imports ... is a defeat'. The resultant inter-state politics has generally been highly complex, with arcane technicalities often acquiring unexpected political significance.

The background against which contemporary trade negotiations have taken place is constituted by the so-called Uruguay Round conducted under the auspices of the GATT. As was explained earlier, from its establishment in 1947 the GATT presided over a series of 'rounds' of international negotiations within which the post-war trade regime was initially agreed, extended and successively modified, generally in the direction of greater non-discrimination and liberalization between trading parties (Gilpin 1987; Jackson 1989; Ostry 1997; Wilkinson 2000). The Uruguay Round was the eighth round and lasted from September 1986 until April 1994. It was much the most difficult of all the GATT rounds to bring to conclusion, in good part because so many more countries were involved in the negotiations than had previously been the case. For the first 40 years after the end of the Second World War most non-industrialized countries did not see the GATT as a fruitful arena in which to pursue their interests. They signed the agreement as a symbol of political independence, but were often frustrated by the culture of the debates that took place and preferred on the whole to adopt 'a "passive" or "defensive" attitude, refraining from significantly engaging in the exchange of reciprocal concessions' (Tussie and Lengyel 2002: 485). At that time, as Wade (2003: 629) has noted, 'the general push towards trade liberalization was conditioned by recognition that developing countries ... needed "special and differentiated" (S&D) treatment by definition of their being developing countries'. However, by the late 1980s the picture had changed. Many more such countries had become contracting parties to the GATT, along with several post-communist 'transition economies' (Michalopoulos 1999); the shift of thinking towards more overtly export-oriented development strategies, albeit under the pressure of IMF and World Bank 'structural adjustment', had also generated more awareness in the minds of their governments and leaders of the need to create trade openings for their products

(Drabek and Laird 1998); by the same token, as the economies of former colonies and other new states were increasingly opened up and some indeed moved into the ranks of 'newly industrializing countries', access to their markets became more attractive to the major trading players, which obviously made the case for drawing them fully into multilateral trade negotiations more and more compelling.

As already indicated, the actual talks were protracted in the extreme. They spread into new, highly complex areas such as services and intellectual property and frequently appeared to be on the point of collapsing. In fact, they were only brought to a conclusion in 1994 as a result of a decision to treat all the facets of the negotiations as contributing to a 'single undertaking', namely, acceptance that *all* of the agreements were to apply to *all* of the countries. This represented a major shift of approach by countries which had hitherto largely 'opted out' of GATT in favour of what T.N. Srinivasan (1999: 1,052) referred to as occasional ' "crumbs from the rich man's table" ... and a permanent status of inferiority' under the terms of the S&D clause. For this reason, the total package embraced as the outcome of the Uruguay Round has often been characterized, in the words of Sylvia Ostry (2000), as a 'North–South Grand Bargain' mutually agreed by all the various interests. In her view, it was built around 'an implicit deal', which could be summarized as follows:

> The opening of OECD markets to agriculture and labor intensive manufactured goods, especially textiles and clothing, for the inclusion into the trading system of trade in services (GATS), intellectual property (TRIPS) and (albeit to a lesser extent than originally demanded) investment (TRIMS) ... and also – as a virtually last minute piece of the deal – the creation of a new institution, the WTO, with the strongest dispute settlement mechanism in the history of international law (Ostry 2000: 4).

Since the deal was struck and the Round finally 'signed off' in Marrakesh in 1994, a huge amount of discussion has been devoted to attempts to assess whether the various undertakings really did connote a fair bargain. Some analysts at least acknowledged 'the extension of certain developmentally-sensitive provisions' throughout the legal framework enacted by the Uruguay Round (Wilkinson 2001: 407), including such features as reduced levels of obligation, more flexible implementation of time-tables and more favourable treatment for the 'least developed'. Others took the view that the outcome was 'unbalanced against the developing countries', especially in relation to the inclusion of the new rules relating to services, trade-related investment measures and intellectual property, and asked, perhaps rather naively, 'why was such an outcome offered and why was it accepted?' (Finger and Nogués 2002: 321, 332). For their part, in a fair and judicious evaluation, Diana Tussie and Miguel Lengyel (2002: 486) recognized that 'developing countries learned in the early stages of the Uruguay Round that greater participation did not translate automatically into leverage' and fully acknowledged that this failure had an impact on the final results. In their view, there were gains that these countries could chalk up: the agreement on agriculture which at least partly brought this area of trade under the same disciplines as applied to manufactures; the commitment to phase out the restrictions on trade in textiles enshrined in the infamous Multi-Fibre Arrangement (MFA); and the creation of a usable dispute settlement mechanism within the new WTO. But there were also losses that, ultimately, were the greater. In this category, they identified as the most significant: a more restrictive approach to S&D, the commitments made in the GATS and TRIMS agreements, the 'binding' (which means the setting of a maximum level) of many of their tariffs and the imposition of new disciplines on subsidies and customs valuation. Furthermore, they argued that it could already be seen that the creation of the WTO changed the nature of the game in international trade politics: the establishment of a new, much stronger institutional apparatus not only altered the parameters and patterns by which trade negotiations had hitherto taken place, but also meant that, in contrast to the GATT era, they would in effect be ongoing, requiring on the part of weaker, poorer countries a constant watchfulness and further commitments of scarce technical and political resources.

This last point is very important and opens the way to the discussion of this chapter. As we noted in Chapter 5, the foremost decision-making organ of the WTO is its biennial Ministerial Conference. It has met thus far only five times. The first two meetings (which took place in Singapore in December 1996 and in Geneva in May 1998) were important gatherings and were not without their controversies; yet they did not command the centre-stage of global politics. However, the next three Ministerials, as they have come to be abbreviated, each generated massive political interest and have constituted the key moments by which global trade diplomacy has, or has not, progressed since the culmination of the Uruguay Round. They took place in Seattle in the United States in November–December 1999, in Doha in Qatar in November 2001 and in Cancún in Mexico in September 2003. In effect, the five conferences represent a series of periodic 'climaxes' within the ongoing negotiation of the current international trade regime and provide the obvious means to structure our analysis of this important aspect of the contemporary global politics of development.

Singapore

The Singapore Ministerial sowed many of the seeds of future conflict. It was immediately forced to address what became known as the 'implementation issue', by which was meant the perception, already taking hold in the thinking of a number of governments, that the Uruguay Round settlement was asymmetric as between the interests of 'developed' and 'developing' countries, precisely along some of the lines already discussed. Some of the expected benefits of accepting the WTO and all of its rules – in respect of which, it should be noted, countries may have been misled or made misjudgements – were not apparent, at least as yet, and dissatisfaction was expressed by some member countries with this lack of 'implementation' of the agreement, as it was described. At this stage there was little organization behind the protest and, in the reckoning of Chakravarthi Raghavan (2000: 499), 'the major industrial nations summarily dismissed the issues and concerns', holding out as concessions no more than 'possible time extensions for compliance with obligations, and that too given on a case-by-case basis', and some extra technical assistance. Certainly, the official Ministerial Declaration in its brief reference to the matter was crisply dismissive.

As one might expect, the questions that dominated the Singapore Ministerial Conference were brought forward by the major post-industrial countries that had always dominated the politics of the GATT and had conventionally set the agenda of international trade negotiations. They principally concerned the extension of the WTO's remit to new issue areas, in particular the relationship between trade and investment; the interaction between trade and competition policy; transparency in government procurement practices; and trade facilitation. In response to these pressures, a group of eight countries formed the Like-Minded Group (LMG) with the specific purpose of blocking their acceptance as matters for future negotiation. The LMG was led by India and also included Cuba, Egypt, Indonesia, Malaysia, Pakistan, Tanzania and Uganda (Narlikar and Odell 2003). The Group was successful in its initial ambition, for the Ministerial Declaration included these four issues (henceforth the 'Singapore issues') in paragraphs 20 and 21 only as items for further study and analysis, not as parts of an unfolding negotiating agenda. This was a holding operation and at this time was accomplished without too much political difficulty.

The issue at Singapore that did attract political controversy concerned the potential inclusion of a reference to core labour standards in the WTO regime. As Charnowitz (1987) and Hughes and Wilkinson (1998) have both shown, the debate about the attachment of such a 'social clause' to international trade agreements has a long history, dating back to discussions of the ill-fated Havana Charter in the immediate post-1945 era. It also cropped up quite forcefully in the very last stages of the Uruguay Round, almost derailing the final settlement and only not doing so because it was decided to pass the matter on to the first Ministerial. In Singapore a specific proposal to create a WTO working group to examine the whole issue of international labour standards and global trade was tabled by the US and Norway. This idea was fiercely opposed by the LMG, led strongly on this particular issue by India and Malaysia, but also by several older industrialized countries, which meant that the argument could not accurately be interpreted via the old vocabulary of 'North–South' international relations. It also drew much of its energy from the more vocal representation of the contending positions by the organized labour movement (led by the International Confederation of Free Trade Unions) on one side, and a collection of development organizations and social movements (led by the Malaysia-based Third World Network) on the other. In general, proponents of a 'social clause' argued in favour of the universality of core labour standards and the rights of workers all over the world to enjoy the fruits of increased trade, rather than become victim to ever more aggressive economic competition between states. Opponents attributed the new push to enact a 'social clause' to persistently high levels of unemployment amongst G7 countries and a growing belief that the rapid growth of some newly industrializing countries had been achieved on the back of the exploitation of labour and a suppression of workers' rights. In effect, the latter claimed that the whole argument about labour standards concealed a disguised protectionism; the former responded by asserting that the NICs were simply seeking to hold on to the comparative advantage hitherto represented by cheap labour costs.

The debate about all of this in and around Singapore was unquestionably acrimonious, but it did lead to a compromise, albeit an uneasy one. Paragraph 4 of the Ministerial Declaration (World Trade Organization 1996) read:

> We renew our commitment to the observance of internationally recognized core labour standards. The International Labour Organization ... is the competent body to set and deal with these standards, and we affirm our support for its work in promoting them. We believe that economic growth and development fostered by increased trade and further trade liberalization contribute to the promotion of these standards. We reject the use of labour standards for protectionist purposes, and agree that the comparative advantage of countries, particularly low-wage developing countries, must in no

way be put in question. In this regard, we note that the WTO and ILO Secretariats will continue their existing collaboration.

There was something here for everyone: a broad but vague commitment to labour standards and a reiteration of the potential contribution of trade liberalization to the maintenance of those standards; a passing of the buck to the ILO; a rejection of protection and a recognition of the advantage offered by low wages; and an enigmatic reference to continuing WTO/ILO collaboration. The last sentence nearly unravelled, because some delegations quickly expressed the view that it committed the WTO to establishing a linkage between trade and labour standards. This forced the Singaporean chairman of the conference, Yeo Cheow Tong, to include in his summary statement a strong denial that the text gave any such authorization or undertaking (cited in Hughes and Wilkinson 1998: 378–9). In reality, there is no legal foundation for institutionalized cooperation between the WTO and the ILO, and any suggestion in the Declaration to the contrary has been aptly described as no more than a 'throw away line' (Stigliani 2000: 188).

Geneva

The Geneva Ministerial was held at a time when the consequences of the Asian financial crisis were still working their way through the global political economy. Perhaps unsurprisingly in these circumstances, it was a relatively uncontentious affair. The labour standards issue was raised again, with the US and the EU once more coming out in favour of a formal linkage of the issue to trade matters; they were backed on this occasion by South Africa. Brazil led the opposition, its President Fernando Henrique Cardoso asserting strongly that the issue of working conditions was alien to the 'philosophy' of the WTO (Wilkinson 1999, 2001). Significantly, however, no mention was made of any of this discussion in the resultant Ministerial Declaration. What did appear there (in paragraphs 8, 9 and 10) with a much greater degree of recognition was the 'implementation issue'. The LMG had recognized the importance of being defined by a positive agenda, rather than just suspicion of the 'Singapore issues', and in all the preparatory sessions in the run-up to Geneva, as well as at the conference itself, it focused actively on the problems its members and many other countries were having in implementing the various Uruguay Round agreements. As a result, the Declaration openly acknowledged the 'problems' that were being encountered and 'the consequent impact on the trade and development prospects of Members', and it promised that 'a process will be established … to ensure full and faithful implementation of existing agreements' by virtue of decisions to be taken at the next Ministerial in two years' time. In the intervening preparatory period, the WTO's work programme would focus on the making of recommendations on the 'implementation issue', the various ongoing negotiations already mandated at Marrakesh and the four 'Singapore issues' which had been consigned to working groups and thus put on hold politically since December 1996. In short, the stage was being set for what became known as the 'battle of Seattle'.

Seattle

The pressure, in fact, grew. By the beginning of 1999 there was increasing talk in government and media circles within the 'Quad' of the merits of using Seattle to launch a whole new round of trade negotiations, quickly dubbed by some a 'millennium round'. It had already been agreed at the end of the Uruguay Round that there would be new negotiations, starting in 2000, in the areas of agriculture and services. Article 20 of the WTO Agreement on Agriculture specifically promised to consider what else needed to be done to achieve the long-term objective of 'substantial progressive reductions in support and protection leading to fundamental reform'; and Article 19 of the GATS opened the way for a further widening and deepening of the commitments already made on market access and national treatment. These were the agreed components of the 'built-in agenda' (Laird 2002). In addition, several Asian and Latin American countries argued that this agenda also encompassed certain aspects of the TRIPS Agreement, notably the articles relating to the protection of traditional geographical indications (such as *basmati* and *tequila*), exceptions to 'patentability', dispute settlement and general implementation. Other countries, however, contested the claim that further negotiations on these issues had been promised.

Even without TRIPS, the 'built-in agenda' was substantial and it was in the end more or less sufficient for the United States at Seattle. The Clinton administration had been struggling for two or three years to get so-called 'fast track authority' for trade negotiations from the US Congress, whereby it would be enabled to negotiate an agreement which Congress could only pass or reject, not amend. It knew too that agriculture and services were areas where, in general, the US stood to gain from further liberalization. By contrast, the EU and Japan had emerged as the main proponents of a 'comprehensive' round, covering all aspects of existing WTO agreements but also taking on the new issues they had pushed in Singapore, notably investment and competition policy. The core idea at the heart of the EU's position was that its member countries would need to be 'compensated' for any concessions they might make on the protected status of their agricultural sectors with big market openings in other areas. For its part, Japan was in the end probably even more insistently opposed to further liberalization of agriculture. Its stance was the product of fierce intra-bureaucratic conflict within the Japanese government in which its Ministry of Agriculture successfully asserted itself over the Ministries of International Trade and Industry and Foreign Affairs. Japan's reticence on agricultural liberalization did not, however, prevent it pressing strongly for other new issues to come within the WTO's orbit.

It was also the case that the 'implementation issue' had not gone away. On the contrary, it had crystallized by the time of Seattle around three main areas of dissatisfaction. First, the Agreement on Agriculture had required signatories to convert all non-tariff barriers into tariff equivalents before reducing them by the agreed amounts. Perhaps predictably, in a process condemned by critics as 'dirty tariffication', the US and the EU countries, in particular, 'chose' tariff equivalents for their non-tariff barriers in the base period that were far higher (44 per cent and 61 per cent respectively, according to one study, cited in Panagariya 2002: 1,219) than was merited. Along with other technical manipulations of the agreement, this in effect meant that the prospect of effective agricultural liberalization emerging from the Uruguay Round settlement was eliminated. Members of the Cairns Group of Fair Traders in Agriculture, which had played such a prominent part in the Uruguay Round negotiations and which included countries such as Brazil, Chile, Colombia, Fiji, Hungary, Indonesia, Malaysia, the Philippines, Thailand and Uruguay as well as Australia, Canada and New Zealand, felt especially bitter. Second, many countries which had anticipated that the new WTO Agreement on Textiles and Clothing (ATC) would bring them substantial new access to the markets of MFA beneficiaries, such as the US, the EU and Canada, were disappointed to realize that the promised phase-out of quotas by 2005 was being 'back-loaded' and that no gains had as yet come their way. Third, many, many poorer countries had at last come to understand the implications and the costs of some of the new agreements, notably GATS, TRIPS and TRIMS, which they had signed up to as part of the Uruguay Round 'single undertaking'. Even supporters of free trade have recognized that, on their part, this was 'a colossal mistake' (Srinivasan 1999: 1,053). It meant that they were required to adopt standards in these policy areas that were already largely prevalent in the post-industrial world. One study, by Finger and Schuler (2000), calculated that implementation in just three areas – customs valuation, TRIPS and sanitary and phytosanitary measures – would cost each country approximately US$150 million. Moreover, there was to be added to this the economic cost of TRIPS in relation, for example, to paying royalties for the use of intellectual property patented in the scientifically advanced countries.

The point is that, by the opening of the Seattle conference, these issues were not only well understood, and the source of much anger, but also the basis for a series of quite specific proposals for redress. The LMG was the prime actor here (Narlikar and Odell 2003). By this time, its membership had been expanded to include the Dominican Republic, Honduras and Zimbabwe, which meant that it represented countries from a significant cross-section of regions (Africa, the Caribbean and Central America, South Asia and Southeast Asia) and with varying material capabilities, including two LDCs. The Group also became better institutionalized in this period, meeting on a weekly basis and dividing up tasks. Although proposals were generally submitted in the names of different combinations of countries, rather than the LMG as a whole, the Group in effect put forward numerous drafts in the preparatory process leading up to Seattle. These covered a whole range of matters, running from reform of TRIPS, the accelerated integration of textiles into the GATT and the elimination of export subsidies and domestic supports in agriculture to the creation of a 'development box' that would allow countries to deviate from their commitments in order to meet 'development' and food security needs. A common theme in all of them was 'the proposal to "operationalize" the provisions of each agreement for Special and Differential Treatment to developing countries – provisions that had been so worded as to remain "good intentions" with no obligations, as "best endeavour" clauses' (Raghavan 2000: 500). The LMG also sought to move beyond the 'implementation issue' itself by urging other actions designed to benefit the position within the WTO system of three other groupings of countries: the LDCs, the 'Small and Vulnerable Economies' and the HIPC group. It suggested, for example, the establishment of a working group to examine the relationship between trade and finance. Finally, and decisively, the Like-Minded Group remained firm in its hostility to the proposed negotiation of the 'Singapore issues', at least until the imbalances of the Uruguay Round had been corrected. To that extent, it was resistant to the whole notion of a comprehensive, new 'millennium round' being initiated at Seattle.

In other words, by the time that the Ministerial Conference opened in November 1999, it was obvious that there were vast gaps between the positions of the main contending parties and coalitions. The US and the EU initially tried to keep the various LMG proposals off the official agenda, but failed when the Chairman of the General Council of the WTO, Ambassador Ali Mchumo of Tanzania, disregarding the advice of the Secretariat and these pressures, tabled a draft text which incorporated ideas from every quarter. Although this was helpful in not immediately closing down the debate, it only highlighted the fact that no issue had been resolved in advance and that, instead, everything had been left to the ministers to decide. It is difficult to be sure quite what the negotiating tactics of the US and the EU were supposed to be. The US perhaps thought that, as the host country and chair of the meeting, it was well placed to push through a final declaration that suited its purposes. The EU may also have thought that, by avoiding attempts to forge compromises in advance amongst WTO ambassadors in Geneva, it could more easily press the LMG and others into agreeing to negotiate its favoured new issues of investment and competition policy. Neither seems to have appreciated in advance the extent of the new determination of the LMG and several other recently-formed groupings, such as the Group of Small and Vulnerable Economies, the LDCs (no fewer than 30 of which were members of the WTO at the time of Seattle), the Friends of the Development Box Group, the G24 on Services and the Friends of Geographical Indications. Region-based coalitions of states, notably the African Group and the Caribbean Community, were also very active and willing to stand up to pressure (Narlikar 2003: 182–94).

A further issue resurfaced in the last moments before Seattle opened and contributed to the growing sense of impending impasse, and that was the question of labour standards. The prompt here was the domestic political agenda of the Clinton White House, in particular its attempt to improve the presidential election chances of Vice-President Al Gore by playing to the sympathies of organized labour, one of the key constituencies in the US Democratic Party. However, Clinton's strategy was put together late and executed poorly. Despite having talked about trying once more to link trade rights with labour standards within the WTO for the best part of the year before Seattle, the US tabled a specific proposal to this effect only at the very end of the preparatory process, leaving no time for serious discussion (and persuasion) in advance of the meeting. Although the delay was probably a consequence of the priority which the administration had been giving to securing normal trading status for China within the US, opponents naturally formed the view that the US, and its allies on the labour rights issue, were hatching a strategy to bounce them into agreeing to something they had long opposed – and they were undoubtedly annoyed. This feeling was further exacerbated by US talk of imposing sanctions against countries which violated core labour standards, a threat which Clinton reiterated in an interview given just before he arrived in Seattle for the meeting.

All in all, given these various background circumstances, it would have been remarkable if the conference had agreed to launch a new trade round. Few expected success as the meeting opened; yet nobody quite envisaged the spectacular nature of the failure that unfolded. What happened was that the conference proceedings themselves became a cause of controversy and discord. The problems derived, in part, from the arrogant style of the chairperson, US Trade Representative (USTR) Charlene Barshefsky, who made little effort to acquaint herself with all the delegations and their positions. In other respects, they reflected an apparent willingness of the WTO Secretariat and representatives of the major trading states to bend and disregard frequently the rules of the organization on the conduct of meetings. Some of the ill-feeling here was carried over from the bitter clash that had taken place earlier in the year over the succession to the Director-Generalship of the WTO following Ruggiero's retirement. Michael Moore had been seen as the candidate of the 'Quad', especially the US, and consequently did not have the necessary authority amongst the membership as a whole to guide the meeting to some kind of consensus. In practice, too, many ministers found themselves either excluded from vital 'Green Room' meetings and other private consultations or simply unaware that they were taking place (Kwa 2002). In the end, it could be said that the bulk of the WTO's membership rebelled against the illegitimacy of the process in which they were involved. The African countries caught the mood of many in a formal statement issued on the third day of the conference in which they drew attention to the fact that there was 'no transparency in the proceedings' and expressed their concern over 'stated intentions to produce a ministerial text at any cost including at the cost of procedures designed to secure participation and consensus' (cited in Page 2002: 63). At the same time as discontent was growing inside the conference hall, protesters from assorted civil society groups were being chased and 'tear-gassed' by the Seattle police, giving rise to all the press stories about 'battle' in the streets. These latter events, although of great relevance to arguments about an emergent global civil society and the role played within it by international NGOs, were only really a side-show as far as global trade negotiations were concerned. They did not derail the meeting, even though some participants in the protests subsequently proclaimed their 'victory'.

Seattle broke down because of substantive differences between states, which remain the only bodies that can sign global trade deals. The hard reality is that there was nothing approaching a consensus within the meeting. Wilkinson (2001) has shown this in an interesting way by surveying all of the 132 official country statements made at the Ministerial. Only 48.5 per cent viewed a new round favourably; 16.6 per cent were unfavourable; and the remainder were either non-committal or did not express an opinion. On new issues, 30.3 per cent were unfavourable, 20.5 per cent favourable, and the remainder (nearly 48 per cent) non-committal or did not express an opinion. On the inclusion of labour standards, over 68 per cent of those delegations that expressed an opinion either perceived the Singapore Ministerial Declaration to be the definitive statement or expressed hostility. Viewed regionally, the picture presented was even more illuminating. Support for a new round was completely absent in South Asia and North Africa and registered only limited support in the Caribbean, Sub-Saharan Africa, the Middle East and the Pacific. A similar pattern was reflected in support (or lack of it) for the embrace of new issues. Finally, the only countries to register significant support for a degree of WTO involvement in labour standards were to be found in Western Europe and North America. Nevertheless, notwithstanding all this evidence of indifference (and, indeed, opposition) to the launch of a new round, it is quite conceivable that the 'Quad' would still have prevailed *if* it had been united. From this perspective, Seattle failed principally because the principal movers of all previous GATT rounds, the US and the EU, did not manage on this occasion to align their particular trade priorities sufficiently (Laird 2001).

Thus, on the last day of the conference – by which time it had become clear that the US administration's narrow domestic objective of shoring up Gore's presidential candidacy by means of the establishment of a WTO working group on trade and labour rights was not going to be achieved – Barshefsky allegedly rang Clinton (by now back in the White House) to get his agreement to her summoning a plenary session of the conference to announce its suspension and the 'freezing' of all proposals (Raghavan 2000). Neither, strictly speaking, was permitted by WTO rules, thereby creating a set of awkward legal uncertainties for the organization. The WTO Secretariat eventually posted on its web-site the edited version of Barshefsky's final statement, but it was unable to publish any official text or declaration at the conclusion of the WTO's Third Ministerial Conference.

Doha

There is no doubt that the outcome of the Seattle Ministerial badly damaged the perceived legitimacy of the WTO, then still a relatively new body. The self-confidence of the organization and its senior staff was also badly shaken. A number of responses were forthcoming, including a general public relations initiative to improve the WTO's image by means of wider release of documents and attempts to quell popular misconceptions about the powers and role of the organization. More substantively, talks on agriculture and services were begun under the rubric of the 'built-in agenda' mandated by the Uruguay Round. Although of importance in their own right, they were seen to open up the potential for cross-sector trade-offs to be made over the course of time in more extensive negotiations. A further review of the 'implementation issue' was set in train, charged with reaching decisions by the end of 2000 and presenting a final report to the next full Ministerial meeting. Just as importantly, the General Council under the chairmanship of Norway's ambassador to the WTO, Kåre Bryn, signalled its intention to try to address the many complaints about the lack of inclusivity and transparency in the WTO negotiation process which had arguably wrecked the Seattle meeting. Bryn in fact issued a set of new negotiating guidelines which urged that member states be advised of the intention to hold informal consultations, that they be given the right to make their views known on an issue of concern, that no assumption should be made that one member 'represented' any others, and that the outcome of all informal discussions be always and expeditiously reported back to the full membership (see Kwa 2002: 15). These proposals, if fully implemented, would have checked some of the abuses of power carried out by influential WTO members in Seattle, but they were not adopted as binding rules and, although many dissatisfied member states pressed for a firmer commitment, the reality was that this was as far as the WTO was prepared to go in reforming its own internal habits and procedures.

Having thereby made some gestures to 'rebuild trust', the 'Quad', with the active support of Moore and the Secretariat, set about renewing the momentum towards the launch of a new trade round. At the beginning of 2001 it was announced that the next Ministerial would be held in November in Doha in Qatar, a country whose political traditions did not exactly facilitate widespread public demonstration. The incoming George W. Bush administration in the US indicated that it was dropping the labour rights issue, thus taking off the table possibly the most contentious of all the points of conflict at Seattle, and the EU hinted at a softening of its position on the Singapore issues. It was widely reported too that the lead trade negotiators of these two key actors, Pascal Lamy as EU Trade Commissioner and Robert Zoellick as the new head of the office of the USTR, had a good personal relationship. The opportunities offered by a new round – as well as the alleged dangers to global prosperity of not embarking on one – were also deliberately talked up. Kofi Annan argued on several occasions that the launch of a round was essential if the further marginalization of the Least Developed Countries was to be avoided and, in an orchestrated statement, Moore's three predecessors as Director-General of the GATT/WTO warned that the 'undermining of the WTO and the notion of a rules-based trading system has gone too far' and needed to be arrested by new trade talks (*Financial Times*, 29 January 2001). Yet, in a candid speech to the General Council in July 2001, Moore admitted that serious political impediments still stood in the way of a new round. Political pressure was being built and was applied in two unorthodox 'mini-ministerials' held in Mexico and in Singapore in August and October 2001 respectively. These were informal gatherings, like the 'Green Rooms', to which only 20 or so countries were invited. One significant difference, post-Seattle, was that the coordinator of the LDC Group, Tanzania, and of the African Group, Nigeria, were included. The problem was that the Secretariat and the leading trading countries clearly presumed that this was sufficiently inclusive and that the support of Tanzania and Nigeria would deliver that of all the countries they were being deemed to represent. This was manifestly questionable, but nevertheless made it harder for these groups of countries to complain that they had been left out of the pre-politics of Doha.

One other event crucially shaped the run-up to the Doha Ministerial, and that was 9/11. Fear of another attack briefly threatened the cancellation of the whole meeting and the subsequent US military intervention in Afghanistan, which was mounted from a US base in Qatar, gave rise to suggestions that the WTO should shift venue, even in the last stages of planning. In the event, Doha went ahead and was convened in a political climate utterly changed by the aftermath of September 11. Prior to the attacks, the leading trading states had in effect acknowledged the existence of a political space in global trade negotiations within which dissident countries could operate, at least to some effect. After the attacks, they saw their opportunity and moved ruthlessly to close it off. Zoellick, Lamy and Moore toured the world, proclaiming that freer trade would underpin the war on terrorism and was thus directly linked to the new security agenda. This greatly increased the vulnerability of all the countries that had hitherto been opposed to the launch of a new round. As Aileen Kwa (2002: 35) put it, 'no matter how ludicrous the linking of a new round was to the fight with terrorism, countries were tiptoeing around the threat of possibly being implicated as supporting or harbouring terrorists'. The effect was also to involve heads of state in the politics of the WTO in a much more overt way, which served to diminish the impact of Geneva-based representatives and thereby negate some of the impact of the work that had been done at that level to rebuild a measure of confidence in the negotiation process.

Doha was undoubtedly a tough meeting. Largely because of the mood created by 9/11 and its aftermath, there was not generated the open anger on the part of many participating delegates which so characterized Seattle. But, that said, the tactics deployed by the 'Quad' were strikingly similar and certainly did not live up to the promises made in Ambassador Bryn's guidelines. According to Bello (2002: 276–7), they included the following:

- Pushing a highly unbalanced draft declaration and presenting it to the ministerial as a 'clean text' on which there allegedly was consensus, thus restricting the arena of substantive discussion and making it difficult for developing countries to register fundamental objections without seeming 'obstructionist'.
- Pitting developing country representatives from capitals against their counterparts from Geneva, with the latter being characterized as 'recalcitrant' or 'narrow'.
- Employing direct threats, as the United States did when it warned Haiti and the Dominican Republic to cease opposition to its position on government procurement or risk cancellation of their preferential trade arrangements.
- Buying off countries [Bello described Pakistan as being notably quiet at Doha and Nigeria as reversing its earlier hostility to the draft declaration, both as a result of receipt of substantial economic and military aid from Washington].
- Reinstituting the infamous 'Green Room' on 13 and 14 November [the last and the extra spill-over day of the conference], when some 20 handpicked countries were isolated from the rest and 'delegated' by the WTO Secretariat, the United States, the EU and the other big trading powers, to come up with the final declaration. These countries were selected undemocratically, and efforts by some developing country representatives to insert themselves into this select group were rebuffed, some gently, others quite explicitly, as was the case with a delegate from Uganda ... [and] ...
- Pressuring developing countries by telling them they would bear the onus for causing the collapse of another Ministerial, the collapse of the WTO, and the deepening of the global recession that would allegedly be the consequence of these two events.

Even this list does not exhaust the tricks that were deployed to secure an agreement. Delegates learned on arrival in Doha that the chairman of the conference, the Qatari Minister of Finance, Economy and Trade, Youssef Hussain Kamal, had appointed, without consultation with the whole membership, six 'friends of the chair' to act as facilitators for each of the key negotiating areas. All came from countries known to be sympathetic to the launch of a round: namely, Singapore, Switzerland, Chile, South Africa, Canada and Mexico. By dint of these and other manoeuvres, allied with much fuller technical preparation of the ground for agreement than had occurred in Seattle, the resistance of those countries opposed to a new round (notably the members of the LMG) was slowly and painfully worn down and their fragile unity eventually broken.

What, then, was the ultimate Doha deal which, according to Mike Moore, 'saved' the WTO? The conference produced three major documents signed by all of the then 142 members of the WTO – the Declaration on the TRIPS Agreement and Public Health, the Decision on Implementation-related Issues and Concerns, and the Doha Ministerial Declaration itself – as well as two 'waivers' from GATT articles designed to benefit specific groups of countries. In deference to the concerns of opponents, the Doha Declaration referred to a work programme, not a round. But, in the neat phrasing of Sam Laird (2002: 60), what was agreed was 'a round by any other name'. For this reason, we need to make sense of each of these documents in turn.

The Declaration on TRIPS and Public Health (World Trade Organization 2001b) was a purely political statement. It arose out of the apparent conflict within the TRIPS Agreement between patent protection and the obvious, urgent need for access to drugs to cope with major health epidemics such as HIV/AIDS. This was brought to a head during 2001 following the South African government's decision to permit local manufacture of generic anti-HIV/AIDS drugs (Cullet 2003; Odell and Sell 2003). Publicized in advance of Doha by an energetic NGO campaign, the cause acquired a strong emotional appeal and was pushed at the Ministerial by the African Group in particular. The resulting Declaration is generally considered to effect some slight weakening of the TRIPS Agreement in that it recognized each member's right to issue compulsory licences to manufacture patented drugs in a 'national emergency or other circumstances of extreme urgency, it being understood that public health crises, including those relating to HIV/AIDS, tuberculosis, malaria and other epidemics' could represent just such circumstances (WTO document WT/MIN(01)/DEC/W/2, Clause 5c). It was obvious that the precise extent of the leeway that this created was likely to be tested in due course within the WTO's dispute settlement procedure, and may in practice be found to be limited. After all, there was nothing in the statement that promised or even held out the possibility of a change to the text of TRIPS, rendering it (in the longer term) 'a victory for Washington' (Bello 2002: 274). But, in Doha at the time, the publication of the Declaration, which also gave the LDCs an extra ten years (until 2016) to implement that part of TRIPS which related to pharmaceutical products, was seen as a minor triumph by those hostile to a new round and it unquestionably contributed to the dynamics of their ultimate acquiescence in that outcome.

For its part, the Decision on Implementation-related Issues and Concerns (World Trade Organization 2001a) sought in effect to close the debate about implementation of various Uruguay Round provisions which had run, as we have seen, since the moment that that package of agreements had been concluded in 1994. It tried to do so by passing all the substantive implementation issues forward to the negotiating agenda summarized in the Doha Declaration, with the 'Decision' in the main offering only further promises to 'take note', deploy 'best endeavours' and act in 'good faith'. For example, in the reference to the Agreement on Agriculture, members were merely urged to 'exercise restraint in challenging measures ... by developing countries to promote rural development and adequately address food security concerns' (WTO document WT/MIN(01)/W/10, Clause 2.1). In the reference to the ATC, it was again agreed that those provisions 'relating to the early integration of products and the elimination of quota restrictions should be effectively utilised' (WTO document WT/MIN(01)/W/10, Clause 4.1). These were typical of the tenor of the document. At best, it can be said to have added modestly to the moral pressure on the US, the EU and Japan to carry through past undertakings; at worst, it constituted what the Pakistani representative at Doha reportedly described as 'almost a bare cupboard' (cited in Panagariya 2002: 1,207).

The Doha Ministerial Declaration (World Trade Organization 2001c) was obviously the cornerstone of the Doha deal. In his analysis of the work programme which it laid out, Arvind Panagariya (2002) has usefully drawn attention to the fact that it fell into three categories: an agenda with a clear negotiating mandate, an agenda with an 'ambiguous' mandate, and a study programme. The first of these, the core negotiating agenda, wrapped together six issues (implementation, agriculture, services, market access for non-agricultural products, trade and environment, and WTO rules) as the elements of another putative 'single undertaking', which was to be agreed by a deadline of no later than 1 January 2005. The negotiations themselves were to be bound by certain specific commitments made in the Declaration, some of which were highly controversial and only agreed after intensive bargaining. As regards agriculture, for example, the objectives were specified as 'substantial improvements in market access; reductions of, with a view to phasing out, all forms of export subsidies; and substantial reductions in trade-distorting domestic support' (WTO document WT/MIN(01)/DEC/W/1, Clause 13). The EU initially objected to the expression 'with a view to phasing out', but was ultimately prevailed upon to accept it by the US and the Cairns Group. In return, as it were, the EU insisted on the reference to 'all forms of export subsidies', which was more than the US wanted. 'Developing countries', as they were described in this part of the Declaration, won the concession that S&D treatment should be 'an integral part' of all aspects of the agricultural negotiations. They also secured a similar commitment within the decision to open up talks on market access for industrial products. The other aspect of the agreed negotiating agenda worth highlighting relates to trade and the environment, which had been under study at the WTO for some time but was brought forward for negotiation at Doha for the first time. The EU pressed the issue as hard as it could in the face of objections from the LMG and other groupings and got its way, although the scope of the actual agreement was quite limited, being in essence talks about the relationship between WTO rules and the trade obligations set out in existing multilateral environmental agreements.

The agenda where there was only an ambiguous mandate was that relating to the Singapore issues. The battle-lines in Doha were just as before – the EU insisting on their inclusion, while many countries in Africa, the Caribbean and Asia were determined to keep them out of the negotiations – and the argument was as fierce as ever. The eventual compromise was unavoidably delphic for, in each of the relevant clauses of the Declaration, it was stated that members 'agree that negotiations will take place after the Fifth Session of the Ministerial Conference on the basis of a decision to be taken, *by explicit consensus*, at that Session on modalities of negotiations' (WTO document WT/MIN(01)/DEC/W/1, Clauses 20, 23, 26 and 27, my emphasis). From one perspective, this could be read to mean that only the modalities remained to be settled, with the decision to draw these issues into the prospective single undertaking already taken; from the other perspective, the requirement that the modalities be decided by explicit consensus created the opportunity for a veto by any country at the Fifth Ministerial. India took the latter view and insisted before it signed up to the Declaration that Youssef Hussain Kamal, as the chairman of the Doha conference, clarify in his concluding remarks the meaning of the language being used. He obliged with the following statement:

> Let me say that with respect to the reference to an 'explicit consensus' being needed ... for a decision to be taken at the Fifth Session of the Ministerial Conference, my understanding is that, at that Session, a decision would indeed need to be taken, by explicit consensus, before negotiations on Trade and Investment and Trade and Competition Policy, Transparency in Government Procurement, and Trade Facilitation could proceed.
>
> In my view, this would give each Member the right to take a position on modalities that would prevent negotiations from proceeding after the Fifth Session of the Ministerial Conference until that Member is prepared to join in an explicit consensus.

This statement was appended to the Declaration and in that sense formed part of the official conference proceedings; yet it did not and could not have the same legal standing as the Declaration itself. In other words, although the Chair's clarification was itself quite clear in its interpretation of the wording, the argument about the incorporation of the Singapore issues into the Doha 'round' had not been resolved and would be re-run at the next Ministerial.

Finally, the Doha Declaration embraced a study programme. This was of significance because WTO practice already showed that this was a route by which issues could eventually find their way into active negotiation. The topics covered were wide-ranging and included the initiation of new work on trade and investment, on the interaction between trade and competition policy and on trade and the environment, all of which satisfied EU concerns. At the same time, the LMG secured the establishment of working groups on trade, debt and finance and on technology transfer; the Group of Small and Vulnerable Economies lobbied successfully for a work programme designed to bring about their 'fuller integration ... into the multilateral trading system' (WTO document WT/MIM(01)/DEC/W/1, Clause 35); and the LDCs expressed a range of anxieties which led to the Director-General being asked to report directly to the General Council and the Fifth Ministerial on all issues affecting this group of countries. Also, on S&D, the Declaration took formal note of a proposed framework agreement proposed by some member countries and agreed that all S&D provisions would be reviewed, with a view to 'making them more precise, effective and operational' (WTO document WT/MIN(01)/DEC/W/1, Clause 44). Of course, in one sense these various commitments to study issues meant very little; they could just have been short-term ways of buying off dissent and shifting it into the future. Equally, they could provide the space within which political cases could be argued and pressure built. Only the outcome of subsequent meetings would reveal which was the case.

The last pieces of the Doha jigsaw were the two waivers: one waiving Article X111 of GATT in relation to the EU's recently revised banana regime which continued to offer a measure of protection to the small Eastern Caribbean banana-producing islands, the other waiving Article 1 of GATT in relation to the Cotonou Convention signed in 2000 between the EU and the African, Caribbean and Pacific (ACP) grouping which also continued to offer trade and aid benefits to former colonies of EU member states. Neither had any direct link to the Doha Declaration and could have been handled as normal WTO business, but they were deliberately brought forward to Doha so that the ACP countries, in particular, could be tied into support for the launch of the new round. Agreement to the waiver was the pre-eminent goal of the ACP countries throughout the conference, and it is known that on the last day of the meeting six African countries within the ACP went to Moore and threatened to block the whole outcome unless it was approved. Having achieved their specific objective, the ACP countries then softened their stance on many of the other matters on which the wider LMG was trying to hold the line (Narlikar and Odell 2003). It is a moot point whether the ACP gained something it might not otherwise have done, or whether it gave away other causes in exchange for something that would in any case have been conceded in due course.

As can be seen, the politics of Doha spread over many issues that were interrelated in a most complex fashion. This makes it difficult to interpret. The final deal was energetically presented by Moore and the WTO as a 'Doha Development Agenda', and there is no doubt that a range of rhetorical devices were deployed to sustain this impression. Panagariya (2002: 1,223) noted, for example, that the main Ministerial Declaration used the phrase 'least developed' countries 29 times, 'developing' countries 24 times and 'LDC' 19 times, although he quickly went on to say that such a 'pro-development' reading does not stand up to close, critical scrutiny. Whatever the specific and/or rhetorical commitments made to countries within these categories, the fact remains that they conceded the launch of a new 'round' without prior correction of the imbalances of the Uruguay Round. That said, in Panagariya's (2002: 1,226) judgement at least, the 'bottom line' is that the Doha outcome was 'an unambiguous improvement' over the Uruguay deal. Labour rights were excluded; so, arguably, were the Singapore issues (although, if one took a more cynical view and assumed that they would in some way form part of future negotiations, then the balance of the argument would move against Panagariya's reading); and greater trade liberalization, which was the core of the actual Doha negotiating agenda, did offer opportunities for gains for at least some poorer countries or groups of countries. It would be wrong, though, to conclude that there occurred some softening of stance on the part of the leading post-industrial trading states. To quote Panagariya (2002: 1,226) one more time, they remained as 'hard-nosed' in Doha as they had been throughout the Uruguay Round. He has pointed out that on most of the occasions when demands from 'developing countries' led to positive outcomes it was because they received support from one or more of the major players, as when the US insisted on the phasing-out of export subsidies or the EU also pressed the Cotonou waiver. As we noted too, the Declaration on TRIPS and Public Health was really the product of civil society pressure, mainly from within the rich world. By contrast, on matters where they had to fight alone, such as implementation, the LMG countries were generally ground down and had to content themselves with the partial blocking, at best, of the Singapore issues and the insertion of some items into the study programme.

In the final analysis, then, perhaps the real political story of Doha is that, after 9/11, the United States needed to show that it could maintain an open global economy and therefore made rather more concessions than it might have done in more normal circumstances. By the same token, it also realized that it had to ensure the participation of at least the bigger non-OECD countries, which gave India, in particular, just enough room for manoeuvre to be able to hold out in the final 'Green Room' and insist on 'explicit consensus' before the Singapore issues could be incorporated. India's Minister of Commerce, Murasoli Maran, was much abused as 'the villain of the piece' in US and European press coverage of Doha, even though he was supported by the representatives of several African and Caribbean countries until the very last moment of the conference. But there was a pointer here to some of the new realities of WTO politics: a country of the power of India cannot shape the agenda, but it can almost break deals if its leaders and representatives can keep their nerve for long enough. In that sense one further significant feature of the Doha Ministerial was that, in the interstices of the meeting, China formally acceded to membership of the WTO, becoming the organization's 143rd and most populous member (Breslin 2003). At this time its role in the negotiation of the round could not be predicted with any confidence, but after Doha it was apparent that it would matter.

Cancún

Slipped into the Doha Ministerial Declaration in the rush to bring the conference to a conclusion was a statement that the overall conduct of the forthcoming negotiations should be supervised by a Trade Negotiations Committee (TNC) operating under the authority of the WTO General Council. Although such a committee had run the Uruguay Round, thereby establishing the precedent for its creation, many LMG states took the view that it was no longer necessary because the General Council had now been established and given the specific authority under the Marrakesh Agreement to make decisions on negotiations between ministerials. They also objected strongly to the proposal made by the 'Quad' as soon as the whole trade caravan returned to Geneva that Moore (or rather, to be precise, the Director-General *ex officio*) be asked to chair the TNC (Kwa 2002: 71–9). Moore's style and his perceived bias in favour of the 'Quad' had become increasingly controversial as his period in office proceeded and it took the familiar panoply of techniques, from the convening of 'Green Room' meetings to pressure placed on national ministers in their capitals, to push through his appointment, which was formally agreed to be 'an exceptional arrangement'. The LMG also managed to get agreement on another set of guidelines that sought to address the systemic WTO problems of inclusiveness and transparency, but the reality was that it had been badly divided at Doha and was further split on the issue of the TNC chairmanship by the fact that Southeast Asian countries knew that Panitchpakdi was soon to become Director-General (and thus also TNC chairman) as a consequence of the original compromise on the appointment in 1999. It is noteworthy, though, that China openly backed LMG calls for officials in future to produce negotiating texts that accurately reflected differences of position when and where they existed.

All in all, the first few months after Doha saw very little progress made on any part of the WTO's agenda. Meetings, both formal and informal, came and went, with neither the US nor the EU, the normal instigators of movement, making any effort to set out a seductive negotiating stance. In fact, the reverse looked to be the case. The Bush administration, in particular, took a number of protectionist measures. For example, in March 2002 it succumbed to the US steel industry's long-standing demands and imposed punitive tariffs on foreign steel imports, justifying its action by reference to the WTO's safeguards provisions. Two months later it substantially increased government support for US farmers in a new farm bill, again claiming that these subsidies were compatible with WTO rules. As Jagdish Bhagwati (2004: 57) noted, even if these claims were true (and the steel tariffs were later deemed to be illegal by a WTO panel), 'the symbolism was bad: one cannot start negotiations to reduce protection and then follow immediately by raising subsidies and trade barriers'. But, as he went on also to argue, the Bush administration realized that its free trade credentials had been more severely damaged than it had anticipated and 'beat a rapid retreat' (Bhagwati 2004: 57) on the most damaging of the measures, those relating to agriculture. Zoellick and the US Agriculture Secretary, Ann Veneman, were thus able to unveil a proposal for the planned post-Doha farm trade talks which involved cutting back US trade-distorting agricultural subsidies to roughly what US farmers received before the farm bill had been passed. At the same time the US also announced an extension of its review of exemptions from the steel tariffs and, in a telling success, managed in August 2002 to get Congress to renew the President's fast-track negotiating authority, something that had been denied Clinton on at least two occasions. For its part, the EU led the attacks on the US steel tariffs and farm bill, but in July 2002 produced a scheme to 'reform' its own Common Agricultural Policy that was, by general consent, remarkably unambitious. Although the plan proposed at last to weaken the direct link between production and subsidies under the EU's agricultural regime, it did not cut the overall size of the available support for EU farmers and it was apparent that the opposition of France in particular, but also Ireland, Greece and Portugal, had limited the EU Commission's scope for change.

By early 2003 the next Ministerial – the WTO's Fifth – due to be held in Cancún in September at what was meant to be the mid-point of the 'round', was beginning to come dangerously close and there was much press discussion of the causes and consequences of a 'stalled' process. The growing Iraq crisis also diverted the political attention of the 'Quad' and was of itself hardly conducive to consensus building. As regards the interests of the non-'Quad' countries, the early draft papers tabled within the TNC on agriculture only revealed how far apart the freer traders and the continuing protectionists still were on this issue; no progress was being made either on the implementation agenda, or on S&D; this left the matter of TRIPS and public health as the one area where the post-Doha log-jam could conceivably be broken. The issue was the detail of the implementation of the agreement, forged at Doha, to weaken the strength of patent protection under TRIPS in the midst of national health emergencies in poor countries. The negotiation centrally involved the Bush administration because of its close economic and political ties, via campaign funding, to the leading US pharmaceutical companies. The companies feared that generic drugs producers in countries such as Brazil and India would be able to flood the market with cheap versions of their patented products. A draft agreement along the lines of the Doha deal was single-handedly blocked by the US from December 2002 until just two weeks before ministers were due to gather in Cancún when, in a significant concession, the US withdrew its objections, having won commitments that the accord would be implemented 'in good faith to protect public health' and not for 'commercial policy objectives', and that most OECD countries, as well as many of the Eastern and Central European countries soon to join the EU, would opt out of the system (*Financial Times*, 28 August 2003). The US hoped that its gesture would enable it to win support on other issues in Cancún itself, but perhaps forgot that 'a concession made can no longer be used as a bargaining chip' (Bhagwati 2004: 57).

With this TRIPS-related controversy resolved, at least to an extent, the Cancún Ministerial was dominated by four areas of dispute: agriculture, the particular position of cotton, what came to be referred to as Strategic Products (SPs) and Special Safeguard Mechanisms (SSMs), and – as ever – the Singapore issues. Of these, agriculture appeared to be the key to success or failure. The first important move was made by the US and the EU when they jointly tabled a proposed text on agricultural trade approximately a month before Cancún opened. Prior to this, some Cairns Group members had hoped that the US would lean closer to their free trade stance; equally, some countries with a more defensive outlook on agriculture had looked forward to the EU aligning itself with their viewpoint. Both were therefore disappointed when the 'two subsidizing superpowers', as they were described by the Brazilian Foreign Minister, Celso Amorim (*Wall Street Journal*, 25 September 2003), sought essentially to consolidate their historically protectionist stances on agriculture by offering only limited concessions to agricultural exporters elsewhere. The US in fact backed off its earlier, rather more generous, proposals in order to stand with the EU, a tactic that only served to remind many non-'Quad' members of the secret and decisive 'Blair House accord' reached by the same two key players in the final stages of the negotiation of the Uruguay Round. The effect was certainly to embitter still further the agricultural talks.

In response, Brazil and China drafted an alternative text that was then signed by another 18 countries: Argentina, Bolivia, Chile, China, Colombia, Costa Rica, Cuba, Ecuador, El Salvador, Guatemala, Mexico, Pakistan, Paraguay, Peru, the Philippines, South Africa, Thailand and Venezuela. Although there had not been an explicit intention to form a new negotiating group, the signatories eventually came to be called the Group of 20 (G20). The draft itself took a positive line, calling for significant cuts in the domestic support for farmers provided by the big post-industrial states, substantial improvements in market access for the products of 'developing countries' and the elimination of export subsidies by 'developed countries' over a specified time period (WTO document WT/MIN(03)/W/16). The document was also careful to include a number of references to S&D and the special concerns of the LDCs. These added to the breadth of the support that was quickly generated. In the light of the effective disintegration of the LMG in the last phase of Doha, the emergence of the G20 constituted an absolutely critical moment in global trade politics. Its membership combined some of the largest and most powerful states outside the OECD (Brazil, India, South Africa and, notably, China) with many others much smaller; it cleverly incorporated aggressive Cairns Group agricultural traders (such as Chile) with defensive food importers (such as India); and it had unquestionable moral authority in that it claimed to represent the interests of over half the world's population and over 60 per cent of its farmers. Moreover, in all of its presentations it was technically highly competent. In short, in the words of Narlikar and Tussie (2004: 953), 'here was a coalition that was capable of making a difference, through the logic of its argument but also the sheer strength of its weight'.

Neither was the G20 the only new grouping to come into being just before Cancún and thereafter play a significant role in the politics of the Ministerial. There was also the group of four cotton-producing West and Central African countries: Mali, Benin, Chad and Burkina Faso. They were exercised in particular by the protection that the US gave to its domestic cotton growers and proposed a complete phase-out of subsidies on cotton, together with financial compensation for cotton-producing LDCs until the subsidies had disappeared (WTO document TN/AG/GEN/4). Their plight attracted a lot of attention and sympathy. Another new force was the Alliance on Strategic Products and Special Safeguards Mechanisms (SP/SSM), led by Indonesia and the Philippines and drawing on the support of no fewer than 33 countries by the end of the conference (hence G33). Prompted by the continuing failure of the post-Doha talks to come up with adequate S&D provision, its original idea was to allow poor countries to define unilaterally what was their special product and be awarded special treatment of it. Finally, there emerged a so-called Core Group of countries determined to resist the full inclusion in the WTO process of the Singapore issues. This initially included 12 countries: Bangladesh, Cuba, Egypt, India, Indonesia, Kenya, Malaysia, Nigeria, Pakistan, Venezuela, Zambia and Zimbabwe. It responded to an EU paper which arrogantly presumed that negotiation on the Singapore issues would start after Cancún by reiterating its understanding of the need for 'explicit consensus' on the modalities of negotiation, as secured at Doha, *before* talks could begin (WTO document WT/GC/W/501). It also suggested that the four issues did not necessarily have to be treated in the same way. As will be seen, this stance grew in support as the conference proceeded.

In the event, it was indeed the running sore of the Singapore issues, not agriculture as many had assumed, which became the 'deal-breaker' at Cancún. By the time the last day was reached the G20 had succeeded in blocking the preferred US/EU agricultural deal, sustained to a significant extent by the moral support of the Africa Group, the ACP and the LDCs, even though many of these countries were concerned about the impact of further agricultural trade liberalization on their existing preferences within the markets of 'Quad' countries. There had also been only the most minimal movement on cotton. The major items left on the agenda were the Singapore issues, which the EU was still pressing as hard as it could. In these circumstances the coordinators of the African Group, the ACP and the LDCs all indicated that they were not prepared to agree to a deal which included even one of the four issues. The South Korean representative responded by saying that his country could not accept any deal without all four issues and was backed in this stance by Japan. Faced with this situation, Lamy consulted with EU government representatives about 'unbundling' the issues and offered to take two of them (investment and competition policy) off the table in exchange for agreement to initiate negotiations on the remainder. Some participants even thought that he might withdraw a third (government procurement) in order to salvage agreement on trade facilitation talks, but it was all too late and clouded in too much suspicion. Although Panitchpakdi was reported to have pressed India and Malaysia, in particular, to respond positively to the EU's olive branch, they would not break ranks, and neither would the new Africa Group/ACP/LDC alliance, which was already being called the Group of 90 (G90) and being described by its adherents as the majority grouping in an organization with 146 member states! At this point, even though discussion could have been extended into the next day, the conference chairman, the Mexican Minister of Foreign Affairs, Luis Ernesto Derbez, called proceedings to a close. There was agreed a short six-paragraph ministerial statement (which was an improvement at least on Seattle). It cheekily claimed that 'considerable progress' had been made, but accepted that 'more work needs to be done in some key areas'. Acknowledging 'this setback', it urged that work continue on outstanding issues 'with a renewed sense of urgency and purpose and taking fully into account all the views ... expressed in this conference' (WTO document WT/MIN(03)/W/24). Specifically, the chairman of the General Council was asked to work closely with the Director-General with a view to convening a meeting of senior officials by the end of 2003 in order to set the Doha 'round' back on track.

Cancún thus collapsed, which meant that yet another WTO Ministerial had failed to reach a consensual conclusion. It is true that the complaints about illegitimate procedure that had hampered both Seattle and Doha were still present, although they were perhaps more muted (Narlikar and Wilkinson 2004). In particular, the draft texts circulated in advance of, and then during, the meeting by the chairman of the General Council were widely seen by the representatives of non-'Quad' countries as being biased in favour of US and EU positions and as effectively ignoring the diligent work of the G20, the SP/SSM alliance and others. But these concerns did not wreck Cancún as they had Seattle; the problem was much more the core politics. On the one hand, it has been argued that the US and the EU did not want to make progress with the 'round' sufficiently badly, certainly not enough to face down their powerful farm lobbies at a time of slow domestic economic growth and generally uncertain political prospects (specifically, the 2004 presidential election in the US and the accommodation of new member states in the EU as of May 2004) (Garten 2003: 49). In particular, it could be said that the Bush administration was insufficiently focused on the WTO. As a consequence, therefore, the 'Quad' did not strive to break the G20 in the way it had the LMG in Doha. On the other hand, it has been just as forcefully suggested that the impressive and striking solidarity of the 'developing country coalitions', especially but not exclusively the G20, was 'a significant new development' reflective of an adjustment in 'the global balance of forces' (Bello 2003). In reality, both interpretations were somewhat exaggerated. The US and the EU were far from indifferent to the future of the 'round'. Equally, the unity of the G20 was not tested to the bitter end because of the focus given to the Singapore issues on the last day of the meeting. The reality is that there are real divisions of interest between so-called 'developing countries' over agriculture; these run through even the G20, let alone the wider body of support – the 'alliances of sympathy' (Narlikar and Wilkinson 2004: 457) – that it was able to assemble in Cancún. To take just the most striking example of this, it is unavoidably the case that producers of temperate products will gain much more from agricultural liberalization than those countries that only grow tropical commodities and/or are net food importers (Morrissey 2003).

In the end, the best explanation for the break-up of the Cancún Ministerial can be found in flaws in the tactics of all the parties. The US conceivably misjudged the extent of the impact of its TRIPS concession and perhaps would have been better negotiating separately from the EU on agriculture. The EU only sought to break up the Singapore issues when trust in its approach had virtually evaporated. The leaders of the G20 made no attempt to offer reductions in their countries' own levels of domestic agricultural protection and could plausibly have put more pressure on the US if they had done so. Finally, the nascent G90 could have seized the opportunity to agree to the dropping from the WTO agenda of two, perhaps three, of the Singapore issues. Much of the immediate press commentary after the end of the Ministerial was highly pessimistic in tone. It made rather too much of Zoellick's assignation of blame to the 'won't do' countries and apparent desire to press ahead with alternative bilateral trade deals with 'can-do' countries (*Financial Times*, 22 September 2003); interpreted Lamy's call for a 'moment of reflection' (*Financial Times*, 4 November 2003) as a disinclination to return to the talks; and generally erred in attributing the collapse of Cancún to an oversimplistic polarization of 'North' and 'South'. Although it was obviously true that the round was unlikely to be wrapped up by 1 January 2005, as initially proposed, the point about bad tactics is, of course, that they can be changed. More astute observers of the long history of global trade talks noted that the Uruguay Round had been punctuated by 'breakdowns', was not concluded on schedule and yet was still brought to consummation in the end (Bhagwati 2004; Wilkinson 2004). They argued, in other words, that Cancún was actually no more than the temporary setback that the departing ministers had claimed in their brief summary statement.

Events proved this point of view to be correct. Although no agreement on a future negotiating framework (which in essence was what Cancún was about) was reached by the initial post-Ministerial deadline of mid-December 2003, the next target – the end of July 2004 – was achieved. The US demonstrated more active engagement and increasingly disassociated itself from the EU on the key matters of domestic agricultural support payments and the Singapore issues; it also rescinded its steel tariffs in the face of the censure of a WTO dispute panel. The EU overrode French opposition to shift its position also on agriculture and eventually agreed to drop all the Singapore issues except trade facilitation. The G20 did not disintegrate, although its membership fell for a period before growing again; it, too, worked its way towards a compromise on agriculture, facilitated by the election of a different government in India in May 2004. The G90, in turn, was prevailed upon by all of the parties (including the G20) not to wreck the emerging deal. In general, the 'Quad' had come to the realization that the plethora of new 'developing country coalitions' could no longer effectively be excluded, but had instead to be brought into the game if another break-down was to be avoided. More broadly, it was grasped on all sides of the debate that the WTO could not afford another failure without its credibility and perhaps its very existence being threatened, especially amidst an ideological climate in which US neoconservatism viewed all multilateral bodies with suspicion.

The resulting 'July package' certainly did not resolve all the problems of the 'Doha Development Agenda'. It cleared the blockage of the four Singapore issues; adopted a 'tiered' formula for the elimination of agricultural subsidies whereby countries promised to make qualitatively and quantitatively different reductions according to their historic levels; came up with a compromise whereby cotton would be negotiated within the overall agricultural talks but would be handled 'ambitiously, expeditiously and specifically'; and incorporated a commitment to the designation of strategic products and special safeguards largely satisfactory to the G33. The rest, broadly speaking, was left to the next WTO Ministerial, to be held in Hong Kong in December 2005 (although, significantly, this was not set as the time by which the negotiations had to be completed). Some difficult process issues will also travel to the next ministerial meeting. Although the July deal was ultimately signed off by all the WTO's member states, the reality is that it was struck in effect by an informal group of 'five interested parties', – the representatives of the US, the EU, Australia, Brazil and India – who met frequently in Geneva, over dinner in London and in the sidelines of other meetings until they found a way to come together on the necessary negotiating framework. Brazil and India kept in close touch with their G20 allies, but that did not prevent many other countries, as diverse as Switzerland and some G90 participants, expressing considerable disquiet about their exclusion from these vital talks. Indeed, in a pointer to conflicts to come, some informed observers have expressed doubt as to whether the G90 can really be said to have obtained enough from the deal (Page 2004).

Conclusion

As we have seen, the global politics of trade is now conducted wholly within the framework of the WTO. All the key issues are brought to this particular table. This means that, as an arena of political contestation, trade is more confined and more structured than, say, finance. The rules, habits and general style of the WTO clearly have a significant effect on the politics that takes place in and around the organization, and here it has been a problem that several of the techniques most frequently used in WTO meetings (the 'Green Rooms', chair's drafts, 'friends of the chair' and so on) have been viewed with suspicion and growing hostility by many member states. They smack of manipulation, not facilitation. Even the Secretariat, which ought in theory to act as a source of neutral support for all WTO members, has come to be widely seen, certainly during the period of Moore's leadership, as institutionally prejudiced in favour of the positions of the 'Quad'. These are all important features of the contemporary trade negotiation process, but they are not necessarily fundamental to the character of the WTO as an institution in the sense that they could never be changed. Amrita Narlikar has, however, recently made the interesting argument that the ministerial process itself (by which she means the central role played within the WTO by these biennial meetings) has perhaps sabotaged the working of the organization by creating periodic crescendos in the negotiation of trade which serve only to expose, and conceivably heighten, the 'power asymmetries' between the many participants (Narlikar 2004: 414). This takes us close to the nub of the matter, which is the power politics that goes on inside the WTO. The WTO may indeed be a 'mediaeval' body, the phrase used to describe it by Lamy in moments of exasperation at the end of both Seattle and Cancún; its procedures may be open to malpractice, with those best placed to exploit them reluctant to countenance reform; but at the end of the day the WTO remains a member-driven organization charged with hosting and resolving the confrontational politics which has always been provoked by the negotiation of global trade rules.

The key point about such negotiations in the contemporary WTO era is that just about every state in the world is involved, albeit with markedly different levels of commitment and resource. The days when the GATT was a 'rich man's club' outside which 'developing countries' quietly waited for crumbs are comprehensively over. Many of these countries are now fully engaged in the global negotiation of trade and have created a diverse array of coalitions that in their intricacy shatter the notion of any single, or even overriding, 'developing countries' (or G77) position. The larger ones, such as Brazil, China and India, are not only very alert to their trading interests but also possessed of enough strength to pursue them increasingly vigorously. What counts in trade politics is share of the global market. Obviously, the US, the EU and Japan continue to account for the bulk of world trade, which still gives them most of the carrots and sticks they need to dominate negotiations. They have generally worked to build what Peter Drahos (2002) has called 'circles of consensus'. First, the US and the EU have come together around a common position; this has subsequently been extended to the rest of the 'Quad', namely, Japan and Canada; other OECD countries will then be brought on board, followed by 'friends' such as South Africa, Chile or Singapore; finally, an attempt is made to win over more awkward potential partners such as India, Pakistan and Malaysia, and lately China; at this point the rest are expected to follow and in practice have little choice but to do so if they want to stay a part of the trading system. What is striking, though, is that these concentric circles have come to be harder and harder for the 'Quad' to close. There are still massive disparities in the size of delegations which countries take to WTO Ministerials: according to one account, the US and the EU had over 800 officials each in Cancún, Japan between 300 and 400, and Australia and New Zealand had 30, compared to Nigeria with 12, Barbados with 8 and the Central African Republic with 3; Malawi had 'learnt' from experience and took 30 people (Narlikar and Wilkinson 2004: 452). Other disparities exist in the amount of research and strategic thinking which can be put into the formation of negotiating stances before meetings begin. There also exist, of course, huge power inequalities between key protagonists; these remain fundamental. But, all that said, the record of Seattle and Cancún, and even Doha up to a point, shows that key non-'Quad' countries – specifically those now grouped in the G20 – fight their positions much more determinedly and effectively than ever before and have just about enough clout to stop or hold up deals that are disproportionately tipped against their interests.

A final observation worth making is that, amidst all the conflicts and jockeying for advantage that take place within the global politics of trade, no country really challenges the ideological case for the liberalization of the system. Strong moves have clearly been made by some states to keep certain areas out of the WTO (most obviously, the Singapore issues). Much is said about the need for S&D and those countries with ongoing advantages from past protective or preferential options manoeuvre and lobby to hang on to them (as the ACP did over Cotonou at Doha and France has repeatedly done within internal EU discussions of agricultural policy). But all of this is undertaken alongside a presumption that trade is a key aspect of the development strategy of all countries – from the richest to the poorest – and that the trend towards further opening up is inexorable.

Chapter 8

Environment

The environment is the third and final policy arena to which we turn in our elaboration of contemporary development diplomacy. Although it has not historically been the case, the pursuit of a coherent approach towards environmental concerns has increasingly come to be seen as a necessary part of any country's strategy of development. The explicit link, which had long been latent in much of the debate about both development and environment, was forged by the work of the Brundtland Commission. Set up by the UN General Assembly and reporting in 1987, the Commission famously coined the concept of 'sustainable development'. Briefly defined, this meant 'development that meets the needs of the present without compromising the ability of future generations to meet their own needs' (World Commission on Environment and Development 1987: 43). This formulation cleverly drew the two themes together and was as widely praised for its farsightedness as it was criticized for its vagueness (Redclift 1987; Lipschutz 1991). The point was that the concept 'remained sufficiently fluid to appeal to a broad range of interests' (Meadowcroft 1996: 409). It gained an immediate political resonance in that it held sway over the United Nations Conference on Environment and Development (UNCED) – popularly known as the 'Earth Summit' – held in Rio de Janeiro in June 1992. Rio was the largest conference of its kind in history, attracting a huge number of national delegations and unofficial NGO personnel and gaining an unprecedented worldwide audience for matters of environmental concern. It certainly did not provide consensual resolution to the question of the relationship between environment and development, and some thought that it notably failed to bring about any satisfactory integration between the two concepts (Rowlands 1992). But what Rio did at least achieve was a reinforcement of Brundtland's positioning of the environment as a central feature of the debate about development.

Rio also shaped the way that global environmental diplomacy has subsequently been conducted. It was in format a United Nations conference summoned into being by the UN General Assembly and it is highly significant that since that moment the environment (unlike finance and trade) has been handled politically within the UN setting. What is more, a vast range of different environmental matters came up for deliberation at Rio. They included protection of the atmosphere, freshwater and ocean resources, land resources, biological diversity and biotechnology, waste management (including toxic wastes) and several other issues related to urban settlement, poverty and human health. Yet, sensibly enough, no attempt has at any time been made to address these concerns within a single environmental regime. Although to some extent linked scientifically, the various presenting issues have generally been viewed as a collection of environmental problems that necessitate different and separate responses. In this spirit UNCED further confirmed an emerging paradigm for the making of environmental agreements, which had been shaped in the main by the way that stratospheric ozone depletion had been tackled in the mid- to late 1980s. In Vogler's (2000: 128) words, this paradigm embraced 'the principle of a "framework convention" … which establishes the problem and an international commitment to take action in a subsequent and more specific protocol which would be designed to allow frequent updating and amendment'. There was thereby provided 'an open-ended and adjustable agreement, responsive to changes in scientific understanding of the causes and dimensions of the problem'. In the case of ozone depletion a convention was signed in Vienna in 1985 that definitively established the nature of the problem and committed signatories to a programme of observation and information exchange. However, although it envisaged control measures, it did not contain them; these were agreed subsequently in a protocol signed in Montreal in 1987 (Benedick 1991; Thomas 1992). As we shall see shortly, Rio fitted into this pattern because it provided a target-date by which framework conventions on climate change and on biodiversity were negotiated and presented for signature.

There was a further significance to the UNCED summit to which we should draw attention. It produced the Rio Declaration on Environment and Development (UNEP 1992), a document that set out a number of 'principles' by which states and peoples were henceforth supposed to cooperate in order to protect 'the integrity of the global environmental and developmental system'. More than a decade later, these principles can be seen to have elaborated at least two vital aspects of the ideational context in which negotiations thereafter took place. In the first place, there was contained in the Declaration a statement of faith in the role of the market in development that was wholly in keeping with the neoliberal norms of the early 1990s. Notwithstanding any apparent contradictions in the ambitions set out, states were urged to 'cooperate to promote a supportive and open international economic system that would lead to economic growth and sustainable development in all countries, better to address the problems of environmental degradation'. In the second place, and of particular significance for the theme of this book, it was recognized that states have made 'different contributions to global environmental degradation' and accordingly have 'common but differentiated responsibilities' for its repair. Even more to the point, the Declaration identified two categories of countries: 'developed countries', which were called upon to 'acknowledge the responsibility that they bear in the international pursuit of sustainable development in view of the pressures that their societies place on the global environment and of the technologies and financial resources they command'; and 'developing countries', which were characterized by a 'special situation and needs' which required that they be given 'special priority'. Again, as we shall see, this simple (and simplistic) bipolar distinction was not fully maintained amidst all the complexities of actual negotiations, and indeed it may well be seen as something of an old-fashioned, even romantic, take upon the problem, but it did nonetheless reflect one of the dominant organizing perceptions that ran through global environmental politics throughout the 1990s and beyond. In this important respect, therefore, this arena of development diplomacy has been structured differently from the others under review in this part of the book.

In this chapter we focus on just two of the issues that have preoccupied the post-Rio global environmental agenda. Although many environmental problems have been addressed by the world's states over the last few years, the main issues that have come to the fore and preoccupied negotiating time and energy have undoubtedly been climate change and biodiversity. Climate change has always been regarded as both more important scientifically and more difficult politically, and it is discussed here at greater length than biodiversity. In the final section of the chapter we also assess Rio's successor ('Rio + 10'), the World Summit on Sustainable Development (WSSD), which met in Johannesburg in August–September 2002 just over ten years after UNCED set in train an intensive decade of global environmental politics. The timing of the summit in relation to Rio offers an obvious benchmark against which to judge what has, or has not, changed in this sphere of development diplomacy over the course of the intervening decade.

Climate change

Climate change only became a major political issue in the mid-1980s. Several scientific conferences during the course of the decade built up a growing consensus that human emissions of carbon dioxide (CO_2) and other 'greenhouse gases' were leading to an 'enhanced greenhouse effect' that would cause a warming of the earth's surface and other associated climatic changes likely to be detrimental to human society (Jäger and

O'Riordan 1996). Potential impacts were thought to be widespread, including on worst-case scenarios significant rises in sea levels with consequent coastal erosion and salt-water intrusion of inland waterways. Likely to be worst hit were many countries that were already economically and politically weak. For example, Bangladesh, Egypt, the Gambia, Indonesia, Mozambique, Pakistan, Senegal, Suriname and Thailand were all at risk because of their coastal concentrations of population and economic activity. Even worse, low-lying island states, such as Kiribati, the Maldives, the Marshall Islands, Tonga and Tuvalu, might become uninhabitable and conceivably disappear altogether. The science was, and to some extent remains, uncertain, but it was thought to be sufficiently compelling by 1988 for the UN Environmental Programme and the World Meteorological Organization (WMO) to establish the Intergovernmental Panel on Climate Change to review and assess the available scientific knowledge in this area. Although the work of the IPCC was criticized by some for representing in the main the agenda of the leading post-industrial countries (Wynne 1994), the results of its First Assessment Report raised enough alarm to prompt the UN General Assembly to initiate formal international negotiations on climate change. The Intergovernmental Negotiating Committee for a Framework Convention on Climate Change (INC/FCCC) accordingly met for the first time in February 1991.

As Paterson and Grubb (1992: 294) immediately observed, cooperation on the management of climate change was 'particularly difficult because serious responses could reach into the heart of countries' political and economic structures'. Three areas of contention, in particular, framed the political reaction (Elliott 1998). The first concerned the costs of stabilizing and eventually reducing greenhouse gas emissions. The task was posed in formidable terms because the IPCC estimated that, even to hold concentrations at 1990 levels, emissions would need to be reduced by over 60 per cent for CO_2, 15–20 per cent for methane, 70–80 per cent for nitrous oxide and varying, but generally high, amounts for chlorofluorocarbons (Houghton, Jenkins and Ephraim 1990). The sources of greenhouse gases are also varied. CO_2, which is the main single contributor accounting for some 70–72 per cent of the additional greenhouse effect since industrialization, arises primarily from the burning of fossil fuels and from deforestation; methane is a by-product of agriculture, especially paddy and livestock, and is leaked during the extraction and transportation of fossil fuels; nitrous oxide emanates from biomass burning, fertilizer use, fossil fuel combustion, land clearing and deforestation. What is obvious instantly is that all these activities are intimately related to the pursuit of economic growth and the interests of some of the most powerful political lobbies, both agricultural and industrial, that exist in all countries. Various strategies are technically available to achieve reductions in emissions of these gases, but all involve financial costs, whether in the form of new taxes, new investments or the payment of penalties, and consequent political costs in implementing them.

The second broad area of dispute was the matter of whose was the responsibility to act. As Elliott (1998: 64) has noted, 'countries vary not only in their contributions to greenhouse emissions, but also in the ease with which they can reduce emissions, in their capacity to pay for response policies and in their degree of resilience or vulnerability to impacts'. The allocation of obligation is thus controversial: 'it depends on which gases are counted and how they are counted: on a total output basis, a per capita basis, or a per GNP basis; on the basis of current levels of exploitation, historical contributions or projected future emissions' (Elliott 1998: 64). Yet, notwithstanding these undoubted complications, the emission figures showed that for 1990, the year of publication of the first IPCC report, the OECD countries were responsible for more than 50 per cent of global fossil fuel CO_2 emissions and the Central and Eastern European countries, including the then Soviet Union, for another 20 per cent. Thus, in Grubb's (1999: 27–9) words, 'the quarter of the world's population in the industrialized countries ... accounted for about three-quarters of the fossil fuel CO_2 emissions, and well over half the total global greenhouse emissions including deforestation and other gases'. By comparison, average per capita emissions of fossil fuel CO_2 from 'developing countries' were barely one-tenth of the OECD average, whilst per capita emissions from regions such as the Indian subcontinent and Africa were about one-twentieth of those of the United States (Paterson and Grubb 1992: 297). Nevertheless, it was also the case that most calculations showed that greenhouse emissions from the 'developing countries' were predicted to increase considerably in the future and thereby contribute a growing relative percentage of overall emissions over time, with China, for example, likely to supersede the US as the world's biggest emitter by around 2020. From these data there obviously emerged differing political assessments. The dominant view in the US, for example, argued that any amelioration of damaging forms of climate change required the participation of the 'developing countries'. This logic was generally resisted by analysts from such countries, who suggested that such an attitude smacked of 'environmental colonialism' and was an attempt not only to shift the blame but also to retard the economic growth of the poorest parts of the world (Agarwal and Narain 1991). A number of academic commentators gave further support to this position by proposing that there was an important ethical distinction to be drawn between 'luxury emissions' and 'subsistence emissions' (Shue 1993).

The third area of dispute related to the extent, if at all, to which scientific uncertainty should be incorporated into potential responses. On one side of the argument, the 'precautionary approach' enunciated the case for not postponing cost-effective measures to prevent climate change, even in circumstances where certain knowledge was not available, for fear that delay would only worsen the problem and intensify the costs of remedial action. On the other side, the so-called 'no regrets' view cautioned against extensive, expensive commitments and called for measures which were also justified on other grounds beyond climate change considerations and which would incur only minimal costs if the gloomiest predictions turned out to be exaggerated (Gray and Rivkin 1991). This fissure tended to replicate the previous argument about the location of the responsibility to act, given that analysts in 'developing countries' mostly saw the ostensible fear of acting with 'regrets' as no more than an excuse not to meet their due obligations by the major emissions culprits.

This was the general political context in which the INC/FCCC set about the task of producing, in barely 18 months, a convention on climate change that would be ready to be signed at the Rio Conference in June 1992. From the beginning of the negotiations, however, it was apparent that, although much of the early discussion of the politics of climate change had, as we have seen, been constructed around the presumption of a fundamental divide between 'developed' and 'developing' countries, the reality of the positions actually taken up by participating governments was much more subtle and differentiated. Both generic camps contained important divisions which, with just a few exceptions, have 'proved remarkably resilient' over the course of the subsequent period during which climate change has been discussed (Grubb 1999: 29). At this point, therefore, we need to sketch out the core views and positions of the main protagonists. No fewer than seven different stances can be discerned: four amongst the general category of 'developed countries', namely, those of the EU, the US, Japan and other OECD countries, and the 'countries with economies in transition' (CEITs) of Russia and Central and Eastern Europe; and three amongst the equivalent loose category of 'developing countries', namely, the Group of 77 and China, the OPEC countries and the members of the Alliance of Small Island States (AOSIS). Each is briefly considered.

European Union countries have generally been at the forefront of demands for strong action to be taken on climate change. The reasons for this are various. At their root is the fact that all, except the UK, are net energy importers. They thus saw a competitive economic case for acting in relation to the prospect of improved energy efficiency, as well as potential technological leadership in this whole field. West Germany had, for example, reaped considerable economic gains during the 1980s from being the first major European country to take steps to control acid rain. It was also a factor that EU member governments came under public pressure to deal with environmental problems earlier than other parts of the world (including the US). The result was that, by 1990, a number of EU countries had already set indicative targets for limiting their own CO_2 emissions and wanted to press similar policies on the rest of the world. At the same time the EU as a grouping faced the constraint that its constituent countries, like the world as a whole, had varying levels of responsibility for, and capacity to address, the greenhouse gas problem. This obviously made agreement on the specifics of concerted action as an institutional entity a testing matter.

The United States was more hesitant about responding to climate change. It was concerned about the economic consequences of carbon dioxide abatement in particular and at times has been overtly hostile to the whole process. This has mattered considerably, not just because of the sheer economic and political power of the US in global affairs generally, but specifically because of the weight of its CO_2 emissions which comprise almost 25 per cent of the global total. Add to this the size and wealth of the US economy generally and it is clear why so many other countries demanded from the outset that the US contribute substantially to the amelioration of the problem. The difficulty is, as Paterson and Grubb (1992: 306) put it, that 'US development has known few limits, and popular culture tends to assume that every constraint can be overcome with a technical fix without affecting resource-intensive US lifestyles'. At the beginning of the 1990s the country was the world's second largest oil producer, the second largest natural gas producer and the largest coal producer, a position which generated an extraordinary array of powerful corporate interests in the energy policy field. As many have observed, the US economy is in effect addicted to cheap energy, which feeds the widespread conviction in US governmental circles that the costs of reducing greenhouse gas emissions, especially carbon dioxide, would be very high, possibly even prohibitively so (Andreson 1991). Accordingly, official spokesmen have often sought to divert attention from US domestic energy consumption by emphasizing the role of other emissions sources (such as deforestation and rice cultivation) and of the general threat posed by the future economic growth of 'developing countries'. It is also worthy of note in assessing the US position that the executive branch of its government, which is tasked by the US constitution with conducting international negotiations, has for this reason been more likely to be sympathetic to global compromise than the legislative branch, which has not only always been more open to the influence of the special interests of the energy sector but also has the crucial responsibility for ratifying international agreements.

Japan's stance was initially ambiguous, exhibiting a tendency to seek out middle positions. During the course of its own industrialization it had made itself one of the most energy-efficient countries in the world and thus had cause to worry about its capacity to make additional emissions reductions. Yet it saw the potential gain from technological leadership in energy conservation and, according to some accounts, also identified the environment as the arena in which it could best make its own 'international contribution' (Kawashima 1997). In 1990 it thus followed the EU lead and adopted a CO_2 emissions target. Other OECD countries took up varying positions. Canada had an energy-intensive economy and, like the US, was concerned about the economic consequences of emission constraints; yet it also had a compensating tradition of popular environmental awareness. Australia was heavily dependent on exports of coal and other heavy industry products to non-industrialized Asian countries, and was consequently suspicious of action to limit emissions. By contrast, New Zealand, Norway and Switzerland were amongst the lowest per capita carbon dioxide emitters in the OECD thanks to their hydro-dominated economies, which served of course to make the prospect of bringing down existing emission levels appear more demanding than it did in the historically coal-based EU member countries. In sum, in Grubb's (1999: 33–4) balanced evaluation, the position of non-EU OECD countries presented 'a complex network of resource-based interests and historically acquired attitudes towards environment, technology and internationalism', with their main characteristic in common being 'greater difficulty than the EU in reducing emissions below 1990 levels'. In climate change terms these countries were the 'industrialised laggards' (Oberthür and Ott 1999: 17).

During the initial phase of the INC/FCCC talks Russia, the other states of the former Soviet Union and the various Eastern and Central European countries were preoccupied with their own internal processes of economic and political change and did not play a very active role. Over time, however, they grew to be more involved and their interests became clarified as 'economies in transition'. Almost all of these CEITs shared the experience of building heavily energy-intensive economies during the Soviet era and then of seeing more or less their entire economic apparatus collapse amidst the disintegration of the Soviet system. This at least meant that by the early 1990s their greenhouse gas emissions had already fallen substantially against historical levels, a trend which placed them in a more advantageous position *vis-à-vis* likely future emissions targets than any other grouping of countries and gave them a distinctive stance in the negotiations. Nevertheless, divergences within this group also existed. They derived from varying orientations after transition, both on the economic front, with Russia remaining a prospective energy exporter of some scale and many of the others having to think more about the future sources and costs of their energy imports, and on the political front, with Russia forming closer political ties with the US than the EU and some Central and Eastern European states signalling instead that they looked in the long term to full EU membership.

The Group of 77 has sought to represent the collective interests of 'developing countries' in all UN bodies and conferences since its formation in UNCTAD in 1964 and it is true, notwithstanding the earlier point made about the problems involved in exaggerating the extent of the 'developed world' versus 'developing world' character of climate change politics, that at the broadest level this wide-ranging alliance of disparate countries did seek to operate as a coherent force in the many rounds of talks. The grouping was certainly united around the principle that 'the developed countries bear the main responsibility for the degradation of the global environment' (Group of Seventy-Seven 1991: paragraph 6) and stuck to its determination not to make any negotiating commitment which infringed the notion of sovereignty over natural resources or was not linked to the provision of financial resources and the transfer of technology. However, G77 unity did not stretch much further than these largely rhetorical postures, although, in truth, it did not need to do so as long as the countries historically responsible for greenhouse gas emissions could be kept, as it were, in the dock. India, Brazil and Indonesia nevertheless often struck individual notes within G77 positions, and China was officially distinct from the G77, although it generally attached itself to the grouping. Discrete sub-regional groups within the G77 also gave voice to African and Latin American countries.

More to the point, two other groups of countries broke ranks from the G77/China to articulate powerful separate positions on climate change. OPEC, formed as long ago as 1960, represented an obvious and recognizable interest. Fearful that efforts to limit CO_2 emissions would depress global oil consumption, OPEC opposed all attempts to institute formal controls. Led by Saudi Arabia and Kuwait, these countries highlighted the extent of scientific uncertainty about the causes and direction of climate change and repeatedly urged that more research be done before definitive steps were taken. In their view, the emphasis in any action contemplated should be placed on the protection and extension of the 'carbon sinks' (primarily forests and oceans) that naturally absorb carbon dioxide. OPEC countries blatantly sought to slow the pace of the talks and quickly earned a reputation for obstructionism. At the opposite end of the spectrum were the countries newly organized within AOSIS. Formed in November 1990 at a WMO World Climate Conference, this grouping comprised 42 tiny states mainly located in the Caribbean Sea and the Pacific, Indian and Atlantic Oceans. Some of them lay only a few metres above sea level at their highest point and were without question the countries of the world most vulnerable to climate change. This existential danger made them the 'ecological conscience' (Oberthür and Ott 1999: 26) of the international climate talks. As a body AOSIS proved to be both vocal and organized, pushing for early and strong action to reduce CO_2 emissions and halt deforestation, and calling for financial help in taking the measures needed to adapt to the climatic changes they argued were already in train.

To put it modestly, the gulf between these various negotiating positions at the beginning of the talks was enormous. Some favoured only a framework convention, the vaguer the better; others wanted an immediate agreement with binding commitments to limit emissions; others still recognized the seriousness of the problem and the need for specific targets but accepted the political case for moving forward incrementally. There was far from unanimity on the science and there could not even be guaranteed a basic goodwill which acknowledged the sincerity of all positions. Yet, somewhat against the odds, the UN Framework Convention on Climate Change (UNFCCC) was established as the basic international commitment within which to address the risks posed by human-induced climate change. It was finalized just weeks before Rio, was quickly ratified by the necessary 50 countries (including the US very early in the process) and thus came into being in March 1994. As of the end of 2004 it had been signed by no fewer than 189 parties. It is not a long document, containing only a preamble, 26 articles and two important annexes (United Nations Framework Convention on Climate Change Secretariat 1992). The key features included:

- the objective of achieving 'stabilisation of greenhouse gas concentrations in the atmosphere at a level that would prevent dangerous anthropogenic interference with the climate system', albeit without a tightly specified time-frame;
- guiding 'principles' which included variously 'equity', 'common but differentiated responsibilities and respective capabilities', precaution, the promotion of 'sustainable development' and support for an 'open international economic system';
- a commitment from all parties to take action to deal with climate change which included the preparation of programmes for mitigation and adaptation, the encouragement of scientific research, and submission of reports on national emissions and response efforts;
- a specific obligation for 'developed country parties' (as listed in Annex I) to take the lead in mitigation efforts by agreeing to set an indicative (and thus non-legally binding) target to return their greenhouse gas

emissions to 1990 levels by the year 2000; and a further obligation for the most prosperous of these parties (as listed in Annex II) to assist 'developing country parties', especially those that were 'particularly vulnerable to the adverse effects of climate change', in meeting the costs of their general obligations under the Convention;

- the establishment of UNFCCC institutions, including the Conference of the Parties (COP) that would meet annually, two specialist bodies – the Subsidiary Body for Scientific and Technological Advice and the Subsidiary Body for Implementation – that would meet twice a year, and a permanent international secretariat; and
- the elaboration of a financial mechanism enabling 'the provision of financial resources on a grant or concessional basis' to be operated, at least on 'an interim basis' by the Global Environmental Facility housed within the World Bank and jointly overseen by the UNEP and UNDP.

As indicated, the Convention contained no authoritative targets or deadlines, chiefly because of the opposition of the US and OPEC. The key article, 4.2, which expressed the extent of the commitments undertaken, was long and convoluted, containing what one commentator called possibly 'the most impenetrable treaty language ever drafted' (Sands 1992: 273). One passage spoke only of the contribution that a return to 'earlier levels' of emissions would bring; another identified the 'aim' (a soft word) of achieving 1990 levels. Even if it had been agreed as a binding target, the latter would have come nowhere near to the 60 per cent reduction that the IPCC had previously suggested was necessary merely to stabilize concentrations. In the long run the main significance of the article was that it locked parties into a process of reporting and reviewing their emissions. It was also important in that Annexes I and II actually named the countries that were expected to take the lead in addressing climate change. Annex I was made up of the member countries of the OECD in 1992 and those Central and Eastern European countries, including Russia but excluding Yugoslavia, formally classified as undergoing the process of 'transition to a market economy'; Annex II was the more exclusive precisely because it did not include the transition group.

All in all, despite its vacuities of expression and its internal contradictions, the Convention was 'probably as successful as could reasonably be expected' for its moment in time (Grubb 1999: 43). What was not known, in the light of the perceived lack of strong public concern and the growing opposition of vested interests, was whether or not the bargaining would continue seriously thereafter. The first COP was held on schedule in March 1995 in Berlin. It was convened by the German government, a proponent of strong action on climate change, especially given the fact that it was well placed, since re-unification and its absorption of the declining industrial economy of the former East Germany, to be able to reduce its overall emissions to 1990 levels. As expected, though, the meeting was polarized around the extent of the adequacy of commitments, especially after 2000. AOSIS and EU members favoured more stringent targets, with the former submitting a bold proposal calling on Annex I countries to cut their CO_2 emissions by 20 per cent by 2005. Other OECD countries, especially Japan, the US, Canada, Australia and New Zealand, worked together as an emerging JUSCANZ group. They were unwilling to accept further obligations beyond the voluntary 'back to 1990' commitment contained in the UNFCCC – which in any case they were generally far from being likely to attain – and focused instead on pressing their case that the 'developing countries' should now be required to adopt commitments as part of a more comprehensive approach to climate change management. OPEC remained opposed to any action at all. Deeply and increasingly painfully split between its AOSIS and OPEC wings, the G77/China gave birth in Berlin to a majority 'Green Group', led by India, which accepted that current commitments were inadequate and joined with the EU in demanding tougher future targets for Annex I countries provided that no commitments were required of its members, a position which the EU accepted. The JUSCANZ grouping felt the pressure mounting and eventually signed up to what became known as the 'Berlin Mandate'. Without reference to any specific details, this recognized the inadequacy of the commitments in the UNFCCC and set in motion a process to agree 'quantified limitation and reduction objectives within specified time-frames' for Annex I – but importantly no other – countries. The work was to be taken forward at a second COP to be held a year later and completed in time for a protocol to be adopted at the third COP in 1997.

The road to Kyoto was thereby laid down. In the intervening period countries and groupings considered their options and strategies. The Clinton/Gore administration in the US (within which the Vice-President, Al Gore, in particular was known for his interest in environmental issues) had not initially been able to effect any significant shift in the US stance. But, as it grew in confidence with the experience of office, it moved to embrace the idea of seeking targets that were 'realistic, verifiable and binding' (Wirth 1997: 6–9), although it has correctly been observed that 'this seems to have been linked to its preference for the introduction of a system of tradeable permits' (Elliott 1998: 72). Russia remained hostile to binding targets (Oberthür 1996), but under US pressure slowly came to see that, with its falling emissions, it could be one of the principal beneficiaries of a trading system. Within OPEC, the Saudi Arabian government in particular realized that continued obstructionism was not an option and came up with the idea of a fund to recompense OPEC countries for lost revenues. This provided an opening for the G77 to reunite around the idea that *all* of the categories of 'developing countries' recognized in the UNFCCC as being adversely affected by climate change should receive financial compensation. For its part, the EU continued to try to lead the process by proposing that all Annex I countries should commit to reducing their combined emissions to 15 per cent below 1990 levels by 2010 and devising an internal redistributive mechanism (later dubbed a 'bubble' in the peculiar jargon of climate change politics) by which it proposed to deliver its own collective commitment. The Japanese administration was internally divided and increasingly unwilling to cause offence, and eventually put forward a highly complex scheme that sought to offer a modest something to all interests. It also felt some pressure, as host, to secure a successful outcome.

By this stage it was indeed the detail of the compromises that mattered. The Kyoto COP in December 1997 was a gruelling affair, with bargaining going on through the nights and continuing right until the last moment. No rules on procedure were in fact ever agreed, which paradoxically served to create the opportunity for the unorthodox and forceful Argentinian chairman of the conference, Raúl Estrada-Oyuela, to push through controversial draft clauses by in effect denying opponents opportunities to block them any further. In the end an extraordinarily complex deal was struck. Its key positive feature was the commitment of Annex I countries to meet legally binding quantitative emissions targets during a first commitment period (defined as 2008–12) for a 'basket' of the six main greenhouse gases. Each country was given a separate, specified target (ranging from an 8 per cent reduction on 1990 levels for Switzerland, most CEITs and the EU as a bloc to a 10 per cent increase on 1990 levels for Iceland) which, taken together, would result in a 5.2 per cent reduction in total Annex I country emissions. The quantified commitments were stronger than many expected, but they were only agreed in conjunction with three novel 'flexibility mechanisms' – joint implementation, the clean development mechanism (CDM) and emissions trading – which had been deliberately designed to allow countries to lessen the costs of meeting their commitments by cooperating in different ways to achieve their emissions reductions. In addition, in what was in essence another offsetting measure, it was agreed that there should be included within the accounting framework certain 'land-use, land-use change and forestry' (LULUCF) activities that could either reduce emissions from forest clearances or increase long-term storage in 'carbon sinks'.

This was the basic architecture of the Kyoto Protocol (United Nations Framework Convention on Climate Change Secretariat 1997). It unavoidably reflected a mass of uneasy compromises between the contending parties. The EU can be said to have obtained the binding regime for which it (and AOSIS) had pushed since the beginning of climate change talks. Indeed, the US and the other OECD countries had signed up for tougher commitments than they really wanted: in the US case a 7 per cent reduction on 1990 levels, in Canada's and Japan's cases a 6 per cent reduction. In return, the US, backed by the rest of the JUSSCANNZ countries (suitably renamed to reflect the additional involvement of Switzerland and Norway), obtained nearly all of the flexibility arrangements that they had sought, notably emissions trading. The US also insisted on including in the regime all the major greenhouse gases (which it favoured because attention was thereby diverted somewhat from carbon dioxide emissions, the principal problem) and the various LULUCF activities (Harris 2000). The EU was generally sceptical of the flexibility mechanisms and sought, as best it could, to fix limits to the extent to which they could be used to meet mandatory targets. It was, for example, able to head off some of the more extensive proposals from JUSS-CANNZ countries regarding the way that 'sinks' might be incorporated into the overall regime, but often lost the initiative in the heady last few days of Kyoto because its own internal decision-making procedures were insufficiently adept at coping with the speed and intensity of the negotiations. Russia and the Central and Eastern European countries 'maintained their status as part of the industrialized world's institutional structures' (Grubb 1999: 151) and gained potential benefits too from the flexibility mechanisms, especially emissions trading, which opened up the potentially lucrative prospect of being able to sell off to other richer states the excess allowances ('hot air') over the benchmark emission levels which they had been conceded.

The AOSIS and OPEC countries saw Kyoto as delivering less and more respectively than they desired, but were consoled by the Protocol's continuing recognition (in Article 2) of the need to 'minimize ... the adverse effects of climate change' on the categories of countries with 'specific needs' identified in the original UN Convention. For their part, the bulk of the countries in the G77/China achieved their core dual aims of strengthening Annex I commitments *and* avoiding new commitments themselves. On the debit side they felt that their objections to emissions trading had been brusquely overridden (although several South American countries, South Korea, the Philippines and AOSIS members did not fully share this hostility) and were disappointed that a Brazilian proposal for the creation of a clean development fund, to be stocked by the imposition of financial penalties on Annex I countries for non-compliance with their Protocol commitments and to be spent on projects in G77 countries, was eventually replaced by the CDM, which was quite different in that it was a mechanism which allowed investments in non-Annex I countries to contribute to compliance, thereby still winning support from at least some G77 countries. Nevertheless, the key achievement of this group was the success of its stand against what was euphemistically described in one particular US proposal as 'the evolution of commitments' to *all* countries over the course of a later period of time (Gupta 2000). By the same token, of course, the latter was seen in the US as the main failure of the whole Kyoto deal (Müller 2001).

In assessing the complex amalgam of measures represented by Kyoto it is also worth commenting briefly on the ideological character of the whole package. The flexibility mechanisms are fundamental to this argument. They effectively allow the leading market economies of the world to meet a substantial part of their emission commitments by means of bilateral trading of assigned amounts between themselves and through corporate investments all over the world. They reflect the growing acceptance of the developmental role of private capital, the perceived desirability of attracting in foreign companies and the sense that corporate investment can often facilitate international problem-solving. In that sense Kyoto was very much a product of its times: as Grubb (1999: 137) put it in his summary evaluation, 'the Protocol is essentially an agreement to extend economic globalization to environmental policy: to establish a global emissions market to counter the global environmental consequences of global economic growth'. It is telling indeed that it was conceived and negotiated just before the Asian financial crisis started to undermine some of the legitimacy of neoliberal globalization.

For all its technical complexity and interminable discussion of the flexibility mechanisms, Kyoto was not able to settle many of the practical arrangements by which they would actually work. In fact, as Victor (2001: 26) noted, 'agreement in Kyoto was possible only because a great veil of uncertainty put all the critical details in the shadow'. The whole climate change caravan therefore moved relentlessly on to COP-4 in Buenos Aires in November 1998. The objective here was to lay the basis for a new agreement on the implementation of the mechanisms. Quite a lot of progress was made on matters such as the role of the GEF, the arrangements by which the Annex II countries would transfer technology and the planning of pilot activities under joint implementation. For the most part the EU and the US agreed to defer until later their differences on emissions trading. This meant that the main line of division occurred within the G77 around the perennial, but nevertheless vexed, question of voluntary commitments by these countries. The Carlos Menem government in Argentina, as host, tried unsuccessfully to put this issue on the agenda and later indicated that it intended to take on a binding emissions commitment under the Protocol. Kazakhstan also announced that it wished to apply to join Annex I, attracted no doubt by the prospect of selling its 'hot air'. But they were the only 'developing countries' to break ranks on this matter and COP-4 was generally considered to have maintained the momentum of Kyoto. COP-5 in Bonn in late 1999 continued the process. Thereafter, however, difficulties mounted as the JUSSCANNZ countries, which were by this stage tending to align themselves more and more with Russia and the Ukraine, the two CEITs with the highest greenhouse emissions and the greatest interest in 'hot air' trading, in a new Umbrella grouping, demanded a range of detailed concessions on implementation in the light of what they increasingly perceived as the excessively strict emission targets they had been persuaded to accept at Kyoto. As a result COP-6 (held in The Hague in November 2000) broke up with the bulk of its business unfinished.

All of these talks were conducted in the shadow of one crucial issue: whether (and, if so, when) the Kyoto Protocol would gather sufficient ratifications to enter into force. The relevant article set the hurdle at ratification by 55 parties, including Annex I countries accounting for 'at least 55 per cent of the total carbon dioxide emissions for 1990'. The first part of this formula was unproblematic: failure would have required more than 120 countries not to ratify, which would have rendered the treaty irrelevant in any case. However, the minimum fraction of CO_2 emissions requirement necessitated in practice that two out of the three major emitters – the US, the EU and Russia – endorse the regime before it could come into force legally. Ratification was not a foregone conclusion in any of these cases, but it was especially uncertain in the US, given longstanding Congressional opposition linked to the interests of both big business and the trade unions. Indeed, as early as July 1997 the US Senate had passed a resolution, 95–0, opposing US acceptance of a binding agreement unless it could be shown that no additional costs would be imposed on the US economy and that a 'meaningful commitment' to greenhouse gas reduction had been secured from 'developing countries' (US Senate 1997). Therefore, even though it could fairly be argued that Kyoto was negotiated so as to be acceptable to the Clinton/Gore administration, the likelihood of US ratification of the Protocol was arguably small even before George W. Bush assumed office in early 2001. As discussed in Chapter 4, Bush led a right-wing team with close links to the oil and energy business and he only waited until March 2001 before publicly repudiating the US commitment to Kyoto. In an open letter to four US senators, he declared that he opposed the Protocol 'because it exempts 80 per cent of the world, including major population centers such as China and India, from compliance, and would cause serious harm to the U.S. economy' (Bush 2001). No amount of public criticism or diplomatic pressure from all parts of the world was able thereafter to shift the US position.

The US disavowal of Kyoto did at least serve to galvanize the other parties. The failed COP-6 was recalled and the Kyoto 'rulebook' was eventually agreed in the Marrakesh Accords signed at COP-7 in

November 2001. This meant that the operational details of the flexibility mechanisms were at last finalized, including the important proviso that reductions thereby achieved should be 'supplemental to domestic action'. Three new funds were set up to assist the G77 countries in their adjustment and mitigation efforts; a compliance procedure was adopted, although not as tough as the EU desired; and the range of LULUCF activities allowable within the accounting framework was further broadened, to the particular advantage of Russia which won an increased forest management allowance. Politically, Marrakesh was a product of the joint desire of the EU and the G77 not to see all their previous gains thrown away, even if the price paid was a *de facto* weakening of some of the Kyoto goals. It also cannot be denied that the US announcement that it would not seek to ratify the Kyoto Protocol has had damaging consequences. The absolute emission reductions secured during the first commitment period will be substantially less than originally anticipated. There will be less demand for credits obtained via the three flexibility mechanisms and the associated financial flows will be reduced. Indeed, some studies quickly estimated that the traded price of carbon could be close to zero without US demand, which might mean that Russia, for example, would be forced to hold over until the next commitment period a substantial proportion of its excess reserves if it wished to make the gains it anticipated (den Elzen and de Moor 2001). In sum, the US defection from Kyoto has bifurcated the nascent global regime on climate change. Whilst the vast majority of countries have continued to indicate that they will partake of a diminished Kyoto system, the US has set out on its own course, as enunciated by Bush in February 2002 in his proclaimed 'Climate Change Initiative', a plan to reduce the greenhouse gas intensity of the US economy – but not the absolute levels of US emissions – by means largely of voluntary action in the corporate sector (de Moor *et al.* 2002). Although this initiative did at last admit the importance of climate change and provide for the establishment of accurate emissions inventories, the Bush administration manifestly has no appetite for mandatory controls of greenhouse emissions and its approach cannot but function as 'a drag on the efforts of states that are prepared to act within the Kyoto framework' (Meadowcroft 2002: 20).

Strictly speaking too, the saga of the ratification of the Kyoto Protocol was not fully brought to completion until early 2005. The situation had been reached by the end of 2002 whereby 100 countries, incorporating Annex I countries accounting for 43.7 per cent of 1990 CO_2 emissions, had ratified the agreement, which meant that Russia's 17.4 per cent then became essential for pushing the tally over the required hurdle. Its increased bargaining power in this context had already been visible at Marrakesh. However, although Russia's president, Vladimir Putin, first promised in September 2002 that his government would soon table the papers needed to initiate the ratification process in the Russian Parliament, a long period of prevarication ensued. Although some attributed this delay to secret US pressure on Putin on the grounds that the US administration would be less embarrassed by its decision to opt out of Kyoto if the whole protocol never came into effect, it is more likely that major disagreement emerged within the Russian government as to the impact that compliance with Kyoto's targets might have on Russia's own development strategy. It is quite possible, too, that Russia sought to take advantage of its indispensability to Kyoto to bargain hard on other international issues, such as the terms of the EU's support for its admission into the WTO (Grubb and Safonov 2003). At any rate, for a period of over two years varying signals and statements from different Russian spokespersons held the rest of the increasingly anxious Kyoto signatories hostage to the eventual Russian decision.

In the meantime, the COPs rolled on, but to no great effect. The eighth meeting took place in Delhi in late 2002. With only minor technical matters on the table, the vacuum was filled by a vigorous debate over the next steps to be taken in the progression of the climate change regime. The Indian government prepared a 'Delhi Declaration' that predictably was silent on the question of abatement efforts beyond the end of the first Kyoto commitment period in 2012. In his address Atal Bihari Vajpayee, the then Indian Prime Minister, rejected as 'misplaced' calls for a process leading to commitments by the G77/China. He argued that per capita incomes and emissions were still much lower in these countries and that the 'developing country' contribution to atmospheric concentrations of greenhouse gases would remain small compared to that of Annex I countries 'for several decades to come' (Vajpayee 2002). In a reversal of past roles the EU delegation objected strongly to this argument, while the US representatives (who still attend COPs because the US remains a signatory of the UNFCCC) spoke with apparently much greater understanding of the difficulties faced by the G77, motivated largely, one presumes, by a desire to avoid a post-Kyoto strengthening of the management of climate change which would in time put pressure on the US to reconsider its position. In the end, both parties subscribed to an Umbrella Group paper calling loosely for 'global participation' in addressing climate change in the future (Pew Center for Global Climate Change 2002). COP-9, held in Milan in December 2003, also tried to get talks going on the next stage of the Kyoto process – the so-called second commitment period running from 2012 onwards – but in the face of continuing contradictory indications of Russia's intent failed to make any significant progress. Indeed, a plan to delay the next COP until mid-2005 was only just blocked by AOSIS which, as ever, was the country grouping that continued to press the case for climate change management with the greatest urgency.

In the end, in October 2004, Putin acceded to the external pressure being exerted upon him and placed the necessary legislation before the Russian Parliament. It was approved and Kyoto duly came into force as a legal entity on 16 February 2005. On the same basis the EU's emissions trading scheme was able to open for business, albeit somewhat tentatively in its early days, in January 2005. The news of Russia's decision also came in time to galvanize the next COP, which gathered in Buenos Aires in late 2004. In the circumstances delegates had no real alternative but to begin to confront the prospects for international climate change policies after 2012. However, the US representative made it plain that his country considered it to be premature to think about the post-2012 era, whilst the Indian and Brazilian ministers, amongst others, reiterated their insistence that their governments would not accept future mandatory restrictions on greenhouse gas emissions if this undermined their paths to economic growth. As we have seen, the approach of the bigger 'developing countries' to the next phase of Kyoto has long been critical, not only because of the stance taken up on this matter by the Bush administration but also because of their growing contribution to the problem. A new study undertaken by the US-based Pew Center for Climate Change, tabled at the conference, found that in 2000 China was already the world's second biggest emitter with 14.8 per cent of the world's total emissions, compared to the US with 20.6 per cent and the EU with 14 per cent. India, in turn, produced 5.5 per cent and Brazil 2.5 per cent (Boumert and Pershing 2004). Such figures were telling, but did not shape the mood of the meeting, which was set by the opening speech of the Argentinian President, Nestor Kirchner, in which he demanded that rich countries pay their 'environmental debts' in the same way that they asked poorer countries to meet their financial debts. The talks in fact came close to collapsing completely, although eventually a compromise was agreed around the EU's idea of holding an informal 'seminar' in May 2005 at which discussion, but not negotiation, about next steps could take place.

Biodiversity

Like climate change, biodiversity only emerged as an explicit issue in global environmental politics in the 1980s. The concept referred to the number and variability of living organisms in the world, highlighting particularly diversity both between and within species. Concern about the loss of biodiversity had been present within an earlier conservation agenda, but was given added impetus by the appearance of a number of studies which suggested that the rate of species extinction was higher than ever before, and accelerating (Porter and Brown 1991; Reid 1992). The causes were various, ranging from habitat destruction and disturbance to resource overexploitation to pollution, each arguably generated by the pursuit of development of some form or another. The scientific debate was also increasingly characterized by a sense of despair. It was admitted that it was not accurately known how many species there were in the world, which meant that some were being lost even before they had been identified and classified. The question that arose was whether this mattered. In this mood of heightened urgency the answer generally given was that biodiversity is 'valuable for three reasons' (Rajan 1997: 153). First, it has economic value, especially for pharmaceutical and medicinal purposes but also for agriculture; second, it provides a crucial (and free) contribution to balancing the ecosystem; and, third, it embodies aesthetic, ethical and cultural values for many communities, including that of humankind's responsibility to future generations. In short, by the end of the 1980s biodiversity had come to be seen almost universally as a cause that needed to be addressed. In the words of the executive director of UNEP (1989: 4), 'biological diversity is a common global resource, like the atmosphere, from which all nations benefit'.

However, such a view severely underestimated the political difficulties that lay in train. They derived in good part from the fact that biodiversity is not uniformly distributed throughout the world (Shiva 1990): it is overwhelmingly concentrated in the poorer countries located between the Tropic of Cancer and the Tropic of Capricorn, of which, according to UNDP, there are some 116 in total. Indeed, according to Brenton (1994: 198), over half of all species live in the mere 6 per cent of the earth's surface that is covered by tropical forest. Some studies also refer to the existence of 12 'mega-diverse' countries, namely, Australia, Brazil, China, Colombia, Ecuador, India, Indonesia, Madagascar, Malaysia, Mexico, Peru and Zaire (now known as the Democratic Republic of Congo) (Brenton 1994: 201). Of these countries, none was a founder member of the OECD (although Australia joined in 1971 and Mexico in 1994); none is a member of the G7; and all except Australia belong to the G77/China grouping within the UN. The 'mega-diversity' of the tropical countries is further illustrated in the astonishing statistics produced by the World Rainforest Movement (1990, cited in Elliott 1998: 74) that one river in Brazil alone contains more fish species than are found in the whole of the United States and that a tiny reserve in Costa Rica contains more plant species than the whole of the United Kingdom.

At the same time it is also the case that nearly all of the world's largest pharmaceutical and biotechnology industries, which manifestly have an interest in accessing and exploiting the diversity of species, are based in the core OECD countries. A clear picture thus emerges of the kind of political cleavages which a serious attempt to protect biodiversity was bound to encounter.

The negotiation of a new global convention for the conservation of biodiversity began in late 1990. The process was initiated by UNEP and conducted under its auspices, with a view to having a document ready to be signed alongside a framework convention on climate change at Rio in June 1992. Perhaps unsurprisingly, at this early and exploratory stage in the process, the talks were marked by what Mukund Govin Rajan (1997: 191) described as divisions between the 'North' and the 'South'. The former position took the view that genetic resources were a 'common heritage' either owned by everyone or no one; companies could thus treat species and genes as free resources and go on to sell the derivatives which they had extracted and synthesized at their own considerable expense. The latter position argued that a country's genetic stock was protected by the doctrine of national sovereignty and could accordingly be utilized in line with its own chosen developmental and environmental priorities; companies from outside interested in the exploitation of these resources should only be able to do so on the basis of mutual agreement and an equitable sharing of the benefits. The Indian delegation's confidential assessment of the state of play after the first negotiating session summed up 'the battle-lines' (its phrase) as follows:

The developed countries are going to push very hard for easy access to germplasm (both domestic and wild) and regulatory regimes for the protection of forests and other habitats, but are going to drag their feet about (i) transfer of technology, specially biotechnology and (ii) sharing of profits. The developing countries will push equally hard in the other direction seeking adequate guarantees for technology transfer, financial assistance and profit sharing (Rajan 1997: 205).

The organizational structure of the G77/China was used to push the arguments of the leading 'mega-diverse' countries such as India and it is the case that the tone of the talks was often heated and some of the language used harsh and divisive (Hendrickx, Koesler and Prip 1993; Rajan 1997). Nevertheless, the Convention on Biological Diversity (CBD) was adopted, just in time, in May 1992 and opened for signature, as planned, at the Rio summit.

The CBD was written on parallel lines to the UNFCCC. Its main features included:

- the objectives of 'the conservation of biological diversity, the sustainable use of its components and the fair and equitable sharing of the benefits arising out of the utilisation of genetic resources';
- the adoption of national strategies, with appropriate monitoring and impact assessment, but only 'as far as possible and as appropriate', thereby preserving a fundamental independence of action at country level;
- acceptance of the 'sovereign right' of states to exploit their own resources in the context of a recognition that the conservation of biological diversity is a common 'concern' (*not* heritage) of humankind;
- specification of (undefined) categories of 'developed country parties' and 'developing country parties' accompanied by acknowledgement that the extent to which the latter will implement their commitments will depend on the 'effective implementation' by the former of 'new and additional financial resources';
- provision that access to genetic resources should be on 'mutually agreed terms' and access to and transfer of technology to 'developing countries' should be on 'fair and most favourable terms'; and
- the establishment of CBD institutions, including a COP, a secretariat, a subsidiary body on scientific, technical and technological advice, and the GEF as the financial mechanism, albeit – again – only on an interim basis.

As can be seen, the G77/China countries obtained most, but not all, of their demands. They did not achieve as firm a commitment on the application of intellectual property rights as they desired and they were forced to accept the GEF as the mechanism for the provision of financial resources, rather than a separate 'biodiversity fund' with compulsory contributions from 'developed country parties' for which they lobbied. Nevertheless, the overall tenor of the CBD was undoubtedly biased more in the direction of Rajan's 'Southern' position.

Some environmentalist critics lambasted the Convention as a 'pastiche of vague commitments, ambiguous phrases and ... awkward compromises' (Raustiala and Victor 1996: 19). But, as tends to be the case with this genre of analysis, the condemnatory tone missed the extent of the political achievement. By the end of the Rio conference 157 countries had signed the CBD and it came formally into being at the end of 1993. Significantly, the US was not one of the signatories. In remarks that uncannily foreshadowed his son's later rejection of the Kyoto Protocol, President George H. Bush argued that the Convention threatened to 'retard biotechnology and undermine the protection of ideas' and conceded too much to the gene-rich countries of the tropics; in any event, he would not sign 'a treaty that ... throws many Americans out of work' (cited in Rajan 1997: 239). His stance drew its force from the influence of the US biotechnology industry lobby and was a sign of a tougher politics in the offing. The incoming Clinton administration did make an attempt to reverse US policy: it formally added the signature of the United States to the Convention but never seriously pressed the merits of ratification upon the US Senate. However, US objections have not stopped the CBD continuing to be refined. As provided for, a series of post-Rio COPs tidied up several ongoing matters. Montreal was designated the site of the secretariat and the GEF re-endorsed as the continuing, but still interim, financial mechanism. A substantial work programme was also set out, including the extension of biodiversity conservation to the spheres of forestry, agriculture and fisheries and the incorporation of the highly sensitive matter of indigenous people's rights.

However, the key new commitment to emerge from these COPs was the decision to embark upon the negotiation of a biosafety protocol. Article 19.3 of the CBD provided for the parties to consider 'the need for and modalities of' a protocol setting out procedures in the field of 'the safe transfer, handling and use' of living modified organisms (LMOs) that might have an adverse effect on biodiversity and its components. An *ad hoc* working group on biosafety was convened in November 1995, but found it difficult to proceed quickly in the face of increasingly polarized positions being taken up by the main protagonists. The process came dramatically to a head at a series of meetings in Cartagena in Colombia in February 1999. It is particularly striking that, by this stage, the initial bipolar division in the CBD negotiations – broadly 'North' versus 'South' – had broken up into a much more nuanced array of positions. By the time of the final, tense moments at Cartagena no fewer than five groups could be discerned (Cosbey and Burgiel 2000). Coming out fully into the open was the Miami Group (so called because of the location of an initial group meeting), led by the US and composed additionally of Argentina, Australia, Canada, Chile and Uruguay. They were all major producers and exporters of genetically modified (GM) seed and crops, with the US and Canada in particular possessing some of the world's most advanced biotechnology industries. The Group's core interest was to enable free trade in GM products without burdensome bureaucratic approval procedures and/or protectionist barriers masquerading as environmental measures. It relied heavily for technical material on the biotechnology industry lobby. At the opposite end of the debate was the Like-Minded Group, which was essentially the G77/China, minus the three South American member states that had defected to the Miami Group.

This Group varied considerably in the regulatory capacity of its countries and the level of their involvement with biotechnology, but was united by the perception that a strong protocol was needed in the light of the unknown effects of LMOs on the environment and human health. It relied in turn on the support of several environmental NGOs. The EU negotiated as a unit, generally taking positions on the middle ground, whilst the Central and Eastern European countries mostly fell into line with either the EU or the Like-Minded Group. Last, but definitely not least, a so-called Compromise Group, composed of Japan, Mexico, Norway, Singapore, South Korea and Switzerland, came into being late in the process with the explicit aim of articulating positions which bridged the gap between the other participants.

In the end the talks failed, blocked by the continuing objections of the Miami Group (Rajamani 1999). Although delegates decided to call the protocol, as and when agreed, the Cartagena Protocol, they could not settle on a text at the Cartagena meeting and the gathering was eventually suspended amidst some discord. However, the project was slowly rebuilt by the chair of the COP, the Colombian Minister of the Environment, Juan Mayr, in a series of informal consultations where only two representatives of each group sat and talked in a round-table format. It was also significant that the resumed 'extraordinary COP', which assembled in Montreal in January 2000, came just a month or so after the disputatious and equally unsuccessful WTO trade talks in Seattle. This increased the pressure on the various groups to come to a deal, and they did (Falkner 2000). The Cartagena Protocol on Biosafety was duly agreed and immediately signed by more than 130 countries. Its main elements were:

- the creation of an 'advance informed agreement (AIA)' procedure that in effect requires exporters to seek consent from importers before the first shipment of LMOs for intentional introduction into the environment, explicitly excepting those to be used in food, feed or processing;
- the requirement that bulk shipments of LMOs, such as corn or soya beans that are intended to be used for these latter purposes, be accompanied by documentation stating that the shipments 'may contain' LMOs;
- the establishment of an internet-based 'Biosafety Clearing House' to facilitate the exchange of information about LMOs between countries; and
- the inclusion of a 'savings clause' which says that the protocol is neither subordinate to nor alters countries' rights and obligations under other international treaties and bodies, notably the WTO.

Some immediate judgements attributed the deal to a US retreat from some of its earlier positions. This was true relative to Cartagena, but should not obscure the reality that the Miami Group gained most of what it wanted in the Protocol. It kept LMOs intended for direct use in food, feed or processing out of the AIA, which means that the procedure only covers a small percentage of traded LMOs; it pushed the discussion of mandatory labelling into the future; and it achieved enough of a compromise in the language used in the 'savings clause'. The Like-Minded Group secured a strong version of the precautionary principle as set out originally in the Rio Declaration, which it felt opened up room for further strengthening of the Protocol in due course, and it obtained some promises of assistance in building the capacity of its member countries to manage modern biotechnology. Beyond that, it was largely disappointed. The other groups at least got an agreed protocol.

As ever, then, the Cartagena Protocol was a mixed package, with discussion of some issues in effect postponed, some remaining unsettled by virtue of ambiguity and some resolved as a consequence of complicated bargains struck between different groups of countries. In general, too, it can be said to have reconciled some trade and environmental arguments. It was prescribed that the Protocol would formally come into force after it had been ratified by 50 parties to the CBD. The US could not therefore sign it, even if it had wanted to do so, but this could not, and did not, imperil its eventual ratification, which occurred in September 2003. As of the end of 2004, no fewer than 111 countries had signed up to its terms.

The World Summit on Sustainable Development

Finally, we turn, as promised, to a brief review of the World Summit on Sustainable Development held in 2002. According to the UN General Assembly resolution which called it into being, the purpose of the WSSD was to hold a decennial review of the Rio 'Earth Summit' with the objective of reinvigorating global commitment to sustainable development. As such, it constituted an obvious, indeed self-proclaimed, staging point in the unfolding of the global environmental diplomacy that this chapter has set out to analyse. What is more, in the months running up to Johannesburg, UN publicists took to presenting the WSSD as the third (after Doha and Monterrey) in a series of major summits devoted to the global negotiation of development. In the event the gathering, although huge and generally well attended by heads of state, failed to live up to these expectations and has been subjected to a good deal of withering criticism, especially from the NGO community. Barry Coates (2002: 1), director of the World Development Movement, wrote, for example, that the outcome had set back the environmental agenda to such an extent that the WSSD, rather than being known as 'Rio plus ten', should 'more accurately be termed Rio minus ten'. Some of the immediate post-Johannesburg commentary did have an excessively bitter tone, for the conference was not without achievement. At the same time it can clearly be seen that too ambitious and too amorphous an agenda was set. In particular, the explicit link made to Doha and Monterrey meant that a whole range of issues pertaining to trade and finance was intermingled with more explicitly environmental themes. Given, too, the raw nerves generated by some of the post-Kyoto politics of climate change, it becomes somewhat easier to see why meaningful commitments in the WSSD's two main documents – the Plan of Implementation and the Johannesburg Declaration – proved to be so hard to secure.

As indicated, the talks at Johannesburg extended over an extraordinary array of complex and contentious matters. The list included not only what were dubbed the 'WEHAB' issues (Water and sanitation, Energy, Health and environment, Agriculture, and Biodiversity and ecosystem management), but also: poverty eradication, governance, trade, finance and globalization, climate change, health and human rights, 'small island developing states' and Africa. The WSSD was deliberately conceived as a 'catch-all' conference and it accordingly caught all of the existing tensions in global development diplomacy. Yet, precisely because the agenda was so dispersed, countries did not form into tight negotiating groups. The US delegation generally sought to block formal commitments and targets, especially if they necessitated financial expenditure. Having been lobbied hard not to attend by the neoconservative right in the US, President Bush did in the end absent himself, and was widely condemned elsewhere for doing so. This left the then US Secretary of State, Colin Powell, to speak on behalf of the US in the 'high-level segment' where his remarks were received with open disdain in some parts of the audience. However, the US was not alone in approaching the WSSD cautiously. On several issues its line was backed by a loose version of the JUSSCANNZ alliance of countries which had made its mark at Kyoto, as well as by OPEC members, vocal as always on energy and climate change matters. The EU endeavoured to operate as a bloc, but it was divided on trade and unable to make the concessions on that front which could have built support for its approach to other issues. Consequently, it was not able to assert effective leadership on the environmental agenda. This ruled out the emergence of the kind of *de facto* working arrangement with the G77/China that, at different moments, had helped to shape climate change politics. The truth about Johannesburg was that most delegations were driven more by negative than positive ambitions. They travelled principally in order to keep items out of the Plan of Implementation. In fact, it was only really South Africa, as host, which had a strong stake in getting agreement on the WSSD documents.

Unsurprisingly, in such a context, the outcomes represented little that was really new (International Institute for Sustainable Development 2002). The most significant of the deals struck included the setting of a target of halving the number of people without basic sanitation (about 2.4 billion people, or 40 per cent of the world's population) by 2015; the establishment of a commitment to restore fish stocks to their maximum sustainable level 'on an urgent basis and where possible not later than 2015'; a plan to reduce use of toxic chemicals by 2005; and an agreement, albeit weaker than many desired, to increase 'substantially' and 'with a sense of urgency' the global share of renewable energy sources. This last form of words in fact highlighted a key failure of Johannesburg. One of the most delicate issues in all the preparatory meetings before the WSSD and at the summit itself revolved around the linked questions of reducing subsidies on the use of fossil fuels and setting specific targets for increased use of renewable energy. The EU was in the vanguard of the debate, keen to see its strong renewable energy companies expand and proposing that countries aim to use renewable energy for 15 per cent of their needs by 2015; by contrast, the US, Japan and the OPEC countries, all of which feared for the position of their fossil fuel companies, were hostile. Brazil, supported by Argentina, Colombia, Norway, Switzerland and Sweden, proposed a compromise. The G77 came up with a different compromise. The EU then sought to work with the G77, but could not ultimately shift Japan from its support for the US line. Fearing that the earlier deal on water and sanitation targets might also unravel, delegates in the end could not get beyond the bland phrases cited above (Vidal 2002). For the rest, the Plan of Implementation largely reiterated the conclusions of other meetings: for example, it restated many of the Millennium Development Goals and drew heavily on the language used in the summary documents of Doha and Monterrey precisely in order to preserve the careful compromises of those negotiations. It also confirmed two of the principles of the 1992 Rio Declaration, those of principle 7 on 'common but differentiated responsibilities' in respect of global environmental degradation and principle 15 on the 'precautionary approach' to threats of serious or irreversible damage to the environment. However, this was only achieved after much argument between countries that wanted alternatively to weaken and strengthen these commitments. As for the new Johannesburg Declaration on Sustainable Development, this emerged from the bargaining as an eminently forgettable and thankfully short piece of prose.

The one, final dimension of the WSSD which it is important to highlight concerns the extensive presence in Johannesburg not only of NGO personnel with developmental and environmental interests, but also of business figures representing some of the biggest multinational companies in the world. This was planned. As Mark Malloch Brown, the UNDP's chief administrator at the time of the conference, revealingly put it, 'the Johannesburg Summit may disappoint now but surprise with its follow-up. There is an energy between governments, the private sector and civil society. It's been the world's biggest trade fair and it will bear fruit' (*Financial Times*, 4 September 2002). Although, of course, this remains to be seen over the longer span of time he identified, what he was referring to were the substantial number of 'partnership initiatives', or in WSSD jargon 'Type-II outcomes' (in contrast to the traditional multilateral Type-I outcomes already discussed), which were proclaimed during the course of the summit in a range of project areas connected broadly to sustainable development. The US government made much of these initiatives, announcing modest direct funding, intended to draw in private sector contributions, for projects related to water, clean air, farming, forest preservation and disease prevention. As implied, advocates of these various partnerships stressed that private finance was the best way to lever new money into environmental projects; opponents condemned them as means to 'deflect criticism over the failure of governments to deliver' (Coates 2002: 4). What is clear is that their centrality to the work of the WSSD offers still more evidence of the extent of the contemporary hold of market ideology on key elements of the global environmental agenda.

Conclusion

The environment is different again from both finance and trade as an arena of development diplomacy. As Marc Williams (1993: 8) reminds us, various writers on global environmental negotiations have long noted 'the importance of the North–South dimension and have speculated on a return to the focused political activity of the NIEO'. The former has certainly been apparent as a dimension of the political process: as we have seen, the Rio Declaration, the UNFCCC and the CBD all deployed in their texts the contrasting categories of 'developed' and 'developing' countries. Certain common themes can also be identified across various environmental issues which might be presented as constituting the essence of a 'Southern' position: that responsibility for global environmental problems lies with the industrial and post-industrial countries, that these countries should take at least the first steps towards amelioration, that any such measures should not hinder the development prospects of poorer countries, and that resource transfers from the rich world should accompany and facilitate all environmental protection activities. Such an emphasis does undoubtedly capture something of the background shape of the picture, but at the same time it misses much of the complexity of the action in the foreground. In relation to climate change and biodiversity, and even at the WSSD, the detailed bargaining has actually been organized around cross-cutting coalitions. Although the G77 has probably been more active and cohesive in the environmental arena than in other spheres of contemporary development diplomacy, its unity has been fractured at several key points in the various negotiations. None of this is to say that G77 countries, in their different guises and subgroups, have not been able to obtain gains of significance from the politics that we have examined. The key difference with the arenas of finance and trade is that in respect of the environment it has been the G7 countries which have been asking them to take action, rather than the other way round. Elizabeth DeSombre (2000: 39) has argued that 'developing countries were most able to achieve their goals when the environmental problems in question were rival, giving them the power to undermine any co-operative efforts by not participating'. This is a plausible thesis and draws attention to the most distinctive feature of this particular arena: the fact that most environmental issues concern what are sometimes called 'common pool resources' (Barkin and Shambaugh 1999). This means that they cannot be satisfactorily provided – although they can be significantly damaged – by one set of actors, thereby creating the need to engineer much wider involvement in environmental problem-solving across the international community.

As suggested at the beginning of this chapter, the concept of sustainable development has been widely criticized for its vacuity. It can also be argued that it has not even come close to being an ideological match for neoliberalism and that Johannesburg in particular showed up the respective political weight of these two world-views. Yet it remains the case that the Brundtland rhetoric, summed up in the notion of a 'common future' and carried through into UN conferences and the work of bodies such as UNEP, has had a marked impact on the conduct of global environmental negotiations. It has served to strengthen and legitimize the right of all countries, no matter how poor or vulnerable, to be taken seriously in relation to environmental concerns. As we have seen, the specific principle that has been laid down, and successfully defended, has been that of 'common but differentiated responsibilities' for the maintenance of environmental well-being. It has not even been unusual for G77 countries to make their arguments about climate change or biodiversity by appealing to the ideals of justice and equity. To that not inconsiderable extent, the environmental strand of the contemporary global politics of development has been conducted on an ideological playing field that has been markedly more level than in the cases of either finance or trade.

Part IV

Conclusion

Chapter 9

Unequal Development

So, what did happen to 'North–South' politics? We posed this question in the Preface at the very beginning of this book and suggested that it was a pithy way of expressing the essential point of entry into what was to follow. At that stage we offered as an answer no more than the assertion that it remained one of the central issues facing the contemporary world order and the hint that that phrase might no longer be the most appropriate way to frame the issue. We have covered a lot of ground in the intervening eight chapters and have now reached the point in this concluding chapter where we must firm up the argument that underpinned those initial observations and that has subsequently been made at length in the core parts of the book. Broadly speaking, the conventional wisdom of our time suggests that a 'North' and a 'South', or their equivalents in other terminologies, still exist, but that 'North–South' politics has largely disappeared, at least by comparison with the high profile that it attained in the 1970s. We disagree with this reading of contemporary global politics in relation to both aspects of the argument.

First, we reject the idea that a simple bifurcated view of the world – as in developed/developing, core/periphery, North/South – is capable of capturing the many nuances, the many complicated dynamics of actual events and situations. In fact, we do not even think that it comes close to doing so. We tried to explain in Chapter 1 why none of these pairs of terms travelled well into the new contours of a globalizing era and it is to be hoped that such an argument proves persuasive. It has been made before and has perhaps not had as much impact as it might, as the briefest perusal of many academic and journalistic writings quickly reveals. Their pages are still littered with references to the position of the 'developing countries', the intransigence of the 'North' or the problems of the 'periphery'. Indeed, new pretenders have arisen over the last few years which are just as simplistic. Within mainstream thinking, both conservative and liberal, the favoured bifurcation of the moment has become 'The West versus the Rest'. In a section entitled precisely that within his famous 'Clash of Civilizations?' article, Samuel Huntington (1993: 39) announced that the 'West' had ascended to 'an extraordinary peak of power in relation to other civilizations', with its leading countries maintaining 'extraordinarily [that emphasis again] close relations with each other to the exclusion of lesser and largely non-Western countries'. Robert Kaplan (2000) drew an even more dramatic distinction between the comfortable world of settled, peaceful, 'Western' liberal democratic states and the dark world of 'gangster states' undermined by the combined stresses of population growth, urbanization, environmental degradation and failed development. Writing not long after 9/11, Martin Wolf (2001), the influential *Financial Times* columnist, asked us to 'think of a limousine driving through an urban ghetto'. 'Inside', he went on, 'is the post-industrial world of western Europe, North America, Australasia, Japan and the emerging Pacific Rim. Outside are all the rest.' The imagery in all of this is strikingly clear. Interestingly, much the same mind-set, albeit from a diametrically opposed moral stance, can be seen in the thinking that has lately identified and made fashionable the notion of a 'Global South'. Beloved by the NGO movement and some of its academic followers despite the obvious linguistic contradiction at the heart of the term, the concept of the 'Global South' also sweeps up a mass of divergent cultures, histories and predicaments into one problematic, which is then distinguished, at least implicitly, from the historic role and responsibilities of the 'Global North'. It should hardly need saying by now that none of this will really do as sophisticated analysis of an enormously variegated world.

Second, we reject just as emphatically the claim that the essential elements which gave meaning to what we used to call 'North–South' politics have departed the global political scene. In effect, we conceived this book as a means by which to search some of the key diplomatic arenas of global politics for evidence that, if found, would comprehensively undermine such a thesis. We think that that evidence has been assembled. Chapters 6, 7 and 8 show beyond doubt that there still exists a plethora of inter-state conflicts around the issues of finance, trade and the environment (to name but three arenas) which resemble in their core dynamics some of the key characteristics of the 'North–South' relations of old. The point is, however, that the patterns of conflict and negotiation, as revealed in these chapters, are much, much more complex than we used to think they were in the heady days of the clashes of the 1970s. It may be, of course, that such a reading of those events was flawed, and that they were never that straightforward. That is not something that we have investigated here. The positive claim that we make in relation to the 1990s and early 2000s is that the interests of 'richer' countries and of 'poorer' countries can still, broadly speaking, be seen to generate political tensions in a variety of key areas of global policy making. Yet this statement must be immediately followed by an important qualification, which is that the precise patterns of state strategy, of international coalition-building, of diplomatic move and counter-move, do not fall according to a neat 'richer–poorer' bifurcation. Put differently, there is a crude spectrum which has the 'richer' and the 'poorer' countries at the two ends; yet that does not mean that 'richer' countries do not disagree on major issues or that 'poorer' countries are always united by their poverty. Crucially, it does not draw sufficient attention to all the activity that takes place in the middle of the spectrum, undertaken by countries that are neither 'rich' nor 'poor' in any simplistic sense. In sum, there is a lot going on politically in these particular arenas of the contemporary global order. We need to do these events justice by finding an analytical method that does not close our minds to complexity by forcing us to think in the excessively crude, dichotomous manner that we criticized so extensively at the outset of this analysis. We have tried in this book to work our way towards such a method by rethinking the key concept that in practice drives the whole of this debate, which is, of course, development.

Development as country strategy

How did we proceed? We argued in Chapters 1 and 2 that we needed to free the concept of development from its distinctive and traditional base in what has, of course, long been specified as development studies and to re-engage with it within the context of those wider discussions of global economic and political change that have lately been taking place in exciting fashion inside the emergent field of critical political economy. In particular, we drew from this latter literature a number of founding theses. We interpreted the end of United States hegemony in the 1970s as the beginning of a new phase in the world order; conceptualized globalization as a process of ongoing structural change in the world economy; and insisted upon the continuing centrality of states (or, as we preferred to call them, following Cox, varying state-society complexes). Stimulated by these insights we were able to identify as follows the four necessary features of a new approach to development:

(a) a rejection of a special category of countries deemed to be in need of development, and a recasting of the whole question of development on a universalist basis;
(b) a focus upon development strategy, principally as still pursued by a national economy, society and/or polity;
(c) a recognition that such a strategy for all countries necessarily involves the interaction, and appropriate meshing, of internal and external elements; and
(d) a recognition of the many variants of time, place and history in development predicaments.

On this platform we redefined development for the contemporary era. It is probably worth reiterating the definition proposed. It was the collective building by the constituent social and political actors of a country (or at least in the first instance a country) of a viable, functioning political economy, grounded in at least a measure of congruence between its core domestic characteristics and attributes and its location within a globalizing world order and capable on that basis of advancing the well-being of those living within its confines. The salient point underpinning this definition was that it refocused the discussion of development on countries but argued, perhaps distinctively, that *all* countries in the world should be seen as having to pursue development. In other words, we suggested that it no longer made sense to think of development as something that only 'developing countries' needed to worry about. By the same token, the so-called 'developed countries' could not be thought somehow to have completed their development, for they too manifestly still had to engage with the world order and chart domestic strategies for so doing. In short, the argument we mounted was that development was an issue for every country.

It has to be conceded that the case for rethinking development in this way (which we have advanced in earlier presentations and publications) has, as yet, been insufficiently recognized. Indeed, the truth is that it has been perceived in some quarters as a hurtful critique. Some scholars working in development studies have turned out to be conservatives in radical clothing, determined to hang on to the proclaimed special nature of their field of study long after the rationale for its distinctiveness has been undercut. There is no denying that development studies has had an heroic history. We have argued previously that, in its heyday, it was an exemplar of all that was best about the social sciences: interdisciplinary, focused on big questions, engaged with them, political in the most generous sense of the word. But that phase has passed and development studies, for all its continuing merits, is no longer quite such a vibrant field of enquiry and debate, as many of its adherents openly admit. In fact, we saw that fully 20 years ago David Booth (1985) declared that an 'impasse' had been reached in the field, a claim which quickly became the new orthodoxy. What is more, the harsh truth is that, despite the efforts of Schuurman (1993) and others to break out beyond this impasse, no basis on which to organize this advance has been found that has proved to be acceptable across the subfield. This, in essence, is why we have argued here and elsewhere that the way forward is to bring about a fruitful marriage between development studies and critical political economy and thereby ground a new post-impasse conception of development in the universalist terms set out above.

Such an approach has another considerable merit, at least as we see it. This is that it enables the study and discussion of development to escape from what we believe to have been almost a moral trap. Although the precise normative content of the term has always been hotly debated between modernization, dependency and the many other assorted theoretical formulations that have been advanced over the years, development has traditionally and unquestioningly been seen as a 'good' – something better than 'mere' economic growth, incorporating perhaps an additional commitment to freedom, embracing the empowerment of the people, bringing about self-respect and the fulfilment of human talents, and so on and so forth. Although the particular normative components of development varied considerably in the hands of different thinkers in different periods of time, what such approaches had in common was a commitment to a moral end. In effect, development was always defined in moral terms. This often had unfortunate consequences analytically because it fostered a tendency in development studies to make moral, rather than what one might call scientific, critiques of actually existing development strategies. The rethinking of development proposed and utilized in this book certainly does not eliminate the possibility of engaging in moral condemnation of a country's development priorities. Indeed, it can be argued that it facilitates such an enterprise because it provides a common base for that critique: namely, prior study and analysis of different *actual* developments based on a review of what countries have sought to do in the real world in respect of building their own national political economies. The important point is that such an approach does not require that the moral critique be made as part and parcel of the analysis. Instead, we can behave more like the good social scientists that we should be aspiring to be, studying in the first instance what country development strategies are being essayed in a given era, assessing what works and what does not and exploring why, and then – *but only then* – considering the implications of what we have found for the moral questions in which we are interested. In intellectual terms we at least have found this way of proceeding to be genuinely liberating.

In this book we have focused on the global politics of development. We have in effect conceived of certain major strands of inter-state conflict as emerging from the intrinsically competing development strategies of the whole range of states now in existence in the world. As we said in Chapter 2, country development strategies have to be seen as inevitably having a critically important external dimension. As such, they cannot avoid reaching outwards in pursuit of advantage, interests and position and, in so doing, they come into conflict with the strategies of other countries working to exactly the same dynamic. Yet these countries do not fall neatly into 'developed' or 'developing', 'North' or 'South', or even 'richer' and 'poorer' packages; instead, they spread across the full spectrum of material capabilities, they are located in different regions of the world, they have experienced different histories and they are characterized by different state–society relationships. Here, of course, are to be found some of the sources of the huge complexity of the politics that then emerges and which the earlier chapters of the book have sought to describe and analyse.

Finally, in this reprise of the method of analysis we have deployed, it is perhaps useful to repeat and justify one more time the argument, initially made in Chapter 1, that what we are endeavouring to dissect here is 'the politics of critical political economy'. This phrase was used to reflect a commitment to try to give due weight to both structure and agency in explanations, rather than privileging one to the exclusion of the other. We thus talked of 'structural context' as the source of both opportunities and constraints, as being both enabling and binding, as permitting agency within bounds. Put another way, agency-oriented (i.e. politics and/or international relations) concepts have necessarily to be embedded within structural (i.e. political economy) concepts. For organizational reasons, the book has been divided into two core parts that broadly reflect these two emphases, with Part II examining the structural context of development and Part III examining the arenas of development diplomacy. Although we will now report the main conclusions of each part of the book under these two headings, it should always be remembered that the two methodologies need to be wrapped up together, for structure shapes agency and agency shapes structure. In other words, the next two sections of this concluding chapter need very much to be read as a whole.

The structural context of development

We organized Part II of the book around Robert Cox's conception of the three key component elements of the historical structures that shape the framework of action within the global political economy: material capabilities, ideas and institutions. We sought to interrogate the first element by examining in detail various aspects of the material capabilities of the 191 countries that presently constitute the full membership of the United Nations. As indicated, countries are still the main protagonists of development strategy in the current era and it therefore seemed most appropriate to begin by trying to set out their most basic material capabilities in relation to size, gross national income and human development. We then explored the important role that ideas play in setting the structural parameters within which country actors, and indeed all actors, have to operate. But ideas are never absolutely dominant and so we pursued this question by reference to the notion of contending ideas. We sought in effect to assess the contemporary global balance of ideological power. Finally, we focused our analysis of the role of institutions within the global political economy on the many international organizations that now adorn the global stage. Recognizing that institutions are often widely, and understandably, defined in broader terms as structured rules of behaviour, it nevertheless made sense in the particular context of our concerns in this book to try to get a handle upon the powers possessed by such critical global institutions as the IMF, the World Bank and the WTO, not to mention the many agencies of the UN system. In short, in Part II of the book we endeavoured to paint in the structural context of development by grappling with the interlinked material, ideational and institutional dimensions of structural power.

What we found was a complex pattern of structural inequalities. In the first place, in reviewing the material capabilities of the many countries of the world, we certainly saw enough to realize that the whole business of categorizing countries is unavoidably political. It did not matter whether the category in question was a 'big emerging market' or a 'small state', whether it was the low income, lower middle income, upper middle income and high income classification deployed by the World Bank, or even whether it was the notion of an LDC, as calculated quite cleverly by the UN Committee for Development Planning on the basis of a mix of criteria. Politics always emerged within the mode of categorization. We thus concluded that we needed to proceed in the main by analysing what countries did and said, rather than by reference to which category of country they could be said to belong. This usefully reinforced our earlier theoretical doubts about the supposed merits of thinking about country strategies in terms of their notional level of development or location in either the 'North' or the 'South', or even the 'West' or the 'Rest'. All that said, this examination of multiple indicators of size, gross national income and human development could not but highlight the huge disparities that exist in these respects in the contemporary world order. There is no need to repeat much of the detail here. One only has to think of the gap between the Russian Federation and Nauru in surface area, between China and Tuvalu in population, between the United States and São Tomé and Principe in GNI, or between Norway and Sweden on the one hand and Niger and Sierra Leone on the other in respect of measures of human development to grasp the point. Yet it is perhaps just as important to note that all the indicators that we scrutinized genuinely ran from top to bottom via all points in between. Indeed, we deliberately highlighted the middle, as well as the upper and lower, tiers in all of the tables to emphasize precisely this point. Although it does not matter, other than to the statistically minded, exactly which countries were the medians in the various tables, it does matter politically that countries were placed in these tables in a most complex fashion. We cannot read off their power in global politics from the indicators in any direct way, but we did nevertheless get an early sense of what quantity and quality of capabilities their leaders can potentially bring to the negotiating table when development issues are being discussed. It is also the case, given the sheer number of countries that now exist, that the dominance of the largest or the richest can never be more than a relatively modest proportion of *total* surface area, population or GNI. In short, some countries do dominate and inequalities abound, but the latter cannot be depicted in simple fashion and the scale of the current global system of countries inevitably places limits on the extent of that dominance, at least in raw statistical terms.

Second, we saw that the terrain of contemporary ideological debate was also structured on a profoundly unequal basis, indeed much more so than the sphere of material capabilities. We examined in turn the ways that the Washington Consensus and the post-Washington Consensus reshaped modes of thinking about development strategy across much of the world, initially bringing to bear upon divergent countries a stark new neoliberal paradigm and then subsequently qualifying the core tenets of that model by the incorporation of other considerations relating to governance, social capital and so on. Many older competing development models, which were very fashionable and indeed moderately successful in the 1950s and 1960s, came under great pressure to concede ground in the face of these ideological juggernauts and over time most fell by the wayside. We now hear almost nothing of the merits of 'import-substitution industrialization', let alone 'state socialism'; we hear much less about the 'developmental state'; and we detect a lot of anxious concerns about the continuing viability of 'welfare capitalism' or 'social democracy'. The point is that the main sources of these ideas have been the US and the UK – the Anglo-American world – and, even here, it has to be said that the contribution played by UK thinkers and ideologues has been minor by comparison with their US counterparts. Ideologically, the global order danced increasingly to the tunes of one powerful country over the course of the 1980s and 1990s. In that sense the successive phases of consensus were aptly named by reference to its capital city, even though this descriptor was initially adduced to reflect the location in Washington, DC, of key global institutions as well as key departments of the US state. However, since 2001 the growing influence in the US of even harsher neoconservative ideas has altered this situation somewhat, moving the debate into relatively uncharted waters. To put it mildly, neoconservative thinking has not proved to be as persuasive globally: in fact, it has set in train a good deal of resistance, causing European politicians and thinkers to rally in support of softer

Third Way neoliberalisms and encouraging others in Asia and Latin America to show interest in the merits of an emerging 'Beijing Consensus'. To this extent, the field of ideas can perhaps be said to be slightly less unequally structured than it has been for some time. Nevertheless, the fact remains that the vast majority of the countries of the world contribute nothing to the way that the ideational debate about development, political economy and international relations is conducted on the global stage.

Third, we noted varying patterns of inequality in the way that the global institutions work. With the exception of the Security Council, the UN operates under a voting system that gives each country a single vote. But the price it pays for this is that the stronger states, most notably the US, frequently ignore the resolutions passed and the stances taken up by the UN. As a result, it can often appear more to be the debating chamber of the world order, rather than its key decision-making body. The WTO also operates notionally on the basis of country consensus, which means that it is harder for the most powerful countries to force through decisions, although at the same time, as we have seen, that does not mean that there do not exist and are not deployed some quite rough ways of bringing power to bear on awkward or reluctant members. By contrast, the weighted voting mechanisms used in the decision-making apparatuses of the IMF and the World Bank entrench the position of the wealthiest countries, again most notably the US, which has in both bodies what is, to all intents and purposes, a veto in key spheres of decision. Indeed, we argued that the US was able to use its position within these two organizations to augment its external reach as a nation-state. Underpinning all of this is the increasing centrality of the G7/G8 system, which seems to be taking on more and more of the role of an organizing political directorate of the global order. Here the numbers do not lie: only seven countries, all of them rich and powerful, are really involved, Russia being incorporated for mainly historical and symbolic reasons. For its part, the G77 was formed at the first meeting of UNCTAD in 1964 as a means to give voice in global politics to what were then generally seen as 'Third World' countries. Its membership now stands as high as 131 countries, even though the original name has been retained, and as a grouping it continues to take up positions on all manner of issues, especially within the UN system. But what it is manifestly not capable of doing is redressing in any significant way the deeply unequal hold which a few leading countries have imposed on those global institutions which they consider to matter the most in the present era.

In sum, then, Chapters 3, 4 and 5 cumulatively exposed a complex pattern of structural inequalities in the very context within which the global politics of development has lately taken place. None of this was easy to express neatly, although it was apparent that ideational and institutional power is being used by a number of leading countries to entrench still further the dominance that they enjoy, albeit to a lesser extent, in respect of raw material capabilities. Certainly, the 'level playing field' much discussed and lauded within liberal political ideology is nowhere to be seen when it comes to assessing what we have called the structural context of development.

The arenas of development diplomacy

We organized Part III of the book around a discussion of what we argued were the three most important arenas of development diplomacy within this general structural context. These were deemed to be finance, trade and the environment, each arena being conceived as a sphere of global policy making that countries could not but enter as a consequence of their pursuit of a particular development strategy. In other words, development strategy was seen as unavoidably having financial, trade-related and environmental dimensions. It would have been possible, of course, to have extended the analysis to include other dimensions, but it seemed to us that these were three of the most important considerations and would provide enough evidence on which to draw conclusions. We were also clear that in this part of the book we were seeking primarily to understand agency, conceived in conventional international relations terms as the pursuit by countries of their perceived national interests, although manifestly, as already argued, it was recognized that all countries, even the most powerful, experience structural constraints on their freedom of action and thus only have a certain room to manoeuvre in seeking to pursue their interests. In short, in Part III of the book we explored the recent global politics of finance, trade and the environment with a view to establishing the nature and effectiveness of the bargaining, coalition-building and deal-making engaged in by the many, many countries willing and able to participate in these diplomatic arenas.

What, again, we found was a complex pattern of agential inequalities. Of itself, this may be thought to be unsurprising since one of the axioms of the realist view of international politics has always been that it is the disparities of power between states that determine outcomes. It was, nevertheless, very revealing of the complexities of these patterns that significant differences emerged between the power relations at work in the three diplomatic arenas we examined. Reviewing each in turn, finance was seen as an arena where there presently exists sustained evidence of domination of the agenda by the richest and most powerful countries of the world grouped together within the G7. The meetings of the G7 finance ministers are now by far the most important inter-state gatherings to take place in this sphere of policy. The G20, formed in 1999 by these very finance ministers specifically to draw into the international financial architecture other 'systemically important countries', has yet to establish a distinctive role for itself beyond providing legitimation and support for G7 efforts to contain threatening financial crises. As for other countries, they have been shown to participate in global financial politics only on terms set by the G7. As we saw, the OFCs were mostly pressed into signing up for 'list politics'; the HIPCs have been led down a tortuous path to limited debt relief as determined in the main by the IMF; and the LDCs still wait like supplicants to see whether the G7 countries and others will provide the funds required to bring them within touching distance of the Millennium Development Goals. In this context the G24 is the dog that did not bark in the night. Established to concert the positions of the 'Third World' countries in advance of the regular IMF and World Bank meetings, it has failed to make an impact.

By comparison, trade appears to be a diplomatic arena in which a tough form of inter-state power politics is the characteristic feature. We saw that for many years global trade politics was dominated by the 'Quad' countries: the US, the EU, Japan and Canada. Once they managed to reach agreement amongst themselves (and here bargaining between the US and the EU was what really counted), they were generally able, eventually, to bring on board enough other significant trading countries to force all the others into a final deal. It is their capacity to continue doing this that has been called into question at meetings of the WTO in Seattle, Doha and Cancún. Many more countries are now fully engaged in the global negotiation of trade and have deployed themselves within an intricate set of shifting coalitions which expresses something much more complicated than the existence of a single, coherent response to the preferred strategy of the 'Quad' and certainly gives the lie to the frequently-touted idea that the 'developing countries' adopt a common position. Of these coalitions, the (other) G20, the grouping formed by Brazil, China, India and others at Cancún, has attracted the greatest attention because it seemed that it had, at least for a while, prevented agreement on the conclusion of the Doha 'Round'. It is unquestionably true that this grouping, as well as others like the G90, the G33 and the Core Group opposed to the inclusion of the Singapore issues within the WTO, has fought its corner with greater skill and resolve than we have seen in previous international trade talks. To that extent, the power relations at work in the trade arena are less unequal than those at play in relation to finance. That said, stark disparities remain; many small and/or poor countries struggle to achieve any impact; and at the end of the day the US and the EU, if they can come to a deal, are still well placed to bring talks to a conclusion on their terms. Indeed, it has lately been suggested that the 'July package' agreed in mid-2004 is evidence that the unity of the G20 has at last been broken (since Brazil and India were two of the five 'interested parties' which brokered this interim deal) and that the WTO is back on track to bring the latest round to a successful conclusion in at least the foreseeable future. This remains to be seen, but is possibly the case.

The environment, at first sight, can seem as if it is an arena of development diplomacy that is redolent of the old 'North–South' battles of the NIEO era of the 1970s. We noted that the Rio Declaration, the UNFCCC and the CBD all referred in their texts to the twin categories of 'developed' and 'developing' countries. By contrast, in the arenas of finance and trade we have been insistent that such turns of phrase do not in any way match the complex realities at work; indeed, that they mislead more than clarify. In the final analysis, the same also applies to the environmental arena. The G77 has been more cohesive in this policy sphere than the others we have examined and it has, quite importantly, been able to harness a collective emotional resonance to the predicament of countries asked to pay in some way for the environmental damage caused by the richest and most powerful early industrialising countries. But, in practice, in relation to climate change and biodiversity, as well as at the WSSD in Johannesburg in 2002, G77 unity has been routinely split, with China also always officially distinct from it, and the serious bargaining has taken place between several coalitions which cut across the 'developed/developing country' divide. The final discussions that led to the signing of the Kyoto Protocol thus involved the interplay of the different perceived interests of the EU, the JUSSCANNZ countries (which included the US and Japan), the CEITs of Russia and Central and Eastern Europe, the AOSIS grouping, OPEC and a rather disparate G77/China alliance. In similar fashion, the final signing of the Cartagena Protocol depended upon a complex deal struck between the Miami Group, the EU, the CEITs, a Compromise Group and the Like-Minded Group, which was in essence the G77/China minus three South American countries that had defected to the Miami Group. Perhaps the key difference between the environmental diplomatic arena and those of finance and trade is that in the former the G7 countries cannot force their interests upon other countries as effectively as they have been able to do in these latter spheres. They are required to ask them to take action in favour of the environment: no agreement means no response, which is thus a defeat for the countries that want to see environmental controls imposed. It is perhaps revealing that the G7 forum has scarcely ever discussed environmental issues.

In sum, then, Chapters 6, 7 and 8 set out a series of complex patterns of agential inequality in the three major arenas of development diplomacy. Once more, the pattern is not easy to express neatly, mainly because it varies from arena to arena and from time to time. It is apparent that the US, the EU and Japan (albeit in varying combinations) are the key drivers of these agendas and that they can often, but not always, assert their core interests. Equally, the emerging role of China, Brazil and India, in particular, is notable and a sign that other national centres of power are increasingly making their presence felt within the global politics of development. By the same token, many other countries, although they are not necessarily all that successful in delivering their negotiating ambitions, are no longer as passive in these arenas as once was the case. Each chapter in turn told an interesting and complex story about contemporary global politics; cumulatively, they certainly suggest that many of the simple pictures that many tend still to use to portray the current era are either out-of-date or have indeed always been fundamentally flawed.

Bringing inequality (fully) in

The big lesson that we draw from these summaries of the conclusions reached in earlier chapters of the book is that we need urgently to bring the concept of inequality fully into the debate about the global politics of development. We have identified the existence on this terrain of complex patterns of structural and agential inequalities and have suggested that these are mutually reinforcing in the ways that structure and agency are always mutually reinforcing. But we have still to explore how best to conceptualize the issue of inequality in global politics.

The question that arises is whether there is much on which to build in embarking upon this endeavour. The brief answer is not much. There is in fact an interesting and lively debate taking place mainly within economics about inequalities within the global economy, but it is doubtful if it is actually of much use to our concerns here. It involves an intricate set of statistical considerations about the income distribution of all the world's people. On one side of the argument the claim is made that world poverty and world inequality have both fallen during the past 20 years, thanks in large part to the rising economic openness generated by neoliberal globalization (World Bank 2002). This conclusion is reached principally by comparing the average incomes over time of each country and then weighting by population, thereby bringing into the analysis and gaining the benefit accordingly of the fast recent economic growth of China and India in particular. On the other side of the argument there sits the work of critical economists such as Robert Wade, who counter-claim that both world poverty and world inequality may actually have been increasing, rather than decreasing, over this period, and certainly during the early to mid-1990s. This calculation is made differently, mostly on the basis of household income and expenditure surveys and using current exchange rates rather than purchasing-power-parity terms. Wade (2004: 164) concludes that 'at the level of the world economy as a whole increasing returns in income generation – the positive feed-back of the Matthew effect, "To him that hath shall be given" – prevails over diminishing returns, despite the third wave [1980 to the present] of globalisation'. As already indicated, the debate is a subtle one and depends on a number of quite sophisticated, and highly questionable, methodological presumptions. It is not going to be resolved quickly or easily (Wade vs Wolf 2002). But, from our point of view that does not matter too much because it does not centrally address our more political or international relations-oriented concerns.

Within the fields of study of international relations and international political economy there is, disappointingly, much less active discussion of the impact and role of inequality. Steve Smith has forcefully made the argument that international relations is predominantly an American social science and shown, *inter alia*, that this genealogy has had a specific impact on the kinds of inequalities 'seen' by its dominant theories and methodologies. 'Put simply', he writes, 'the mainstream of the U.S. dis-cipline sees political and military inequalities, but it does not deem other forms of inequality as relevant to the discipline' (Smith 2002: 82). Nicola Phillips (2005) has equally effectively argued that mainstream US-based international political economy has a similar general tendency systematically to neglect issues of inequality. More importantly from the perspective adopted in this book, she has been almost as critical of the treatment of inequality in critical globalization studies, partly for its tendency still to think in continuing 'North–South' terms, as extensively criticized here, but also because 'inequality is understood predominantly as an effect or a consequence of globalisation' (Phillips 2005a: 45). She rightly highlights an important article by Andrew Hurrell and Ngaire Woods (1995) that is probably the best effort yet made within critical international political economy to think through the relationship between globalization and inequality. They insist that 'inequalities among states *both* shape the process of globalisation *and* are affected by it' (Hurrell and Woods 1995: 447, my emphases). They go on to illustrate their argument by drawing attention to four areas which illustrate the link-ages between inequality and globalization, namely, state strength, inter-national institutions, values and norms, and non-state actors. As such, they take us nicely beyond those liberal approaches that either ignore or downplay inequality. Yet Phillips' comment upon their argument is apposite and worthy of quotation. She observes that, for all their good work, Hurrell and Woods still 'tend to treat inequality primarily as a condition which influences responses to globalization rather than genuinely tracing the ways in which globalization is itself intrinsically structured by inequality' (Phillips 2005a: 45).

We have here an important insight. We must do more than conceive of inequality as just an outcome of global politics; we must also go further even than seeing it as a condition that shapes global politics. The latter is an improvement, but still not adequate. What we must surely seek to do is to bring inequality *fully* into the discussion by thinking of it as something that is fundamentally *constitutive* of contemporary global politics. This means that we cannot think of what global politics is without situating inequality at the very core of our understanding of that reality. We are therefore arguing quite explicitly that marked inequalities of power of both a structural and an agential nature limit the capacity of countries to pursue and deliver successfully their preferred national development strategies, and that this is absolutely central to understanding the core dynamics of contemporary global politics. We choose to think of this as the global politics of *unequal development* and recommend this form of words as the best, certainly the most nuanced, way of capturing these inequalities in a shorthand phrase. The argument, in summary, is that *all* countries (the most powerful and the least powerful, the largest and the smallest, the richest and the poorest) seek to achieve development as we have redefined it. They cannot but take their country development strategies to the global stage because such goals cannot sensibly be pursued in isolation in a globalizing order. In so doing, they confront complex structural inequalities in respect of their possession of material capabilities, their production of key ideas and their capacity to play a significant role within global institutions. They start, in effect, from positions marked by unequal access to development resources. They can of course play their hands with varying degrees of skill in pursuit of their development objectives, but they still find that they end up playing out severe agential inequalities when they press their development strategies in key global diplomatic arenas. They live as a consequence with outcomes that emerge from inter-state political bargaining in these arenas that are profoundly unequal. In a nutshell, then, we can and do say that all countries experience the constraints and the opportunities of what we have called unequal development.

The point is that the politics generated by these patterns of unequal development does not operate in a form that can be expressed in a simple formula. The reality is that contemporary global politics is characterized not just by inequality, but by a very complex inequality.

This complexity can only be unpicked structure by structure and arena by arena, as we have tried to do in preceding chapters. We have to take on the task of getting to grips with the detail and of examining what particular countries, or groupings and alliances of countries, actually do, not what we presuppose they do in the light of flawed organizing assumptions. We cannot in all honesty substitute for such a 'bottom-up' approach a simplistic 'top-down' set of expectations about what the 'First World' or the 'Third World', or the 'North' or the 'South', or even less the 'West' or the 'Rest', are or should be doing *if* we want to understand fully and properly the interactions of no fewer than 191 separate countries. To the extent that we do, we only delude both ourselves and those who read what we write.

Conclusion

We could end the journey that the writing (and reading) of this book has involved with a plea that an ethic of equality be placed at the centre of global political debate at the beginning of the new century. For example, J. Mohan Rao (1999) has argued to good effect that equity is not just a means better to effect cooperation between countries but is actually a valuable end in itself: in his preferred phrase, it is a 'global public good'. Others have made the same argument in different ways and in different vocabularies. From a normative viewpoint, we are entirely in sympathy. It would seem a very attractive prospect to look forward to living in a world marked by equal development but, unfortunately, this seems rather to miss the point. We have argued that, at root, the contemporary global politics of unequal development is embedded within and dependent upon 'hierarchies of power' (Mittelman 2000: 5) which remain understudied and underemphasized in many existing accounts of globalization. Politics is thus the problem, but it is also perhaps the solution. We should not assume for a moment that powerful countries that gain hugely from patterns of unequal development will be likely to give up voluntarily the benefits that this brings to their peoples. They may decide to 'pay off' some of the worst excesses of this inequality in relation to HIV/AIDS, or Africa in general, or even in respect of the worst, or most visible, forms of poverty wherever they occur in the world. They are certainly likely to be willing to bring closer to the centre of global politics a modest number of countries that appear to have the capacity to disrupt the system as a whole. But they will not embark seriously upon the politics of global equality, no matter how much occasional rhetorical flourishes to that effect suggest otherwise. Such gains as will be made over the next period of years in the direction of more equal development will be made by disadvantaged countries, operating mostly in shifting alliances, forcing concessions and changes of current policy in finance or trade or the environment by harnessing and deploying effectively the resources of power, however limited, that they do have at their disposal.

Viewed optimistically, there are some signs that this is beginning to happen. As we have seen, over the last few years the tectonic plates of the global politics of development have been shifting slowly. The US is dominant but not hegemonic; the EU is often distracted by internal concerns; Japan is an uncertain player on the global stage; meanwhile, China, India, Brazil, and others too, are asserting themselves more and more. Moreover, within the spaces opened up by these subtly shifting hierarchies, smaller, weaker, poorer countries look for and occasionally find enhanced room for manoeuvre in a mood that does not reflect a sense of hopelessness. After all that we have said, there can be no denying that the contemporary world of development is riven by many complex inequalities. But, as ever, there are political responses that can be, and increasingly are being, made to this reality.

Statistical Appendix

| | Size | | Gross National Income | | Human Development Index (HDI) | | | | |
Country	Surface area (thousands of sq. km.)	Population (millions, 2002)	Billions of dollars, 2002	Per capita dollars, 2002	Life expectancy at birth (years, 2002)	Adult literacy rate (% ages 15 and above, 2002)	Combined gross enrolment ratio for primary, secondary and tertiary schools (%, 2001–2)	GDP per capita (PPP US$, 2002)	HDI value, 2002
Afghanistan	652	28	n.a.	n.a.	n.a.	n.a.	n.a.	n.a.	n.a.
Albania	29	3	4.4	1,380	73.6	98.7	69	4,830	0.781
Algeria	2,382	31	53.8	1,720	69.5	68.9	70	5,760	0.704
Andorra	0.5	0.07	n.a.	n.a.	n.a.	n.a.	n.a.	n.a.	n.a.
Angola	1,247	14	9.2	660	40.1	42.0	30	2,130	0.381
Antigua and Barbuda	0.4	0.07	0.6	9,390	73.9	85.8	69	10,920	0.800
Argentina	2,780	38	154.1	4,060	74.1	97.0	94	10,880	0.853
Armenia	30	3	2.4	790	72.3	99.4	72	3,120	0.754
Australia	7,741	20	386.6	19,740	79.1	99.0	113	28,260	0.946
Austria	84	8	190.4	23,390	78.5	99.0	91	29,220	0.934
Azerbaijan	87	8	5.8	710	72.1	97.0	69	3,210	0.746
Bahamas	13.9	0.31	4.5	14,860	67.1	95.5	74	17,280	0.815
Bahrain	0.7	0.67	7.2	11,130	73.9	88.5	79	17,170	0.843
Bangladesh	144	136	48.5	360	61.1	41.1	54	1,700	0.509
Barbados	0.4	0.27	2.6	9,750	77.1	99.7	88	15,290	0.888
Belarus	208	10	13.5	1,360	69.9	99.7	88	5,520	0.790
Belgium	33	10	239.9	23,250	78.7	99.0	111	27,570	0.942
Belize	23	0.25	0.7	2,960	71.5	76.9	71	6,080	0.737
Benin	113	7	2.5	380	50.7	39.8	52	1,070	0.421
Bhutan	47	0.85	0.5	590	63.0	47.0	n.a.	1,969	0.536
Bolivia	1,099	9	7.9	900	63.7	86.7	86	2,460	0.681
Bosnia and Herzegovina	51	4	5.2	1,270	74.0	94.6	64	5,970	0.781

Continued

Country	Size		Gross National Income		Life expectancy at birth (years, 2002)	Human Development Index (HDI)			
	Surface area (thousands of sq. km.)	Population (millions, 2002)	Billions of dollars, 2002	Per capita dollars, 2002		Adult literacy rate (% ages 15 and above, 2002)	Combined gross enrolment ratio for primary, secondary and tertiary schools (%, 2001–2)	GDP per capita (PPP US$, 2002)	HDI value, 2002
Botswana	582	2	5.1	2,980	41.4	78.9	70	8,170	0.589
Brazil	8,547	174	497.4	2,850	68.0	86.4	92	7,770	0.775
Brunei	5.8	0.35	n.a.	n.a.	76.2	93.9	73	19,210	0.867
Bulgaria	111	8	14.1	1,790	70.9	98.6	76	7,130	0.796
Burkina Faso	274	12	2.6	220	45.8	12.8	22	1,100	0.302
Burundi	28	7	0.7	100	40.8	50.4	33	630	0.339
Cambodia	181	12	3.5	280	57.4	69.4	59	2,060	0.568
Cameroon	475	16	8.7	560	46.8	67.9	56	2,000	0.501
Canada	9,971	31	700.5	22,300	79.3	99.0	95	29,480	0.943
Cape Verde	4	0.46	0.6	1,290	70.0	75.7	73	5,000	0.717
Central African Republic	623	4	1.0	260	39.8	48.6	31	1,170	0.361
Chad	1,284	8	1.8	220	44.7	45.8	35	1,020	0.379
Chile	757	16	66.3	4,260	76.0	95.7	79	9,820	0.839
China	9,598	1,281	1,209.5	940	70.9	90.9	68	4,580	0.745
Colombia	1,139	44	80.1	1,830	72.1	92.1	68	6,370	0.773
Comoros	2.2	0.59	0.2	390	60.6	56.2	45	1,690	0.530
Congo, Dem. Rep.	2,345	54	5.0	90	41.4	62.7	27	650	0.365
Congo, Rep.	342	3	2.2	700	48.3	82.8	48	980	0.494
Costa Rica	51	4	16.2	4,100	78.0	95.8	69	8,840	0.834
Côte d'Ivoire	322	17	10.3	610	41.2	49.7	42	1,520	0.399
Croatia	57	4	20.3	4,640	74.1	98.1	73	10,240	0.830

Cuba	110.9	11	n.a.	n.a.	76.7	96.9	78	5,259	0.809
Cyprus	9.3	0.76	9.3	12,320	78.2	96.8	74	18,360	0.883
Czech Republic	79	10	56.7	5,560	75.3	99.0	78	15,780	0.868
Denmark	43	5	162.7	30,290	76.6	99.0	96	30,940	0.932
Djibouti	23.2	0.66	0.6	900	45.8	65.5	24	1,990	0.454
Dominica	0.8	0.07	0.22	3,180	73.1	76.4	74	5,640	0.743
Dominican Republic	49	9	20.0	2,320	66.7	84.4	77	6,640	0.738
Ecuador	284	13	19.0	1,450	70.7	91.0	72	3,580	0.735
Egypt	1,001	66	97.6	1,470	68.6	55.6	76	3,810	0.653
El Salvador	21	7	13.5	2,080	70.6	79.7	66	4,890	0.720
Equatorial Guinea	28.1	0.48	0.3	700	49.1	84.2	58	30,130	0.703
Eritrea	118	4	0.7	160	52.7	56.7	33	890	0.439
Estonia	45	1	5.6	4,130	71.6	99.8	96	12,260	0.853
Ethiopia	1,104	67	6.4	100	45.5	41.5	34	780	0.359
Fiji	18.3	0.82	1.77	2,160	69.6	92.9	73	5,440	0.758
Finland	338	5	122.2	23,510	77.9	99.0	106	26,190	0.935
France	552	59	1,342.7	22,010	78.9	99.0	91	26,920	0.932
Gabon	267.7	1.2	4.0	3,120	56.6	71.0	74	6,590	0.648
Gambia	11.3	1.3	0.4	280	53.9	37.8	45	1,690	0.452
Georgia	70	5	3.3	650	73.5	100.0	69	2,260	0.739
Germany	357	82	1,870.4	22,670	78.2	99.0	88	27,100	0.925
Ghana	239	20	5.4	270	57.8	73.8	46	2,130	0.568
Greece	132	11	123.9	11,660	78.2	97.3	86	18,720	0.902
Grenada	0.3	0.1	0.4	3,500	65.3	94.4	65	7,280	0.745
Guatemala	109	12	20.9	1,750	65.7	69.9	56	4,080	0.649
Guinea	246	8	3.1	410	48.9	41.0	29	2,100	0.425
Guinea-Bissau	36.1	1.25	0.2	150	45.2	39.6	37	710	0.350

Continued

| | Size | | Gross National Income | | | | | | |
Country	Surface area (thousands of sq. km.)	Population (millions, 2002)	Billions of dollars, 2002	Per capita dollars, 2002	Life expectancy at birth (years, 2002)	Adult literacy rate (% ages 15 and above, 2002)	Combined gross enrolment ratio for primary, secondary and tertiary schools (%, 2001–2)	GDP per capita (PPP US$, 2002)	HDI value, 2002
Guyana	215	0.77	0.7	840	63.2	96.5	75	4,260	0.719
Haiti	28	8	3.7	440	49.4	51.9	52	1,610	0.463
Honduras	112	7	6.2	920	68.8	80.0	62	2,600	0.672
Hungary	93	10	53.7	5,280	71.7	99.3	86	13,400	0.848
Iceland	103	0.28	7.9	27,970	79.7	99.0	90	29,750	0.941
India	3,287	1,048	501.5	480	63.7	61.3	55	2,670	0.595
Indonesia	1,905	212	149.9	710	66.6	87.9	65	3,230	0.692
Iran	1,648	66	112.1	1,710	70.1	77.1	69	6,690	0.732
Iraq	438.3	24	n.a	n.a.	n.a.	n.a.	n.a.	n.a.	n.a.
Ireland	70	4	92.6	23,870	76.9	99.0	90	36,360	0.936
Israel	21	6	n.a.	n.a.	79.1	95.3	92	19,530	0.908
Italy	301	58	1,097.9	18,960	78.7	98.5	82	26,430	0.920
Jamaica	11	3	7.4	2,820	75.6	87.6	75	3,980	0.764
Japan	378	127	4,265.6	33,550	81.5	99.0	84	26,940	0.938
Jordan	89	5	9.1	1,760	70.9	90.9	77	4,220	0.750
Kazakhstan	2,725	15	22.3	1,510	66.2	99.4	81	5,870	0.766
Kenya	580	31	11.3	360	45.2	84.3	53	1,020	0.488
Kiribati	0.7	0.09	0.08	810	n.a.	n.a.	n.a.	n.a.	n.a.
Korea, Dem. Rep.	120.5	22	n.a.	n.a.	n.a.	n.a.	n.a.	n.a.	n.a.
Korea, Rep.	99	48	473.0	9,930	75.4	97.9	92	16,950	0.888
Kuwait	18	2	n.a	n.a	76.5	82.9	76	16,240	0.838
Kyrgyzstan	200	5	1.5	290	68.4	97.0	81	1,620	0.701

Lao PDR	237	6	1.7	310	54.3	66.4	59	1,720	0.534
Latvia	65	2	8.1	3,480	70.9	99.7	87	9,210	0.823
Lebanon	10	4	17.7	3,990	73.5	86.5	78	4,360	0.758
Lesotho	30	2	1.0	470	36.3	81.4	65	2,420	0.493
Liberia	111.4	3.2	0.48	150	n.a.	n.a.	n.a.	n.a.	n.a.
Libya	1,759.5	5.5	n.a.	n.a.	72.6	81.7	97	7,570	0.794
Liechtenstein	0.2	0.03	n.a.	n.a.	n.a.	n.a.	n.a.	n.a.	n.a.
Lithuania	65	3	12.7	3,660	72.5	99.6	90	10,320	0.842
Luxembourg	2.6	0.44	17.2	38,830	78.3	99.0	75	61,190	0.933
Macedonia, FYR	26	2	3.5	1,700	73.5	96.0	70	6,470	0.793
Madagascar	587	16	3.9	240	53.4	67.3	45	740	0.469
Malawi	118	11	1.7	160	37.8	61.8	74	580	0.388
Malaysia	330	24	86.0	3,540	73.0	88.7	70	9,120	0.793
Maldives	0.3	0.28	0.6	2,090	67.2	97.2	78	4,798	0.752
Mali	1,240	11	2.8	240	48.5	19.0	26	930	0.326
Malta	0.3	0.39	3.6	9,200	78.3	92.6	77	17,640	0.875
Marshall Islands	0.2	0.05	0.1	2,350	n.a.	n.a.	n.a.	n.a.	n.a.
Mauritania	1,026	3	1.0	340	52.3	41.2	44	2,220	0.465
Mauritius	2	1.2	4.7	3,850	71.9	84.3	69	10,810	0.785
Mexico	1,958	101	596.7	5,910	73.3	90.5	74	8,970	0.802
Micronesia, Fed. States	0.7	0.12	0.2	1,980	n.a.	n.a.	n.a.	n.a.	n.a.
Moldova	34	4	1.7	460	68.8	99.0	62	1,470	0.681
Monaco	0.2	0.03	n.a.	n.a.	n.a.	n.a.	n.a.	n.a.	n.a.
Mongolia	1,567	2	1.1	440	63.7	97.8	70	1,710	0.668
Morocco	447	30	35.4	1,190	68.5	50.7	57	3,810	0.620
Mozambique	802	18	3.9	210	38.5	46.5	41	1,050	0.354
Myanmar	677	49	n.a.	n.a	57.2	85.3	48	1,027	0.551
Namibia	824	2	3.3	1,780	45.3	83.3	71	6,210	0.607

Continued

| Country | Size | | Gross National Income | | Human Development Index (HDI) | | | | |
	Surface area (thousands of sq. km.)	Population (millions, 2002)	Billions of dollars, 2002	Per capita dollars, 2002	Life expectancy at birth (years, 2002)	Adult literacy rate (% ages 15 and above, 2002)	Combined gross enrolment ratio for primary, secondary and tertiary schools (%, 2001–2)	GDP per capita (PPP US$, 2002)	HDI value, 2002
Nauru	0.02	0.01	n.a.	n.a.	n.a.	n.a.	n.a.	n.a.	n.a.
Nepal	147	24	5.6	230	59.6	44.0	61	1,370	0.504
Netherlands	42	16	386.8	23,960	78.3	99.0	99	29,100	0.942
New Zealand	271	4	53.1	13,710	78.2	99.0	101	21,740	0.926
Nicaragua	130	5	n.a.	n.a.	69.4	76.7	65	2,470	0.667
Niger	1,267	12	2.0	170	46.0	17.1	19	800	0.292
Nigeria	924	133	38.7	290	51.6	66.8	45	860	0.466
Norway	324	5	171.8	37,850	78.9	99.0	98	36,600	0.956
Oman	309.5	2.5	19.1	7,720	72.3	74.4	63	13,340	0.770
Pakistan	796	145	59.2	410	60.8	41.5	37	1,940	0.497
Palau	0.5	0.02	0.1	7,140	n.a.	n.a.	n.a.	n.a.	n.a.
Panama	76	3	11.8	4,020	74.6	92.3	73	6,170	0.791
Papua New Guinea	463	5	2.8	530	57.4	64.6	41	2,270	0.542
Paraguay	407	6	6.4	1,170	70.7	91.6	72	4,610	0.751
Peru	1,285	27	54.7	2,050	69.7	85.0	88	5,010	0.752
Philippines	300	80	81.5	1,020	69.8	92.6	81	4,170	0.753
Poland	323	39	176.6	4,570	73.8	99.7	90	10,560	0.850
Portugal	92	10	108.7	10,840	76.1	92.5	93	18,280	0.897
Qatar	11	0.61	n.a.	n.a.	72.0	84.2	82	19,844	0.833
Romania	238	22	41.3	1,850	70.5	97.3	68	6,560	0.778
Russian Federation	17,075	144	307.9	2,140	66.7	99.6	88	8,230	0.795

Rwanda	26	8	1.9	230	38.9	69.2	53	1,270	0.431
Samoa	2.5	0.17	0.2	1,420	69.8	98.7	69	5,600	0.769
San Marino	0.1	0.03	n.a.	n.a.	n.a.	n.a.	n.a.	n.a.	n.a.
São Tomé and Principe	1.0	0.15	0.04	290	69.7	83.1	62	1,317	0.645
Saudi Arabia	2,150	22	n.a.	n.a.	72.1	77.9	57	12,650	0.768
Senegal	197	10	4.7	470	52.7	39.3	38	1,580	0.437
Serbia and Montenegro	102	11	11.6	1,400	n.a.	n.a.	n.a.	n.a.	n.a.
Seychelles	0.5	0.08	0.5	6,530	72.7	91.9	85	18,232	0.853
Sierra Leone	72	5	0.7	140	34.3	36.0	45	520	0.273
Singapore	1	4	86.1	20,690	78.0	92.5	87	24,040	0.902
Slovak Republic	49	5	21.4	3,950	73.6	99.7	74	12,840	0.842
Slovenia	20	2	19.6	9,810	76.2	99.7	90	18,540	0.895
Solomon Islands	28.9	0.44	0.3	570	69.0	76.6	50	1,590	0.624
Somalia	637.7	9.3	n.a.	n.a.	n.a.	n.a.	n.a.	n.a.	n.a.
South Africa	1,221	44	113.5	2,600	48.8	86.0	77	10,070	0.666
Spain	506	41	594.1	14,430	79.2	97.7	92	21,460	0.922
Sri Lanka	66	19	15.9	840	72.5	92.1	65	3,570	0.740
St Kitts and Nevis	0.4	0.04	0.3	6,370	70.0	97.8	97	12,420	0.844
St Lucia	0.6	0.15	0.6	3,840	72.4	94.8	74	5,300	0.777
St Vincent	0.4	0.11	0.3	2,820	74.0	83.1	64	5,460	0.751
Sudan	2,505.8	32.3	11.4	350	55.5	59.9	36	1,820	0.505
Suriname	163.3	0.42	0.8	1,960	71.0	94.0	74	6,590	0.780
Swaziland	17.4	1	1.3	1,180	35.7	80.9	61	4,550	0.519
Sweden	450	9	221.5	24,820	80.0	99.0	114	26,050	0.946
Switzerland	41	7	274.2	37,930	79.1	99.0	88	30,010	0.936
Syria	185	17	19.2	1,130	71.7	82.9	59	3,620	0.710
Tajikistan	143	6	1.1	180	68.6	99.5	73	980	0.671

Continued

Country	Size		Gross National Income		Human Development Index (HDI)				
	Surface area (thousands of sq. km.)	Population (millions, 2002)	Billions of dollars, 2002	Per capita dollars, 2002	Life expectancy at birth (years, 2002)	Adult literacy rate (% ages 15 and above, 2002)	Combined gross enrolment ratio for primary, secondary and tertiary schools (%, 2001–2)	GDP per capita (PPP US$, 2002)	HDI value, 2002
Tanzania	945	35	9.6	280	43.5	77.1	31	580	0.407
Thailand	513	62	122.2	1,980	69.1	92.6	73	7,010	0.768
Timor-Leste	14.9	0.78	n.a.	n.a.	49.3	58.6	75	n.a.	0.436
Togo	57	5	1.3	270	49.9	59.6	67	1,480	0.495
Tonga	0.8	0.1	0.1	1,410	68.4	98.8	82	6,850	0.787
Trinidad and Tobago	5.1	1.3	8.5	6,490	71.4	98.5	64	9,430	0.801
Tunisia	164	10	19.6	2,000	72.7	73.2	75	6,760	0.745
Turkey	775	70	174.0	2,500	70.4	86.5	68	6,390	0.751
Turkmenistan	488	6	6.7	1,200	66.9	98.8	81	4,300	0.752
Tuvalu	0.03	0.01	n.a.	n.a.	n.a.	n.a.	n.a.	n.a.	n.a.
Uganda	241	23	5.9	250	45.7	68.9	71	1,390	0.493
Ukraine	604	49	37.7	770	69.5	99.6	84	4,870	0.777
United Arab Emirates	83.6	3	n.a.	n.a.	74.6	77.3	68	22,240	0.824
United Kingdom	243	59	1,486.2	25,250	78.1	99.0	113	26,150	0.936
United States of America	9,329	288	10,110.1	35,060	77.0	99.0	92	35,750	0.939
Uruguay	176	3	14.8	4,370	75.2	97.7	85	7,830	0.833
Uzbekistan	447	25	11.5	450	69.5	99.3	76	1,670	0.709
Vanuatu	12.2	0.2	0.2	1,080	68.6	34.0	59	2,890	0.570

Venezuela	912	25	102.6	4,090	73.6	93.1	71	5,380	0.778
Vietnam	332	81	34.9	430	69.0	90.3	64	2,300	0.691
Yemen, Rep.	528	19	9.4	490	59.8	49.0	53	870	0.482
Zambia	753	10	3.5	330	32.7	79.9	45	840	0.389
Zimbabwe	391	13	n.a.	n.a.	33.9	90.0	58	2,400	0.491

n.a. = not available

Sources: Compiled by Chris Payne from data in The World Bank, *World Development Report 2004* (Oxford University Press for the World Bank, Oxford, 2004), Tables 1 and 7; and United Nations Development Programme, *Human Development Report 2004* (Oxford University Press for the UNDP, Oxford, 2004), Table 1.

References

Abugre, C. and Alexander, N. (1998) 'Non-governmental Organizations and the International Monetary and Financial System', in *International Monetary and Financial Issues for the 1990s*, Vol. IX (Geneva: United Nations Conference on Trade and Development), pp. 107–25.

Adams, J. (1989) 'Review of R.W. Cox, *Production, Power and World Order: Social Forces in the Making of History*', *Annals of the American Academy*, No. 501, pp. 224–5.

Agarwal, A. and Naraim, S. (1991) *Global Warming in an Unequal World: A Case of Environmental Colonialism* (New Delhi: Centre for Science and Environment).

Albert, M. (1992) 'The Rhine Model of Capitalism: An Investigation', *European Business Journal*, No. 2, pp. 8–22.

Albert, M. (1993) *Capitalism against Capitalism* (London: Whurr).

Amoore, L., Dodgson, R., Gills, B.K., Langley, P., Marshall, D. and Watson, I. (1997) 'Overturning "Globalization": Resisting the Teleological, Reclaiming the "Political" ', *New Political Economy*, Vol. 2, No. 1, pp. 179–95.

Amsden, A. (1989) *Asia's Next Giant: South Korea and Late Industrialization* (Oxford: Oxford University Press).

Anderson, P. (2000) 'Editorial: Renewals', *New Left Review*, Second Series, No. 1, pp. 5–24.

Andresen, S. (2000) 'The Financial Stability Forum', *CESifo Forum*, Vol. 1, No. 4, pp. 18–20.

Andreson, S. (1991) 'US Greenhouse Policy: Reactionary or Realistic?', *International Challenges*, Vol. 11, No. 1, pp. 17–24.

Annan, K. (2002) *First Progress Report on the Implementation of the Millennium Development Goals*, Office of the Secretary-General, UN, New York, 1 October.

Armstrong, J.D. (1996) 'The Group of Seven Summits', in D.H. Dunn (ed.), *Diplomacy at the Highest Level: The Evolution of International Security* (London: Macmillan), pp. 41–52.

Arrighi, G. (1991) 'World Income Inequalities and the Future of Socialism', *New Left Review*, No. 189, pp. 39–65.

Arrighi, G., Silver, B.J. and Brewer, B.D. (2003) 'Industrial Convergence, Globalisation, and the Persistence of the North–South Divide', *Studies in Comparative International Development*, Vol. 28, No. 1, pp. 3–31.

Ashman, S. (2004) 'Resistance to Neoliberal Globalisation: A Case of "Militant Particularism"?', *Politics*, Vol. 24, No. 2, pp. 143–53.

Aysha, E.E. (2001) 'The United States Boom, "Clintonomics" and the New Economy Doctrine: A Neo-Gramscian Contribution', *New Political Economy*, Vol. 6, No. 3, pp. 341–58.

Baker, A. (2000) 'The G7 as a Global "Ginger Group": Plurilateralism and Four-dimensional Diplomacy', *Global Goverance*, Vol. 6, No. 2, pp. 165–89.

Balaam, D.N. and Veseth, M. (1996) *Introduction to International Political Economy* (Saddle River, NJ: Prentice Hall).

Baldwin, D. (ed.) (1993) *Neorealism and Neoliberalism: The Contemporary Debate* (New York, NY: Columbia University Press).

Baran, P. (1967) *The Political Economy of Growth* (New York, NY: Monthly Review Press).

Barkin, S.J. and Shambaugh, G. (eds) (1999) *Anarchy and the Environment: The International Relations of Common Pool Resources* (Albany, NY: State University of New York Press).

Bayne, N. (2000) *Hanging in There: The G7 and G8 Summit in Maturity and Renewal* (Aldershot: Ashgate).

Bello, W. (2001) 'UNCTAD: Time to Lead, Time to Challenge', mimeo, available at http://www.lbbs.org/crisescurevts/globalism/unctadbello.html.

Bello, W. (2002) 'Learning from Doha: A Civil Society Perspective from the South', *Global Governance*, Vol. 8, No. 3, pp. 273–9.

Bello, W. (2003) 'The WTO Cancún Ministerial has Failed: It's Time for Global Civil Society to Work for Bigger Victories', *Bangkok Post*, 21 September, available at http://www.focusweb.org/popups/articleswindow.php?id=371.

Benedick, R.E. (1991) *Ozone Diplomacy: New Directions in Safeguarding the Planet* (Cambridge, MA: Harvard University Press).

Berger, M.T. (1994) 'The End of the "Third World"?', *Third World Quarterly*, Vol. 15, No. 2, pp. 257–75.

Berger, M.T. (ed.) (2004) 'Special Issue: After the Third World?', *Third World Quarterly*, Vol. 25, No. 1.

Berger, S. and Dore, R. (eds) (1996) *National Diversity and Global Capitalism* (Ithaca, NY: Cornell University Press).

Best, J. (2003) 'From the Top-Down: The New Financial Architecture and the Re-embedding of Global Finance', *New Political Economy*, Vol. 8, No. 3, pp. 363–84.

Bhagwati, J. (1998) 'The Capital Myth: The Difference between Trade in Widgets and Dollars', *Foreign Affairs*, Vol. 77, No. 3, pp. 7–12.

Bhagwati, J. (2004) 'Don't Cry for Cancún', *Foreign Affairs*, Vol. 83, No. 1, pp. 52–63.

Bichsel, A. (1994) 'The World Bank and the International Monetary Fund from the Perspective of the Executive Directors from Developing Countries', *Journal of World Trade Law*, Vol. 28, No. 1, pp. 141–67.

Biersteker, T.J. (1995) 'The "Triumph" of Liberal Economic Ideas in the Developing World', in B. Stallings (ed.), *Global Change, Regional Response: The New International Context of Development* (Cambridge: Cambridge University Press), pp. 174–96.

Bird, G. (2001) 'A Suitable Case for Treatment? Understanding the Ongoing Debate about the IMF', *Third World Quarterly*, Vol. 22, No. 5, pp. 823–48.

Birnbaum, N. (1999) 'Is the Third Way Authentic?', *New Political Economy*, Vol. 4, No. 3, pp. 437–46.

Boote, A.R. and Thugge, K. (1997) *Debt Relief for Low-Income Countries and the HIPC Initiatives*, IMF Working Paper WP/97/24, Washington, DC.

Booth, D. (1985) 'Marxism and Development Sociology: Interpreting the Impasse', *World Development*, Vol. 13, No. 7, pp. 761–87.

Booth, D. (1993) 'Development Research: From Impasse to New Agenda', in F. J. Schuurman (ed.), *Beyond the Impasse: New Directions in Development Theory* (London: Zed Books), pp. 49–76.

Boumert, K. and Pershing, J. (2004) *Climate Data: Insights and Observations* (Arlington, VA: Pew Center for Global Climate Change).

Bourantonis, D. and Magliveras, K. (2002) 'The Enlargement of the Security Council: Reflections from the Current Debate', *Politics*, Vol. 22, No. 1, pp. 24–30.

Brandt Commission (1980) *North–South: A Programme for Survival* (London: Pan Books).

Brenton, T. (1994) *The Greening of Machiavelli: The Evolution of International Environmental Politics* (London: Royal Institute of International Affairs and Earthscan).

Breslin, S. (2003) 'Reforming China's Embedded Socialist Compromise: China and the WTO', *Global Change*, Vol. 15, No. 3, pp. 213–29.

Broad, R. and Cavanagh, J. (1999) 'The Death of the Washington Consensus?', *World Policy Journal*, Vol. 16, No. 3, pp. 79–88.

Brown, G. (2001) *Speech to the New York Federal Reserve Bank*, 16 November, New York, available at http://www.hm-treasury.gov.uk.

Brown, G. (2003) *Address to the Chatham House Conference on Corporate Social Responsibility*, Royal Institute for International Affairs, London, 22 January, available at http://www.hm-treasury.gov.uk.

Buira, A. (1996) 'The Governance of the International Monetary Fund', in R. Culpeper and C. Pestieau (eds), *Development and Global Governance*, Conference Proceedings, 2 May 1995 (Ottawa: International Development Research Centre/The North–South Institute), pp. 43–53.

Bulmer-Thomas, V. (1999) 'The Brazilian Devaluation: National Responses and International Consequences', *International Affairs*, Vol. 74, No. 4, pp. 729–41.

Bundegaard, A.B., Goerens, C., Herfkens, E., Johnson, H.F. and Klingvall, M.-I. (2001) 'Richest Countries Should Join G-0.7 Club to Fight Poverty', *Financial Times*, 19 November.

Burnham, P. (1991) 'Neo-Gramscian Hegemony and the International Order', *Capital and Class*, No. 45, pp. 73–92.

Burnham, P. (1999) 'The Politics of Economic Management', *New Political Economy*, Vol. 4, No. 1, pp. 37–54.

Bush, G.W. (2001) 'Letter to Senators Hagel, Helms, Craig and Roberts', The White House, Washington, DC, 13 March 2001, available at http://www.whitehouse.gov/news/releases/2001/03/20010314.html.

Buzan, B. (1996) 'The Timeless Wisdom of Realism?', in S. Smith, K. Booth and M. Zalewski (eds), *International Theory: Positivism and Beyond* (Cambridge: Cambridge University Press), pp. 47–65.

Cammack, P. (2002) 'The Mother of All Governments: The World Bank's Matrix for Global Governance', in R. Wilkinson and S. Hughes (eds), *Global Governance: Critical Perspectives* (London: Routledge), pp. 36–53.

Cammack, P. (2004) 'Giddens's Way with Words', in S. Hale, W. Leggett and L. Martell (eds), *The Third Way and Beyond: Criticisms, Futures, Alternatives* (Manchester: Manchester University Press), pp. 151–66.

Caporaso, J.A. and Levine, D.P. (1992) *Theories of Political Economy* (Cambridge: Cambridge University Press).

Cardoso, F.H. and Falletto, E. (1979) *Dependency and Development in Latin America* (translated by M.M. Urquidi) (Berkeley, CA: University of California Press).

Caron, D. (1993) 'The Legitimacy of the Collective Authority of the Security Council', *American Journal of International Law*, Vol. 87, pp. 552–88.

Castells, M. (1996, 1997 and 1998) *The Information Age: Economy, Society and Culture: Vols. 1, 2 and 3* (Oxford: Basil Blackwell).

Castillo-Ospina, O.L. (2002) 'Non-Governmental Organisations and the External Debt Relief Process: The Heavily Indebted Poor Countries Initiative', unpublished PhD thesis, University of Wales, Cardiff, November.

Charnowitz, S. (1987) 'The Influence of International Labour Standards on the World Trading Regime: A Historical Overview', *International Labour Review*, Vol. 126, No. 5, pp. 565–84.

Christian Aid (1998) *Forever in your Debt? Eight Nations and the G-8*, prepared by Matthew Lockwood, May, available at http://www.christianaid.org.

Clark, I.D. (1996) *Should the IMF become More Adaptive?*, IMF Working Paper WP/96/17, Washington, DC.

Coates, B. (2002) 'The World's Biggest Summit – So What? Making Sense of the World Summit on Sustainable Development', mimeo, World Development Movement, London, available at http://www.wdm.org.uk.

Coates, D. (2000) *Models of Capitalism: Growth and Stagnation in the Modern Era* (Cambridge: Cambridge University Press).

Coates, D. and Hay, C. (2001) 'The Internal and External Face of New Labour's Political Economy', *Government and Opposition*, Vol. 36, No. 4, pp. 447–71.

Cohen, R. and Rai, S.M. (2000) 'Global Social Movements: Towards a Cosmopolitan Politics', in R. Cohen and S.M. Rai (eds), *Global Social Movements* (London: Athlone Press), pp. 1–17.

Commission on Global Governance (1995) *Our Global Neighbourhood: The Report of the Commission on Global Governance* (Oxford: Oxford University Press).

Committee for Development Planning (1971) 'Report on the Seventh Session 1971: Document E/4990', mimeo, United Nations, New York.

Commonwealth Secretariat (1985) *Vulnerability: Small States in the Global Society* (London: Commonwealth Secretariat).

Commonwealth Secretariat (1997) *A Future for Small States: Overcoming Vulnerability* (London: Commonwealth Secretariat).

Commonwealth Secretariat/World Bank Joint Task Force on Small States (2000) 'Small States: Meeting Challenges in the Global Economy', Final Report, mimeo, Commonwealth Secretariat and World Bank, London and Washington, DC, March.

Corbridge, S. (1990) 'Post-Marxism and Development Studies: Beyond the Impasse', *World Development*, Vol. 18, No. 5, pp. 623–39.

Cosbey, A. and Burgiel, S. (2000) 'An Analysis of Results' [of the Cartagena Protocol on Biosafety], a Briefing Note, International Institute for Sustainable Development, Winnipeg.

Cox, R.W. (1979) 'Ideologies and the New International Economic Order: Reflections on Some Recent Literature', *International Organization*, Vol. 33, No. 2, pp. 257–302.

Cox, R.W. (1981) 'Social Forces, States and World Orders: Beyond International Relations Theory', *Millennium: Journal of International Studies*, Vol. 10, No. 2, pp. 126–55.

Cox, R.W. (1983) 'Gramsci, Hegemony and International Relations: An Essay in Method', *Millennium: Journal of International Studies*, Vol. 12, No. 2, pp. 162–75.

Cox, R.W. (1987) *Production, Power and World Order: Social Forces in the Making of History* (New York, NY: Columbia University Press).

Cox, R.W. (1989) 'Production, the State, and Change in the World Order', in E.-O. Czempiel and J.N. Rosenau (eds), *Global Changes and Theoretical Challenges: Approaches to World Politics for the 1990s* (Lexington, MA: Lexington Books), pp. 337–50.

Cox, R.W. (1992) 'Multilateralism and World Order', *Review of International Studies*, Vol. 18, No. 2, pp. 161–80.

Cox, R.W. (1993) 'Structural Issues of Global Governance: Implications for Europe', in S. Gill (ed.), *Gramsci, Historical Materialism and International Relations* (Cambridge: Cambridge University Press), pp. 259–89.

Cox, R.W. (2002), with Schechter, M.G., *The Political Economy of a Plural World: Critical Reflections on Power, Morals and Civilisation* (London: Routledge).

Crane, E. and Niskanen, W. (2003) 'Upholding Liberty in America', *The Guardian*, 25 June.

Crane, G.T. and Amawi, A. (eds) (1991) *The Theoretical Evolution of International Political Economy* (New York, NY: Oxford University Press).

Cullet, P. (2003) 'Patents and Medicines: The Relationship between TRIPS and the Human Right to Health', *International Affairs*, Vol. 79, No. 1, pp. 139–60.

Daalder, I.H. and Lindsay, J.M. (2003) *America Unbound: The Bush Revolution in Foreign Policy* (Washington, DC: Brookings Institution).

Davis, M. (1990) *City of Quartz: Excavating the Future in Los Angeles* (London: Verso).

de Moor, A., Berk, M., den Elzen, M. and van Vuuren, D. (2002) 'Evaluating the Bush Climate Change Initiative', RIVM Report 728001019, Bilthoven.

den Elzen, M. and de Moor, A. (2001) 'The Bonn Agreement and Marrakech Accords: An Updated Analysis', RIVM Report 728001017, Bilthoven.

DeSombre, E.R. (2000) 'Developing Country Influence in Global Environmental Negotiations', *Environmental Politics*, Vol. 9, No. 3, pp. 23–42.

Destler, I.M. (1986) *American Trade Politics: System under Stress* (Washington, DC: Institute for International Economics).

de Vries, M. (1986) *The IMF in a Changing World, 1945–85* (Washington, DC: International Monetary Fund).

de Waal, A. (2002) 'What's New in the "New Partnership for Africa's Development"?', *International Affairs*, Vol. 78, No. 3, pp. 463–75.

Dia, M. (1991) 'Development and Cultural Values', *Finance and Development*, Vol. 28, No. 4, pp. 10–13.

Dobson, H. (2004) 'The G8 and Global Governance: Concert Diplomacy in an Age of Globalisation', unpublished paper delivered to a conference on 'Global Governance and Japan', Doshisha University, Kyoto, September.

Doornbos, M. (2001) ' "Good Governance": The Rise and Decline of a Policy Metaphor', *The Journal of Development Studies*, Vol. 37, No. 6, pp. 93–108.

Drabek, Z. and Laird, S. (1998) 'Trade Policy Developments in Emerging Markets', *Journal of World Trade Law*, Vol. 32, No. 5, pp. 241–69.

Drahos, P. (2002) *Developing Countries and International Intellectual Property Standard-setting*, Study Paper No. 8, Commission on Intellectual Property Rights (CIPR), available at http://www.iprcommission.org/graphic/documents/study-papers.

Eichengreen, B. (1999) *Toward a New International Financial Architecture: A Practical Post-Asia Agenda* (Washington, DC: Institute for International Economics).

El Kahal, S. (2001) 'United Nations Educational, Social and Cultural Organization (UNESCO)', in R.J. Barry Jones (ed.), *Routledge Encyclopedia of International Political Economy*, Vol. 3 (London: Routledge), p. 1,639.

Elliott, L. (1998) *The Global Politics of the Environment* (London: Macmillan).

Escobar, A. (1995) *Encountering Development: The Making and Unmaking of the Third World* (Princeton, NJ: Princeton, University Press).

Esquivel, G., Larraín B.F. and Sachs, J.D. (1998) *The External Debt Problem in Central America: Honduras, Nicaragua, and the HIPC Initiative*, Development Discussion Paper No. 645, Central America Project Series, Harvard Institute for International Development, Harvard University, August.

Esteva, G. (1992) 'Development', in W. Sachs (ed.), *The Development Dictionary: A Guide to Knowledge as Power* (London: Zed Books), pp. 6–25.

Evans, H. (1999) 'Debt Relief for the Poorest Countries: Why did it take so Long?', *Development Policy Review*, Vol. 17, No. 3, pp. 267–79.

Evans, P. (1995) *Embedded Autonomy: States and Industrial Transformation* (Princeton, NJ: Princeton University Press).

Evans, P. (1997) 'The Eclipse of the State? Reflections on Stateness in an Era of Globalization', *World Politics*, Vol. 50, No. 1, pp. 62–87.

Falkner, R. (2000) 'Regulating Biotech Trade: The Cartagena Protocol on Biosafety', *International Affairs*, Vol. 76, No. 2, pp. 299–313.

Fidler, S. and Baker, G. (2003) 'America's Democratic Imperialists', *Financial Times*, 6 March.

Financial Stability Forum (FSF) (2000) *Report of the Working Group on Offshore Centres*, 5 April, available at http://www.fsforum.org/Reports/repOFC.pdf.

Fine, B. (1999) 'The Developmental State is Dead – Long Live Social Capital?', *Development and Change*, Vol. 30, pp. 1–19.

Fine, B. (2001) 'Neither the Washington nor the Post-Washington Consensus: An Introduction', in B. Fine, C. Lapavitsas and J. Pincus (eds), *Development Policy in the Twenty-First Century: Beyond the Post-Washington Consensus* (London: Routledge), pp. 1–27.

Fine, B., Lapavitsas, C. and Pincus, J. (eds) (2001) *Development Policy in the Twenty-First Century: Beyond the Post-Washington Consensus* (London: Routledge).

Finger, J.M. and Schuler, P. (2000) 'Implementation of Uruguay Round Commitments: The Development Challenge', *The World Economy*, Vol. 24, No. 4, pp. 511–25.

Finger, J.M. and Nogués, J.J. (2002) 'The Unbalanced Uruguay Round Outcome: The New Areas in Future WTO Negotiations', *The World Economy*, Vol. 25, No. 3, pp. 321–40.

Finlayson, J.A. and Zacher, M.W. (1981) 'The GATT and the Regulation of Trade Barriers: Regime Dynamics and Functions', *International Organization*, Vol. 35, No. 4, pp. 273–314.

Frank, A.G. (1967) *Capitalism and Underdevelopment in Latin America* (New York, NY: Monthly Review Press).

Frieden, J.A. and Lake, D.A. (1991) *International Political Economy: Perspectives on Global Power and Wealth* (London: Unwin Hyman).

Fukuyama, F. (1989) 'The End of History?', *The National Interest*, No. 16, pp. 3–18.

Fukuyama, F. (1996) *Trust: The Social Virtues and the Creation of Prosperity* (Harmondsworth: Penguin).

Fukuyama, F. (2002) 'The Transatlantic Rift', *The Guardian*, 7 September.

Gamble, A. (2001) 'Neo-Liberalism', *Capital and Class*, Issue 75, pp. 127–34.

Gamble, A., Payne, A., Hoogvelt, A., Dietrich, M. and Kenny, M. (1996) 'Editorial: New Political Economy', *New Political Economy*, Vol. 1, No. 1, pp. 5–11.

Gardner, R.N. (1956) *Sterling–Dollar Diplomacy: Anglo-American Collaboration in the Reconstruction of Multilateral Trade* (Oxford: Clarendon Press).

Garten, J.E. (1994) 'Speech to the Foreign Policy Association' by the Undersecretary of Commerce for International Trade, mimeo, Department of Commerce, Washington, DC, 20 January.

Garten, J.E. (1997) *The Big Ten: The Big Emerging Markets and How They Will Change Our Lives* (New York, NY: Basic Books).

Garten, J.E. (2003) 'Cancún: Going up in Flames', *Newsweek*, 29 September, pp. 48–51.

George, S. (1992) *The Debt Boomerang* (London: Pluto Press).

Germain, R.D. (2001) 'Global Financial Governance and the Problem of Inclusion', *Global Governance*, Vol. 7, No. 4, pp. 411–26.

Germain, R.D. (2002) 'Reforming the International Financial Architecture: The New Political Agenda', in R. Wilkinson and S. Hughes (eds), *Global Governance: Critical Perspectives* (London: Routledge), pp. 17–35.

Ghosal, S. and Miller, M. (2003) 'Lenders' Inaction does Little Credit', *The Guardian*, 12 May.

Gianaris, W.N. (1991) 'Weighted Voting in the International Monetary Fund and the World Bank', *Fordham International Law Journal*, Vol. 14, pp. 910–45.

Giddens, A. (1990) *The Consequences of Modernity* (Cambridge: Polity Press).

Giddens, A. (1994) *Beyond Left and Right* (Cambridge: Polity Press).

Gill, S. (1990) *American Hegemony and the Trilateral Commission* (Cambridge: Cambridge University Press).

Gill, S. and Law, D. (1988) *The Global Political Economy: Perspectives, Problems and Policies* (Hemel Hempstead: Harvester Wheatsheaf).

Gilpin, R. (1975) *U. S. Power and the Multinational Corporation: The Political Economy of U. S. Direct Foreign Investment* (New York, NY: Basic Books).

Gilpin, R. (1987) *The Political Economy of International Relations* (Princeton, NJ: Princeton University Press).

Girvan, N. (1999) 'Debate: The Regulation of Global Finance: A Perspective from the South', *New Political Economy*, Vol. 4, No. 3, pp. 415–19.

Gold, J. (1972) *Voting and Decisions in the International Monetary Fund* (Washington, DC: International Monetary Fund).

Goodin, R.E. (1992) *Green Political Theory* (Cambridge: Polity Press).

Gore, C. (2000) 'The Rise and Fall of the Washington Consensus as a Paradigm for Developing Countries', *World Development*, Vol. 28, No. 5, pp. 789–804.

Gowan, P. (2001) 'Explaining the American Boom: The Roles of "Globalisation" and United States Global Power', *New Political Economy*, Vol. 6, No. 3, pp. 359–74.

Gramsci, A. (1971) *Selections from the Prison Notebooks* (New York, NY: International Publishers).

Grant, R. and Nijman, J. (eds) (1998) *The Global Crisis in Foreign Aid* (Syracuse, NY: Syracuse University Press).

Gray, C.B. and Rivkin, D.B. (1991) 'A "No Regrets" Environmental Policy', *Foreign Policy*, No. 83, pp. 47–65.

Greider, W. (1997) *One World, Ready or Not: The Manic Logic of Global Capitalism* (New York, NY: Simon and Schuster).

Green, D. and Griffith, M. (2002) 'Globalization and its Discontents', *International Affairs*, Vol. 78, No. 1, pp. 49–68.

Group of Seven (G7) (1999) *G7 Communiqué Köln*, June, available at http://www. g7.toronto.ca.

Group of Seventy-Seven (G77) (1991) *Beijing Ministerial Declaration on Environment and Development*, mimeo, 19 June, Beijing.

Group of Twenty-Four (G24) (2000) *Communiqué*, 25 September, available at http://www.g24.org.

Grubb, M. and Safonov, Y. (2003) 'Why is Russia Dragging its Feet on Kyoto', *Financial Times*, 15 July 2003.

Grubb, M., with Vrolijk C. and Brack, D. (1999) *The Kyoto Protocol: A Guide and Assessment* (London: Royal Institute of International Affairs and Earthscan).

Grugel, J. and Hout, W. (1999) 'Regions, Regionalism and the South', in J. Grugel and W. Hout (eds), *Regionalism across the North–South Divide: State Strategies and Globalization* (London: Routledge), pp. 3–13.

Gupta, J. (2000) 'North–South Aspects of the Climate Change Issue: Towards a Negotiating Theory and Strategy for Developing Countries', *International Journal of Sustainable Development*, Vol. 3, No. 2, pp. 115–35.

Haggard, S. (2000) *The Political Economy of the Asian Financial Crisis* (Washington, DC: Institute of International Economics).

Hall, P. (1989) *The Political Power of Economic Ideas* (Princeton, NJ: Princeton University Press).

Hall, P.A. and Taylor, R.C.R. (1996) 'Political Science and the Three New Institutionalisms', *Political Studies*, Vol. 44, No. 4, pp. 936–57.

Hamilton, C. (1986) *Capitalist Industrialisation in Korea* (Boulder, CO: Westview Press).

Hampton, M.P. and Abbott, J.P. (1999) 'The Rise (and Fall?) of Offshore Finance in the Global Economy: Editors' Introduction', in M.P. Hampton and J.P. Abbott (eds), *Offshore Finance Centres and Tax Havens: The Rise of Global Capital* (London: Macmillan), pp. 1–17.

Hanlon, J. (2000) 'How Much Debt Must be Cancelled?', *Journal of International Development*, Vol. 12, No. 6, pp. 877–901.

Harris, P.G. (ed.) (2000) *Climate Change and American Foreign Policy* (New York, NY: St Martin's Press).

Harriss, J. and de Renzio, P. (1997) ' "Missing Link" or Analytically Missing? The Concept of Social Capital: An Introductory Bibliographic Essay', *Journal of International Development*, Vol. 9, No. 7, pp. 919–37.

Harvey, D. (2003) *The New Imperialism* (Oxford: Oxford University Press).

Hay, C. and Marsh, D. (eds) (2000) *Demystifying Globalization* (Basingstoke: Palgrave Macmillan).

Hay, C. and Rosamond, B. (2002) 'Globalisation, European Integration and the Discursive Construction of Economic Imperatives', *Journal of European Public Policy*, Vol. 9, No. 2, pp. 147–67.

Held, D., McGrew, A., Goldblatt, D. and Perraton, J. (1999) *Global Transformations: Politics, Economics and Culture* (Cambridge: Polity Press).

Hendrickx, F., Koesler, V. and Prip, C. (1993) 'Convention on Biological Diversity – Access to Genetic Resources: A Legal Analysis', *Environmental Policy and Law*, Vol. 23, No. 6, pp. 250–8.

Hertz, N. (2001) *The Silent Takeover: Global Capitalism and the Death of Democracy* (London: Heinemann).

Hettne, B. (1993) 'Neo-Mercantilism: The Pursuit of Regionness', *Cooperation and Conflict*, Vol. 28, No. 3, pp. 211–32.

Hettne, B. (1995) *Development Theory and the Three Worlds: Towards an International Political Economy of Development* (Harlow: Longman).

Hettne, B., Payne, A. and Söderbaum, F. (1999) 'Rethinking Development Theory: Guest Editors' Introduction', *Journal of International Relations and Development*, Vol. 2, No. 4, pp. 354–7.

Higgott, R. (1998) 'The Asian Economic Crisis: A Study in the Politics of Resentment', *New Political Economy*, Vol. 3, No. 3, pp. 333–56.

Higgott, R. (2000) 'Contested Globalization: The Changing Context and Normative Challenges', *Review of International Studies*, Vol. 26, No. 5, pp. 131–53.

Higgott, R. and Phillips, N.J. (2000) 'Challenging Triumphalism and Convergence: The Limits of Global Liberalisation in Asia and Latin America', *Review of International Studies*, Vol. 26, No. 2, pp. 359–79.

Higgott, R. and Reich, S. (1998) *Globalisation and Sites of Conflict: Towards Definition and Taxonomy*, Centre for the Study of Globalisation and Regionalisation Working Paper No. 1, University of Warwick, March.

Hirst, P. and Thompson, G. (1996 1st edn; 1999 2nd edn) *Globalization in Question: The International Economy and the Possibilities of Governance* (Cambridge: Polity Press).

Hobson, J.M. and Ramesh, M. (2002) 'Globalisation Makes of States What States Make of It: Between Agency and Structure in the State/Globalisation Debate', *New Political Economy*, Vol. 7, No. 1, pp. 5–22.

Hoekman, B. and Kostecki, M. (2001) *The Political Economy of the World Trading System: The WTO and Beyond* (Oxford: Oxford University Press).

Hollingsworth, J.R and Boyer, R. (eds) (1997) *Contemporary Capitalism: The Embeddedness of Institutions* (Cambridge: Cambridge University Press).

Holm, H.-H. (1990) 'The End of the Third World?', *Journal of Peace Research*, Vol. 27, No. 1, pp. 1–7.

Hoogvelt, A. (1997) *Globalisation and the Postcolonial World: The New Political Economy of Development* (London: Macmillan).

Horsefield, J.K. (1969) *The International Monetary Fund, 1945–65: Twenty Years of International Monetary Cooperation*, Vol. 1 (Washington, DC: International Monetary Fund).

Hoselitz, B.F. *et al.* (1960) *The Sociological Aspects of Economic Growth* (New York, NY: Free Press).

Houghton, J.T., Jenkins, G.J. and Ephraims, J.J. (eds) (1990) *Climate Change: The IPCC Scientific Assessment*, Final Report of Working Group I, IPCC (Cambridge: Cambridge University Press).

Hughes, S. and Wilkinson, R. (1998) 'International Labour Standards and World Trade: No Role for the World Trade Organization?', *New Political Economy*, Vol. 3, No. 3, pp. 375–89.

Huntington, S.P. (1988/9) 'The U.S. – Decline or Renewal?', *Foreign Affairs*, No. 67, pp. 76–96.

Huntington, S.P. (1993) 'The Clash of Civilizations?', *Foreign Affairs*, Vol. 72, No. 3, pp. 22–49.

Hurrell, A. and Woods, N. (1995) 'Globalisation and Inequality', *Millennium: Journal of International Studies*, Vol. 24, No. 3, pp. 447–70.

Ignatieff, M. (2003) *Empire Lite: Nation Building in Bosnia, Kosovo, Afghanistan* (London: Vintage).

Ikenberry, G.J. (1989) 'Rethinking the Origins of American Hegemony', *Political Science Quarterly*, Vol. 104, No. 3, pp. 375–400.

Ikenberry, G.J. (2004) 'The Illusions of Empire', *Foreign Affairs*, Vol. 83, No. 2, pp. 144–54.

International Conference on Financing for Development (2002) *Monterrey Consensus*, Monterrey, Mexico, 22 March, available at http://www.un.org/esa/ffd/aac257-32.htm.

International Financial Institutions Advisory Commission (2000) *Report of the International Financial Institutions Advisory Commission (IFIAC)*, US Congress, March, Washington, DC.

International Institute for Sustainable Development (2002) 'Summary of the World Summit on Sustainable Development 26 August–4 September 2002', *Earth Negotiations Bulletin*, Vol. 22, No. 51, pp. 1–37, available at http://www.iisd.ca/linkages/vol22/enb225k.html.

International Monetary Fund (IMF) (2001a) *Debt Relief for Poverty Reduction: The Role of the Enhanced HIPC Initiatives*, prepared 2 August, available at http://www.imf.org/external/pubs/ft/exrp/debt/eng/index.htm.

International Monetary Fund (IMF) (2001b) *IMF Survey*, Vol. 30, No. 7.

Jackson, J. (1989) *The World Trading System* (Cambridge, MA: MIT Press).

Jäger, J. and O'Riordan, T. (1996) 'The History of Climate Change Science and Politics', in T. O'Riordan and J. Jäger (eds), *Politics of Climate Change: A European Perspective* (London: Routledge), pp. 1–31.

James, H. (1996) *International Monetary Cooperation since Bretton Woods* (New York, NY: Oxford University Press for the International Monetary Fund).

Johnson, C. (2000) *Blowback: The Costs and Consequences of American Empire* (New York, NY: Metropolitan Books).

Jones, C.A. (1983) *The North–South Dialogue: A Brief History* (London: Macmillan).

Jowitt, K. (1991) 'After Leninism: The New World Disorder', *Journal of Democracy*, Vol. 2, No. 1, pp. 11–20.

Kahler, M. (1990) 'The United States and the International Monetary Fund: Declining Influence or Declining Interest?', in M.P. Karns and K.A. Mingst (eds), *The United States and the Multilateral Institutions: Patterns of Changing Instrumentality and Influence* (London: Routledge), pp. 91–114.

Kampffmeyer, T. and Taake, H.-H. (1999) *The Indebtedness of the Developing Countries*, German Development Institute Briefing Paper 2/1999, Berlin.

Kamrava, M. (1995) 'Political Culture and a New Definition of the Third World', *Third World Quarterly*, Vol. 16, No. 4, pp. 691–701.

Kaplan, R. (2000) *The Coming Anarchy: Shattering the Dreams of the Post-Cold War* (New York, NY: Random House).

Kapstein, E. (1994) *Governing the Global Economy: International Finance and the State* (Cambridge, MA: Harvard University Press).

Kapur, D., Lewis, J.P. and Webb, R. (1997) *The World Bank: Its First Half Century*, Vols 1 and 2 (Washington, DC: Brookings Institution).

Kaul, I., Grunberg, I. and Stern, M.A. (eds) (1999) *Global Public Goods: International Cooperation in the 21st Century* (Oxford: Oxford University Press for the United Nations Development Programme).

Kawashima, Y. (1997) 'A Comparative Analysis of the Decision-making Processes of Developed Countries towards CO_2 Emissions Reduction Targets', *International Environmental Affairs*, Vol. 9, No. 2, pp. 95–126.

Kenen, P.B. (2001) *The International Financial Architecture: What's New? What is Missing?* (Washington, DC: Institute for International Economics).

Kennedy, P. (1988) *The Rise and Fall of the Great Powers* (London: Unwin Hyman).

Keohane, R.O. (1984) *After Hegemony: Cooperation and Discord in the World Political Economy* (Princeton, NJ: Princeton University Press).

Kerr, W.A. (2002) 'A Club No More – The WTO after Doha', *The Estey Centre Journal of International Law and Trade Policy*, Vol. 3, No. 1, pp. 1–9.

Killick, T. (2000), 'HIPC II and Conditionality: Business as Before or a New Beginning?', unpublished paper commissioned by the Commonwealth Secretariat for Policy Workshop on Debt, HIPC and Poverty Reduction, London, July.

Kindleberger, C.P. (1973) *The World in Depression 1929–39* (Berkeley, CA: University of California Press).

Kirton, J.J. (1999) 'Explaining G8 Effectiveness', in M.R. Hodges, J.J. Kirton and J.P. Daniels (eds), *The G8's Role in the New Millennium* (Aldershot: Ashgate), pp. 45–68.

Klein, N. (2000) *No Logo* (London: Flamingo).

Klein, N. (2001) 'Reclaiming the Commons', *New Left Review*, Second Series, No. 9, pp. 81–9.

Kock, K. (1969) *International Trade Policy and the GATT 1947–1967* (Stockholm: Almqvist and Wicksell).

Köhler, H. (2000) *Statement by the Managing Director of the International Monetary Fund*, statement to the Development Committee 2000–22, 22 September, Prague.

Köhler, H. and Wolfensohn, J. (2000) *The IMF and the World Bank Group: An Enhanced Partnership for Sustainable Growth and Poverty Reduction*, a Joint Statement by the Managing Director of the International Monetary Fund and the President of the World Bank Group, 5 September, Washington, DC.

Korany, B. (1994) 'End of History, or its Continuation and Accentuation? The Global South and the "New Transformation" Literature', *Third World Quarterly*, Vol. 15, No. 1, pp. 7–15.

Krasner, S.D. (ed.) (1983) *International Regimes* (Ithaca, NY: Cornell University Press).

Krueger, A.O. (2002) 'A New Approach to Sovereign Debt Restructuring', mimeo, International Monetary Fund, Washington, DC.

Krugman, P. (1995) 'Dutch Tulips and Emerging Markets', *Foreign Affairs*, Vol. 74, No. 4, pp. 28–44.

Krugman, P. (1997) 'What Should Trade Negotiators Negotiate About?', *Journal of Economic Literature*, Vol. 35, No. 1, pp. 113–20.

Kwa, A. (2002) 'Power Politics in the WTO: Developing Countries' Perspectives on Decision-making Processes in Trade Negotiations', mimeo, Focus on the Global South, Bangkok, June.

Laffey, M. (1992) 'Ideology and the Limits of Gramscian Theory in International Relations', unpublished paper presented at the International Studies Association conference, Atlanta, 1–4 April.

Laird, S. (2001) 'Dolphins, Turtles, Mad Cows and Butterflies – A Look at the Multilateral Trading System in the 21st Century', *The World Economy*, Vol. 24, No. 4, pp. 453–81.

Laird, S. (2002) 'A Round by any Other Name: The WTO Agenda after Doha', *Development Policy Review*, Vol. 20, No. 1, pp. 41–62.

Leaver, R. (1989) 'Restructuring in the Global Economy: From the Pax Americana to Pax Nipponica?', *Alternatives*, Vol. 14, No. 4, pp. 429–61.

Lee, S. (2002) 'The International Monetary Fund', *New Political Economy*, Vol. 7, No. 2, pp. 283–98.

Leonard, M. (2004) 'The Burning of Bush', *Financial Times Magazine*, 26 June.

Lewellen, T.C. (1995) *Dependency and Development: An Introduction to the Third World* (Westport, CT: Bergin and Garvey).

Leys, C. (1996) 'The Crisis in "Development Theory" ', *New Political Economy*, Vol. 1, No. 1, pp. 41–58.

Lipietz, A. (1992) *Towards a New Economic Order: Postfordism, Ecology and Democracy* (Oxford: Oxford University Press).

Lipschutz, R.D. (1991) 'One World or Many? Global Sustainable Economic Development in the 21st Century', *Bulletin of Peace Proposals*, Vol. 22, No. 2, pp. 189–98.

Lister, F.K. (1984) *Decision-Making Strategies for International Organizations: The IMF Model*, Vol. 20, Book 4 (Denver, CO: Graduate School of International Studies, University of Denver).

Loxley, J. (2003) 'Imperialism and Economic Reform in Africa: What's New about the New Partnership for Africa's Development (NEPAD)?', *Review of African Political Economy*, Vol. 30, No. 95 pp. 119–28.

Ma, S.-Y. (1998) 'Third World Studies, Development Studies and Post-Communist Studies: Definitions, Distance and Dynamism', *Third World Quarterly*, Vol. 19, No. 3, pp. 339–56.

Mann, M. (1997) 'Has Globalization Ended the Rise and Rise of the Nation-state?', *Review of International Political Economy*, Vol. 4, No. 3, pp. 472–96.

Mann, M. (2003) *Incoherent Empire* (London: Verso).

Marsh, D. (1995) 'The Convergence between Theories of the State', in D. Marsh and G. Stoker (eds), *Theory and Methods in Political Science* (London: Macmillan), pp. 268–87.

Martin, P. (2000) *Speech to the House of Commons Standing Committee on Foreign Affairs and International Trade*, 18 May, available at http://www.fin.gc.ca.

Mayorbre, E. (ed.) (1999) *G-24: The Developing Countries in the International Financial System* (Boulder, CO: Lynne Rienner).

McMichael, P. (2000) *Development and Social Change: A Global Perspective* (Thousand Oaks, CA: Pine Forge Press).

Meadowcroft, J. (1996) 'Debate: Re-evaluating Rio: Taking Issue with UNCED's Critics', *New Political Economy*, Vol. 1, No. 3, pp. 408–12.

Meadowcroft, J. (2002) 'Next Steps: A Climate Change Briefing Paper', a report of the Transatlantic Programme of the Robert Schuman Centre of the European University Institute, Florence.

Michalopoulos, C. (1999) 'The Developing Countries in the WTO', *The World Economy*, Vol. 22, No. 1, pp. 117–43.

Mikesell, R.F. (1994) 'The Bretton Woods Debates: A Memoir', in C. Gwin and R. Feinberg (eds), *Essays in International Finance No. 192* (Princeton, NJ: International Finance Section, Department of Economics, Princeton University), pp. 21–36.

Mingst, K.A. and Karns, M.P. (eds) (2000) *The United Nations in the Post-Cold War Era* (Boulder, CO: Westview Press).

Mittelman, J.H. (2000) *The Globalization Syndrome: Transformation and Resistance* (Princeton, NJ: Princeton University Press).

Mittelman, J.H. (2004) 'Feature Review: "Globalization and Its Discontents" by Joseph E. Stiglitz', *New Political Economy*, Vol. 9, No. 1, pp. 129–33.

Monbiot, G. (2000) *Captive State: The Corporate Takeover of Britain* (London: Pan).

Monbiot, G. (2003) *The Age of Consent: A Manifesto for a New World Order* (London: HarperCollins).

Moore, D. (1999) ' "Sail on, O Ship of State": Neo-Liberalism, Globalisation and the Governance of Africa', *Journal of Peasant Studies*, Vol. 27, No. 1, pp. 61–96.

Morrissey, O. (2003) 'Cancún, the WTO and Developing Countries', *Wider Angle*, No. 2, pp. 10–11.

Müller, B. (2001) 'Fatally Flawed Inequity: Kyoto's Unfair Burdens on the United States and the Chinese Challenge to American Emission Dominance', unpublished paper presented to the World Bank Climate Change Day, Washington, DC, 14 June and Climate Strategies Review, CEPS, Brussels, 15 June, available at http://www. wolfson.ox. ac.uk/~mueller.

Murphy, C.N. (1999) 'Inequality, Turmoil and Democracy: Global Political-economic Visions at the End of the Century', *New Political Economy*, Vol. 4, No. 2, pp. 289–304.

Narlikar, A. (2003) *International Trade and Developing Countries: Bargaining Coalitions in the GATT and WTO* (London: Routledge).

Narlikar, A. (2004) 'The Ministerial Process and Power Dynamics in the World Trade Organization: Understanding Failure from Seattle to Cancún', *New Political Economy*, Vol. 9, No. 3, pp. 413–28.

Narlikar, A. and Odell, J. (2003) 'The Strict Distributive Strategy for a Bargaining Coalition: The Like Minded Group in the World Trade Organization', unpublished paper prepared for a conference on 'Developing Countries and the Trade Negotiation Process', UNCTAD, Geneva, 6–7 November.

Narlikar, A. and Tussie, D. (2004) 'The G20 at the Cancún Ministerial: Developing Countries and their Evolving Coalitions in the WTO', *The World Economy*, Vol. 27, No. 7, pp. 947–66.

Narlikar, A. and Wilkinson, R. (2004) 'Collapse at the WTO: A Cancún Post-Mortem', *Third World Quarterly*, Vol. 25, No. 3, pp. 447–60.

Nye, J.S. (1988) 'Understating US Strength', *Foreign Policy*, No. 72, pp. 105–29.

Nye, J.S. (2004) 'Neo-Quandaries', *Financial Times Magazine*, 14 August.

Oberthür, S. (1996) 'UNFCCC: The Second Conference of the Parties', *Environmental Policy and Law*, Vol. 26, No. 5, pp. 195–201.

Oberthür, S. and Ott, H.E. (1999) *The Kyoto Protocol: International Climate Policy for the 21st Century* (Berlin: Springer).

O'Brien, R., Goetz, A.M., Scholte, J.A. and Williams, M. (2000) *Contesting Global Governance: Multilateral Institutions and Global Social Movements* (Cambridge: Cambridge University Press).

Odell, J.S. and Sell, S.K. (2003) 'Reframing the Issue: The WTO Coalition on Intellectual Property and Public Health, 2001', unpublished paper prepared for a conference on 'Developing Countries and the Trade Negotiation Process', UNCTAD, Geneva, 6–7 November.

Ogata, S. (1989) 'Shifting Power Relations in Multilateral Development Banks', *Journal of International Studies*, Vol. 22, No. 1, pp. 1–25.

Ohmae, K. (1995) *The End of the Nation State* (New York, NY: Free Press).

Organisation for Economic Cooperation and Development (OECD) (1979) *Report of the Secretary-General* (Paris: OECD)

Organisation for Economic Cooperation and Development (OECD) (1985) *Twenty-five Years of Development Co-operation: A Review* (Paris: OECD).

Organisation for Economic Cooperation and Development (OECD) (1998) *Harmful Tax Competition: An Emerging Global Issue*, April, available at http://www.oecd.org/pdf/M00004000/M00004517.pdf.

Organisation for Economic Cooperation and Development (OECD) (2000) *Toward Global Tax Co-operation: Progress in Identifying and Eliminating Harmful Tax Practices*, Report to the 2000 Ministerial Council Meeting and Recommendations by the Committee on Fiscal Affairs, June (Paris: OECD).

Ostry, S. (1997) *The Post-Cold War Trading System* (Chicago, IL: University of Chicago Press).

Ostry, S. (2000) 'The Uruguay Round North–South Grand Bargain: Implications for Future Negotiations', mimeo, September, available at http://www.utoronto.ca/cis/ostry.html.

Oxfam (1998) *Debt Relief and Poverty Reduction: Strengthening the Linkage*, Oxfam International Paper, August, available at http://www.oxfam.org.

Page, S. (2002) 'Developing Countries in GATT/WTO Negotiations', mimeo, Overseas Development Institute, London, February.

Page, S. (2004) 'Making Doha a Better Deal for Poor Countries', *Financial Times*, 27 July.

Palan, R. (1998) 'Trying to Have Your Cake and Eating it: How and Why the State System has Created Offshore', *International Studies Quarterly*, Vol. 42, No. 4, pp. 625–44.

Panagariya, A. (2002) 'Developing Countries at Doha: A Political Economy Analysis', *The World Economy*, Vol. 25, No. 9, pp. 1,205–33.

Paterson, M. and Grubb, M. (1992) 'The International Politics of Climate Change', *International Affairs*, Vol. 68, No. 2, pp. 293–310.

Payer, C. (1974) *The Debt Trap* (Harmondsworth: Penguin).

Payne, A.J. (1994) 'US Hegemony and the Reconfiguration of the Caribbean', *Review of International Studies*, Vol. 20, No. 2, pp. 149–68.

Payne, A.J. (2005) 'The Study of Governance in a Global Political Economy', in N.J. Phillips (ed.), *Globalizing International Political Economy* (Basingstoke: Palgrave Macmillan), pp. 55–81.

Peterson, M.J. (1986) *The General Assembly in World Politics* (Boston, MA: Unwin Hyman).

Pew Center for Global Climate Change (2002) 'Climate Talks in Delhi – COP 8: Summary', available at http://www.pewclimate.org/cop8/summary.cfm.

Phillips, N.J. (2004) *The Southern Cone Model: The Political Economy of Regional Capitalist Development in Latin America* (London: Routledge).

Phillips, N.J. (2005a) 'Globalization Studies in International Political Economy', in N.J. Phillips (ed.), *Globalizing International Political Economy* (Basingstoke: Palgrave Macmillan), pp. 20–54.

Phillips, N.J. (2005b) 'State Debates in International Political Economy', in N.J. Phillips (ed.), *Globalizing International Political Economy* (Basingstoke: Palgrave Macmillan), pp. 82–105.

Pieterse, J.N. (1996) 'The Development of Development Theory: Towards Critical Globalism', *Review of International Political Economy*, Vol. 3, No. 4, pp. 541–64.

Pieterse, J.N. (2003) 'Hyperpower Exceptionalism: Globalisation the American Way', *New Political Economy*, Vol. 8, No. 3, pp. 299–319.

Porter, G. and Brown, J.W. (1991) *Global Environmental Politics* (Boulder, CO: Westview).

Porter, R.B. (2001) 'Progress, Development and Change', *Progress in Development Studies*, Vol. 1, No. 1, pp. 1–4.

Porter, T. and Wood, D. (2002) 'Reform without Representation? The International and Transnational Dialogue on the Global Financial Architecture', in L.E. Armijo (ed.), *Debating the Global Financial Architecture* (Albany, NY: State University of New York Press), pp. 236–56.

Putnam, R.D. and Bayne, N. (1987) *Hanging Together: Cooperation and Conflict in the Seven-Power Summits* (London: Sage).

Putzel, J. (1997) 'Accounting for the "Dark Side" of Social Capital: Reading Robert Putnam on Democracy', *Journal of International Development*, Vol. 9, No. 7, pp. 939–49.

Raghavan, C. (2000) 'After Seattle, World Trade System Faces Uncertain Future', *Review of International Political Economy*, Vol. 7, No. 3, pp. 495–504.

Rajamani, L. (1999) 'The Cartagena Protocol – A Battle over Trade or Biosafety?', *Third World Resurgence*, No. 104/105, available at http://www.twnside.org.sg/title/lavanya-en.htm.

Rajan, M.G. (1997) *Global Environmental Politics: India and the North–South Politics of Global Environmental Issues* (Delhi: Oxford University Press).

Ramo, J.C. (2004) *The Beijing Consensus* (London: The Foreign Policy Centre), available at http://www.fpc.org.uk.

Randall, V. (1992) 'Third World: Rejected or Rediscovered?', *Third World Quarterly*, Vol. 13, No. 4, pp. 727–30.

Randall, V. and Theobald, R. (1998) *Political Change and Underdevelopment: A Critical Introduction to Third World Politics* (London: Macmillan).

Rao, J.M. (1999) 'Equity in a Global Public Goods Framework', in I. Kaul, I. Grunberg and M.A. Stern (eds), *Global Public Goods: International Cooperation in the 21st Century* (Oxford: Oxford University Press for the United Nations Development Programme).

Raustiala, K. and Victor, D.G. (1996) 'Biodiversity since Rio: The Future of the Convention on Biological Diversity', *Environment*, Vol. 38, No. 4, pp. 17–20, 37–45.

Ravenhill, J. (1990) 'The North–South Balance of Power', *International Affairs*, Vol. 66, No. 4, pp. 731–48.

Redclift, M. (1987) *Sustainable Development: Exploiting the Contradictions* (London: Methuen).

Reid, W.V. (1992) 'Conserving Life's Diversity: Can the Extinction Crisis be Stopped?', *Environmental Science and Technology*, Vol. 26, No. 6, pp. 1,090–5.

Rice, S.E. (2003) 'The New National Security Strategy: Focus on Failed States', *Policy Brief No. 116*, Brookings Institution, Washington, DC, February.

Riddell, R. (1987) *Foreign Aid Reconsidered* (Baltimore, MD: The Johns Hopkins University Press).

Robinson, W.I. (1998) 'Beyond Nation-State Paradigms: Globalization, Sociology, and the Challenge of Transnational Studies', *Sociological Forum*, Vol. 13, No. 4, pp. 561–94.

Robinson, W.I. (2004) *A Theory of Global Capitalism: Production, Class, and State in a Transnational World* (Baltimore, MD: The Johns Hopkins University Press).

Robison, R., Beeson, M., Jayasuriya, K. and Kim, H.-R. (eds) (2000) *Politics and Markets in the Wake of the Asian Crisis* (London: Routledge).

Roddick, J. (1988) *The Dance of the Millions: Latin America and the Debt Crisis* (London: Latin America Bureau).

Rosenau, J. (1997) *Along the Domestic–Foreign Frontier: Exploring Governance in a Turbulent World* (Cambridge: Cambridge University Press).

Rostow, W. (1960) *The Stages of Economic Growth* (Cambridge: Cambridge University Press).

Rowlands, I. (1992) 'The International Politics of Environment and Development: The Post-UNCED Agenda', *Millennium: Journal of International Studies*, Vol. 21, No. 2, pp. 209–24.

Roxborough, I. (1979) *Theories of Underdevelopment* (London: Macmillan).

Ruggie, J.G. (1982) 'International Regimes, Transactions and Change: Embedded Liberalism in the Postwar Economic Order', *International Organization*, Vol. 36, No. 2, pp. 379–415.

Ruggie, J.G. (ed.) (1993) *Multilateralism Matters: The Theory and Praxis of an Institutional Form* (New York, NY: Columbia University Press).

Rupert, M. (1995) *Producing Hegemony: The Politics of Mass Production and American Global Power* (Cambridge: Cambridge University Press).

Sachs, J. (1989) 'Conditionality, Debt Relief, and the Developing Country Debt Crisis', in J. Sachs (ed.), *Developing Country Debt and the World Economy* (Chicago, IL: University of Chicago Press), pp. 275–84.

Sachs, J. (1998) 'The IMF and the Asian Flu', *American Prospect*, March–April.

Sachs, J. (2003) 'A Miserly Response to a Global Emergency', *Financial Times*, 17 July.

Said, E. (1992) *Culture and Imperialism* (London: Chatto and Windus).

Sanders, R. (2002) 'The Future of Financial Services in the Caribbean', in R. Birwas (ed.), *International Tax Competition: Globalisation and Fiscal Sovereignty*, Commonwealth Secretariat, London, pp. 48–58.

Sands, P.J. (1992) 'The United Nations Convention on Climate Change', *Review of European Community and International Environmental Law*, Vol. 1, No. 3, pp. 270–7.

Sen, A. (1999) *Development as Freedom* (Oxford: Oxford University Press).

Scholte, J.A. (1997) 'Global Capitalism and the State', *International Affairs*, Vol. 73, No. 3, pp. 427–52.

Scholte, J.A. (2000) *Globalisation: A Critical Introduction* (Basingstoke: Palgrave Macmillan).

Schuurman, F.J. (ed.) (1993) *Beyond the Impasse: New Directions in Development Theory* (London: Zed Books).

Shiva, V. (1990) 'Biodiversity, Biotechnology and Profit: The Need for a People's Plan to Protect Biodiversity', *The Ecologist*, Vol. 20, No. 2, pp. 44–7.

Shue, H. (1993) 'Subsistence Emissions and Luxury Emissions', *Law and Policy*, Vol. 15, No. 1, pp. 39–59.

Sinclair, T.J. (1996) 'Beyond International Relations Theory: Robert W. Cox and Approaches to World Order', in R.W. Cox, with T.J. Sinclair, *Approaches to World Order* (Cambridge: Cambridge University Press), pp. 3–18.

Sjoeberg, H. (1994) *From Idea to Reality: The Creation of the Global Environment Facility*, United Nations Development Programme/United Nations Environment Programme Working Paper No. 10, Washington, DC.

Smaghi, L.B. (2004) 'A Single EU Seat in the IMF?', *Journal of Common Market Studies*, Vol. 42, No. 2, pp. 229–48.

Smith, S. (2002) 'The United States and the Discipline of International Relations: "Hegemonic Country, Hegemonic Discipline" ', *International Studies Review*, Vol. 4, No. 2, pp. 67–85.

Snidal, D. (1985) 'The Limits of Hegemonic Stability Theory', *International Organization*, Vol. 39, No. 4, pp. 579–614.

Soederberg, S. (2001) 'The Emperor's New Suit: The New International Financial Architecture as a Reinvention of the Washington Consensus', *Global Governance*, Vol. 7, No. 4, pp. 453–67.

Soederberg, S. (2002) 'On the Contradictions of the *New* International Financial Architecture: Another Procrustean Bed for Emerging Markets?', *Third World Quarterly*, Vol. 23, No. 4, pp. 607–20.

Soederberg, S. (2004) 'American Empire and "Excluded States": The Millennium Challenge Account and the Shift to Pre-Emptive Development', *Third World Quarterly*, Vol. 25, No. 2, pp. 279–302.

Srinivasan, T.N. (1999) 'Developing Countries in the World Trading System: From GATT, 1947, to the Third Ministerial Meeting of the WTO, 1999', *The World Economy*, Vol. 22, No. 8, pp. 1,047–64.

Standing, G. (2000) 'Brave New Worlds? A Critique of Stiglitz's World Bank Rethink', *Development and Change*, Vol. 31, No. 4, pp. 737–63.

Staniland, M. (1985) *What is Political Economy? A Study of Social Theory and Underdevelopment* (New Haven, CT: Yale University Press).

Stelzer, I. (ed.) (2004) *Neo-Conservatism* (London: Atlantic Books).

Stern, N. and Ferreira, F. (1993) *The World Bank as Intellectual Actor*, Development Economics Research Programme Discussion Paper DEP/50, STICERD, London School of Economics, London.

Stigliani, N.A. (2000), 'Labor Diplomacy: A Revitalised Aspect of US Foreign Policy in the Era of Globalization', *International Studies Perspectives*, Vol. 1, No. 2, pp. 177–94.

Stiglitz, J.E. (1998a) 'More Instruments and Broader Goals: Moving Toward the Post-Washington Consensus', The 1998 World Institute for Development Economic Research Annual Lecture, Helsinki, 7 January, available at http://www.worldbank.org/html/extdr/extme/js-010798/wider.htm.

Stiglitz, J.E. (1998b) 'Towards a New Paradigm for Development: Strategies, Policies and Processes', The 1998 Prebisch Lecture at UNCTAD, Geneva, 19 October, available at http://www.worldbank.org/html/extdr/extme/jssp101998.htm.

Stiglitz, J.E. (2000) 'What I Learned at the World Economic Crisis', *The New Republic*, 17 April.

Stiglitz, J.E. (2001) 'The IMF's Missed Opportunity', *Project Syndicate*, September, pp. 1–2.

Strange, S. (1971) *Sterling and British Policy* (Oxford: Oxford University Press).

Strange, S. (1990) 'The Name of the Game', in N.X. Rizopoulos (ed.), *Sea-Changes: American Foreign Policy in a World Transformed* (New York, NY: Council on Foreign Relations), pp. 238–73.

Taylor, I. (2003) 'Global Monitor: The United Nations Conference on Trade and Development', *New Political Economy*, Vol. 8, No. 3, pp. 409–18.

Teunissen, J.J. and Akkerman, A. (eds) (2004) *HIPC Debt Relief: Myths and Reality* (The Hague: FONDAD).

Thacker, S.C. (1999) 'The High Politics of IMF Lending', *World Politics*, Vol. 52, No. 1, pp. 38–75.

Thérien, J.-P. (1999) 'Beyond the North–South Divide: Two Tales of World Poverty', *Third World Quarterly*, Vol. 20, No. 4, pp. 723–42.

Thérien, J.-P. (2002) 'Debating Foreign Aid: Right and Left', *Third World Quarterly*, Vol. 23, No. 3, pp. 449–66.

Thomas, C. (1992) *The Environment in International Relations* (London: Royal Institute of International Affairs).

Thomas, C. (2000) *Global Governance, Development and Human Security: The Challenge of Poverty and Inequality* (London: Pluto Press).

Thompson, G.F. (2003) 'Globalisation and the Total Commercialisation of Politics?', *New Political Economy*, Vol. 8, No. 3, pp. 401–8.

Thompson, G.F. (2004) 'Feature Review: "The Age of Consent: A Manifesto for a New World Order" by George Monbiot', *New Political Economy*, Vol. 9, No. 1, pp. 134–44.

Toye, J. (1987) *Dilemmas of Development: Reflections on the Counter-revolution in Development Theory and Policy* (Oxford: Basil Blackwell).

Triffin, R. (1961) *Gold and the Dollar Crisis* (New Haven, CT: Yale University Press).

Tussie, D. and Lengyel, M.F. (2002) 'Developing Countries: Turning Participation into Influence', in P. English, B.M. Hoekman and A. Mattoo (eds), *Development, Trade and the WTO: A Handbook* (Washington, DC: The World Bank), pp. 485–92.

United Nations (1995) *Report of the World Summit for Social Development*, A/CONF, 166/9, 19 April (New York, NY: United Nations).

United Nations (1999) *The Global Compact: Shared Values for a Global Market* (New York, NY: UN Department for Public Information, DP1/2075).

United Nations Development Programme (1997) *Human Development Report 1997* (New York,. NY: Oxford University Press for UNDP).

United Nations Development Programme (2001) *Human Development Report 2001* (New York, NY: Oxford University Press for UNDP).

United Nations Environmental Programme (1989) *Annual Report of the Executive Director – 1988* (Nairobi: UNEP).

United Nations Environmental Programme (1992) *Rio Declaration on Environment and Development*, available at http://www.unep.org/unep/rio.htm.

United Nations Framework Convention on Climate Change Secretariat (1992) *United Nations Framework Convention on Climate Change*, Bonn, available at http://www. un/ccc.def.fccc/conv/convtoc.htm.

United Nations Framework Convention on Climate Change Secretariat (1997) *The Kyoto Protocol to the United Nations Framework Convention on Climate Change*, Bonn, available at http://unfccc.int/resource/docs/convkp/kpeng.pdf.

United Nations General Assembly (2000) *Resolution 55/2: United Nations Millennium Declaration*, issued 8 September, UN, New York.

United Nations Research Institute for Social Development (1995) *States of Disarray: The Social Effects of Globalization* (Geneva: UNRISD).

United States Government (2002) 'National Security Strategy of the United States of America', The White House, Washington, DC, September, available at http://www. whitehouse.gov/usc/nss1.html.

United States Senate (1997) 'The Byrd–Hagel Resolution', sponsored by Senator Robert Byrd and Senator Chuck Hagel, Senate Resolution No. 98, 105th Congress, 25 July.

United States Treasury Department (2001) 'Treasury Secretary O'Neill Statement on OECD Tax Havens', US Treasury Department Press Release No. PO366, 10 May.

Vajpayee, Shri Atal Bihari (2002) 'Speech at the High Level Segment of the Eighth Session of the Conference of the Parties to the UN Framework Convention on Climate Change', New Delhi, 30 October, available at http://www.unfccc.int/cop8/latest/ 9_shi.pdf.

van der Pijl, K. (1984) *The Making of an Atlantic Ruling Class* (London: Verso).

Victor, D.G. (2001) *The Collapse of the Kyoto Protocol and the Struggle to Slow Global Warming* (Princeton, NJ: Princeton, University Press).

Vidal, J. (2002) 'A Diplomatic Chess Game that could not End in Stalemate', *The Guardian*, 4 September.

Vogler, J. (2000) *The Global Commons: Environmental and Technological Governance*, 2nd edn (Chichester: John Wiley).

Wade, R. (1990) *Governing the Market: Economic Theory and the Role of Government in East Asian Industrialization* (Princeton, NJ: Princeton University Press).

Wade, R. (1996) 'Japan, the World Bank, and the Art of Paradigm Maintenance: *The East Asian Miracle* in Political Perspective', *New Left Review*, No. 217, pp. 3–36.

Wade, R. (2001) 'Making the World Development Report 2000: Attacking Poverty', *World Development*, Vol. 29, No. 8, pp. 1,435–41.

Wade, R. (2002) 'US Hegemony and the World Bank: The Fight over People and Ideas', *Review of International Political Economy*, Vol. 9, No. 2, pp. 201–29.

Wade, R. (2003) 'What Strategies are Viable for Developing Countries Today? The World Trade Organization and the Shrinking of "Development Space" ', *Review of International Political Economy*, Vol. 10, No. 4, pp. 621–44.

Wade, R. (2004) 'On the Causes of Increasing World Poverty and Inequality, or Why the Matthew Effect Prevails', *New Political Economy*, Vol. 9, No. 2, pp. 163–88.

Wade, R. vs Wolf, M. (2002) 'Prospect Debate: Are Global Poverty and Inequality Getting Worse?', *Prospect*, March, pp. 16–21.

Wallerstein, I. (1974) *The Modern World System: Capitalist Agriculture and the Origins of the European World Economy in the Sixteenth Century* (London: Academic Press).

Watkins, K. (2004) 'Africa's Burden of Debt is still Far Too Heavy', *Financial Times*, 22 September.

Weir, M. (2001) 'The Collapse of Bill Clinton's Third Way', in S. White (ed.), *New Labour: The Progressive Future?* (Basingstoke: Palgrave Macmillan), pp. 137–48.

Weiss, L. (1997) 'Globalization and the Myth of the Powerless State', *New Left Review*, No. 225, pp. 3–27.

Weiss, L. (1998) *The Myth of the Powerless State: Governing the Economy in a Global Era* (Cambridge: Polity Press).

Wendt, A. (1992) 'Anarchy is What States Make of It: The Social Construction of Power Politics', *International Organization*, Vol. 46, No. 2, pp. 335–425.

Wendt, A. (1999) *Social Theory of International Politics* (Cambridge: Cambridge University Press).

Westergaard, J. (1999) 'Where does the Third Way Lead?', *New Political Economy*, Vol. 4, No. 3, pp. 429–36.

White, G. (1987) *Development States in East Asia* (New York, NY: St Martin's Press).

White, H. (2001a) 'Development Assistance Committee (DAC)', in R.J. Barry Jones (ed.), *Routledge Encyclopedia of International Political Economy*, Vol. 1 (London: Routledge), pp. 340–1.

White, H. (2001b) 'Paris Club', in R.J. Barry Jones (ed.), *Routledge Encyclopedia of International Political Economy*, Vol. 3 (London: Routledge), pp. 1,196–7.

Wilkinson, R. (1999) 'Labour and Trade-Related Regulation: Beyond the Trade-Labour Standards Debate?', *British Journal of Politics and International Relations*, Vol. 1, No. 2, pp. 165–91.

Wilkinson, R. (2000) *Multilateralism and the World Trade Organisation: The Architecture and Extension of International Trade Regulation* (London: Routledge).

Wilkinson, R. (2001) 'The WTO in Crisis: Exploring the Dimensions of Institutional Inertia', *The Journal of World Trade Law*, Vol. 35, No. 3, pp. 397–419.

Wilkinson, R. (2002) 'The World Trade Organization', *New Political Economy*, Vol. 7, No. 1, pp. 129–41.

Wilkinson, R. (2004) 'Crisis in Cancún', *Global Governance*, Vol. 10, No. 2, pp. 149–56.

Willetts, P. (1978) *The Non-Aligned Movement: The Origins of a Third World Alliance* (London: Frances Pinter).

Williams, D.G. (1996) 'Governance and the Discipline of Development', *The European Journal of Development Research*, Vol. 8, No. 2, pp. 157–77.

Williams, D. and Young, T. (1994) 'Governance, the World Bank and Liberal Theory', *Political Studies*, Vol. 42, No. 1, pp. 84–100.

Williams, M. (1993) 'Re-articulating the Third World Coalition: The Role of the Environmental Agenda', *Third World Quarterly*, Vol. 14, No.1, pp. 7–29.

Williams, M. (1994) *International Economic Institutions and the Third World* (Hemel Hempstead: Harvester Wheatsheaf).

Williamson, J. (1990) 'What Washington Means by Policy Reform', in J. Williamson (ed.), *Latin American Adjustment: How Much has Happened* (Washington, DC: Institute of International Economics), pp. 5–20.

Williamson, J. (1993) 'Democracy and the "Washington Consensus"', *World Development*, Vol. 21, No. 8, pp. 1,329–36.

Wirth, T. (1997) 'Speech delivered to COP2 by US Under Secretary of State for Global Affairs', reprinted in *Global Issues: Confronting Climate Change* (electronic journal of US Information Agency), Vol. 2, No. 2, pp. 6–9.

Wolf, M. (2001) 'The View from the Limousine', *Financial Times*, 7 November.

Wolfe, R. (2001) 'Organisation for Economic Co-operation and Development (OECD)', in R.J. Barry Jones (ed.), *Routledge Encyclopedia of International Political Economy*, Vol. 2 (London: Routledge), pp. 1,179–82.

Wolfensohn, J. (1999) 'A Proposal for a Comprehensive Development Framework: Discussion Draft', mimeo, World Bank, Washington, DC, 21 January.

Wolf-Phillips, L. (1987) 'Why "Third World"?: Origin, Definition and Usage', *Third World Quarterly*, Vol. 9, No. 4, pp. 1,311–27.

Woods, N. (1999) 'Good Governance in International Organizations', *Global Governance*, Vol. 5, No. 1, pp. 39–61.

Woods, N. (2000) 'The Challenge of Good Governance for the IMF and the World Bank Themselves', *World Development*, Vol. 28, No. 5, pp. 823–41.

Woods, N. and Narlikar, A. (2001) 'Governance and the Limits of Accountability: The WTO, the IMF and the World Bank', *International Social Science Journal*, Vol. 53, No. 170, pp. 569–83.

Woodward, R. (2002) 'Offshore or "Shorn Off"? The Impact of the OECD's Harmful Tax Competition Initiative on Development in Small Island Economies', unpublished paper delivered to the conference on 'Towards a New Political Economy of Development: Globalisation and Governance', Political Economy Research Centre, University of Sheffield, Sheffield, 4–6 July.

Woodward, R. (2004) 'Global Monitor: The Organisation for Economic Cooperation and Development', *New Political Economy*, Vol. 9, No. 1, pp. 113–27.

Woolcock, M. (1998) 'Social Capital and Economic Development: Toward a Theoretical Synthesis and Policy Framework', *Theory and Society*, Vol. 27, No. 2, pp. 151–208.

World Bank (1979) *World Development Report 1979* (Washington, DC: World Bank).

World Bank (1992) *Governance and Development* (Washington, DC: World Bank).

World Bank (1993) *The East Asian Miracle: Economic Growth and Public Policy*, A World Bank Policy Research Report (Oxford: Oxford University Press for the World Bank).

World Bank (1995a) *Global Economic Prospects and the Developing Countries 1995* (Washington, DC: World Bank).

World Bank (1995b) *The World Bank Annual Report 1995* (Washington, DC: World Bank).

World Bank (1997a) 'Social Capital: The Missing Link?', in World Bank, 'Monitoring Environmental Progress: Expanding the Measure of Wealth', mimeo, World Bank, Washington, DC.

World Bank (1997b) *World Development Report 1997: The State in a Changing World* (New York, NY: Oxford University Press for the World Bank).

World Bank (1998) *Global Development Finance 1998* (Washington, DC: World Bank).

World Bank (2002) *Globalization, Growth, and Poverty: Building an Inclusive World Economy* (Oxford: Oxford University Press for the World Bank).

World Commission on Environment and Development (1987) *Our Common Future* (The Brundtland Report) (Oxford: Oxford University Press).

World Rainforest Movement (1990) *Rainforest Destruction: Causes, Effects – and False Solutions* (Penang: WRM).

World Trade Organization (1996) *Singapore Ministerial Declaration*, adopted on 13 December 1996, available at http://www.wto.org/english/thewto_e/minist_e/min96_e/wtodec_e.htm.

World Trade Organization (2001a) *Decision on Implementation-related Issues and Concerns*, WTO document WT/MIN(01)/W/10, 4th Ministerial Conference, Doha, 14 November.

World Trade Organization (2001b) *Declaration on the TRIPS Agreement and Public Health*, WTO document WT/MIN(01)/DEC/W/2, 4th Ministerial Conference, Doha, 14 November.

World Trade Organization (2001c) *The Doha Ministerial Declaration*, WTO document WT/MIN(01)/DEC/W/1, 4th Ministerial Conference, Doha, 14 November.

Wynne, B. (1994) 'Scientific Knowledge and the Global Environment', in M. Redclift and T. Benton (eds), *Social Theory and the Global Environment* (London: Routledge), pp. 168–89.

Zedillo, E. *et al.* (2001) *Report of the High-Level Panel on Financing for Development*, presented to the UN Secretary-General, UN, New York, 28 June, available at http://www.un.org/reports/financing.

Ziai, A. (2004) 'The Ambivalence of Post-Development: Between Reactionary Populism and Radical Democracy', *Third World Quarterly*, Vol. 25, No. 6, pp. 1,045–60.

Zysman, J. (1996) 'The Myth of the Global Economy: Enduring National Foundations and Emerging Regional Realities', *New Political Economy*, Vol. 1, No. 2, pp. 157–84.

Index